John Muir

Metrical Translations from Sanskrit Writers

John Muir

Metrical Translations from Sanskrit Writers

ISBN/EAN: 9783337177775

Printed in Europe, USA, Canada, Australia, Japan

Cover: Foto ©ninafisch / pixelio.de

More available books at **www.hansebooks.com**

"Φησὶ δ' Ἀριστόξενος ὁ μουσικὸς Ἰνδῶν εἶναι τὸν λόγον τοῦτον. Ἀθήνησι γὰρ ἐντυχεῖν Σωκράτει τῶν ἀνδρῶν ἐκείνων ἕνα τινά, κἄπειτα αὐτοῦ πυνθάνεσθαι, τί ποιῶν φιλοσοφοίη. Τοῦ δὲ εἰπόντος, ὅτι ζητῶν περὶ τοῦ ἀνθρωπίνου βίου, καταγελάσαι τὸν Ἰνδὸν, λέγοντα μὴ δύνασθαι τινα τὰ ἀνθρώπινα καταλαβεῖν, ἀγνοοῦντά γε τὰ θεῖα. Τοῦτο μὲν οὖν εἰ ἀληθές ἐστιν οὐκ ἂν δύναιτό τις διατεινόμενος εἰπεῖν."—*Aristokles in Eusebius' Præparatio Evangelii*, xi. 3.

"But Aristoxenus the musician says that this doctrine [of Plato, that human things could not be perceived, unless divine things had first been seen] comes from the Indians; for that one of those men fell in with Sokrates in Athens, and asked him what was the substance of his philosophy; and that when Sokrates answered that it consisted of an enquiry regarding human life, the Indian laughed, and said that no one who was ignorant of divine things could comprehend things relating to man. No one, however, could very strongly affirm that this statement is true."

METRICAL TRANSLATIONS.

"*Φησὶ δ' Ἀριστόξενος ὁ μουσικὸς Ἰνδῶν εἶναι τὸν λόγον τοῦτον. Ἀθήνησι γὰρ ἐντυχεῖν Σωκράτει τῶν ἀνδρῶν ἐκείνων ἕνα τινὰ, κἄπειτα αὐτοῦ πυνθάνεσθαι, τί ποιῶν φιλοσοφοίη. Τοῦ δὲ εἰπόντος, ὅτι ζητῶν περὶ τοῦ ἀνθρωπίνου βίου, καταγελάσαι τὸν Ἰνδὸν. λέγοντα μὴ δύνασθαι τινα τὰ ἀνθρώπινα καταλαβεῖν, ἀγνοοῦντά γε τὰ θεῖα. Τοῦτο μὲν οὖν εἰ ἀληθές ἐστιν οὐκ ἂν δύναιτό τις διατεινόμενος εἰπεῖν.*"—*Aristokles in Eusebius' Præparatio Evangelii*, xi. 3.

"But Aristoxenus the musician says that this doctrine [of Plato, that human things could not be perceived, unless divine things had first been seen] comes from the Indians; for that one of those men fell in with Sokrates in Athens, and asked him what was the substance of his philosophy; and that when Sokrates answered that it consisted of an enquiry regarding human life, the Indian laughed, and said that no one who was ignorant of divine things could comprehend things relating to man. No one, however, could very strongly affirm that this statement is true."

METRICAL TRANSLATIONS

FROM

SANSKRIT WRITERS

WITH

AN INTRODUCTION, MANY PROSE VERSIONS,

AND

PARALLEL PASSAGES FROM CLASSICAL AUTHORS.

BY

J. MUIR, C.I.E., D.C.L., LL.D., PH.D.

LONDON:

TRÜBNER & CO., LUDGATE HILL.

1879.

PREFACE.

The present Volume embraces the contents of the little work entitled "Religious and Moral Sentiments, metrically rendered from Sanskrit Writers," &c., published by Messrs Williams & Norgate in 1875, together with three collections of versified translations subsequently printed, but not published, and a reprint of the metrical pieces contained in Volumes II. and V. of my "Original Sanskrit Texts," &c.

In the notice prefixed to the former publication I have acknowledged my obligations to Dr O. Böhtlingk's large collection of maxims. All the quotations from works of a more recent date than the Mahâbhârata, and many from that great epic poem itself, are drawn from his book.

The sources to which I am indebted for the parallel passages from classical writers, are mostly indicated at the head of each quotation. In the previous published collection I stated that almost all those then given from Latin writers had been taken from Wuestemann's "Promptuarium Sententiarum," &c.

I am indebted to Dr E. L. Lushington for revising the greater portion of the supplement to the Appendix, and suggesting emendations; and to Professor E. B. Cowell for correcting the translation in page 249 f.

CONTENTS.

	PAGE
INTRODUCTION, ...	
MISCELLANEOUS METRICAL TRANSLATIONS—	
1. Consequence of the knowledge of the self-existent Soul,	1
2. The Great Spirit, ...	1
3. Devotion to the God of gods, ...	2
4. Hymn addressed to Vishnu by the Deities, . . .	2
5. Impeachment, and vindication. of the Divine government,	4
6. The Divine sovereignty, ...	7
7. All sins known to the gods, ...	7
8. Secret sin not unobserved, ...	8
9. The wise corrected by advice : the bad checked by punishment,	8
10. Ill-gotten gains fail to benefit, ...	8
11. The genesis of Rudra, ...	8
12. The gods give wisdom to those whom they favour, and conversely, ...	9
13. Good and evil not always apparent at first sight, . .	9
14. The same, ...	9
15. Fools mistake evil for good, ...	10
16. A doomed man is killed by anything, ...	10
17. The same, ...	10
18. "Take no thought for your life, what ye shall eat," &c., .	10
19. The same, ...	11
20. Faith in Holy Scripture, ...	11
21. An Indian Free-thinker's fate, ...	11
22. The Indian Rationalist in ancient times, ...	12
23. Denial of a future life and of a God; and ridicule of the doctrine of final liberation as nothing else than annihilation,	13
24. Jabali's Sophistical discourse and Rama's reply, . .	14
25. Virtue unreal and useless, ...	21
26. The Rule of Duty difficult to ascertain, . . .	22
27. Preparation for Death, ...	22
28. The only inseparable friend, ...	26
29. "What is your life? It is even a vapour," . .	26
30. No distinctions in the grave, ...	27
31. "For we brought nothing into this world, and it is certain we can carry nothing out,"	28
32. How the wise ought to live : a Dialogue,	28
33. "Take thine ease, eat, drink, and be merry,"	33

MISCELLANEOUS METRICAL TRANSLATIONS—*continued.*

PAGE

34. Final overthrow of the wicked, ... 34
35. Good and bad seem to be equally favoured here: not so hereafter, ... 35
36. "Strait is the gate and narrow is the way which leadeth unto life," 35
37. No second youth to man, ... 36
38. The lapse of time not practically noticed, ... 36
39. "All men think all men mortal but themselves," . . 36
40. Who are the really blind, deaf, and dumb? 36
41. Remember thy mortality, ... 37
42. Sin removed by repentance, ... 37
43. Never do what would distress thee on a sick-bed, . . 37
44. Men should think on their end, ... 38
45. Men devout when in distress, ... 38
46. Men love the fruits of virtue, not virtue itself, . . 38
47. Effects of habitual sin and virtue respectively, . . . 38
48. A small part of the toil endured in gaining wealth would ensure final emancipation, ... 39
49. Action keeping in view the future, ... 39
50. Daily self-examination, ... 39
51. Improvement of time, ... 39
52. Virtue difficult; vice easy, ... 40
53. "Gutta cavat lapidem," &c., good slowly acquired, . . 40
54. The condition of acquiring knowledge, ... 40
55. Knowledge a treasure which cannot be lost, ... 40
56. Ars longa, vita brevis: The essence of books to be got, . 41
57. The condition of mortality, ... 41
58. The mysteries of destiny, ... 42
59. The same, ... 44
60. Contrasts of life, ... 44
61. Means do not always lead to the desired ends, . . . 45
62. The same, ... 45
63. Poverty lends a relish to food, ... 45
64. The vanity of human ambition, ... 46
65. The path of salvation, ... 47
66. Sanctitas via intelligentiæ: Holiness the road to knowledge, 48
67. The extinction of sin leads to knowledge, ... 48
68. Final beatitude; and the self-evidencing power of the doctrine regarding it, ... 48
69. A guide through the gloom, ... 49
70. Janaka's saying: The blessedness of dispassion, . . . 50
71. Whither knowledge leads, ... 50
72. Death is not the extinction of the good, ... 50
73. The watchtower of wisdom, ... 51
74. The Indian Martha and Mary, ... 51
75. Nachiketas: a theosophic story, ... 54
76. Wonderful attributes of the Brahmans, ... 60
77. Diversities among Brahmans, ... 64

MISCELLANEOUS METRICAL TRANSLATIONS—*continued.*

PAGE

78. Knowledge to be sought from all castes, which all spring from Brahmā, ... 65
79. No distinction of castes, ... 66
80. Final beatitude attainable even by low caste men and by women, 67
81. Honour due not to class, but to character, ... 68
82. The nobility of manhood, ... 68
83. Generous impartiality, ... 69
84. Virtue of more value than high birth, ... 69
85. The true Brahman, ... 69
86. The same, ... 69
87. What makes a man a Brahman, ... 70
88. The true Brahman, ... 70
89. Goodness essential to a Brahman, ... 71
90. The same, ... 71
91. Profession without practice, ... 72
92. Great wealth injurious to Brahmans, ... 72
93. Brahmans should shun honour, ... 72
94. The real ascetics, ... 73
95. The recluse less meritorious than virtuous men who live in the world, ... 73
96. Retirement from the world not necessary for self-control, . 73
97. Condemnation of premature asceticism, ... 74
98. What determines the character of actions, ... 75
99. The inefficacy of mere theological knowledge, . . . 75
100. Austerities and rites unavailing without inward purity, . 75
101. Truth better than sacrifice, ... 76
102. The same, ... 76
103. Results of truth and falsehood, ... 76
104. Sweet savour of good deeds: Falsehood to be shunned, . 77
105. Loss of virtue the only real loss, ... 77
106. The righteous always prosper, ... 77
107. Righteousness more valuable than riches, ... 78
108. The value of rites depends on the inward purity of the performer, ... 78
109. Fate of those who have no belief in virtue; benefits of faith, 78
110. Moral goodness essential, ... 79
111. True piety and righteousness, and their fruits, . . . 80
112. The most meritorious gifts, ... 80
113. Two inheritors of paradise, ... 80
114. The best use of wealth, ... 81
115. Good practised because it is duty, ... 81
116. Good easy, evil difficult, to a noble man, ... 81
117. Effort, not success, the test of goodness, ... 81
118. Evil intentions, if relinquished, not punished, . . . 82
119. Virtue lies in the thought, not in the act, ... 82
120. Virtue must be a man's own unaided act, ... 82
121. Kind and heartless men, ... 82
122. The humble are wise, ... 83

MISCELLANEOUS METRICAL TRANSLATIONS—*continued.*

		PAGE
123.	Marks of a virtuous man,	83
124.	Selfishness,	83
125.	"If any provide not for his own, . . . he is worse than an infidel,"	84
126.	Disinterestedness; "Do good and lend, hoping for nothing again,"	84
127.	Do to others as ye would that they should do to you,	84
128.	Marks of a good man,	85
129.	The same,	85
130.	Beneficence a duty,	85
131.	The prosperity of others not to be envied,	85
132.	The requiter, not equal to the doer, of good acts,	86
133.	"This is the law and the prophets,"	86
134.	Do not to others what thou would'st not have done to thee,	86
135.	"If ye love them which love you what reward have ye,"	87
136.	The highest worship of the Deity,	87
137.	The proper aim of life,	87
138.	The means of attaining to final liberation,	87
139.	"Overcome evil with good,"	88
140.	"Who when he was reviled, reviled not again,"	88
141.	"If thine enemy hunger, feed him,"	88
142.	Forgiveness of injuries,	88
143.	Suppliants not to be sent empty away,	89
144.	The same,	89
145.	Narrow and large heartedness,	89
146.	Compassion should be shown to all men,	89
147.	A man may learn from the humblest, &c.,	90
148.	Good may be gained from everything,	90
149.	Men are formed by their associates,	90
150.	Evil men to be avoided,	91
151.	How the wise and foolish respectively are affected by society,	91
152.	Effects of good and bad company,	91
153.	Undiscerning men's praise worthless,	92
154.	"The tongue can no man tame,"	92
155.	"Casting pearls before swine,"	92
156.	Hopelessness of reclaiming the bad,	92
157.	Good advice not to be wasted on fools,	93
158.	Ability necessary for acquiring knowledge,	93
159.	The pain inflicted by harsh words,	93
160.	The same,	94
161.	Harsh speech,	94
162.	Disregard of good advice,	94
163.	The same,	95
164.	The claims and duties of friendship,	95
165.	A real friend,	95
166.	Broken friendships never thoroughly cemented,	96
167.	Honest advice,	96
168.	Dishonest eulogists and secret detractors,	97

MISCELLANEOUS METRICAL TRANSLATIONS—*continued.*

		PAGE
169.	Evil of revengefulness,	97
170.	Results of foresight and courage and their contraries,	97
171.	Conditions of success,	98
172.	Boldness necessary to success,	98
173.	Self-respect essential to success,	98
174.	What energy can effect,	99
175.	Fearlessness,	99
176.	Procrastination,	99
177.	Evil of indecision,	100
178.	Promptitude necessary,	100
179.	Study beforehand the consequences of action,	100
180.	The best remedy of grief,	100
181.	The cure for grief,	101
182.	The wise superior to circumstances,	101
183.	Marks of a wise man,	101
184.	Appearances not always to be trusted,	101
185.	Content and final blessedness,	102
186.	The foolish discontented; the wise content,	102
187.	Discontent,	102
188.	No perfect happiness in the world,	102
189.	Desire insatiable,	103
190.	The same,	103
191.	Evils of wealth: praise of contentment,	104
192.	A man's aims vary with his time of life,	105
193.	Wealth and poverty,	105
194.	Wealth often injurious,	106
195.	The same,	107
196.	What will not men do to get wealth!	107
197.	The same,	107
198.	The rich hath many friends,	107
199.	The same,	108
200.	Heirs of the rich often spendthrifts,	108
201.	Self-exaltation, and censure of others condemned,	108
202.	Bad men pleased to hear ill, not good, of others,	109
203.	The bad like, the good dislike, to censure others,	109
204.	Men of merit alone can appreciate merit,	109
205.	Censoriousness and self-deception,	109
206.	Men see other's faults, but are blind to their own,	110
207.	"Why beholdest thou the mote that is in thy brother's eye," &c.,	110
208.	Want of self-knowledge,	110
209.	Conceit difficult to cure,	110
210.	To give advice easy; to act well difficult,	111
211.	To boast easy; to act difficult,	111
212.	Union is strength,	111
213.	The same,	112
214.	The same,	112
215.	Mutual help,	112

MISCELLANEOUS METRICAL TRANSLATIONS—*continued.*

	PAGE
216. Weak foes not to be despised,	112
217. Caution in dealing with a foe,	113
218. The same,	113
219. Machiavellian counsel,	113
220. How women ought to gain and keep their husband's affections,	113
221. A Kshatriya heroine's exhortation to her son,	120
222. Praise of women,	133
223. The same,	135
224. The bachelor only half a man,	137
225. The best cure for misfortune,	137
226. Reward of a wife's devotion,	137
227. Women naturally pandits,	138
228. Women's wiles,	138
229. A spell to promote concord in a family,	139
230. Description of a good king,	139
231. Self-conquest must precede other conquests,	140
232. Mercy should be shown to ignorant offenders,	142
233. A king's best treasures and castles,	142
234. "Vixere fortes ante Agamemnona," &c.,	142
235. Love of home,	142
236. Untravelled men's horizon contracted,	143
237. "The wolf also shall dwell with the lamb,"	143
238. The saint should patiently await the hour of his departure,	143
239. What is injurious, though dear, is to be abandoned,	144
240. "A prophet has no honour in his own country,"	144
241. ASITA AND BUDDHA, OR THE INDIAN SIMEON,	145
242. RAVANA AND VEDAVATI,	154
VERSIFIED TRANSLATIONS FROM THE RIGVEDA—	
243. Varuna,	159
244. Indra,	164
245. Parjanya, the Rain god,	177
246. Vâta or Vayu, the Wind god,	178
247. Sūrya, the Sun,	179
248. Ushas, the Indian Aurora,	180
249. Agni, the god of Fire,	183
250. Yama, and a future life,	186
251. Nonentity, Entity, and the One,	188
252. Aranyânî, the Forest goddess,	189
253. Men's various tastes,	190
254. The gambler,	190
255. Praise of liberality,	192
256. The same,	193
257. The frogs in autumn,	194
258. The warrior,	195
APPENDIX, CONTAINING PROSE TRANSLATIONS, ETC.,	197
SUPPLEMENT TO APPENDIX, CONTAINING PARALLEL PASSAGES FROM THE CLASSICAL AUTHORS,	337

INTRODUCTION.

ERRATA AND CORRECTIONS.

Introduction, p. xliv., line 13, for 360 read 363.

Page 31, place a mark of reference to the note (*) after "main" at the end of line 5.

Page 64, note, line 4, *for* "below," *read* "in the Appendix."

Page 74, line 11 from foot, put a comma after "gain."

Page 87, line 11, *for* "still men's grief," *read* "share men's grief."

Page 94, line 8 from foot, omit Psalms li. 2, and lv. 21.

Page 112, line 14, put full stop after "aid."

Pages 113, 3rd line from the foot; 114, lines 15 and 17; 115, line 2, for Kṛishṇā read Kṛishṇa, the masculine form with a short *a* at the end.

In pp. 114, line 1, 115, line 12, and 116, line 3, the feminine form Kṛishṇā is correct.

Page 119, line 9, *for* "hordes," *read* "hoards."

Page 215, *read* Śārṅgadhara's.

Page 271, line 20, *read* ὅταν τις.

Page 277, line 23, *for* "author," *read* "drama."

quote from this translation, p. 286, the following sentences of Dr Lorinser:—"If now we can find in the Bhagavad Gītā passages, and these not single and obscure, but numerous and clear, which present a surprising similarity to passages in the New Testament, we shall be justified in concluding that these

* Die Bhagavad Gitā uebersetzt und erläutert von Dr F. Lorinser, Breslau, 1869.

INTRODUCTION.

It will be noticed that not a few of the religious and moral maxims which are metrically rendered in this volume bear a striking resemblance to some of the most admired texts of the New Testament. With the view of affording the reader the means of judging with what degree of exactness the metrical versions reproduce the sentiments and expressions of the Indian writers, I have given in an Appendix a faithful prose version of the passages, to which, in some cases, the contexts have been added.

It has been supposed that an influence has been exercised on the religious ideas of the Indians by the introduction of a knowledge of Christianity into India in the earlier centuries of our era. This has been argued at length in regard to the "Bhagavad Gītā" (a theosophical episode of the Mahābhārata), by Dr Lorinser, who in the Appendix to his German translation of that work,* presents us with a collection of passages from the work in question, which he regards as borrowed from, or influenced by, the New Testament, and alongside of which he places the texts which he regards as having exercised this influence. The "Indian Antiquary," a monthly journal published at Bombay, contains in the number for October 1873, pp. 283—296, a translation of this Appendix. I quote from this translation, p. 286, the following sentences of Dr Lorinser:—"If now we can find in the Bhagavad Gītā passages, and these not single and obscure, but numerous and clear, which present a surprising similarity to passages in the New Testament, we shall be justified in concluding that these

* Die Bhagavad Gītā uebersetzt und erläutert von Dr F. Lorinser, Breslau, 1869.

coincidences are no play of chance, but that taken altogether they afford conclusive proof that the composer was acquainted with the writings of the New Testament, used them as he thought fit, and has woven into his own work numerous passages, if not word for word, yet preserving the meaning, and shaping it according to his Indian mode of thought, a fact which till now no one has noticed. To put this assertion beyond doubt, I shall place side by side the most important of these passages in the Bhagavad Gitā, and the corresponding texts of the New Testament. I distinguish three different kinds of passages to which parallels can be adduced from the New Testament: First, such as with more or less of verbal difference, agree in sense, so that a thought which is clearly Christian appears in an Indian form of expression. These are far the most numerous, and indicate the way in which the original was used in general; Secondly, passages in which a peculiar and characteristic expression of the New Testament is borrowed word for word, though the meaning is sometimes quite changed; Thirdly, passages in which thought and expression agree, though the former receives from the context a meaning suited to Indian conception."

Although the influence of the Christian Scriptures may not be considered to extend to the religious and moral ideas, not of a specifically Christian character—such as are adduced in the present volume—which are found in the Indian writers, and to affect their originality, I regard the question raised by Dr Lorinser as of sufficient interest to induce me to reproduce here, with modifications, the discussion of the subject which appeared in the introduction to my little work, "Religious and Moral Sentiments, metrically rendered, from Sanskrit Writers" (published in 1875), which is incorporated in the present volume.

In order, if possible, to reach a solution of the problem propounded by Dr Lorinser, three points must be considered and settled:—1*st*, the age of the Bhagavad Gitā; 2*dly*, whether, supposing its antiquity not to be such as to guarantee its originality, any Christian doctrines could, at the date of its composition, have been imported into India and promulgated in an oral or written form so as to be accessible to the author, if his mind was open to their reception; and *3dly*, whether his work, when compared with the Christian Scriptures, or doctrines, manifests any such similarity to their ideas as to justify the supposition of their being borrowed.

Without myself offering any definite opinion on this intricate problem, the solution of which depends on the answers to be given to these various questions, I shall refer the reader to what has been said on the first two points by the different writers quoted further on, and myself offer some remarks on the third point.

In forming an opinion on a question of this kind, we should, supposing the alleged resemblances to be admitted, consider, first, whether the ideas, sentiments, or figures of speech supposed to be borrowed by the Indians from the west are not such as might naturally arise in the human, or at least in the oriental, mind; secondly, whether they cannot be traced, at least in germ, in Indian writers of such antiquity as to exclude the supposition of foreign influence; thirdly, whether they do not so pervade the Indian writings as to be manifestly indigenous and original; fourthly, whether the writings of any other countries, known to be independent of Christian influences, contain ideas or sentiments supposed to be exclusively or peculiarly Christian; and fifthly, what probability there is that the Brahmans of the period in question could have been brought into contact with foreign ideas, and whether they would have been intellectually and morally open to, and susceptible of, such influences.

I venture to make the following remarks on this subject. There is, no doubt, a general, or perhaps I might say, a striking, resemblance between the manner in which Kṛishṇa asserts his own divine nature, enjoins devotion to his person, and sets forth the blessings which will result to his votaries from such worship, on the one hand, and, on the other, the strain in which the founder of Christianity is represented in the Gospels, and especially in the Fourth, as speaking of himself and his claims, and the redemption which will follow on their faithful recognition. At the same time, the Bhagavad Gîtâ contains much that is exclusively Indian in its character, and which finds no counterpart in the New Testament doctrine.

Some of the texts in the Indian poem also present a resemblance more or less close to some in the Bible. Perhaps the most striking are the declarations of the Bhagavad Gītā, ix. 29, "They who devoutly worship me are in me, and I in them;" and xii. 8, "Repose thy mind upon [or in] me, fix thine understanding on me, and thou shalt thereafter* dwell in me," as compared with John vi. 56, "He that eateth my flesh and drinketh my blood abideth in me and I in him;" and John xvii. 20 f., "Neither pray I for these alone, but for them also which believe on me through their word; that they all may be one, as thou, Father, art in me, and I in thee, that they also may be in us." Here, however, it will be observed, that the condition of indwelling in the speaker is not the same in all the cases; and, in particular, that the Indian work neither recognises the idea of eating his flesh and drinking his blood, nor the existence of two divine persons.

In the Ṛigveda some passages occur which in part convey the same or a similar idea. Thus in ii. 11, 12, it is said: *tve Indra apy abhūma viprāḥ*, "O Indra, we sages have been in thee;" and in x. 142. 1, *Ayam Agne jaritā tve abhūd api sahasaḥ sūno nahy anyad asty āpyam*, "This worshipper, O Agni, hath been in thee: O son of strength, he has no other kinship;" and in viii. 47. 8, *Yushme devāḥ api smasi yudhyantaḥ iva varmasu*, "We, O gods, are in you, as if fighting in coats of mail." In the Sanskrit and German Lexicon compiled by Dr Böhtlingk and himself, Professor Roth assigns to the words *api smasi* in the last passage the sense of "being in anything," being closely connected with it. To the similar phrases, *apy abhūma* and *abhūd api*, in the other two texts, he ascribes the sense of "having a share in," which seems to be the meaning in one passage at least, (*Aitareya Brāhmaṇa*, vii. 28), where the compound verb occurs. In any case, close connection is

* Lorinser translates the words *ataḥ ūrddhvam*, here rendered "thereafter," by "in the height" (*in der Höhe*). He here follows Schlegel, who has, *apud superos*, and Thomson, whom he cites as having "on high after this life." The words, however, usually mean "after this," and K. T. Telang gives "hereafter." With this passage Dr Lorinser compares Colossians iii. 1, "Seek those things which are above," etc.

intended. And in viii. 81. 32, the worshipper says to Indra, *tvam asmâkam tava smasi*, "thou art ours, and we are thine."

The following are some other remarks which I have to make upon Dr Lorinser's renderings :—

Ind. Ant., as above quoted, p. 288: "He is far from darkness" (viii. 9).

P. 289: "Light of lights, far from darkness is his name" (xiii. 17).

Which he compares with "God is light, and in him is no darkness at all" (1 John i. 5).

The words here translated "far from darkness" (*tamasaḥ parastât*) would be better rendered by "beyond the darkness." They are not peculiar to this passage, but occur also in the *Muṇḍa Upanishad*, ii. 2. 6, and *Mahâbhârata*, v. 1712. The words, *tamasas pari*, meaning "above, or beyond, the darkness," occur also in *Ṛigveda*, i. 50. 10: "Gazing towards the upper light beyond the darkness, we have ascended to the highest luminary, Sûrya (the Sun), a god among the gods." In the lines of the *Bhagavad Gîtâ*, the words, *tamasaḥ parastât*, are immediately preceded by *âditya-varṇam*, "the sun-coloured," "beyond the darkness." The Indian writer had thus no need to borrow this epithet from the Bible. It may be remarked, besides, that the verse Bh. G. viii. 9 contains many other epithets of Kṛishṇa as the supreme deity.

P. 291: "But if I were not constantly engaged *in work*, unwearied . . . these worlds would perish *if I did not work my work*" (iii. 23, 24).

Which is compared with "My Father worketh hitherto, and I work." (John v. 17).

This is quoted as one of the "passages which contain a characteristic expression of the New Testament with a different application;" but as the author translates it, the application seems to be nearly the same, as he renders the words, *utsîdeyur ime lokâḥ*, "these worlds would perish," or "would sink" (*versanken*); whereas it appears that the whole context (verses 21 ff.) points to the influence exercised by the example of an eminent man on the people around him, and leads to the conclusion that the words should be rendered "these men would be discouraged," or led into error, if I did not perform good works as an example for their imitation. In Râmânuja's commentary the words are paraphrased *sarve śishṭalokāḥ*, &c., "all good people would be destroyed."* The sentiment expressed in Bhag. Gītā iii. 21 is also to be found in *Rāmāyaṇa* ii. 109. 9 (Bombay edition. See Appendix to this volume, p. 220, line 7 f.)

P. 292: "*Dead in me*" (x. 9).
"Ye are dead, and your life is hid with Christ in God" (Col. ii. 3).

The phrase here rendered "dead in me" is *mad-gata-prāṇāḥ*. It is explained by Râmânuja as *mad-gata-jīvitāḥ* | *mayā vinā ātma-dhāraṇam alabhamānāḥ ity arthaḥ* | "'Having your life gone to me.' The sense is, 'not obtaining a support for your soul or self without me.'" The participle *gata*, followed by *prāṇa* (*gata-prāṇa*), undoubtedly means "dead," *i.e.*, one whose breath is gone, just as *gatāsu* (*i.e.*, *gata* + *asu*) does. But compounded with a word preceding it, *gata* means "gone to;" thus *hṛid-gata* means, "gone to, or abiding in, the heart." The compound before us therefore signifies, "whose breath resorts to, and rests in, me.' It is preceded by *mach-chittaḥ*, "having your hearts in me." Lorinser quotes Mr Cockburn Thomson as supporting the sense he gives, but it is not adopted by Schlegel or Burnouf.

P. 291: "I who am the highest *way*," (vii. 18).

P. 293: "I am the way, beginning, and end" (ix. 18). [The German of the last two words should be rendered "origin and dissolution,"]—compared with:

"I am the *way* . . . No man cometh unto the Father but by me" (John xiv. 6). "I am the first and the last." (Rev. i. 17).

The word here translated "way" is in both passages of the Sanskrit, *gati*. This I regard as incorrect. *Gati*, it is true, primarily means "going," and so, no doubt, stands for "path," but here, as in many other passages of the Indian writings, it

* I should observe, however, that this is not the sense assigned to *ime lokāḥ* in Kāshināth Trimbak Telang's translation, p. 22, where they are rendered "these worlds," on the authority of Śankara and Śrīdhara. If he is right, there would be more similarity between the two passages compared by Dr Lorinser.

certainly signifies "the place reached by going," "resort," "refuge." Râmânuja explains *gati* in the second passage thus: *gati—Śakra-loka-prabhṛiti-prâpya-sthânam, i.e.*, "the heaven of Śakra (Indra), and other abodes which are to be attained."

It is further to be observed that whilst Jesus designates himself as "the way, the truth, and the life," Kṛishṇa, in one of the verses referred to, calls himself only the "unequalled abode or resort;" and in the other, "the resort, the sustainer, the lord, the witness, the abode, the refuge, the friend, the source, the dissolution, the stay, the receptacle, the undecaying seed;" so that, in any case, the resemblance would be but partial, while some of the ideas in the Bh. G. are foreign to the New Testament.

It is, perhaps, superfluous to remark that there is found in the Gitâ no such idea as that Kṛishṇa should suffer for the sins of mankind; while Jesus repeatedly affirms this of himself (John x. 11, 15, 17 f.; xi. 50; xii. 23—33; xv. 18—20). It can scarcely be considered as an approach to such an idea that Kṛishṇa says of himself in ix. 11, that foolish men despise him in his human form, being ignorant of his higher nature, as lord of all beings. He is, in fact, described in the Mahâbhârata ii. 1338 ff., as having been treated with contempt by Śiśupâla, whom he slew. See Prof. Monier Williams' "Indian Epic Poetry," p. 102 f.; and my "Original Sanskrit Texts," iv. 205 ff. (2d ed.)

It is also to be remarked, as another difference between the Christian and the Indian doctrines, that while in the fourth Gospel Christ asserts his oneness with the Father (John x. 30), and speaks of the Father as being in him, and of himself as being in the Father (xiv. 10, 11), he yet declares himself to be in some sense distinct from him, as being the Son (v. 19), as being sent into the world by the Father (x. 36; xii. 49), as having received of the Father the prerogative of having life in himself (v. 26), and as not doing anything of himself, but doing the Father's will (v. 30). Whereas in the Bhagavad Gîtâ we find no reference to any similar relation subsisting between Kṛishṇa and any other person in the godhead, or in fact any reference to a distinction of persons in the godhead at all. He is represented as himself the Supreme

Deity. In vii. 6 f. he says of himself: "I am the generator and the destroyer of the entire universe. Than me there is nothing higher. On me all this universe is woven, as gems on a string. I am the flavour in water, the light in the sun and moon," &c.; and in ix. 4 he says: "By me, imperceptible in form, this universe is pervaded [or spread out?] All existences abide in me, but I do not abide in them; and yet they do not abide in me." After hearing Krishna's own account of himself, Arjuna says, x. 12: "Thou art the Supreme Brahma, the highest essence (*dhāman*), the eternal divine Purusha, unborn, all-pervading."

Two modes of attaining to oneness with Krishna are described as follows at the beginning of sect. xii., verses 2 ff.: "Those who, fixing their minds on me with the completest faith, worship me with constant devotion, are esteemed by me the most devoted: 3, 4, But I am the goal at which those arrive who, controlling their senses, maintaining in all circumstances the same dispositions, bent upon the good of all creatures, worship the indestructible, indescribable, imperceptible, all-pervading, unthinkable, absolute (*kūṭastha*), immovable, unchanging (Being). But [the latter], those whose minds are fixed on the imperceptible, experience greater difficulty; since the imperceptible goal is hard to be attained by embodied beings." Here there seems to be no subordination of Kṛishṇa to the Supreme Spirit, as described in verses 3 and 4. But it appears as if in this passage it were intended to represent the attainment of final liberation by means of devotion to Kṛishṇa as an easier method of gaining that end, by substituting in the interest of simple-minded worshippers,—who were not to renounce the world, though they were, like king Janaka, to regard it and all its interests with perfect indifference,—a visible, incarnate object of meditation, for the impalpable and abstract object of contemplation to which the thoughts of devotees had formerly been directed by scholastic theologians.* In a verse of a previous section (viii. 14)

* King Janaka is celebrated in the Gītā, iii. 20, as having attained perfection by the method of works, the system preferred by Krishṇa. In the passage of the Mahābhārata, abstracted in the Appendix, pp.

Kṛishṇa had said: "I am easily attained by the steadfast devotee who thinks of me, with a soul fixed on me exclusively."

It thus appears, that while the doctrine of Kṛishṇa regarding his own nature is pantheistic, his pantheism differs in its accompaniments from the older pantheism of the Upanishads, and many parts of the Mahābhārata. In the Upanishads, the Supreme Spirit is neither represented as incarnate in a human person, nor made the object of passionate devotion. The absence of all emotion, indeed, is regarded as an essential element in that perfection which leads to final liberation from earthly bonds, and identification with the Supreme Spirit. But may not the doctrine of the Bhagavad Gītā have arisen naturally, and without the intervention of any foreign influence, from a fusion of the transcendental and popular elements which both existed in the anterior Hinduism? In the hymns of the Ṛigveda we find devotion and affection to the gods expressed in a variety of terms, which are adduced in the latter part of this volume, pp. 314 ff. and 327 ff. Is there, as has been asserted by Dr Lorinser ("Indian Antiquary" for 1873), anything essentially new in the conception of *bhakti* (devotion) which was not contained in these Vedic expressions? And it is scarcely necessary to say that a popular worship and adoration of various deities must have prevailed all along from the Vedic age down to that of Kṛishṇa, among those sections of the people which were inaccessible to abstract speculation and to pantheistic ideas. And might not the speculative and popular conceptions have been blended in the minds even of members of the learned class, and have found their expression in such systems as the Bhagavad Gītā?*

I may mention here (although the question before us is not

251 ff., however, his course of life, though at first vindicated by himself, is declared by the female devotee Sulabhā to be inconsistent with real renunciation of the world. Here, therefore, we seem to have the views of a writer opposed to Krishna's system, whether the passage be more recent, or earlier in date than the Bhagavad Gītā.

* The remarks of Kāshināth Trimbak Telang (whose book will be noticed below), in pp. xxxii., bear on this question. See below an account of the stages by which Prof. Weber considers that Kṛishṇa was elevated to the dignity of identification with Vishṇu.

discussed in it), that in a dissertation just issued on "Arjuna, a contribution to the reconstruction of the Mahābhārata,"* in which the Pāṇḍu prince's career, and his relations with Kṛishṇa, are traced throughout the great Epic, Professor Adolf Holtzmann remarks as follows (p. 20 f.) on the Bhagavad Gītā: "A conversation on the spirit in which men should fight may in the old poem (*i.e.*, the poem in its earliest form, before it had been modified by later influences,) have found a place before the beginning of the great battle; only it was probably not carried on between Arjuna and Kṛishṇa, but rather between Duryodhana and his learned teacher Droṇa. Even now the Bhagavad Gītā begins with a short talk between these two; and then passes to Arjuna and Kṛishṇa. Such hints are always significant. The beautiful verses, which, proceeding on a pantheistic view of the world, point out the folly of all dread of death, the profound reflections on energy and resignation, the mutual relation of which was always an attractive mystery to the Indian mind, are certainly old; but not so the identification of the pantheistic soul of the world with Vishṇu, and then that of the latter with Kṛishṇa." Of Kṛishṇa, Professor H. says further on, p. 59: "In the old poem he is a [mere] man; and indeed a man who does not stand high, either by birth, or by nobility of sentiment. He is the charioteer, and, no doubt, also the brother-in-law, of Arjuna, his best friend, and crafty adviser. All the schemes which, according to the ancient doctrine of warfare, were [held to be] dishonourable or faithless, were planned by Kṛishṇa,† and were, after some resist-

* This is the third essay which Professor Holtzmann has published on the Mahābhārata. One on "Agni nach den Vorstellungen des Mahābhārata," (pp. 36), appeared in 1878. Another on Indra is to be found in the second number of the Journal of the German Oriental Society for the same year. In these valuable dissertations, the author seeks to discover and adduce the ideas entertained of the deities in those parts of the great Epic which appear to be the most ancient, and to distinguish them from the new or modified conceptions which are found in those passages which may reasonably be held to have been produced and inserted in it at a later period.

† Compare the passage from the Mahābhārata ix. 3445 ff., translated by me in the Indian Antiquary for November 1876 (p. 311), where Kṛishṇa defends unfair fighting with their adversaries, on the ground that they could not otherwise have been overcome.

ance, either carried out by Arjuna himself, ... or permitted to take effect." In p. 61, Professor H. remarks: "What fatality impelled the Indians to elevate such a man into an incarnation of the supreme Deity, is an, as yet, unsolved enigma. There must have been powerful political, as well as religious, revolutions which brought about this result. The old Kṛishṇa of the Mahābhārata must have been fused with a quite different Kṛishṇa, such as, (*e.g.*) he is represented in the Harivanśa, the deified tribal hero of a brave and victorious population, to whose mythological conceptions the old Indian pantheon had to adjust itself." . . . . . P. 62, "The deification of Kṛishṇa is as yet unknown to the older portion of the Mahābhārata; but everywhere later pieces, which teach that doctrine, are interpolated; so that, looking to the whole, we must say that this doctrine of the identity of Kṛishṇa with the supreme Being,—a doctrine which, so to speak, has turned the entire old poem upside down,—has penetrated the whole of the existing Mahābhārata."

Besides the Bhagavad Gītā, there is another part of the Mahābhārata to which I wish to refer, as it also has been adduced to prove that a knowledge of Christianity existed in India in the early centuries of our era,—I mean the passages in which the Śveta-dvīpa, the white island (or continent), and its inhabitants are referred to. This account is considered by Professor Lassen (Indische Alterthumskunde, 2d Ed., ii. 1115, Note 1) to be one of the latest additions made to the great epic poem.* In M. Bh. xii. 12702 ff., we are told that the sage Nārada flew up into the sky, and alighted on the top of Mount Meru; and looking towards the northwest, saw the great island, Śvetadvīpa, to the north of the ocean of milk, 22,000 yojanas (a yojana is at least several miles) higher than Meru, inhabited by white men, without organs of sense, free from sin, with bodies of adamant, umbrella-shaped heads, and a hundred lotus-feet; who with their tongues † continually, and devoutly,

* The reason assigned for this opinion is that the account is inserted in the narrative adduced in the Appendix to Professor L.'s first volume, p. xxxvi., Note, regarding Uparichara Vasu.

† How had they tongues, if they had no organs of sense?

licked the universal-faced God of sun-like brightness. (Here the story of Nārada stops, to be resumed afterwards.) These inhabitants of Śveta-dvīpa are again described in verses 12778 ff. as being moon-like in brilliancy, devoted to Nārāyaṇa and Purushottama (both names of Vishṇu), worshippers of one Deity, or monotheists (*ekāntinaḥ*), and as entering into (or becoming absorbed in) the eternal god of a thousand rays. The island was visited by three sages, Ekata, Dvita, and Trita, who, however, could not see the God, being blinded by the blaze of his glory (verse 12784). After performing austerities for a hundred years, they saw the white men, who, as a reward of the concentration of their minds on the Deity, obtain each from Vishṇu a lustre equal to that of the sun as it shines at the end of the yugas (great mundane periods). Then was beheld a glory equal to a thousand suns, and the white men all run up, crying out, "Adoration!" (to the God). The God comes, but the three visitors are unable to see him (12798), and are told by a god (12804 ff.) that the Deity could be seen only by those white men, and that they (the visitors) might depart; that the Deity, who could with difficulty be viewed owing to his intense brightness, could not be beheld by any one destitute of devotion (*abhakta*), but only by those who after a length of time had attained to the capacity of worshipping one God. The account of Nārada's visit to the white island (which had been broken off at verse 12707) is resumed at verse 12861. After paying homage to, and receiving homage from, the white men, he addresses a hymn to the Deity, who appears to him, universal-formed, showing different colours in different parts of his manifestation, with a thousand eyes, a hundred heads, and a thousand feet, uttering the sacred syllable Om, the Gāyatrī, many Vedas, an Âraṇyaka, and bearing various objects connected with the ritual of sacrifice. He tells Nārada that Ekata, Dvita, and Trita had been unable to see him, and that no one could behold him but a worshipper of one God, such as he (Nārada) was. He then desires Nārada to ask a boon; but Nārada replied that the vision which he had obtained was a sufficient boon. The Deity then says he may go, hinting that his continued presence might disturb the devout contemplations of the white men, who are now perfect, and were formerly worshippers of one God; and who, being free from passion and darkness (rajas and tamas), will certainly enter into (or be absorbed in) him (verse 12884).* His address is continued down to verse 12973; and Nārada goes, after being told, in verse 12971, that not even Brahmā had obtained such a vision of the Deity as he had had.

Another passage which has been cited as bearing upon the question under discussion is the following:—In the Mahābhārata, xii. 5675, Yudhishṭhira asks Bhīshma (without there being in the immediate context, so far as I can see, anything to occasion the question) whether he had ever seen or heard of a dead person being raised to life? In reply, Bhīshma tells him a story of a conversation between a jackal and a vulture. A Brahman's son had died, and was taken to the cemetery by his relations, who were hesitating to leave him there, when they were addressed by a vulture, which tells them to go, as no dead person had ever been restored to life. The friends were then about to leave the body, and depart, when they were stopped by a jackal, who charged them with want of affection. They accordingly remained. The vulture replies and the jackal rejoins; and then the former says (verse 5728) that he had lived a thousand years and never seen a dead person live again. The jackal in answer asserts (verses 5742 ff.) that it was reported that, after slaying Śambuka, a Śūdra, Rāma had restored a Brahman's son to life,† and that the son of the

---

* Compare verse 12913 and verse 12907. "Men devoted to me, entering into me, are freed." In verse 12911 it is said, "I am called the life (*jīva*); in me the life is reposed; never think to thyself 'The life has been seen by me,'"—a passage in which a follower of Dr Lorinser might see a reflection of Christianity. See St John's Gospel, i. 4 and xi. 25. The life (*jīva* or *jīvātman*), the individual soul, is a term which frequently occurs in Indian philosophy.

† See the Rāmāyaṇa, Uttarakāṇḍa, sections 73—76. A Brahman's son had died young; his death was ascribed by Nārada to the enormity of a Śūdra presuming to perform austerities (74, 27 ff.) Rāma goes and finds the Śūdra in the act, and kills him (sect. 75, 14 ff.; 76, 1 ff.). The gods applaud the deed, and on being solicited to restore the Brahman's boy to life, say that he had recovered his life as soon as the Śūdra had been killed.

royal ṛishi Śveta had been raised to life again by his righteous father; and he adds that perhaps some saint (*siddha*) or sage (*muni*) or god may take pity on them also. The advocates of the two opposite views are still disputing when the god Śankara (Śiva) arrives (5788 ff.), sent by his wife, his eyes moistened with tears of compassion; and on their solicitation restores the boy to life for a hundred years.

On the first of these passages regarding Śveta-dvīpa, Professor Weber (Indische Studien, i. 400, Note) builds the conjecture that "Brahmans went by sea to Alexandria, or Asia Minor, at the period when early Christianity flourished, and that on their return home they transferred the monotheistic doctrine, and certain legends connected with it, to their own indigenous sage or hero Kṛishṇa Devakī-putra (son of Devakī, the divine), who by his name reminded them of Christ, the son of the divine virgin, and who had perhaps been previously worshipped as a god; substituting, however, for the Christian doctrines the philosophical principles of the Sānkhya and Yoga schools; as the latter may, on the other hand, have influenced the formation of the Gnostic sects."

In a note to page 421 of the same volume Professor Weber refers to a note of the late Professor H. H. Wilson in his Sketch of the religious sects of the Hindus (see his collected works, Vol. I. p. 210 f.), in which we read:—"Śiva, it is said, appeared in the beginning of the Kali age as Śveta, for the purpose of benefiting the Brahmans. He resided on the Himālaya mountains, and taught the Yoga. He had four chief disciples, one also termed Śveta, and the others, Śveta-śikha, Śvetāśva [V. L., Śvetāsya],* and Śvetalohita. . . . The four primitive teachers may be imaginary; but it is a curious circumstance that the word Śveta, *white*, should be the leading member of each appellation, and that in the person of Śiva and his first disciple it should stand alone as Śveta, the white. Śiva, however, is always painted white, and the names may be contrived accordingly; but we are still at a loss to understand why the god himself should have a European complexion." On this Weber remarks:—"Are we to suppose here a Syrian

* The word in parenthesis is added by the editor, Dr R. Rost.

Christian mission ?* That its doctrines should be clothed by its Indian disciples in a Brahmanical dress, and that the monotheism of Christianity alone should remain, is natural." Professor Weber then proceeds to refer thus to the second passage above quoted :—" In the Mahābhārata, xii. 5743, the case of a white king (*Śvetasya rājarsheḥ*)—who because he was dharmanishṭha (devoted to righteousness) had restored his son to life—is referred to in proof of the possibility of such restoration. A Christian legend may perhaps form the basis of this story, unless we should compare with it the legend of Sṛinjaya Śvaitya (in the M. Bh. xii. 906 ff.), to whom Nārada gave by sanjīvana (restoration to life) a new son, Hiraṇyanābha, in lieu of Suvarṇashṭhīvin, a son whom he had lost."

The story last referred to is told in two places of the Mahābhārata. According to vii. 2155 ff., King Sṛinjaya obtained as a boon from the sage Nārada that he should have a son, whose nature was such that all that issued from his body was of gold. The king's wealth in consequence increased enormously. The son was, however, carried off, and killed by robbers, who hoped to get gold from his body, but were disappointed. The king laments him, and is told by Nārada that he shall die as many famous kings, whom he goes on to

* Professor Weber returns to this subject in the second volume of his Ind. Stud., pp. 168 f., where he supposes that a number of Christian missionaries came to India both by sea (of whose agency traces still remain on the Malabar coast), and also through High Asia,—those who arrived from this side being at first confined to the north-west of India. If no Christian colonies are now to be met with there, he finds the reason of this partly in the fact that this tract has been the battlefield of foreign invaders, but especially in the circumstance that the communication of these Christians with their home was cut off, and they could receive thence no fresh spiritual force, nor any other resources, —while the case was different with the Christians of Malabar. He then proceeds :—" Although it is consequently inconceivable *à priori* that Christian colonies should have been able to maintain themselves in the north-western parts of India, I have nevertheless, in Vol. I. 421, indicated from a legend adduced by Wilson the remembrance retained of the fact that five Christians—this meaning probably a mission of five Christian priests—had at one time settled on the Himālaya, and there preached monotheism ;" though the result was that the worshippers of Siva regarded this mission as a revelation of their own god.

enumerate, have died before him. At the end of his discourse, which had a sanctifying effect on Sṛinjaya, Nārada restores to him his son, delivering him from hell (verses 2458 f.). Vyāsa, who tells the story to Yudhishṭhira, adds that those who have gone to heaven do not desire to return to earth, and that therefore the slain who are in paradise should not be lamented; while the lot of the living, on the contrary, should be a cause of grief. The tale is repeated in a quite different form in M. Bh. xii. 1041 ff., and 1102 ff. Sṛinjaya asks the sages Nārada and Parvata for a long-lived son. Parvata promises a son, but not a long-lived one, as he says the father, in making his request, designed that his son should overthrow the god Indra; and when entreated to change his decision, remains silent. The king is, however, assured by the narrator of the story (Nārada) that he himself, if called upon after the boy's death, would restore him to life (verses 1107 f.) A son is accordingly born to Sṛinjaya. Indra, however, being afraid of him, and being a follower of Vṛihaspati's doctrine, plans the young prince's death, and commands his thunderbolt to take the form of a tiger and kill him (1113 ff.) This accordingly takes place when the boy was five years old, and was playing in the wood, attended by his nurse (1118 ff.) The king comes to the spot, and calls Nārada to mind, who appears and restores the boy to life (1126 ff.)

The views of Professor Weber above referred to are discussed by Professor Lassen in the second volume of his Indische Alterthumskunde, second edition, pp. 1118 ff. (1), He concurs in the belief that some Brahmans became acquainted with Christianity in some country lying to the north of India, and brought home some Christian doctrines. This he considers to be supported (*a*) by the name of the white island, and the colour of its inhabitants, so different from that of the Indians;* (*b*) by the ascription to these people of the worship of an unseen God, while the Indians of the same period had images

---

* A learned correspondent is of opinion that no such conclusion can be drawn from this story. He thinks that Śveta Dvīpa bears about the same relation to the Syrian Christians as Swift's Brobdignag or the Nephelokokkygia of Aristophanes does.

of their deities; (*c*) by the attribution to them of faith, the efficacy of which is not an ancient Indian tenet;* (*d*) by the value attributed to prayer, which is a less important element in Indian than in Christian rites; and (*e*) by the fact that the doctrine which they learned is described as one only made known to the Indians at a late period. He holds it as the most likely supposition that Parthia was the country where the Brahmans met with Christian missionaries. (2), Professor Lassen thinks that the proof drawn from the passage about Śiva and his four disciples, referred to by Prof. Weber (see above) in favour of the supposition of the presence of Christian missionaries in India, rests on no firm foundation; and believes that this story owes its origin to the other passage in the M. Bh. about the Śveta Dvipa. Prof. Lassen does not think that any influence was exercised by Christian missionaries or their disciples on the religious views of the Indians, because (*a*) the Christians occupied a very subordinate position in India, and were at a distance from the centres of Indian science and religious life; (*b*) because the Brahmans actually persecuted the Christians; and (*c*) because both the Brahmans and other Indians are opposed to the reception of anything offered to them by the Mlechha (*i.e.*, degraded foreigner). The only knowledge of Christianity which the Indians have yet been shown to have possessed during the first three centuries of our era is confined to the meagre acquaintance with it contained in the narrative of the Mahâbhârata, to which reference has been made. (3), Lassen does not consider that the Pāncharātra doctrines arose from an acquaintance with Christianity, but thinks that the narrator of the story about the White Island employed this

* See, however, the reference made above (p. xxi.) to the occurrence in the ancient hymns of the Veda of frequent allusions to faith in the gods. In the Chhândogya Upanishad, ii. 1, 10, it is said: "Whatever is done with knowledge, with faith, with esoteric science, is more efficacious." In the Taittirîya Sanhitâ it is said, i. 6, 8, 1: "They have no faith in that man's sacrifice who sacrifices without the exercise of faith; and in the Śatapatha Brâhmaṇa, xiv. 6, 9, 22 (= Brihad Âraṇyaka Upanishad, iii. 9, 21): "On what are largesses based? on faith; for when a man has faith he bestows largesses; so it is on faith that largesses are based. On what is faith based? on the heart; for it is through his heart that a man has faith." See below, p. 327 ff. of this volume.

name to intimate what he had heard about the journey of some Brahmans to a Christian country, and the doctrines there prevalent; but does not correctly represent the religious and philosophical tenets of the Pāncharātras, ascribing to them beliefs which are not theirs. This, he proceeds, has been perceived by the latest editors of the Mahābhārata, who found it necessary to add a true account of their doctrines. This has been done by the introduction of Nārada, who is said to have gone to the Śveta Dvīpa after Ekata, Dvita, and Trita, and to have received from Vāsudeva himself the Pāncharātra doctrine. Lassen is further opposed to the supposition (see Weber's Indische Studien, i. 423) that the Indian monotheism resulted from an acquaintance with Christianity; for (*a*) the Pāncharātras did not adore a single God, but Vāsuveda, as the highest, to whom the others were subordinated; (*b*) the Brahmans had already a highest god in Brahmā, and the adherents of the Yoga system had a single highest god in their Íśvara, making Brahmā a created being. The Indian tendency to monotheism was based, he considers, on the character of the sects, which involved an exclusive adoration either of Vishṇu or Śiva. Further, Lassen does not consider it permissible to hold that the ideas of the Brahmans regarding prayer and faith were at all influenced by any acquaintance with Christianity. He is further of opinion that a belief in the incarnations of Vishṇu existed three centuries before the Christian era, an opinion which he bases on what Megasthenes relates of the Indian Hercules; and thinks that there is no valid ground for admitting that in the early ages of Christianity any Christian legends were transferred and applied to Kṛishṇa.

Professor Weber, in a note in the second vol. of his Ind. Stud., pp. 409 ff., replies to Lassen's argument—derived from the account given by Megasthenes regarding the Indian Hercules—that in the age of that Greek author the Indians already possessed the conception of incarnations of the Deity. He considers that Lassen is wrong in supposing that Megasthenes had Kṛishṇa in view in his account of the Indian Hercules, and thinks rather that the Videha Māthava mentioned in the Śatapatha Brāhmaṇa [i. 4, i. 10 ff.] is alluded to, or that if not he, then Balarāma, Kṛishṇa's brother, is more likely to be meant (as Wilson decides in his Preface to the Vishṇu Purāṇa, vol. i. of Dr Hall's Edition, p. xii.)

Kṛishṇa was, Weber continues, regarded at the period in question as a purely human personality, a character which he bears in the Chhāndogya Upanishad [Bibliotheca Indica, pp. 220 ff.]. The peculiarity of the system of Avatāras (incarnations) consists, Weber considers, not in the assumption by a god of an animal or a human form, which is common to almost all mythologies, but,—apart from the number and series of the incarnations,—essentially in the circumstance that it is out of compassion to the suffering, and from anger towards sinful humanity, that the god is born as a man, and leads a human life. Admitting even—what Prof. Weber does not believe—that this conception was current among the Indians before they became acquainted with Christianity, it was only after this period that it acquired such force as to become formed into a complete system.

In a paper by Professor Bhāṇḍārkar in the Indian Antiquary for January 1874, headed "Allusions to Kṛishṇa in Patanjali's Mahābhāshya," pp. 14-16, the author, after adducing the passages on which he relies, concludes as follows: "I have thus brought together seven passages from a work written in the middle of the second century before Christ, which show that the stories about Kṛishṇa and his worship as a god are not so recent as European scholars would make them. And to these I ask the attention of those who find in Christ a prototype of Kṛishṇa, and in the Bible the origin of the Bhagavad Gītā, and who believe our Puranic literature to be merely a later growth."

Prof. Weber had previously referred to these passages in pp. 348 ff. of his paper on the Mahābhāshya (Indische Studien, vol. xiii.) finished in October 1873. But (on the uncertain supposition that these references go back to Patanjali's time) he does not consider that the application to Vishṇu of the word "bhagavat" (on which Prof. Bhāṇḍārkar relies, and to which the Commentator Kaiyaṭa gives the sense of the supreme Spirit) means anything more than that he was regarded as a demi-god, a character intermediate between his position as a hero in the epic story, and his identification with Vishṇu. (Ind. Antiq. iv. 246 f.)

In his dissertation on the Kṛishṇajanmāshṭamī festival, pp. 316 ff., Prof. Weber refers to the earlier stages by which Kṛishṇa was gradually elevated to the character of the Supreme Deity. We first, he says, find Kṛishṇa, son of Devakī, mentioned in the Chhāndogya Upanishad (iii. 17, 4), as receiving instruction from Ghora Āngirasa, which made him indifferent to other knowledge. *2dly.* He appears in the Mahābhārata, ii. 1332, 1378, 1384, where he receives, though not a king, the present suitable to a person of the highest dignity.* *3dly.* He appears, further, as a demigod, the friend and adviser of the Pāṇḍus, possessed of supernatural power and wisdom. How he attained this elevation Prof. Weber regards as, for the present, inexplicable. *4thly.* The pilgrimage of some Indian sages to Śvetadvīpa, and their discovery there of the worship of Christ, the son of the divine virgin, led to the further development of the worship of Kṛishṇa, and to his eventual exaltation to the dignity of Vishṇu. This result was not so much, Prof. Weber considers, due to direct Christian influences as to independent appropriations, leading to a special Indian growth.

This question of the originality or otherwise of the Bhagavad Gītā has been treated at length by the Kāshināth Trimbak Telang, in an introductory essay of cxix pages, prefixed to his English metrical translation of the Bhagavad Gītā, published at Bombay in 1875. Some of the contents of this introduction are as follows. The author discusses the grounds alleged by Dr Lorinser for his opinions, combats the proposition that the Gītā is certainly subsequent to Buddha, and holds, as a sort of provisional hypothesis, that it is older (pp. ii–vii). He denies the sufficiency of the evidence that Christian communities existed in India before the third century A.D. (pp. xi–xv), or that a translation of the Christian

---

* Immediately after, in line 139 ff., a divine character is distinctly ascribed to him, as he is called the originator and ender of the worlds. This, however, may be an interpolation. See the pages of my Sanskrit Texts, iv. 205 ff., referred to in a previous page (xix.)

Scriptures into any Indian language had then been made (pp. xvi ff.). He does not allow that the ascription of a divine character to Kṛishṇa is an idea derived from Christianity, and holds that it is as old as the Mahābhāshya of Patanjali, (pp. xxvi–xxxi). In pp. xxxvii–lvii he examines the passages adduced by Dr Lorinser to prove that the Gītā borrows from the Bible, together with some other passages not adduced by him which exhibit a similarity, and decides that they do not bear out his conclusion. Nor does he admit that the scene in which Kṛishṇa manifests his glory is derived from the transfiguration of Christ (pp. lviii f.). In pp. lxxix ff. the author combats Dr Lorinser's idea that the terms *śraddhā* and *bhakti* (faith and devotion) are borrowed from Christianity. In p. lxxxvii he gives it as his opinion that it is more probable that Christianity borrowed from Hinduism than *vice versa.* For details I may refer the reader to the essay itself.

Having adduced these discrepant opinions on the question whether the Indian writers who lived shortly after the rise of Christianity ever acquired any knowledge of that religion, and whether their doctrines were influenced by such knowledge, I may provisionally treat the question as being *adhuc sub judice.* However it may be decided, it becomes of the less consequence, as one of the advocates of an affirmative answer, Prof. Weber holds, as we have seen above, that the Indians modified very much that which he considers them to have adopted. See the quotations above made, pp. xxvi f. from his Ind. Stud., i. 400, 421; and the remarks from his Kṛishṇajanmāshṭamī, p. 321, quoted above in p. xxxii.

But however the question of the obligations of the Bhagavad Gītā, or of some other parts of the Mahābhārata, to Christianity may be decided, the decision can scarcely affect the determination of the further and very different question of the originality or otherwise, as far as any foreign influences are concerned, of the great bulk of the moral and religious sentiments embraced in my collection. These sentiments and observations are the natural expression of the feelings and experiences of universal humanity; and the higher and nobler portion of them cannot be regarded as peculiar to

Christianity. The correctness of this view is placed beyond a doubt by the parallels which I have adduced from classical writers. It is my impression, however, that the sentiments of humanity, mercy, forgiveness, and unselfishness are more natural to the Indian than to the Greek and Roman authors, unless, perhaps, in the case of those of the latter who were influenced by philosophical speculation. This tenderness of Indian sentiment may possibly have been in part derived from Buddhism, which, however, itself was of purely Indian growth.

It is also to be remarked that even supposing the comparatively late date of the Bhagavad Gitā, and any other parts of the Mahābhārata, many other portions of that great work, from which so large a proportion of the maxims collected in the following pages are derived, may be older, and such as, from the age in which they were composed, could not have undergone any influence from Christianity.

What, then, are we to say as to the date of the Mahābhārata? This cannot at present, if it can ever, be determined with any certainty. The great poem is no doubt in its present form made up of materials dating from very different periods. Prof. Lassen is of opinion (Indische Alterthumskunde, 2d edition, I. 589 f.) that, with the exception of pure interpolations which have no real connection with the substance of the work, we have the ancient story of the Mahābhārata before us in its essential elements, as it existed in the pre-Buddhistic period, *i.e.*, several centuries before Christ. The subsequent additions he considers to have reference chiefly to the exclusive worship of Vishṇu, and the deification of Kṛishṇa, as an incarnation of that divinity (p. 586).

In the article Mahābhārata in Chambers's Cyclopædia, which is one of the contributions furnished to that work by the late Professor Goldstücker, the following remarks occur: —"That this huge composition was not the work of one single individual, but a production of successive ages, clearly results from the multifariousness of its contents, from the difference of style which characterises its various parts, and even from the contradictions which disturb its harmony."

The question is also treated by Professor Max Müller in his

"History of Ancient Sanskrit Literature," pp. 36 ff. In pp. 42 ff. he tells us that the name of the Bhārata (in some MSS. of the Mahābhārata) is mentioned in the Sūtras of Âśvalāyana (whom, in p. 244, he conjecturally places about the year 350 B.C.); and that his age "would, therefore, if we can rely on our MSS., furnish a limit below which the first attempt at a collection of a Bhārata or Mahābhārata ought not to be placed. But," he adds, "there is no hope that we shall ever succeed by critical researches in restoring the Bhārata to that primitive form and shape in which it may have existed before or at the time of Âśvalāyana. Much has indeed been done by Professor Lassen, who, in his 'Indian Antiquities,' has pointed out characteristic marks by which the modern parts of the Mahābhārata can be distinguished from the more ancient." . . . In p. 46 he says, "In the form in which we now possess the Mahābhārata, it shows clear traces that the poets who collected and finished it, breathed an intellectual and religious atmosphere very different from that in which the heroes of the poem moved. The epic character of the story has throughout been changed and almost obliterated by the didactic tendencies of the latest editors, who were clearly Brahmans, brought up in the strict school of the laws of Manu."

In a paper published in the 10th Volume of the Journal of the Bombay branch of the Royal Asiatic Society, Prof. R. G. Bhāṇḍārkar examines the question regarding the age of the Mahābhārata; and concludes his investigation by saying, p. 92, "I have thus briefly sketched the principal testimonies to the existence of the Mahābhārata from the time of Pāṇini and Áśvalāyana, *i.e.*, from about the 5th century B.C. to the time of Śārṅgadhara, *i.e.*, the 14th century after Christ." He had previously said in p. 85, "Of course, I do not assert that the poem existed in Patanjali's time in exactly the same form as we have it now. There can be no question that several additions have been subsequently made, and it has undergone a good deal of transformation. . . . But the main story as we now have it, leaving the episodes out of consideration, was current long before Patanjali's time."

The remarks just quoted afford us but little of the special

aid which we require in judging of the age of many of the different parts of the Mahābhārata. Until the poem shall have been subjected to a much closer examination than it has yet received, and of which Prof. Holtzmann has set the example, it must remain uncertain in regard to many portions of its contents, to which of the two classes, of ancient or modern, or to what stage within either, they should be assigned.

I may perhaps hazard the opinion, that such passages as that containing the long collection of maxims uttered by Vidura in the 5 Book, vv. 990—1550,—as interrupting the narrative, if not for other reasons,—are unlikely to have formed a part of the original work. And from their contents, the same is probably true of large portions, at least, of the 12th and 13th Books.

The texts which I have quoted from this great poem are (as remarked in the quotation given above from Professor Goldstücker's article) far from being all in harmony with each other. In a work of such great extent, augmented no doubt by a series of successive additions from the pens of writers of very different dates, a conformity of sentiment was not always to be expected, but development in various directions was a natural result. Perhaps the most distinctly marked diversities are those which relate to the light in which the pretensions of the Brahmans are regarded. In some passages which I have translated in the following pages, these pretensions are stated in their most exaggerated form; whilst in other texts the value of priestly birth is as distinctly depreciated, and moral and religious goodness alone is esteemed as possessing any value. This alteration in sentiment is ascribed to the influence of Buddhism by Professor Ludwig, who considers that other principles of the later Brahmanism also were derived from the same source.* And even contemporaneous writers may have regarded the Brahmanical pretensions differently. Again, the Macchiavellian maxims in *M. Bh.* i. 5548 ff., and xii. 5253 ff., of which one specimen is

* See p. 11 of the 3d volume of his work on the Rigveda. This volume bears the title of "Die Mantralitteratur und das alte Indien."

given in No. ccxix., and others in p. 364, are opposed to the spirit of the better sentiments of the poem, and are even, as observed in p. 365, repudiated by the supposed narrator, or more probably by a subsequent interpolator. There is a class of unscrupulous men whose ideas are expressed in these verses, while they are rejected by men of higher moral feelings. Fair dealing with enemies is expressly enjoined in *M. Bh.* x. 186 ff., and xii. 3558 ff. Further, we find in the different passages which I have adduced, very different sentiments regarding women. It is needless to say that this should be no matter of surprise, and is easily to be accounted for by the differences in the characters of women, and in the experiences of their eulogists or censors.

I must confess, however, that my own examination of the Mahābhārata has been very superficial; and, as above observed, much light yet remains to be thrown upon its discrepancies and developments by a minuter and more careful study of its contents. So much, however, seems to be already clear, that however many of the sentiments and ideas which occur in it may be due to Buddhistic influences which can easily and naturally have acted upon the contributors to its contents, there is no reason for resorting to the supposition that Christian doctrines may have modified any considerable number of its ideas.

The other works from which I have quoted (except the Atharvaveda, the Śatapatha Brāhmaṇa, the Upanishads, Manu, &c., and the Rāmāyaṇa, from which some passages have been taken) are of much more modern date; but the substance of many of the maxims which occur in them is to be found in the older works; and the fact that so many sentiments of the latter should have been repeated in the more modern books, may afford some proof that they are congenial and natural to the Indian mind.

As this question whether the ideas and doctrines of the Indian poem are derived from, or have been influenced by, the New or the Old Testament, is one of great interest and importance, I give below a translation of the latter part of an article by Professor Windisch of Leipzig on Dr Lorinser's book, which appeared in the *Literarisches Centralblatt* for 15th

October 1870, followed by some remarks with which Professor Weber, Dr Böhtlingk, and M. Auguste Barth, have favoured me on the ubject of the dependence or independence of Indian writers on Christian or other foreign sources for any of their ideas. Professor Windisch says:—

"We have not as yet spoken of the object which the book before us has properly in view. This is nothing less than to show that all the nobler thoughts in the *Bhagavad Gîtâ* are derived from Christianity, or from the 'primæval revelation.' It is impossible here to examine minutely Dr Lorinser's process of proof, since it is based upon a large number of particular passages. According to the judgment of the author of this notice, however, the proof has not yet been adduced that in the *Bhagavad Gîtâ* we have a piece of Christianity translated into the form of Indian conceptions.

"To refer to at least some general points of view, Dr Lorinser's failure to make use of Indian commentaries has had first of all, for its result, that he could not always apprehend the Indian thoughts in an Indian spirit. . . . The immediate introduction of the Bible into the explanation of the *Bhagavad Gîtâ* is, therefore, at least premature. Besides, the particular Biblical passages themselves are with too great confidence designated by Dr Lorinser as the sources of the Indian thought or expression. It cannot be denied that he has actually adduced some surprising parallel passages; but the most of the texts which he has cited can at the utmost claim our consideration only after it has been proved in another way that the *Bhagavad Gîtâ* and the Bible stand in a near relation to each other. If the author should think to rely upon the multitude of the passages which he has quoted, it should be recollected that a hundred uncertain references prove no more than a single one of the same character. Has Dr Lorinser noticed that the comparison of the human soul with a team of horses (adduced by him in p. 60, note 59) from the *Kaṭha Upanishad*, corresponds with remarkable exactness to the beautiful myth in Plato's *Phædrus?* This might be regarded as one of the most interesting examples of accidental correspondence. For the rest, it is much to be questioned whether Professor Weber, to whom the author repeatedly appeals, shares his conviction. For Professor Weber's assumption that Christian teachers and doctrines arrived at an early period in India, and that in particular the worship of Krishṇa, and the legends relative to him, were formed under the influence of Christianity, is very widely different from Dr Lorinser's conviction, according to which the composer of the *Bhagavad Gítá* must have learnt at least the New Testament directly by heart. This is the conclusion at which every one would arrive who believingly reads the lists put together in the Appendix of—i. passages which vary in expression but agree in sense (60 in number); ii. passages in which a characteristic expression of the New Testament occurs in a different sense (23); iii. passages in which sense and expression correspond (16). Even the ideas of the Christian Fathers are supposed not to have been unknown to the poet (see, *e.g.*, p. 82, note 56; p. 179, note 6; p. 207, note 27, &c.) So much the more surprising is it, therefore, when Dr Lorinser himself (p. 211, note 54) finds it necessary to refer to the sharp contrast in which Christianity and the Indian conceptions stand to each other in regard to the doctrine of the human soul, and when he further (p. 117, note 1) cannot avoid ascribing to the poet an acquaintance, though a very defective acquaintance, with Christianity. It is impossible to combine Dr Lorinser's ideas into one general picture. Finally, as regards the thoughts in which Dr Lorinser perceives traces of the 'primæval revelation' or 'primæval tradition' (see, *e.g.*, pp. 45, 122, 231, 250), he should first have investigated whether they can be pointed out in the Veda. Had he done this, he would probably have discovered that the contrary is the case.

"The book before us plainly shows how much the text and explanation of the *Bhagavad Gítá* stand in need of a thorough revision on the part of scholars who are familiar with this branch of study. The view of which Dr Lorinser is a representative must be subjected to a closer examination than was here practicable."

In the preceding notice reference is made to the opinions of Professor Weber on the influence exercised by Christianity upon Indian religious ideas. I am indebted to the kindness of this distinguished Sanskritist, with whom I have communicated on the subject of Dr Lorinser's book, for an indication of his views regarding it. He refers me to a brief mention of the work in question in a note to an article republished in his *Indische Streifen*, vol. ii. p. 288, where he speaks of Dr Lorinser's remarkable endeavour to point out in the *Bhagavad Gîtâ* coincidences with, and references to, (*Anklänge und Beziehungen*) the New Testament, and states that although he considers this attempt of Dr Lorinser to be overdone, he is not in principle opposed to the idea which that writer maintains, but regards it as fully entitled to a fair consideration, as the date of the *Bhagavad Gîtâ* is not at all settled, and therefore presents no obstacle to the assumption of Christian influences, if these can be otherwise proved. He adds that he regards Wilson's theory that the *bhakti* of the later Hindu sects is essentially a Christian doctrine, as according well with all that we know already about the Śvetadvîpa, the Kṛishṇajanmâshṭamî, &c. As regards the age of the *Mahâbhârata*, Professor Weber thinks that it should be borne in mind that in the very passages which treat of the war between the Kauravas and Pâṇḍavas, and which therefore appear to be the oldest parts of that vast epic collection, not only is direct mention made of the Yavanas, Śakas, Pahlavas, and the wars with them (see Professor Wilson's *Academical Prelections on Indian Literature*, p. 178), but further that the Yavanâdhipa (Yavana king) Bhagadatta appears there as an old friend of the father of Yudhishṭhira (see *Indische Studien*, v. 152). He concludes that all these passages must be posterior to Alexander the Great, and still continues to regard his calculation that this most original part of the poem was written between the time of Alexander and that of Dio Chrysostom * (see *Hist. of Ind. Lit., Engl. transl.*, p. 186) as the most probable.

The opinion above referred to of Professor Wilson is to be found (as appears from Professor Weber's Dissertation on the Râma-Tâpanîya Upanishad, p. 277, note) in Vol. iii. of the *Oriental Magazine*, and is thus referred to in Mrs Speir's "Life

* The age of this author is there said to be in the second half of the first century of our era.

in Ancient India" (1856) p. 434:—"Professor Wilson notices the resemblance of the doctrines of the Bhagavad Gītā to those of some divisions of the early Christian schools, and hints that the remodelling of the ancient Hindu systems into popular forms, and 'in particular the vital importance of faith, were directly influenced by the diffusion of the Christian religion.'" I find no express reference to this influence of Christianity in Professor Wilson's *Sketch of the Religious Sects of the Hindus*, (Works, vol. i., pp. 160 ff., 368) except that he there says that "the doctrine of the efficacy of *bhakti* seems to have been an important innovation upon the primitive system of the Hindu religion" (p. 161).

On the same general subject Dr Böhtlingk has favoured me with the following expression of his opinion. He writes:—"Neither in the *Mahābhārata* nor in later writers have I found any utterances of moral or religious import which could with any probability be referred back to any foreign source. In this department the Indians have themselves reflected so much, and presented their thoughts in such elegant forms, that with their riches they might easily supply the rest of the world. The ethics and the religion of different peoples are not so different from one another that here and there coincidences should not be expected to be found between them. The line of the *Kaṭha Upanishad*, [i. 6]—*śasyam iva martyaḥ pachyate, śasyam ivājāyate punaḥ*" (like corn a mortal ripens, like corn he is produced again) "sounds as if from the New Testament, but is not therefore borrowed."

M. Barth writes to me as follows:—

"I am entirely of your opinion in regard to the reserves which you make as to the sentiments alleged to be borrowed, which Lorinser adduces from the Bhagavad Gītā. The same resemblances had been indicated in a general way long before him. . . . In collecting these passages, and confronting them with the texts which are asserted to be the originals, Lorinser appears to me rather to have succeeded in proving the contrary of this thesis. The book is Indian, and Indian throughout. The declaration of Kṛishṇa, 'Those who are devoted to me, are in me, and I in them,' is a reproduction of the

Vedantic doctrine in a form adapted to the requirements of practical religion. There would, perhaps, rather be reason for inquiring what is the sense which the corresponding terms bear in the Johannean theology; and interpretations of them have not been wanting. In any case, they have a meaning quite different from that which they bear in the Indian poem; and in order to find them again on Christian ground, invested with a meaning akin to that of the Vedânta, we shall have to descend to the mystics of the middle ages, and to what is nearer to us—the Hegelian theology of Marheinecke; by all of whom, as by the Indian poet, the illusory character, or the non-existence, of the individual being, and the exclusive essential reality of the absolute, is maintained. For them, also, whatever really exists in man, is God: all the rest is illusion, negation; or as they say—employing the same image as the Indians—a mere sport of the Divinity, which is one in many, and in many always the same. Thus Eckart, Tauler, Ruysbroeck, and the other Dominican mystics who preached and wrote on the banks of the Rhine in the fourteenth century, ask themselves: 'How can man love God?' And they answer: 'Why does the burning coal which you place on your hand burn you? Because this coal is in substance the same as your hand. In the same way God burns you, and acts by love within you, because in substance he is identical with you,—because he is in you, and you in him.'*

"As regards the Vedic passages" (see above, p. 8), "I think that we are not to look in them for too much precision. The locative case does not signify merely *in*, but also *with*, *near to*, *for*. 'We are yours; you are ours; thou art with us, thou art for us, thou art near us, as a coat of mail, as a ram-

* M. Barth informs me that those who are interested in the striking resemblances in doctrine between the doctrines of the Bhagavad Gîtâ and those of the Christian mystics of the middle ages, will find an account of the latter in the dissertation of M. Charles Schmidt, Professor of Theology at Strasburg, entitled, "Études sur le Mysticisme Allemand du xivme Siécle," in the Mémoires de l' Institut de France; Mémoires de l' Académie des Sciences Morales et Politiques, t. ii. 1847.

part,' &c. We have not yet got the dogmatic idea of Purusha = pure śâyin.

"As regards *gati*, I agree with you that the essence of the image is rather *end* than *way*. It is sufficient to observe how this word is associated with *kâshṭhâ*, *e.g.*, in the Kaṭha Upanishad, iii. 11; or is simply replaced by the latter, for instance, in the Apastamba-dharma-sûtra, i. 22. 7 (p. 39, Bühler's edition), sa (âtman) sarvam, paramâ kâshṭhâ . . . sa vai vaibhâjanam puram."

I make a further quotation on the same subject from Prof. Monier Williams's work, "Indian Wisdom," &c. (pp. 143 f. note): "Dr Lorinser, expanding the views of Professor Weber, and others, concerning the influence of Christianity on the legends of Kṛishṇa, thinks, that many of the sentiments of the Bhagavad-Gîtâ have been directly borrowed from the New Testament, copies of which, he thinks, found their way into India about the third century, when he believes the poem to have been written.* . . . He seems, however, to forget, that fragments of truth are to be found in all religious systems, however false, and that the Bible, though a true revelation, is still in regard to the human mind, through which the thoughts are transfused, a thoroughly Oriental book, cast in an Oriental mould, and full of Oriental ideas and expressions. Some of his comparisons seem mere coincidences of language, which might occur quite naturally and independently. In other cases, where he draws attention to coincidences of ideas,—as, for example, the division of the sphere of self-control into thought, word, and deed, in chap. xviii. 14-16, &c.; and of good works into prayer, fasting, and almsgiving, how could these be borrowed from Christianity when they are also found in Manu, which few will place later than the fifth century B.C.? . . . Nevertheless, something may be said for Dr Lorinser's theory." Some further remarks are made on the same subject in pp. 153 ff., which are adverse to that theory.

---

* In a previous page (137) Professor Williams says, that the author of the Bhagavad-Gîtâ, "is supposed to have lived in India during the first or second century of our era;" and in a note he adds: "Some consider that he lived as late as the third century, and some place him even later, but with these I cannot agree."

It is, perhaps, but just that, in presenting a collection of some of the best sentiments which are to be found in Sanskrit writers, I should advert to the fact, which, however, is already well known, that the moral and religious ideas of the Indians are not all of the same noble and elevated character, but offer a mixture of good and bad, of pure and impure,

πολλὰ μὲν ἐσθλὰ μεμιγμένα, πολλὰ δὲ λυγρά.

"Many good (things), and many bad, mingled."

The Mahābhārata itself has in two of its books collections, identical in purport, of sometimes immoral Macchiavellian maxims, one of which has been translated in pp. 113 and 293, No. ccxix. Some further specimens of the same kind may be found in the Supplement to the appendix, p. 360 ff. And are not even the literatures, whether sacred or profane, of all countries, more or less, disfigured by something repugnant to the moral sense?

J. M.

EDINBURGH, *July*, 1879.

METRICAL TRANSLATIONS FROM SANSKRIT WRITERS.

I. Consequence of the knowledge of the self-existent Soul.

Atharvaveda x. 8, 44.

The happy man who once has learned to know
The self-existent Soul, from passion pure,
Serene, undying, ever young, secure
From all the change that other natures show,
Whose full perfection no defect abates,
Whom pure essential good for ever sates,—
That man alone, no longer dreading death,
With tranquil joy resigns his vital breath.

II. The Great Spirit.

Śvetāśvatara Upanishad iii. 19.

No hands has He, nor feet, nor eyes, nor ears,
And yet He grasps, and moves, and sees, and hears.
He all things knows, Himself unknown of all;
Him men the great primeval Spirit call.

III. Devotion to the God of gods.

Vikrama-charita 232.

O God of gods, Thou art to me
A father, mother, kinsmen, friends;
I knowledge, riches, find in Thee;
All good Thy being comprehends.

IV. Hymn addressed to Vishnu by the Deities.

Raghuvanśa x. 15, ff.

To Thee, creator first, to Thee,
Preserver next, destroyer last,
Be glory; though but one, Thou hast
Thyself in act revealed as three.

As water pure from heaven descends,
But soon with other objects blends,
And various hues and flavours gains;
So moved by Goodness, Passion, Gloom,*
Dost Thou three several states assume,
While yet Thine essence pure remains.

Though one, Thou different forms hast sought;
Thy changes are compared to those
Which lucid crystal undergoes,
With colours into contact brought.

Unmeasured, Thou the worlds dost mete.
Thyself though no ambition fires,
'Tis Thou who grantest all desires.
Unvanquished, Victor, Thee we greet.

---

* See the prose translation of No. IV. in the Appendix.

A veil, which sense may never rend,
Thyself,—of all which sense reveals
The viewless source and cause—conceals:
Thee saints alone may comprehend.

Thou dwellest every heart within,
Yet fillest all the points of space;
Without affection, full of grace,
Primeval, changeless, pure from sin;

Though knowing all, Thyself unknown,
Self-sprung, and yet of all the source,
Unmastered, lord of boundless force,
Though one, in each thing diverse shown.

With minds by long restraint subdued,
Saints, fixing all their thoughts on Thee,
Thy lustrous form within them see,
And ransomed, gain the highest good.

Who, Lord, Thy real nature knows?
Unborn art Thou, and yet on earth
Hast shown Thyself in many a birth,
And, free from passion, slain Thy foes.

Thy glory in creation shown,
Though seen, our reason's grasp transcends:
Who, then, Thine essence comprehends,
Which thought and scripture teach alone?

Ungained, by Thee was nought to gain,
No object more to seek: Thy birth,
And all Thy wondrous deeds on earth,
Have only sprung from love to men.

With this poor hymn though ill-content,
We cease:—what stays our faltering tongue?

We have not half Thy glories sung,
But all our power to sing is spent.

V. Impeachment, and Vindication, of the Divine Government.

Mahâbhârata iii. 1124 ff.

DRAUPADI *speaks:*

Beholding noble men distrest,
Ignoble men enjoying good,
Thy righteous self by woe pursued,
Thy wicked foe by fortune blest,
I charge the Lord of all—the strong,
The partial Lord—with doing wrong.

His dark, mysterious, sovereign will
To men their several lots decrees;
He favours some with wealth and ease,
Some dooms to every form of ill.

As puppets' limbs the touch obey
Of him whose fingers hold the strings,
So God directs the secret springs
Which all the deeds of creatures sway.

In vain those birds which springes hold
Would seek to fly: so man, a thrall,
Fast fettered ever lives, in all
He does or thinks by God controlled.

As trees from river-banks are riven
And swept away, when rains have swelled
The streams, so men by Time impelled
To action, helpless, on are driven.

God does not show for all mankind
A parent's love, and wise concern;
But acts like one unfeeling, stern,
Whose eyes caprice and passion blind.

YUDHISHTHIRA *replies:*

I've listened, loving spouse, to thee,
I've marked thy charming, kind discourse,
Thy phrases turned with grace and force,
But know, thou utterest blasphemy.

I never act to earn reward;
I do what I am bound to do,
Indifferent whether fruit accrue;
My duty I alone regard.

Of all the men who care profess
For virtue—love of that to speak—
The unworthiest far are those who seek
To make a gain of righteousness.

Who thus—to every lofty sense
Of duty dead—from each good act
Its full return would fain extract;—
He forfeits every recompense.

Love duty, thus, for duty's sake,
Not careful what return it brings:
Yet doubt not, bliss from virtue springs,
While woe shall sinners overtake.

By ships the perilous sea is crossed;
So men on virtue's stable bark
Pass o'er this mundane ocean dark,
And reach the blessed heavenly coast.

If holy actions bore no fruits;
If self-command, beneficence,
Received no fitting recompense;
Then men would lead the life of brutes.

Who then would knowledge toil to gain?
Or after noble aims aspire?
O'er all the earth delusion dire
And darkness deep and black would reign.

But 'tis not so; for saints of old
Well knew that every righteous deed
From God obtains its ample meed:
They, therefore, strove pure lives to lead,
As ancient sacred books have told.

The gods—for such their sovereign will—
Have veiled from our too curious ken
The laws by which the deeds of men
Are recompensed with good and ill.

No common mortal comprehends
The wondrous power, mysterious skill,
With which these lords of all fulfil
Their high designs, their hidden ends.

These secret things those saints descry
Alone, whose sinless life austere
For them has earned an insight clear,
To which all mysteries open lie.

So let thy doubts like vapours flee,
Abandon impious unbelief;
And let not discontent and grief
Disturb thy soul's serenity.

But study God aright to know,
That highest Lord of all revere,
Whose grace on those who love him here
Will endless future bliss bestow.

DRAUPADI *rejoins:*

How could I God, the Lord of all,
Contemn, or dare His acts arraign,
Although I weakly thus complain?
Nor would I virtue bootless call.

I idly talk; my better mind
Is overcome by deep distress,
Which long shall yet my heart oppress:
So judge me rightly; thou art kind.

VI. The Divine Sovereignty.

Mahâbhârata v. 916 f.

The Lord all creatures' fortunes rules;
None, weak or strong, His might defies;
He makes the young and simple wise;
The wise and learn'd he turns to fools.

VII. All sins known to the gods.

Mahâbhârata xii. 7058; iii. 13754.

Poor uninstructed mortals try
Their wilful sins from view to screen:
But though by human eyes unseen,
The gods their guilty deeds descry.

VIII. Secret sin not unobserved.

Manu viii. 84, 91; iv. 161; *Mahābhārata* i. 3015, 3018.

"None sees me": so when bent on sin,
The fool imagines, madly bold;
For gods his evil deeds behold;
The Soul, too, sees, the man within.

IX. The wise corrected by advice: the bad checked by punishment.

Mahābhārata v. 1252.

Their teacher's words correct the wise,
And rulers stern the bad chastise;
The judge who dwells 'mid Hades' gloom
Awards the secret sinner's doom.

X. Ill-gotten gains fail to benefit.

Mahābhārata v. 1251 f.

When men unjustly-gotten gains
Employ unsightly rents to hide,
Each ancient rent unveiled remains,
While new ones gape on every side.

XI. The Genesis of Rudra.

Mahābhārata xii. 2791-3.

Whence springs the god whom mortals fear,
The god with awful form severe?
From sin destroying Rudra springs,
On this our world who ruin brings.

He is that self who dwells within,
In men, the source and seat of sin,
Which plunges both in woe, the good,
As well as all the guilty brood.

XII. The gods give wisdom to those whom they favour, and conversely.

Mahâbhârata v. 1222; ii. 2669 ff.

The gods no club, like herdsmen, wield
To guard the man they deign to shield:
On those to whom they grace will show
They understanding sound bestow;
But rob of sense and insight all
Of whom their wrath decrees the fall.
These wretched men,—their minds deranged,—
See all they see distorted, changed;
For good to them as evil looms,
And folly wisdom's form assumes.

XIII. Good and evil not always apparent at first sight.

Mahâbhârata v. 1451.

That loss from which advantage springs
Can ne'er a real loss be deemed;
And that is not true gain esteemed
Which soon, or later, ruin brings.

XIV. The same.

Mahâbhârata iii. 87; xii. 3855.

Oft ill of good the semblance bears,
And good the guise of evil wears:

So loss of wealth, though bringing pain,
To many a man is real gain;
While wealth to others proves a bane;
Its hoped-for fruits they seek in vain.

XV. Fools mistake evil for good.

Mahābhārata v. 1155.

Esteeming real loss as gain,
And real gain as evil, fools
Whom lawless passion ever rules,
For bliss mistake their greatest bane.

XVI. A doomed man is killed by any thing.

Mahābhārata vii. 429.

When men are doomed without respite,
Even straws like thunderbolts will smite.

XVII. The same.

Mahābhārata xiii. 7607.

A man, until his time arrives,
Though pierced by hundred darts, survives,
While he whose hour of death is nigh,
Touched only by a straw, will die.

XVIII. Take no thought for your life, what ye shall eat, &c.

(Matthew vi. 25 f.)

Hitopadeśa i. 171 (or 189).

Shall He to thee support refuse
Who clothes the swan in dazzling white,
Who robes in green the parrot bright,
The peacock decks in rainbow hues?

XIX. The same.

Vṛiddha Chāṇakya x. 17.

With fervent hymns while I great Vishṇu laud,
The gracious, mighty, all-sustaining god,
How can I, faithless, for subsistence fear?
Does he for babes their mother's milk prepare,
And will he not his ever-watchful care,
Extend o'er all their future life's career?

XX. Faith in Holy Scripture.

Mahābhārata iii. 13461[b], 13463.

Profane, unhappy doubters miss
Both present joy and future bliss.
Faith is that sign by which the wise
A man's redemption recognise.
All baseless, fruitless reasonings leave;
With faith to holy scripture cleave.

[The verses, of which the following is a free translation, and the next citation, have an interest, as showing that the same conflict with which we are familiar in our own day between the vindicators and the opponents of a supernatural revelation, was hotly waged in India in early times.]

XXI. An Indian Free-thinker's Fate.

xii. 6736, ff.; xii. 2980.

While yet a human form I bore,
I loved profane and useless lore;
Contemned the Scriptures, steeped in pride,
And took poor reason for my guide.

In halls where reverend scholars met
To talk, and questions deep debate,
I liked to argue, plied the rules
Of logic, called the Brahmans fools,
Oft battering hard with impious knocks
My grave opponents orthodox.
Untaught in sacred wisdom's school,
A doubter, unbeliever, fool,
In every point the truth I missed,
A vain, pretentious, sciolist,
Who others viewed with scornful eyes,
And deemed myself most learn'd and wise.
Now mark the retribution meet
Of this my doubt and self-conceit!
Behold me here a jackal born,
Who once the Vedas dared to scorn!
But now my hope is this; perhaps
When many, many days elapse,
From this brute form I shall escape,
And gain once more my human shape.
Devoutly then, with right good-will,
Shall I religious rites fulfil,
With liberal gifts the priests delight,
And 'gainst my lawless senses fight,
Will real knowledge seek, and shun
Whate'er I ought to leave undone.

XXII. The Indian Rationalist in Ancient Times.

Mahābhārata xiii. 2194 ff.; xii. 2980.

The man who on the Vedas looks
As unauthoritative books,
Who breaks their rules, and spurns all law,
Down on his head must ruin draw.
The Brahman who, in vain conceit,

With scorn those scriptures dares to treat,
Who shallow, yet acute and smart,
On logic dotes, that worthless art,
Who, versed in all its tactics, knows
His simpler brethren how to pose,
Who subtly syllogizing speaks,
In wordy war to conquer seeks,
Who Brahmans good and true reviles,
At all they say contemptuous smiles,
The truths they urge with doubt receives,
And absolutely nought believes,—
That man, in speech so sharp and wild,
Is nothing better than a child.
Nay worse: the wisest men and best
That wrangler as a dog detest.
For just as dogs assail their prey,
With savage growls, and rending, slay,
So too these noisy scoffers strive
The Scriptures into shreds to rive.

XXIII. **Denial of a future life and of a God; and ridicule of the doctrine of final liberation as nothing else than annihilation.**

Naishadha Charita xvii. 45.

The scripture says, the bad begin,
When dead, with woe to pay for sin,
While bliss awaits—a happier birth—
The good whene'er they quit the earth.
But here the virtuous suffer pain,
The bad by vice enjoyment gain.
How, then, this doubtful case decide?
Tell what is urged on either side.

Did God exist, omniscient, kind,
And never speak His will in vain,
'Twould cost Him but a word, and then
His suppliants all the wish would find.

If God to men allotted woe,
Although that woe the fruit must be
Of men's own actions, then were he
Without a cause his creatures' foe,—
More cruel, thus, than men, who ne'er
To others causeless malice bear.

In this our state of human birth
Man's self and Brahma co-exist,—
As wise Vedantists all insist,—
But when this wretched life on earth
Shall end, and all redemption gain,
Then Brahma shall alone remain.
A clever doctrine here we see!
Our highest good to cease to be!

[In the second paragraph, ending at the top of this page, the atheistic writer assumes, 1st, that finite minds are competent to judge of the acts of an infinite Being, and 2d, that God is indifferent to moral good and evil, both of which assumptions theists deny as unwarranted.

It is unnecessary to answer the reasoning in No. xxv., page 21 f; and the morality of No. xxvi. in page 22, is low; it ignores the "man within," the individual conscience.]

XXIV. Jābāli's Sophistical discourse and Rāma's reply.

Rāmāyaṇa, ii. 108 and 109 (Bombay edition, and ii. 116 and 118, Gorresio's edition).

Rāma, the eldest son of Daśaratha, King of Ayodhyā, by his queen Kauśalyā, and the destined heir of his father, consented to go into banishment, in consequence of the action of Kaikeyī, another of the wives of his father, to whom the latter had once promised that her son should be his successor. Rāma's banishment was very much against his father's will, and occasioned him great grief; but he felt himself obliged to permit the fulfilment of his promise, on which Kaikeyī insisted. Bharata, the son of Kaikeyī, who was absent from Ayodhyā when Rāma left it, and had no desire to supplant his brother, was sent for on his father's death; but refused to be installed as king in his stead, and followed Rāma into exile, with the view of inducing him to return home. Rāma, however, though the kingdom was offered to him by Bharata, refused to accept it, and declared he would abide by his father's decision. (See Prof. Monier Williams' "Indian Epic Poetry," pp. 67-71). The Brahman Jābāli now endeavours to persuade Rāma to disregard his father's decision. The arguments which he employs, founded on immoral principles, are very freely reproduced in the following translation of most of his discourse. They represent the doctrines of the Chārvākas or Lokāyatikas; and tally with those ascribed to the Chārvākas in the Sarvadarśana-sangraha, and to Māyāmoha, the great deceiver, in the Vishṇu Purāṇa, iii. 18, 25 ff.

See my article on these doctrines in the "Journal of the Royal Asiatic Society," vol. xix. 299 ff. (1862), and Prof. Cowell's article on the Chārvāka system of philosophy, in the "Journal of the Asiatic Society of Bengal," for 1862, pp. 371-390; in which a long and elaborate passage from the Uttara Naishadha of Śrīharsha, setting forth the same view, is translated. See also Prof. Cowell's edition of Mr Colebrooke's Essays, i. 426 ff.

When Rāma, loyal, gentle, good,
His brother's pleas had thus withstood,
The priest Jābāli sought once more,
By force of nihilistic lore,
And reasonings false, though kindly meant,
To turn the prince from his intent.

"Let no such thoughts thy conduct sway,
Or lead thee, to thy hurt, astray.
By thinking men despised, such rules
Are only fit for simple fools.
What man by any real bands
To other men related stands?
And so 'tis but a fancy vain,
That one from others aught can gain.
Alone each mortal sees the light;
Alone he disappears in night.

That man, O king, himself deceives,
Whoe'er to others fondly cleaves,
And one with love his mother names,
Another for his father claims.

As men who leave their village home,
In distant lands a while to roam,
In some strange hamlet rest one day,
And in the morning go their way,
So men's relations, too, their ties
With parents, children, all they prize,
Can only for a moment last;
And who would care for what is past?

What is thy father now to thee,
Or thou to him? thy course is free.
His promise now thou needst not heed,
But quit these woods, and homeward speed.
Thy sire has thither gone where all
Must go at fate's resistless call.
No longer weakly play the fool;
The throne is thine; thy people rule,
Who now, thine absence mourning, burn
With strong desire for thy return.
I pity those, who, self-subdued,
In virtue sought their highest good,
Who here misled by lore unsound,
Renounced the bliss they might have found;
And who far, far, from gaining heaven,
For which they long and hard had striven,
Are plunged in dark extinction, sleep
A sleep unending, dreamless, deep.

What fools are men who waste their bread
On senseless offerings to the dead!
The dead no more exist: what good
Can nothings ever get from food?

If food, by one when eaten here,
Another sates, far off or near,
Then why should men provision make
For travel? victuals with them take?
For why not offer Srāddhas,* pray,
To kinsmen journeying far away?
[And might not men upon the roof
Make others eat for their behoof?] †
Why, why, are simple men beguiled
By books which learned men compiled,
Which scores of useless rites ordain,
And swarm with precepts false and vain?
Such books were meant as charms to act
On silly men, and gifts extract,
To fill the coffers of the priests,
Those pampered guests at sumptuous feasts.

[To us no sacred texts are given,
Unerring, perfect, dropped from heaven.
No lore inspired, no truths supplied
From source supernal, men to guide,
Have ever reached this world: in vain
Such fancied aid they seek to gain.
Who this expects, could also dream
The sky with blooming flowers might teem! ‡
Truth only then is gained, when sought
By power of logic, force of thought.
For truth so found alone I care;
And such as you my view will share.] §

---

* This is the Sanskrit word for offerings to the dead.

† This interpolated verse is from the Sarvadarśana-sangraha.

‡ A "sky flower" is in Indian writers an image of impossibility.

§ These twelve lines within brackets are a largely expanded version of a verse in the Vishṇu Purāṇa iii. 18, 30. See my

No heaven, no hell, exists ; believe
Alone in what thine eyes perceive ;
And all as non-existent slight
Whose form eludes thy trusty sight."
[Since life is short, the quest of joy
Should all a mortal's hours employ.
If scanty means the power deny
His cravings all to gratify,
With borrowed money let him feast,
Till all his credit shall have ceased.] *

When thus the unbelieving priest,
His subtle lies to vent had ceased,
Then Rāma made this wise reply,
Unmoved by all his sophistry.
" Thou would'st that I should cast aside
Good faith and truth,—my joy and pride,—
That I may present good secure,
And flee the ills I now endure.
Thou would'st persuade me not to dread
The pains that wait the wicked dead ;
Thou would'st that men should all despise,—
With scorn reject as silly lies,—
The earnest words of all who teach
A future life, and duty preach.
Thy words, I know, are kindly meant,
But thou hast failed in thine intent.
As wholesome words at first they sound,
But proved, are false and noxious found.
A show of right they have, but tried,
They cannot reason's test abide.

---

article in the Journal R. A. S., above referred to, pp. 301 ff., where the verse is numbered as 23.

* These six lines in brackets are paraphrased from a line in the Sarvadarśana-angraha.

Believe me, all the good and wise
That foolish, wilful, man despise,
From virtue's path aside who turns,
And all restraints impatient spurns.
By conduct only men we know,
As pure and noble, vile and low;
Their natures we can only test,
As acts those natures manifest.
Should I the sacred books despise,
And act as thou dost now advise,—
Would I not all the world delude
By seeming noble, pure, and good,
While I was vicious, vile, and base,
A blot upon the royal race?
If virtue's garb assuming, I
Should virtue by my deeds deny,
Should lead a base and vicious life,
With order, law, and right at strife,
How could I, leading men astray,
By such a course, from wisdom's way,
Aught else but condemnation stern
From righteous men and sages earn?
By such a course should I not miss
Both present joy, and heavenly bliss?
The kings their subjects' weal who seek
Should never fail the truth to speak;
Whatever promise once they make,
Though tempted, they should never break.
The good examples rulers give
Direct their people how to live;
For common mortals watch the great,
And all their doings imitate.
A righteous king will rule by truth,
And temper, too, his acts with ruth.
When truth abides its guiding law,
Then kingly sway is free from flaw.

Both gods and holy seers delight
In those who practise truth and right;
Though such on earth no bliss attain,
The highest future good they gain.

Good faith and truth are virtue's root;
From them abundant blessings shoot.
Truth rules supreme on earth, and nought
Surpassing truth can e'er be thought.
All holy rites, all acts austere,
The sacred books which men revere,—
Which duty's laws and forms disclose,—
These books themselves on truth repose.
Why should I then be led astray
My sire's command to disobey?
No fancied good, no dazzling lure,
My sense of right shall e'er obscure,
Or tempt me under foot to tread
My sacred promise to the dead.

As Rāma his advice despised,
Jābāli thus apologised:—

"No nihilistic lore I preach,
That nought exists, I do not teach.
Believe me, prince, I only seek
What suits the occasion best, to speak.
At first I deemed it wise and kind
To try to make thee change thy mind;
But seeing this thy settled mood,
I cannot longer find it good
To play the sceptic, but will now
The old established creed avow.
But should I find it opportune,
I'll turn again a sceptic soon."

[The nine verses with which this section concludes are

marked by Schegel as interpolations; but they are found in the Bombay edition. In one of them (v. 34) Buddha is mentioned and compared to a thief (*Yathā hi choras sa tathā hi Buddhaḥ*). I have not noticed any reference to Buddha in the Mahābhārata, unless there be an allusion to him in the following half verse, xii. 7124, which is repeated in verses 9034 and 10517: *Etad buddhvā* (*buddhyā* in verse 10517) *bhaved buddhaḥ kim anyad buddha-lakshaṇam*: "Understanding this, a man will become intelligent (*buddhaḥ*): What other mark of an intelligent man (*buddhaḥ*) is there?"]

The words of which the following lines are a free translation purport to have been addressed by Lakshmaṇa to his brother Rāma, when the latter was overwhelmed with grief on hearing a false rumour of the death of his wife Sītā. Rāma is not stated to have made any reply; but his answer to Jābāli may be regarded as expressing the sentiments which the poet assigned to his hero, as in consonance with his whole character.

XXV. Virtue Unreal and Useless.

Rāmāyaṇa vi. 83, 14 ff., Bomb. Ed.; and vi. 62, 15 ff., Gorr. Ed.

My brother dear, thy life is pure;
Thou spurnest every sensual lure;
Thy conduct all is noble, just;
The world, secure, thy word can trust.
Yet what does all this virtue boot?
To thee it brings no meed, no fruit;
For thou art crushed by ills: I deem
That virtue is a baseless dream.
Our senses outward objects show;
And thus that such exist we know.
Of virtue no such form I see,
And deem it a nonentity.
Were virtue real, then thy fell
And hateful foe would sink to hell;

Whilst thou, so righteous, true and good,
By ill wouldst be no more pursued.
But now, when he enjoys success,
Whilst thou art plunged in deep distress,
I learn by demonstration strong,
That wrong is right, and right is wrong;
I see,—it needs no insight nice,—
That vice is virtue, virtue vice.
The righteous pine, the wicked thrive;
Why vainly after virtue strive?
   In virtue, then, no more confide;
If thou would'st turn thy fortune's tide,
With vigour act; arise, arise;
And thine own greatness recognise.

XXVI. The Rule of Duty difficult to ascertain.

Mahābhārata iii. 17402.

The principles of duty lie
Enveloped deep in mystery.
On what can men their conduct found?
For reasonings lack all solid ground;
The Veda with itself conflicts,—
One text another contradicts;
No muni old, however wise,
A sure unerring norm supplies.
The only rule is:—ne'er forsake
The beaten road the many take.

XXVII. Preparation for Death.

Mahābhārata xii. 12078 ff.; 12447 ff.

Before King Yama's * awful band
Arrives, to speak its lord's command,

* Yama is the ruler of the dead, the Indian Pluto.

And bear thee to the realms of death,—
Whilst yet thou draw'st thy vital breath,—
My son, in grave and earnest mood,
Strive after right and rectitude.
Before the Ruler of the dead
Resistless, unimpassioned, dread,
Thy life, with every root and stay,
And bond of kinship, tears away;
Before the deadly tempest blows,
Which Yama's near approach foreshows;
Before the regions of the sky
Begin to whirl before thine eye;
Before thine ear to every sound
Is closed, and terror reigns around;
While yet thou art respited, care
For things unseen, for death prepare,
And sunk in meditation deep,
The fruits of holy knowledge reap.
Before the memories of thy life,—
So oft with right and good at strife,—
Of acts of thoughtless folly, rise,
To vex thy soul, now thou art wise,—
That only real treasure store,
Which thou shalt keep for evermore.
Before decay thy body wears,
And with it strength and beauty bears,
Those noblest treasures hoard in haste,
Which neither time nor chance can waste.
Before disease, stern charioteer,
Thy dire destroyer, death brings near,
Whose force thy feeble frame shall rend,—
In rites austere thy moments spend.
Before the hideous wolves which dwell
In mortals' bodies, fierce and fell,
Assail thy life on every side,
On virtue's pathway onward stride.

Make haste, before the fatal gloom
Round thy lone road begins to loom,
Before thine eye the golden trees
Above the mountain's summit sees.*
Before from wisdom's hallowed way
By evil men thou'rt led astray ;—
Misled by foes that look like friends,—
With ardour seek the highest ends.
  With ceaseless care amass that wealth
Which neither thieves can filch by stealth,†
Nor greedy tyrants snatch away,
Which even in death shall with thee stay.
  The treasures which thou thus dost gain
For ever shall thine own remain.
Unshared shalt thou enjoy the meeds
Acquired by thine own righteous deeds.
  Dismissing every vulgar care,
For yonder nobler life prepare.
To earth's attachments bid adieu,
And fix on higher bliss thy view.
The road which thou dost traverse swarms
With foes, with hornets' hideous forms.
Guard, then, thy works, as thou dost go,
Against the assaults of every foe.
  When men with fear and anguished heart,
From hence to worlds unknown depart,
No band of kinsmen dear, or friends
With loving care their path attends.
Of what avail are stores untold,
Of jewels, silver, gems, and gold,
When, as the body's powers decay,

---

* The commentator states that to see golden trees is a sign of approaching death (*Hiraṇya-vṛiksha-darśanam maraṇa-chihnam.*

† Compare Matthew vi. 19 ff. ; Luke xii. 33.

The living spirit flits away?
Not all Kuvera's* wealth could buy
A single hour of bliss on high,
Or those dire future pains avert,
Which justice claims for ill-desert.
When mortals leave behind them here
Their wealth, their friends, their kinsmen dear,
Have they no comrades on the road
Which leads to Yama's dread abode?
Yes, all the deeds that men have done,
In light of day, before the sun,†
Or veiled beneath the gloom of night,
The good, the bad, the wrong, the right,
These, though forgotten, reappear,
And travel, silent, in their rear.
And when—their journey at an end,—
The dead before King Yama bend,
And from his lips the doom await
Which settles all their future fate,
What fittest witness then can rise
To speak the truth without disguise,
And all those deeds and thoughts reveal
Which living men would fain conceal,
As well as those good acts to tell
On which fond memory loves to dwell?
The conscious soul, the past which knows,
Itself that past can best disclose,
And all the secrets bring to light
Which once were closely wrapped in night.
Men living ever sinless here,
Shall soar to yonder higher sphere;
And, clothed in bodies bright and pure,
Shall gain the meeds their deeds ensure.

---

* The god of wealth. † 2 Samuel xii. 12.

XXVIII. The only inseparable Friend.

Manu viii. 17; and iv. 239 ff.

Our virtue is the only friend
That follows us in death:
All other ties and friendships end
With our departing breath.
Nor father, mother, wife, nor son,
Beside us then can stay,
Nor kinsfolk; virtue is the one
Companion of our way.
Alone each creature sees the light,
Alone the world he leaves;
Alone of actions wrong or right
The recompense receives.
Like log or clod, beneath the sod
Their lifeless kinsmen laid,
His friends turn round and quit the ground;
But virtue speeds the dead.
Be then a hoard of virtue stored,
To help in day of doom.
By virtue sped, we cross the dread,
Immeasurable, gloom.

XXIX. "What is your life? It is even a vapour."

(James iv. 14; 1 Peter v. 8.)

Mahābhārata xii. 12050 ff.

The body—is it not like foam
The tossing wave an instant cresting?
In it the spirit, bird-like, resting,
Soon flies to seek another home.
In this thy frail abode, so dear,
How canst thou slumber free from fear?
Why dost thou not wake up, when all

Thy watchful enemies ever seek
To strike thee there where thou art weak,
To bring about thy longed-for fall ?
  Thy days are numbered,—all apace
Thy years roll on,—thy powers decay.
Why dost thou vainly then delay,
And not arise, and haste away
To some unchanging dwelling-place ?

XXX. No distinctions in the grave.

Mahâbhârata xi. 88 ff; 116 ff.

Enslaved by various passions, men
Profound self-knowledge fail to gain.
Some yield to pride of birth, and scorn
All those in humbler stations born.
By wealth elated, some look down
On mortals cursed by Fortune's frown;
While others, trained in learning's schools,
Contemn the unlearned, and call them fools.
All quickly other's faults discern;
Their own to check they never learn.
But soon a time arrives when all
The wise, the foolish, great and small,
The rich, the poor, the high, the low,
The proud, the humble hence must go:
Within the graveyard lone reclined,
Their pomp, their rags, they leave behind.
Soon, soon their lifeless frames a prey
Become to sure and sad decay.
When forms, once fair, of flesh are reft,
And skeletons alone are left,
Say, then, of all the bones around,
That strew the sad funereal ground,
What eye has power to recognize
Those of the rich, the great, the wise?

When all by death's impartial blow
Shall, undistinguished, soon lie low,
Oh, why should now the proud, the strong,
The weak, the lowly, seek to wrong?
Whoe'er, before the eyes of men,
Or when removed beyond their ken,
Will heed this warning kind, though stern,
The highest future good shall earn.

XXXI. "For we brought nothing into this world, and it is certain we can carry nothing out."—(1st Epistle to Timothy vi. 7.)

Mahābhārata xii. 3892 b f.

Wealth either leaves a man, O king!
Or else a man his wealth must leave.
What sage for that event will grieve,
Which time at length must surely bring?

XXXII. How the Wise Ought to Live: a Dialogue.*

Mahābhārata xii. 6526 ff. (= 9932 ff.); 8307 ff.

SON.

Since soon the days of mortals end,
How ought the wise their lives to spend?
What course should I, to duty true,
My sire, from youth to age pursue?

FATHER.

Begin thy course with study; store
The mind with holy Vedic lore.
That stage completed,—seek a wife,
And gain the fruit of wedded life,

* This dialogue is referred to in p. 351 f. of Prof. Max Müller's Hibbert Lectures.

A race of sons, by rites to seal,
When thou art gone, thy spirit's weal.
Then light the sacred fires, and bring
The gods a fitting offering.
When age draws nigh, the world forsake,
Thy chosen home the forest make;
And there, a calm, ascetic sage,
A war against thy passions wage,
That, cleansed from every earthly stain,
Thou may'st supreme perfection gain.

SON.

And art thou then, my father, wise,
When thou dost such a life advise?
What wise or thoughtful man delights
In formal studies, empty rites?
Should such pursuits and thoughts engage
A mortal more than half his age?
The world is ever vexed, distressed;
The noiseless robbers * never rest.

FATHER.

Tell how the world is vexed, distressed;
What noiseless robbers never rest?
What means thy dark, alarming speech?
In plainer words thy meaning teach.

SON.

The world is vexed by death; decay
The frames of mortals wears away.
Dost thou not note the circling flight
Of those still robbers, day and night,

* Literally, "When the unfailing ones ever recur" (*amoghâsu patantîshu*). The Commentator explains *amoghâsu* as *âyur-haraṇe saphâlasu râtrishu*: "The nights, which are efficacious in carrying off life."

With stealthy tread which hurrying past,
Steal all our lives away at last?
When well I know how death infests
This world of woe, and never rests,
How can I still, in thoughtless mood,
Confide in future earthly good?
Since life with every night that goes,
Still shorter, and yet shorter grows,
Must not the wise perceive how vain
Are all their days that yet remain?
We, whom life's narrow bounds confine,
Like fish in shallow water, pine.
While men on other thoughts are bent,—
Like those on gathering flowers intent,—
As lambs by wolves are snatched away,—
They fall to death a sudden prey,
Before they yet the good have gained
For which they every nerve had strained.
No moment lose; in serious mood
Begin at once to practise good;
To-morrow's task to-day conclude;
The evening's work complete at noon:—
No duty can be done too soon.*
Who knows whom death may seize to-night,
And who shall see the morning light?
And death will never stop to ask,
If thou hast done, or not, thy task.
While yet a youth, from folly cease;
Through virtue seek for calm and peace.
So shalt thou here attain renown,
And future bliss thy lot shall crown.
Death interrupts the futile dreams
Of men who, plunged in various schemes,

* Compare Ecclesiastes ix. 10, and xii. 1.

Are thinking: "This or that is done;
This still to do; that just begun."
As torrents undermine the ranks
Of stately trees that crown their banks,
And sweep them downwards to the main,
Death tears from earth those dreamers vain.
While some are all on traffic bent,
And some on household cares intent,
Are fighting hard with pressing need,
And struggling wives and babes to feed,
Or with some other ills of life
Are waging an incessant strife;
Death these hard toiling men uproots,
Before they yet have reaped the fruits
Of all their labour, all their thought,
Of all the battles they have fought.
Death spares no class, no rank, nor age;
He carries off the fool, the sage,
The knave, the saint, the young, the old,
The weak, the strong, the faint, the bold.
As soon as men are born, decay
And death begin to haunt their way.
How can'st thou, thoughtless, careless, rest,
When endless woes thy life infest;
When pains and pangs thy strength consume,—
Thy frame to dissolution doom?
Forsake the busy haunts of men,
For there has death his favourite den.
In lonely forests seek thy home,
For there the gods delight to roam.
Fast bound by old attachment's spell,
Men love amid their kin to dwell.
This bond the sage asunder tears;
The fool to rend it never cares.

---

* This simile is found in *Mahābhārata* xii. 8311.

Thou dost advise that I should please
With sacrifice the deities.
Such rites I disregard as vain;
Through these can none perfection gain.
Why sate the gods, at cruel feasts,
With flesh and blood of slaughtered beasts?
Far other sacrifices I
Will offer unremittingly;
The sacrifice of calm, of truth,
The sacrifice of peace, of ruth,
Of life serenely, purely, spent,
Of thought profound on Brahma bent.*
Who offers these, may death defy,
And hope for immortality.
And then thou say'st that I should wed,
And sons should gain to tend me, dead,
By offering pious gifts, to seal,
When I am gone, my spirit's weal.
But I shall ask no pious zeal
Of sons to guard my future weal.
No child of mine shall ever boast
His rites have saved his father's ghost.†
Of mine own bliss I'll pay the price,
And be myself my sacrifice.

---

* *Brahma-yajṇe sthito muṇiḥ*, *i.e.*, "as a muni practising the Brahma-sacrifice." I have here ventured to take the compound word *Brahma-yajṇe*, as meaning a sacrifice of contemplation on Brahma, as most suitable to the state of a sage. Its recognized sense is that of the Vedic sacrifice, *i.e.*, study of the Vedas, the word *Brahma* having also the meaning of Veda.—*See* Professor M. Müller's "Hibbert Lectures," p. 164.

† By these words (in the original: *na mām tārayati prajā:* "Offspring does not deliver me;") the practice of Śrāddhas, oblations to deceased ancestors, is rejected as useless.

XXXIII. "Take thine ease, eat, drink, and be merry."

Bhagavad Gitâ xvi. 1 ff. = *Mahâbhârata* vi. 1403 ff.

On earth two classes live of men;
And one is devilish, one divine;
In one all noble virtues shine,
In th' other evil passions reign.

From malice free, averse to strife,
Mild, bounteous, humble, calm, sincere,
Kind, holding other creatures dear,
The one are pure in heart and life.

The others differ far from these;
Impure, deceitful, haughty, vain,
Harsh, cruel, causing others pain,
They only care themselves to please.

Such men enjoyment only prize,
And so, to sate impure desire,
By fraud and force they wealth acquire;
And often thus soliloquize:

"This gained to-day; I soon shall more
Acquire, on which my heart is set.
From this and that I hope to get
Yet further means to swell my store.

"One foe I've smitten;—all the rest
Shall undergo a like defeat.
A mighty lord am I, complete
In all that makes a mortal blest.

"I'm rich, can boast my noble birth;
With me what other creature vies?
I'll lavish gold, I'll sacrifice;
And lead a life of ease and mirth."

So these deluded wretches think,
On low and sensual pleasures bent;
But soon,—their brief existence spent,—
They down to hell, condemned, shall sink.

XXXIV. Final overthrow of the wicked.

Manu iv. 170 ff.

Not even here on earth are blest
Unrighteous men, who live by wrong
And guileful arts: who, bold and strong,
With cruel spite the weak molest.

Though goodness only bring distress,
Let none that hallowed path forsake:
Mark what reverses overtake
The wicked after brief success.

Not all at once the earth her fruits
Produces; so unrighteousness
But slowly works, yet not the less
At length the sinner clean uproots.

At first through wrong he grows in strength,
He sees good days, and overthrows,
In strife triumphant, all his foes;
But justice strikes him down at length.

Yes, retribution comes, though slow;
For if the man himself go free,
His sons shall then the victims be,
Or else his grandsons feel the blow.

XXXV. Good and bad seem to be equally favoured here: not so hereafter.

Mahâbhârata xii. 2798.

AILA says:

Both good and bad the patient earth sustains,
To cheer them both the sun impartial glows,
On both the balmy air refreshing blows,
On both the bounteous god, Parjanya, rains.

KASYAPA replies:

So is it here on earth, but not for ever
Shall bad and good be favoured thus alike;
A stern decree the bad and good shall sever,
And vengeance sure at last the wicked strike.
The righteous then in realms of light shall dwell,
Immortal, pure, in undecaying bliss;
The bad for long, long years shall pine in hell,
A place of woe, a dark and deep abyss.

XXXVI. "Strait is the gate and narrow is the way which leadeth unto life."

Mahâbhârata xiv. 2784.

Heaven's narrow gate eludes the ken,
Bedimmed and dull, of foolish men.
Within that portal sternly barred,
To gain an entrance, O how hard!
What forms its bolts and bars? the sin
Of those who seek to enter in.
Men generous, pure, and self-controlled,
Alone that heavenly door behold;
To such 'tis ever opened wide;
They entering there, in bliss abide.

XXXVII. No second youth to man. (Compare Job xiv. 7.)

Kathâsaritsâgara lv. 110.

The empty beds of rivers fill again,
Trees, leafless now, renew their vernal bloom;
Returning moons their lustrous phase resume;
But man a second youth expects in vain.

XXXVIII. The lapse of time not practically noticed.

Subhâshitârṇava 255.

Again the morn returns, again the night;
Again the sun, the moon, ascends the sky:
Our lives still waste away as seasons fly,
But who his final welfare keeps in sight?

XXXIX. "All men think all men mortal but themselves." (Young's "Night Thoughts.")

Mahâbhârata iii. 17041.

Is not those men's delusion strange,
Who, while they see that every day
So many sweeps from earth away,
Can long themselves t' elude all change?

XL. Who are the really blind, deaf, and dumb?

Dampatiśikshâ 26; *Praśnottaramâlâ* 15.

That man is blind whose inner eye
Can nought beyond this world descry;
And deaf the man on folly bent,
On whom advice is vainly spent.
The dumb are those who never seek
To others gracious words to speak.

XLI. Remember thy mortality.

Bhartṛihari's Śāntiśataka, 35.

Thou hear'st that from thy neighbour's stores
Some goods by theft have vanished; so,
That none of thine by stealth may go,
Thou sett'st a watch, and barr'st thy doors.
'Tis well: but know'st thou never fear
When thou dost learn that every day
Stern death from many a dwelling near
A helpless victim tears away?
Deluded mortals, warning take,
From such insensate slumber wake!

XLII. Sin removed by Repentance.

Manu xi. 228; *Mahābhārata* iii. 13751[b] ff; xiii. 5534 ff.

Whenever men with inward pain
And self-reproach their sins confess,
And steadfast never more transgress,
Their souls are cleansed from every stain;
As serpents shed their worn-out skins,
These men are freed from cast-off sins.

XLIII. Never do what would distress thee on a sick-bed.

Mahābhārata v. 1474[b] f; xii. 10559[b] f.

Such deeds as thou with fear and grief
Would'st, on a sick-bed laid, recall,
In youth and health eschew them all,
Remembering life is frail and brief.

XLIV. Men should think on their end.

Vṛiddha Chāṇakya, 14, 6.

Did men but always entertain
Those graver thoughts which sway the heart,
When sickness comes, or friends depart,
Who would not then redemption gain ?

XLV. Men devout when in distress.

Subhāshitārṇava 163 ; *Vṛiddha Chāṇakya*, 176.

In trouble men the gods invoke ;
When sick, submit to virtue's yoke ;
When lacking power to sin, are good ;
When poor, are humble, meek, subdued.

XLVI. Men love the fruits of virtue, not virtue itself.

Subhāshitārṇava 43.

In virtue men have small delight ;
To them her fruits alone are dear ;
The fruits of sin they hate and fear,
But sin pursue with all their might.

XLVII. Effects of habitual sin and virtue respectively.

Mahābhārata v. 1242.

Sin practised oft,—experience shows,—
Men's understanding steals at length,
And understanding gone, the strength
Of sin unchecked, resistless grows.
But virtue ever practised, lends
The understanding firmer sway ;
And understanding day by day
More widely virtue's rule extends.

XLVIII. A small part of the toil endured in gaining wealth would ensure final emancipation.

Panchatantra ii. 127 (117 Bombay Ed.)

Fools endless labour, care and moil,
In storing earthly wealth endure.
A hundredth part of all that toil
Would everlasting calm ensure.

XLIX. Action keeping in view the future.

Mahābhārata v. 1248 f.

Let all thy acts by day be right,
That thou mayst sweetly rest at night;
Let such good deeds thy youth engage,
That thou mayst spend a tranquil age.
So act through life, that not in vain
Thou future bliss may'st hope to gain.

L. Daily self-examination.

Sārngadhara's Paddhati, Nīti 2.

With daily scrutinizing ken
Let every man his actions try,
Enquiring "What with brutes have I
In common, what with noble men?"

LI. Improvement of time.

Śārngadhara's Paddhati, p. 4.

The sage will ne'er allow a day
Unmarked by good to pass away;
But waking up, will often ask,
"Have I this day fulfilled my task?
With this, with each, day's setting sun,
A part of my brief course is run."

LII. Virtue difficult; vice easy.

Hitopadeśa ii. 44.

As stones rolled up a hill with toil and pain,
Come quickly bounding backward o'er its side;
'Tis hard the top of virtue's steep to gain,
But easy down the slope of vice to glide.

LIII. "Gutta cavat lapidem," &c.; good slowly acquired.

Vṛiddha Chāṇakya xii. 22.

As water-drops, which slowly fall,
A pitcher fill by ceaseless flow;
So learning, virtue, riches, all
By constant small accessions grow.

LIV. The condition of acquiring knowledge.

Mahābhārata v. 1537.

How can the man who ease pursues,
The praise of knowledge ever earn?
All those the path of toil must choose—
Of ceaseless toil—who care to learn.
Who knowledge seeks must ease refuse;
Who ease prefers must knowledge lose.

LV. Knowledge a treasure which cannot be lost.

Chāṇakya 5.

With knowledge, say, what other wealth
Can vie, which neither thieves by stealth
Can take, nor kinsmen make their prey;
Which lavish'd, never wastes away.

LVI. Ars longa, vita brevis: The essence of books to be got.

Vṛiddha Chāṇakya xv. 10.

The list of books is long; mishaps arise
To bar the student's progress; life is brief;
Whatever, then, in books is best and chief,
The essence, kernel,—that attracts the wise.

LVII. The Condition of Mortality.

Rāmāyaṇa (Bombay Edition) ii. 105. 16, (= *MBh.* xi. 48, 55; xii. 828; 5683; 8255 ff.; 12501; 12516 ff.).

In scatterings end collections all;
High towering piles at length must fall;
In parting every meeting ends;
To death all life of creatures tends.
  The early fall to earth is sure,
Of fruits on trees that hang mature.
Of mortals here behold a type;
They, too, succumb, for death when ripe.
  As houses fall when long decay
Has worn the posts which formed their stay,
So sink men's frames, when age's course
Has undermined their vital force.
  The nights which once have passed away,
And mingled with the morning ray,
Return no more,—as streams which blend
With ocean, there for ever end.
  Revolving ceaseless, night and day,
The lives of mortals wear away;
As summer's torrid solar beams
Dry up the ever lessening streams.
  In hours when men at home abide,
Death, too, reposes by their side;

When forth they issue, day by day,
Death walks companion of their way;
Death with them goes when far they roam;
Death with them stays, death brings them home.
  Men hail the rising sun with glee,
They love his setting glow to see,
But fail to mark that every day
In fragments bears their life away.
  All nature's face delight to view,
As changing seasons come anew;
Few see how each revolving year
Abridges swiftly man's career.
  As logs that on the ocean float,
By chance are into contact brought,
But, tossed about by wind and tide,
Together cannot long abide;—
So wives, sons, kinsmen, riches, all
Whate'er our own we fondly call,—
Obtained, possessed, enjoyed, to-day,
To-morrow all are snatched away.
  As, standing on the road a man
Who sees a passing caravan,
Which slowly winds across the plain,
Cries, "I will follow in your train;"
So men the beaten path must tread
On which their sires of yore have led.
  Since none can nature's course elude,
Why o'er thy doom in sorrow brood?

LVIII. The Mysteries of Destiny.

Mahābhārata xii. 846 f.; 854 ff.

How strange, to all her course who mark,
Must Fortune's ways appear, how dark!

For those she seems to favour most,
By fatal ills are often crossed.
The man who strongest seems to be,
Is vexed by some infirmity.
Oft rich men pine from lack of health,
And gain scant good from all their wealth.
A prosperous youth, whose hopeful mood
Foresees long years of coming good,
To sudden, early death a prey,
From all his joys is torn away:
While oft a poor man, frail and worn,
Lives out a hundred years, forlorn.
The poor man's wife, son after son
Brings forth although he asks for none.*
The rich man vainly seeks an heir;
No sons are granted to his prayer.
The leech who other men can cure,
Himself must sharp disease endure;
His skill, his learning, nought avail,
His vaunted drugs and potions fail
To ease his frame by pain oppressed,
Or Death's foredoomed approach arrest.
And men whom study, deep and long,
Has taught the rules of right and wrong,
By women lured, misled by knaves,
Of vice are often found the slaves.
No prayers, no rites, no drugs, no spells,
Can save the man whom death assails.
Disease and death like wolves devour,
None, strong or weak, elude their power;
Not even the king whose sway extends
Supreme, to earth's remotest ends.

---

* The original may mean that the poor man does not wish either for so many, or for any, sons.

LIX. The Same.

Mahábhárata iii. 13851 ff; xii. 12521 ff.

Men self-controlled, acute and wise,
Oft fail their aims to realize.
In vain they plan, in vain they strive;
Their schemes are foiled, they never thrive.
While others worthless, base, or weak,
Gain often all the good they seek.
A man the scoundrel's part who plays
Lives on in ease through all his days.
One favouring Fortune's gifts commands,
Although he sits and folds his hands.
Another, every nerve who strains,
Gains no return for all his pains.
A man who offspring lacks, adores
The gods, and humbly sons implores.
At length, in answer to his prayers,
His spouse the longed-for children bears;
But ah! they prove a wicked race,
Who on their parents bring disgrace.*

LX. Contrasts of life.

Bhartṛihari, and *Subháshitárṇava* 28, 313.

Hark! here the sound of lute so sweet,
And there the voice of wailing loud;
Here scholars grave in conclave meet,
There bowls the brawling drunkard-crowd;

* Compare Ecclesiastes ix. 11, "I returned, and saw under the sun that the race is not to the swift, nor the battle to the strong, neither yet bread to the wise, nor yet riches to men of understanding, nor yet favour to men of skill; but time and chance happeneth to them all."

Here charming maidens full of glee,
There tottering, withered dames, we see.
Such light! such shade! I cannot tell
If here we live in heaven or hell.*

LXI. Means do not always lead to the desired ends.

Mahâbhârata xii. 831 (=xii. 6486[b] f).

Friends cannot always bring us bliss,
Nor foes suffice to bring us ill;
Wealth is not always won by skill,
And rich men oft enjoyment miss.

LXII. The same.

Mahâbhârata v. 1430 (compare xiii. 7597—7606).

The clever do not always wealth command,
Nor stupid fools for lack of fortune pine;
The wise the course of mundane things divine;
No other men the secret understand.

LXIII. Poverty lends a relish to food.

Mahâbhârata v. 1144.

The poor man daintier fare enjoys
Than e'er his wealthy neighbours taste;
For hunger lends his food a zest,
While plenty pampered palates cloys.

---

* The expressions in this line are stronger than the original employs. See prose translation in the Appendix.

LXIV. The Vanity of Human Ambition.

Vishṇu Purāṇa iv. 24, 48 ff.

How many kings—their little day
Of power gone by—have passed away,
While yet the stable earth abides,
And all the projects vain derides
Of men who deemed that She was theirs,
The destined portion of their heirs!

With bright autumnal colours gay,
She seems to smile from age to age,
And mock the fretting kings who wage
Fierce wars for Her,—for ampler sway.

"Though doomed," She cries, "to disappear
So soon, like foam that crests the wave,
Vast schemes they cherish, madly brave,
Nor see that death is lurking near.

"And kinsmen, brothers, sons and sires,
Whom selfish love of empire fires,
The holiest bands of nature rend,—
In bloody strife for Me contend.

"O! how can princes, well aware
How all their fathers, one by one,
Have left Me here behind, and gone,
For my possession greatly care?"

King Pṛithu strode across the world,
And all his foes to earth he hurled;
Beneath his chariot wheels—a prey
For dogs and vultures—crushed they lay.

Yet snatched by time's resistless blast,
He long from hence away has past;
Like down the raging flames consume,
He, too, has met the common doom.

And Kârtavîrya, once so great,
Who ruled o'er all the isles, supreme,
Is but a shadow now, a theme
On which logicians subtly prate.

Those Lords of men, whose empire's sheen
Of yore the regions all illumed,
By death's destroying frown consumed,
Are gone; no ashes e'en are seen!

Māndhātṛi once was world-renowned:
What forms his substance now? A tale!
Who hearing this, if wise, can fail
This mundane life to scorn, so frail,
So dreamlike, transient, worthless found?

Of all the long and bright array
Of kings whose names tradition shows,
Have any ever lived? Who knows?
And now where are they? None can say.

LXV. The path of salvation.

Mahâbhârata i. 3176, and 3177; xii. 781—3; xii. 6508[b] ff.

That man with Brahma union wins,—
The highest good by sages sought,—
Who ne'er in deed, or word, or thought,
'Gainst any living creature sins.

LXVI. Sanctitas via intelligentiæ: Holiness the road to knowledge.

Mahâbhârata v. 1382.

The man who every sin forsakes,
Whose breast with love of goodness glows,—
He Nature's primal essence knows,
And all the changing forms she takes.

LXVII. The extinction of Sin leads to Knowledge.

Mahâbhârata xii. 7447.

As sinful passion's fires grow cold,
Men ever deeper knowledge gain,
Until, at length, when free from stain,
They in themselves the Soul behold.

LXVIII. Final beatitude; and the self-evidencing power of the doctrine regarding it.

Mahâbhârata iii. 13982; xii. 8959, ff.; 11380, ff.; 11692, ff. xiv. 1455, ff.

Let men all worldly longings quell,
And, sunk in contemplation, dwell
On th' inmost, deepest truth of things,
From which the spirit's freedom springs.
Composed and calm, ascetics feel
No longer outward woe and weal:
Within themselves enclosed they rest,
And self-sufficing, live most blest.
Their state resembles placid sleep,
'Mid men who troubled vigils keep.
'Tis as,—when winds by night repose,—
A lamp's clear flame unflickering glows.

And thus as seasons onward roll,
The saint, with meagre fare content,
On deep self-contemplation bent,
Within himself beholds the Soul.*

Now see in this most wholesome lore
The Vedas' deep esoteric core.
On no tradition old it rests:
Its truth at once itself attests.
Whatever precious gems you find
In sacred tales, are here combined.
Extracted here, you taste distilled
The nectar thousand verses yield.

LXIX. A guide through the gloom.

Mahābhārata xii. 12064.

The night approaches now: hold fast
The lamp of holy knowledge, bright
With ever slowly kindling light,
To guide thee till the gloom is past.

---

* Compare, though of a different character, the phenomenon described by Professor Reuss, Histoire des Israelites, p. 295, note 3, as quoted in the Appendix.

[Although in subsequent verses (8967 f.), systems founded on reasoning, and ignorance of the Vedas, are condemned, we seem to have in the passage before us a recognition of the self-evidencing power of certain doctrines, independently of any revealed authority. In the pieces preceding, pp. 11-13, entitled "An Indian Free-thinker's fate," and "The Indian Rationalist in ancient times," strict orthodoxy is required.]

LXX. Janaka's saying: The Blessedness of dispassion.

Mahâbhârata xii. 529, 6641, 9917, 9919; (also 7981).

"As having nothing, and yet possessing all things."

How vast my wealth, what joy I taste,
Who nothing own and nought desire!
Were this fair city wrapped in fire,
The flame no goods of mine would waste.

A purer, sweeter bliss he knows
Whom quelled desire no more annoys
Than springs from earth's exciting joys,
Or even than paradise bestows.

LXXI. Whither knowledge leads.

Śatapatha Brâhmaṇa x. 5, 4. 16.

By knowledge mortals thither soar
Where all desires have passed away;
Alms, penance, cannot there convey
The man who lacks this holy lore.

LXXII. Death is not the extinction of the good.

Mahâbhârata xii. 12121.

Let no one deem the wise are dead,
Who've "shuffled off this mortal coil,"
The wise whose lives were pure from soil,
Who never fell, by lust misled.

LXXIII. The Watchtower of Wisdom.*

Mahābhārata xii. 530 (= xii. 5623).

As men who climb a hill behold
The plain beneath them all unrolled,
And thence with searching eye survey
The crowds that pass along the way,
So those on wisdom's mount who stand
A lofty vantage-ground command.
They thence can scan the world below,
Immersed in error, sin and woe;
Can mark how mortals vainly grieve,
The true reject, the false receive,
The good forsake, the bad embrace,
The substance flee and shadows chase.
But none who have not gained that height,
Can good and ill discern aright.

LXXIV. The Indian Martha and Mary.

(Illustrative of the Vedantic doctrine of absorption
into Brahma).

Bṛihad Araṇyaka Upanishad ii. 4, 1, ff; and iv. 5, 1, ff.

Two wives, as Indian rules allowed,
Called pious Yājnavalkya lord.

---

* This passage has some resemblance to Lucretius, ii. 10 f. Sed nil dulcius est, bene quam munita tenere edita doctrinâ sapientum templa serena, despicere unde queas alios passimque videre errare atque viam palantis quærere vitæ, etc. "But nothing is more welcome than to hold the lofty and serene positions well fortified by the learning of the wise, from which you may look down upon others and see them wandering all abroad and going astray in their search for the path of life," etc.—MUNRO.

They dwelt in peace and good accord,
With varying powers and tastes endowed.

Maitrēyī studied, grave and wise,
The depths of sacred lore to sound;
In fair Kātyāyanī were found
Such gifts as women mostly prize.

Now Yājnavalkya longed to gain
A higher stage of saintly life,
And wander far from home and wife,
Domestic ties esteeming vain.

He thus addressed his elder bride:
"I now go forth alone to roam:
So let me, e'er I quit my home,
Between you twain my goods divide."

She asked him then, that thoughtful wife:
"If earth, with boundless treasures filled,
Were mine, should then my fears be stilled,
That Yama * soon will claim my life?"

He said: "Hadst thou such treasures won,
Thy lot would but be that of those
Round whom her halo fortune throws,
Whose life with pleasure overflows:—
The grasp of death thou couldst not shun."

"What profits wealth," Maitrēyī cried,
"If I must die and leave it soon?
Immortal life, that envied boon,
To gain, if thou canst guide me, guide."

---

* The Indian Pluto.

Then Yājnavalkya said: "Though dear
To me, my spouse, thou wast before,
For these thy words I love thee more.
Now ponder well what thou shalt hear:

"A woman holds her husband dear.
'Tis not her lord, as such, that draws
Her love; he's only dear because
In him she sees that Soul appear.

"With others, too, the same is true:
Wife, sons—whate'er our own we call—
Are only dear, because in all
The Universal Soul we view.

"Whate'er we round us see, the whole
Terrestrial system—gods, priests, kings,—
The vast totality of things—
Is nothing else than that one Soul.

"A lump of salt, as soon as cast
Into its primal source, the sea,
Dissolves, and ne'er can cease to be
A part of that salt ocean vast.

"So, sprung from that great Spirit, men,
When once their earthly term is spent,
To him return, and with him blent,
The sense of life no more retain."

"The dark, mysterious words that end
Thy sage discourse," Maitreyī cried,
"Perplex my mind. Oh! guide me, guide;
The Soul I do not comprehend."

"Let not the knowledge I now give
Perplex thee," Yājnavalkya said;

The Soul, as thou appear'st to dread
It may, can never cease to live.

"A baseless, dualistic dream
Indulging, vulgar men suppose
That one another sees, hears, knows.
If 'tis not as the many deem,

"And if that Soul is all, and none
But That exists,—and this is so,—
Whom else can That behold or know?
Since thus, Maitreyī, nought but one

"Great Spirit lives, there cannot be
Of separate being any sense
To mortals left, when they go hence.
That Soul is deathless; therein see
The only immortality."

Thus Yājnavalkya taught his wife,
Who wondering heard his mystic lore,
And left her then, to come no more,
But lead till death a beggar's life.

In quitting those he loved so well,
Showed then the saint a husband's heart;
Or played he, cold, the Stoic's part?
Tradition fails: we cannot tell.

LXXV. Nachiketas: a theosophic story.

Taittirīya Brāhmaṇa iii. 11, 8, 1 ff.; *and Kaṭha Upanishad.*

Desiring heaven, a sage of old
With sacrifice the gods adored;

Devoting to the priests his hoard
Of slowly-gathered goods and gold.

His son, young Nachiketas, stood
And saw the gifts his father brought,
To give the priests: "My Sire," he thought,
"His vow has not made fully good."

"Thou hast not all, my father, given
Thou hadst to give," he calmly said;
One offering more must yet be made,
If thou would'st hope to merit heaven.

"To whom shall I be given, my sire?"
His father deemed the question vain;
Once more he asked, and yet again:
"To Death," his father cried in ire.

He rose to go to Death's abode:
A Voice addressed him from the air,
"Go, seek Death's house, and enter there
What time its lord shall be abroad.

"Three nights within his mansion stay,
But taste not, though a guest, his food;
And if in hospitable mood,
He comes and asks thee, thou shalt say:

"'I in thy house three nights have passed.'
When next he asks, 'what did'st thou eat;'
Say, 'First thy children were my meat,
Thy cattle next, thy merits last.'"

The youth th' aerial Voice obeyed,
And dwelt three nights in Death's abode;
When questioned by his host, the god,
He answered as the Voice had said.

Disturbed that this his youthful guest,
Had not been fitly entertained,
The god, to make amends constrained,
The stranger humbly thus addressed:

"I bow before thee, reverend child;
I pray thee crave a boon of me."
"My father let me, living, see,"
The boy rejoined, "and reconciled."

To whom the god,—"I grant thy prayer;
But ask a second boon"—replied.
"May my good works," the stripling cried,
"Of bliss an endless harvest bear."

This, too, according, Death desired
He yet one boon would choose, the last.
"When men away from earth have past,
Then live they still?" the youth enquired.

"To solve this question dark and grave
Was even for gods too hard a task:
This boon, I pray thee, cease to ask,
Fair youth," said Death, "another crave."

Young Nachiketas, undeterred,
Replied, "The boon I choose, bestow:
Who can like thee the answer know?
No boon like this may be compared."

Death said: "Ask all thine heart's desire;
Sons long-lived, cattle, gold demand,
Elect a wide domain of land,
And length of days from me require;

"Or seek what earth can ne'er supply—
The love of witching heavenly brides,
And all celestial joys besides;
But unto death forbear to pry."

The youth rejoined, "The force of man
Is frail, and all excess of joys
His feeble organs soon destroys:
Our longest life is but a span.

"Wealth cannot satisfy: all zest
Of pleasure flies before thy face;
Our life depends upon thy grace,
Once more, of boons I crave the best.

"For who, with deathless youth though crowned,
And godlike force, if wise, would deign
To spend an endless life in vain
In sensual joy's disturbing round?"

When thus the stripling had withstood,
Though proffered by a god, the lure
Of sensual bliss, and sought the pure
Delight of transcendental good,

Then Death, who knew the unborn soul,
And being's essence, taught the youth
The science of the highest truth,
Through which is reached the final goal.

"Two things for men's regard contend—
The good, the pleasant: he who woos
The good is blest, whilst they who choose
The pleasant miss the highest end.

"The wise between the two discern,
The pleasant spurn, the good embrace,
But fools the pleasant wildly chase:
To love the good they cannot learn.

"The first take knowledge for their guide;
The last by ignorance are led;
Far, far, diverge the paths they tread;
The chasm that parts their goals is wide.

"The fools who ignorance obey,
Conceive they much have learnt and know,
But roam, unwitting where they go,
As blind men, led by blind men, stray.

"With fortune's favours vain elate,
The men whom earthly passions fire,
To no sublimer aim aspire,
Nor dream of any future state.

"Of all the objects men can know,
The highest is the Soul, too high
For common mortals to descry,
Whose eyes are dazzled by outward show.

"Some men have never learnt this lore,
And some whom sages seek to teach,
Possess no faculty to reach
This sacred doctrine's inner core.

"O skilled and wonderful, my son,
Is he the Soul who gains and knows!
This subtle science only those
Can teach who think the Soul as one.

"The sage whose spirit's gaze intense,
This God, the Soul, from fleshly eyes
Impenetrably veiled, descries,
No longer dotes on things of sense.

"Derived from no anterior source,
The Soul, unborn, exempt from all
The accidents that life befall,
Holds on its everlasting course.

The smiter thinks that he can slay;
The smitten fears that he is slain:
The thoughts of both alike are vain,
The Soul survives the murderous fray.

"Steel cannot cut, nor cleave, nor tear,
Nor fire consume, nor water wet,
Nor winds e'er dry it up, nor yet
Aught else its deathless essence wear.

"A man casts from him on the shelf
His garments old, and newer takes;
So bodies worn the Soul forsakes,
And new assumes, unchanged itself.*

"The man who learns the Soul to be
Minute, yet infinitely vast,
He, by his Maker's grace, at last
Its majesty attains to see.

"It travels far and wide, at rest;
Moves everywhere, although asleep.
Say, who but I the secret deep
Of this mysterious God has guessed?

---

* The ideas in this and the preceding verse are taken from the Bhagavad Gitâ. See also Mahâbhârata xi. 91 f.

"By reasoning, thought, or many books,
This hidden Soul is sought in vain.
That man alone the Soul may gain,
On whom the Soul with favour looks,*

"Elected thus, the sage believes
His oneness with the One Supreme;
Awakes for ever from the dream
Which uninstructed men deceives;

"And now from imperfection purged,
And freed from circling life and death,
He calmly yields his vital breath,
And in the Sovereign Soul is merged.†

LXXVI. Wonderful Attributes of the Brahmans.

(*Mahābhārata* i. 3383 f.; 7045 ff.; iii. 50; 1395; 12470 ff.; 13362 ff.; 13427; 13434 ff.; 13676 ff.; 13684 ff.; xii. 6057 ff.; 6951 ff.; xiii. 2084 ff.; 2160 ff.; 7163—7184; 7213 ff.; 7412 ff.; *Manu* ix. 314 ff.)

[It is perhaps not very easy to determine in what sense some of the most extravagant assertions in the verses which I have translated are to be understood. On the one hand it will be seen from one of the notes given below, that the statement there referred to, is regarded by Kullūka the com-

* In regard to the translation of this verse, see the Appendix, and the renderings of Dr Roer and Professor Max Müller there quoted.

† The general substance of the Vedantic doctrine of absorption is here expressed, not in any words of the Katha Upanishad.

mentator as eulogistic and hyperbolical; and from another, that the gods and worlds are in some way regarded as dependent on the sacrifices of the Brahmans. Compare my "Original Sanskrit Texts," Vol. v., where the god Indra is said to be stimulated by the Soma libations which he drank, and strengthened to support the earth and the sky, (p. 88); and where a similar effect is said to be produced by the hymns, prayers, and worship addressed to him, (p. 91). The action of the worshipper and the god on each other, is thus in some measure reciprocal. The worshipper by his offerings and his hymns strengthens the god, and thus enables him to afford the help which the suppliant requires.

Before the Brahmans bow with awe;
Esteem their every word as law;
For they shall prosper all, who treat
The priests with filial reverence meet.

As pure and lustrous gleams the fire,
Which lights the foulest funeral pyre,
As that which household hearths illumes,
Or holy offerings consumes.
No touch of objects base or vile
Can all-destroying fire defile.*
So, though they servile tasks † pursue,
To Brahmans high esteem is due.

---

* Comp. Prof. A. Holzmann's Agni, pp. 10 ff.

† The words in the original are "all undesirable works." By the commentator on Manu ix. 319, where the same verse occurs, "undesirable" is explained as (*kutsita*) bad, or "mean," as it is rendered by Sir W. Jones. The commentator says that as the verse is of an eulogistic character, (*stutyarthatvāt*), it is not to be regarded as contrary to the rules of Scripture, some at least of which forbid a Brahman, unless in cases of necessity, to engage in the occupations of the lower castes.

For be he stolid as a clod,
A Brahman is a mighty god.
How much more, then, should those who shine
By learning be pronounced divine!
By them,—whose might sustains the world,*
It could be into ruin hurled,
And others formed to take its place,
With guardian gods, a younger race.
Could aught the Brahmans overthrow,
The gods themselves would feel the blow,
And fall from heaven, resourceless left,
Of all their best allies bereft.
Through their high grace to gods 'tis given
In bliss serene to dwell in heaven.
By them cast down, the demon host
Lies prostrate on the ocean tost.
By their transforming curse malign,
The sweet sea-waves were turned to brine.
No power could form th' ethereal space,†
Or shake Himālay from its base;
No dam could stem the Ganges' tide;
No might can quell the Brahman's pride.
The dam of law uprearing, they
The surging flood of evil stay,
Which truth and right would sweep away.
Their gold they never grudge to give;
A silent, lovely life they live;
Whate'er may be their outward state,
They never grieve or feel elate.

---

* The commentator on Manu ix. 316, understands the dependence of the worlds, and the gods, on the Brāhmans, to be connected with the sacrifices offered by the latter.

† Yet it is stated in Mahābhārata xii, 6132, that Brahmā created the other (*ākāśa*).

In scented silken robes bedight,
They know no pride, no vain delight.
If wrapped in skins, or coarsely clad,
And smeared with mud, they are not sad.
Nor plenteous fare, nor lack of food,
Affects their calm, unchanging mood.
And thus a sinless life they lead,
From worldly ties and passions freed.
What forms their wealth? this life austere.
Their power? that potent word we hear.
Of other mortals they are guides;
In them all sacred lore resides.
They know the nicest points of right;
No jot eludes their piercing sight.
A heavy yoke sustaining, strong,
They draw the social car along.
Like oxen staunch, though rough their road,
They never sink beneath their load.
With fullest knowledge blest, and free
From doubt, the final goal they see.
The highest good they seek to gain,
And lead on others in their train.
  The Brahman deem a lamp whose light
Can guide athwart the gloom of night;
An eye, through which what else were sealed,—
To even the sagest lies revealed.
Of other causes he the cause,
The proof of proofs, the law of laws.*

---

* The last four words of this line are not in the original; but have been added for the sake of the rhyme they afford, as they harmonise with the two preceding characteristics ascribed to the Brahmans. The words "proof of proofs," (*pramáṇasya pramáṇam cha,*) could perhaps be better rendered "authority of authorities."

The next verses are different in their tendency.

LXXVII. Diversities among Brahmans.

Mahâbhârata xiii. 2092 ff.

After declaring, in verses 2084 ff. that Brahmans should be honoured, and asserting their great powers, Bhîshma refers to their varieties:—

Deem not in character the same
All those who bear the Brahman's name.
Among them every sort you find,
In work, in character, in mind.
Some dangerous, dark, resemble wells,
Whose mouth luxuriant grass conceals;
While others are as clear as day,
When shines the sun's unclouded ray.
Some cattle tend, some till the ground;
Some, begging, roam the country round.
Some fierce, and wild, obey no rule,
While some are soft as cotton-wool.
Some harmless lives ascetic lead,
From earthly hopes and longings freed;
While some, to sordid passions slaves,
Are liars, thieves, and arrant knaves;
And others in the mimic's art *
Adepts, in plays enact their part.
By lives so low, by acts so base,
Some men this highest caste disgrace,

---

* This might have been otherwise rendered:—
And others, leagued with dancers, stoop
To join a dancing, acting, troop.
See, however, the quotation given below from Prof. Wilson's "Theatre of the Hindus," in which he intimates his opinion, that the profession of an actor was not considered disreputable in ancient India; as well as the remarks which precede.

Which other some, not better born,
By virtue, learning, fame, adorn.
But he who virtue's laws obeys,
Howe'er subsisting, merits praise.

LXXVIII. **Knowledge to be sought from all castes, which all spring from Brahma.**

Mahābhārata xii. 11811.

From knowledge springs redemption: seek
That lore in faith, with spirit meek,
From Brahmans, Kshatriyas, Vaiśyas learn,
Nor even the Śūdra's teaching spurn.
This lowest order none should scorn;
For though from different members born,
All castes from Brahmā sprang; the name
Of Brāhman all may fitly claim:
And all by reverent impulse stirred,
Recite aloud the sacred Word.
To thee I tell the inmost core
And sense of this most holy lore:
This world is Brahma: all we see
Around is nothing else than He.

The following is a somewhat different and completer rendering of the same lines.

Through knowledge men redemption earn,
And never more to earth return.
Such knowledge seek,—make this thy task,—
From Brahmans, Kshatriyas, Vaiśyas ask,
Yea, even from lowly Śūdras learn,
And so shalt thou the truth discern.
Be full of faith: whoe'er believes
The fruit of holy lore receives.
The humble Śūdra none should scorn;

For though from different members born,
All castes alike from Brahmā spring,
And so are Brāhmans all, O king.
From lips of all the sacred word,
Recited, too, is ever heard.
Of that blest word now learn the core,
And live in error sunk no more.
This word that deepest truth makes known,
That Brahma and the world are one.
The lack of knowledge know to be
The source of mortals' misery;
This brings them back again to earth
In ever varying forms of birth.
Seek, therefore, knowledge: wheresoe'er
Thou seekest, thou shalt find it there.
To no one class is truth confined;
It lightens even the Śūdra's mind.
Whoever gains it, high or low,
Redeemed, no change shall ever know.

The following remarkable words of the sage Bhrigu are more decided. They are quoted and translated in my "Original Sanskrit Texts," i. 138 ff.

LXXIX. No distinction of Castes.

Mahābhārata xii. 6939.

When Brahmā framed the world of men,
He made it all Brahmanic then.
By no distinction marked of class,
They formed one homogeneous mass.

But when in time they showed diverse
And widely varying characters,
Those men whose natures were the same,
Conjoined, received a separate name.

The following passage is written in a similar spirit.

Mahābhārata xiii. 6612.

The Śūdra pure in all his ways,
Who all his passions sternly sways,
The same respect can rightly claim
As he who bears the Brahman's name.
So Brahmā ruled, and he well knew
To mete to every class its due.

When worthy acts, a nature sound,
Are both in any Śūdra found,
He surely merits more esteem
Than worthless Brahmans;—so I deem.

Nor birth, nor hallowing rites, nor store,
However vast, of sacred lore
Can make a Brahman; nought avails
For this, if virtuous conduct fails.

Good conduct constitutes a man
A Brahman; nought else ever can.
And Śūdras too, whose lives are pure,
The rank of Brahmanhood secure.

Brahmanic nature shows no change,
Wherever found, in all its range.
That man a Brahman deem in whom,
Exempt from goodness, passion, gloom,
The stainless Brahma dwells, serene:—
None else deserves the name, I ween.

LXXX. Final beatitude attainable even by low caste men and by women.

xii. 8801; xiv. 592.

Know this, the highest good, the final rest,
To gain with Brahma union;—this the goal:

Then freed from hard corporeal bonds, the soul
Enjoys immortal life, supremely blest.

This end pursuing, e'en the lowest men,
With women, reach that blissful state; much more
Shall Brahmans, Kshatriyas, versed in sacred lore,
Who Brahma seek, this good transcendent gain.

[This is said after a statement has been made in xiv. 532 ff. of the means by which final redemption, described in v. 543 as *nirvāṇa*, may be obtained. The same promise is made by Kṛishṇa (who is also the speaker here), to the same classes of persons in the Bhagavad Gītā, ix. 32 f.; but it is there made dependent on their being devoted to him, the words *mām hi Pārtha vyapāśritya* standing there in place of *dharmam imam samāsthāya*, the reading of v. 593 in the passage before us].

LXXXI. Honour due not to Class, but to Character.

Mahābhārata xiii. 2610.

No well-born man respect deserves,
Whose life from virtue's canons swerves;
While honour is that Śūdra's due,
Who lives to duty ever true.

LXXXII. The nobility of manhood.

Mahābhārata xii. 10931.

Though joyless, poor, and sad at heart,
Let no man seek with life to part;
For even the humblest, basest state
Of manhood yet is something great.

LXXXIII. Generous impartiality.

Mahâbhârata xii. 8752.

With equal eye the truly wise
View learned Brahmans, nobly born,
Cows, dogs, and outcast men forlorn,
Whom thoughtless fools as vile despise.

For both in objects fixed, and things
Which inward motive force impels,—
In all,—the one great Spirit dwells,
From whom this frame of nature springs.

LXXXIV. Virtue of more value than high birth.

Mahâbhârata v. 1492; iii. 12531.

The man of high or humble birth,
Whose life with virtue's laws accords,—
The righteous, modest man, is worth
A hundred merely high-born lords.

LXXXV. The true Brahman.

Mahâbhârata xii. 9667.

The man who Nature knows, with all
The changing growth that from her springs,
And all the fates of living things,—
That man the gods a Brahman call.

LXXXVI. The Same.

Mahâbhârata xii. 8925.

He whose sole presence fills a place,
Whose absence makes a void in halls
Where thousands throng the ample space,
That man the gods a Brahman call.

LXXXVII. What makes a man a Brahman.

Mahâbhârata iii. 17392; xii. 2363; iii. 12470.

A spirit (Yaksha) asks:

What is it makes a Brahman? birth,
Deep study, sacred lore, or worth?

King Yudhishthira answers;

Nor study, sacred lore, nor birth
The Brahman makes; 'tis only worth.

All men—a Brahman most of all—
Should virtue guard with care and pains.
Who virtue rescues, all retains;
But all is gone with virtue's fall.

The men in books who take delight,
Frequenters all of learning's schools,
Are nothing more than zealous fools;
The learn'd are those who act aright.

More vile than one of Śûdra race
That Brahman deem, whose learned store
Embraces all the Vedic lore,
If evil deeds his life disgrace.

That man deserves the Brahman's name
Who offerings throws on Agni's flame,
And knows his senses how to tame.

LXXXVIII. The true Brahman.

Mahâbhârata iii. 14075.

No better than a Śûdra deem
The Brahman wise in sin, the slave
Of low degrading vice, the knave
Who fain a holy man would seem.

But rank with men of priestly birth,
The Śûdra truthful, self-restrained,
By constant acts in virtue trained:
A twice-born man is he by worth.

LXXXIX. Goodness essential to a Brahman.

Mahābhārata xii. 2363.

The pious man who Soma * drinks,
From all base deeds with horror shrinks,
Calm, unaspiring, tender, mild,
Kind, patient, just, in guile a child,—
Deserves alone the Brahman's name,
Which no bad man can ever claim.

XC. The Same.

Mahābhārata xiii. 1542 f.

KASYAPA *says*:

Nor vedic learning deep, nor store
Of legends, or of Sānkhya lore,
Nor stainless birth, avails to save
The priest who lives to vice a slave.

AGNI *says*:

The man who much has read, and deems
His brain with copious learning teems,
Who yet misusing what he knows,
On worthier men discredit throws,—
By such base arts shall surely miss
In future worlds enduring bliss.

* The juice of the Soma plant, as part of a religious rite.

XCI. Profession without Practice.

Mahâbhârata xiii. 1550 f.

Some Brahmans roam the world around,
And loudly virtue's * praises sound,
Yet fail to practise what they preach;
Nay, vice by vicious living teach.
To honour such let no one think;
Who gives them gifts to hell shall sink.

XCII. Great Wealth injurious to Brahmans.

Mahâbhârata xiii. 3082.

To own too ample stores of wealth
Destroys a Brahman's moral health.
The man who no misfortune knows,
Whose life in bliss unbroken flows,
And who, by Fortune long caressed,
Is deemed by all supremely blest,
Of such success the price must pay,—
By vain conceit be led astray.
But when the Brahmans, filled with pride,
No longer others wisely guide,
Abandoned by its guardians, then
Must virtue cease to govern men.

XCIII. Brahmans should shun honour.

Manu ii. 162 f.; *Mahâbhârata* xii. 8449 f.; 11017; compare 9064.

A Brahman should from honour shrink,
As he would poison dread to drink;

* The original here has *dharma*, which may mean caste and ritual rules, and speaks of the conduct of the persons in question as leading to a confusion of castes, and so is written from a Brahmanical point of view.

And love contempt, as if he quaffed
A sweet celestial nectar-draught.
Though scorned, the wise man sweetly sleeps;
Though scorned, he ever calmly wakes;
And scorned, this course he calmly keeps;
But woe the scorner overtakes.

XCIV. The real ascetics.

Mahābhārata iii. 13448 f.; xii. 343[b] ff.; xii. 2979.

The high-souled men who never sin
In thought, or word, or action—they,
They are the true ascetics: pray,
What virtue's in a shrivelled skin?

XCV. The recluse less meritorious than virtuous men who live in the world.

Mahābhārata xii. 12126.

From every vicious taint though pure,
A hermit's virtue cannot vie
With theirs who ne'er from trials fly,
But face, and conquer, every lure.

XCVI. Retirement from the world not necessary for self-control.

Mahābhārata xii. 5961; (Comp. v. 1680.)

Why, pray, to forests wild repair,
There war against thy senses wage?
Where dwells the self-subduing sage,
The wood, the hermit's cell, is there.

XCVII. Bhima's Condemnation of Premature Asceticism.

Mahābhārata xii. 293 ff.

When old and grey, when strength decays,
By foes when crushed, in evil days,
From fortune's heights when downward hurled,—
Yes, then let men renounce the world;
But not in days of youth and health,
When crowned with glory, blest with wealth.
Those scripture texts which praise as best
A life ascetic, lone, unblest,
Dragged sadly on in gloomy woods,
And dreary, doleful solitudes,
Are fictions hatched in squalid schools
By needy unbelieving fools,
Which look like truth, but proved, are found
To rest on no substantial ground.

To savage beasts it is not given
By forest life to merit heaven;
Yet this same life, by hermits led,
Their future bliss ensures, 'tis said!

When men no pleasure feel, nor pain,
A state of stupid torpor gain.
They then have reached perfection, rise
To heaven, so say the would-be wise.
But should not trees,—if this be true,—
And boulders, gain perfection too?
For they are calm and torpid, feel
Nor pain nor pleasure, woe nor weal;
They dread no want, they seek no ease,
Like self-tormenting devotees.

Abandon, then, thy vain design;
By kingly virtues seek to shine.

See how by acts all mortals strive
Their ends to gain, through effort thrive.
Inaction ne'er perfection brings;
From strenuous deeds alone it springs.

XCVIII. What determines the Character of Actions.

Mahâbhârata xii. 4094.

'Tis from the soul, the man within,
That actions all their value win;
No outward state, whate'er it be,
Affects an action's quality.

Would he not sin, a Brahman sage
Who slew within a hermitage?
Bring gifts no fruit, howe'er profuse,
Unless bestowed by a recluse?

XCIX. The inefficacy of mere theological knowledge.

Mahâbhârata v. 1623.

No varied store of sacred texts has power
To save the man in guile and fraud expert;
His lore forsakes him in his final hour,
As birds, full-fledged, their native nests desert.

C. Austerities and rites unavailing without inward purity.

Mahâbhârata iii. 13445.

The triple staff, long matted hair,
A squalid garb of skins or bark,
A vow of silence, meagre fare,
All signs the devotee that mark,
And all the round of rites are vain,
Unless the soul be pure from stain.

CI. Truth better than sacrifice.

Mahābhārata i. 3094 ff.; xii. 6002; xiii. 3650 [b] ff.

By weighing truth and sacrifice appraise,
A thousand sacrifices truth outweighs.

CII. The Same.

Mahābhārata xiii. 1544; (Comp. xiii. 6073 ff).

In one scale truth, in the other lay
A thousand Aśvamedhas; try;
I doubt if all that pile so high,
Even half as much as truth would weigh.

CIII. Results of Truth and Falsehood.

Śatapatha Brāhmaṇa ii. 2, 2, 19.

Those noble men who falsehood dread,
   In wealth and glory ever grow,
   As flames with greater brightness glow,
With oil in ceaseless flow when fed.

But like to flames with water drenched,
   Which, faintly flickering, die away,
   So liars day by day decay,
Till all their lustre soon is quenched.

CIV. Sweet savour of Good Deeds: Falsehood to be shunned.

Taittirīya Araṇyaka x. 9.

As far and wide the vernal breeze
Sweet odours wafts from blooming trees,
So, too, the grateful savour speeds
To distant lands of virtuous deeds.

As one expert in daring feats
Athwart a pit a sword who lays,
And walking on its edge essays
The chasm to cross, but soon retreats,
With cries, afraid to fall below,
And trembling stands upon the brink,—
So let a man from falsehood shrink,
And guard himself from future woe.

CV. Loss of Virtue the only real Loss.

Mahábhárata v. 1289.

Thy virtue guard at any cost.
  Wealth none can trust; it comes and goes:
  The good survive misfortune's blows;
But virtue lost,—and all is lost.

CVI. The Righteous always Prosper.

Mahábhárata v. 1381; 1223 (comp. v. 4157 ff.).

Whoe'er would wealth abundant earn,
Should first to practise virtue learn.
Success on goodness always waits,
As nectar aye the blessed sates.

CVII. Righteousness more valuable than Riches.

Mahábhárata xii. 9810.

Wealth little satisfaction brings:
The highest bliss from virtue springs.

CVIII. The value of rites depends on the inward purity of the performer.

Vāyu Purāṇa viii. 190.

No sacred lore, howe'er profound,
Nor all the long and varied round
Of sacred rites, can bliss procure
For worthless men, in heart impure.
Although a man with zeal and skill
Should all external rites fulfil,
He reaps no fruit of all his toil,
If sin his inner man should soil.
Ev'n he his all in alms who spends
With heart defiled, secures no meed:
The disposition, not the deed,
Has value,—all on it depends.

CIX. Fate of those who have no belief in virtue; benefits of faith.

Mahābhāvata iii. 13747 f.

The fearful doom of all is sure
Who laugh at men whose lives are pure;
Who duty's binding force deny,
And scout all virtue as a lie.
The man who loves to live in sin
Is like a huge inflated skin;
With wisdom's show himself he cheats,
For vain are all his proud conceits.
No sin can want of faith exceed,
While men by faith from sin are freed.

Believing men throw off their sins,
As snakes cast off their worn-out skins.*

CX. Moral Goodness essential.

Mahábhárata xiv. 2835 (comp. xiii. 5544).

The knaves, untrained in wisdom's schools
Who smile at honest men as fools,
Who never vexed with scruples, long
Have wealth amassed by fraud and wrong,
And then their gains, with hearts elate,
To pious uses dedicate,
On costly sacrifices spend,
Or ample gifts to Brahmans send,—
Such knaves can never gain the meeds
Ordained for truly righteous deeds:
Their riches, sprung from poisoned roots,
Can bear none else than deadly fruits.
Bad men, who goodness only feign.
In hope the world's esteem to gain,
With lavish gifts and dainty feasts
In vain delight a host of priests.
Esteem that Brahman's doom assured,
Whoe'er, by lust of gold allured,
From virtue's hallowed path departs,
And heaps up wealth by wicked arts.
But those who others' wants relieve,
By giving what they have to give,—

---

* The following does not sound so satisfactory, but very Antinomian; but see the context as given in the Appendix:

Sacrifice is everything.

Mahábhárata xii. 2320.

A man of wicked life, a thief—
Of sinners yea the very chief,—
I reckoned good, if so he bring
The gods a fitting offering.

The scantiest harvest-gleanings, roots,
A draught of water, herbs, or fruits,—
These righteous, self-denying men
At length the bliss of heaven attain.

CXI. True Piety and Righteousness, and their Fruits.

Mahābhārata xiii. 7574. (Matthew vi. 19 f.; xix. 21.)

With awe sincere the gods adore,
Meet honour to thy tutor show,
With gifts enrich the good, and so
In heaven enduring treasure store.

Thy pious acts perform apart;
A love for goodness scorn to feign,
And never, as a means of gain,
Parade it with self-seeking art.

[In xii. 1328, it is said, "Let no man bestow gifts in order to gain reputation" (*na dadyād yaśase dānam*)].

CXII. The most meritorious Gifts.

Mahābhārata xiv. 2788.

Rich presents, though profusely given,
Are not so dear to righteous Heaven
As gifts, by honest gains supplied,
Though small, which faith has sanctified.

CXIII. Two Inheritors of Paradise.

Mahābhārata v. 1028.

Two men of heavenly bliss are sure,—
The lordly man who rules a land
With mild and patient self-command,
The man who freely gives, though poor.

CXIV. The best use of Wealth.

Mahâbhârata xii. 795.

For what should wealthy mortals live?
Should such their gains enjoy or hoard?
Not all * should be enjoyed or stored:
Those use wealth best who freely give.

CXV. Good practised because it is duty.

Mahâbhârata xii. 5906 (comp. xii. 1328).

'Tis not for gain, for fame, from fear,
That righteous men injustice shun,
And virtuous men hold virtue dear;
An inward voice they seem to hear
Which tells that duty must be done.

CXVI. Good easy, evil difficult, to a noble man.

Mahâbhârata vii. 5960.

A noble man no effort needs
To make to practice noble deeds;
But, oh! he struggles hard and long
Before he perpetrates a wrong.

CXVII. Effort, not success, the test of Goodness.

Mahâbhârata v. 3313.

A man who toils with all his strength
A high and righteous end to gain,
May fail,—but has not wrought in vain;
His merit gains its meed at length.

* The apparent rigour of the original is modified here.

CXVIII. Evil intentions, if relinquished, not punished.

Mahábhárata v. 3314.

Should thou the base intention nurse
To wrong another, pause and think:
Even then if thou from sin shalt shrink,
Thou shalt of guilt escape the curse.

CXIX. Virtue lies in the thought, not in the act.

Mahābhārata xii. 7063 (comp. xiii. 7593[b] ff.)

The real seat of virtue's in the mind
And not in outward act, so say the wise:
Let therefore every man in thought devise,
With earnest zeal, the good of all mankind.

CXX. Virtue must be a man's own unaided act.

Mahābhārata xii. 7064.

In virtue's practice men alone must stand;
No friends can e'er their moral efforts share:
Wise guides or books the rule of life declare;
But only men themselves their acts command.

(Comp. xiii. 7594[b] ff., translated above, No. cxi., first line of verse second. It is only the first clause which corresponds to this passage, and the meaning is different, though the words correspond.)

CXXI. Kind and Heartless Men.

Mahábhárata xiii. 3010.

That man beloved by other lives
Who kindly acts and kindly gives:
From other men a fitting meed
He gains for every loving deed.

Those who have power to help, but fail
To heed the needy suppliant's wail,
Who treat his prayer with cold disdain,
These justly reprobation gain.
The man who kindly treats a foe
By stern misfortune's stroke laid low,
Who sues for help in humble mood,—
He who so acts is truly good.

CXXII. The humble are wise.

Mahâbhârata v. 1010.

Those men who far 'bove others rise
By learning, wealth, or royal state,
And yet with pride are ne'er elate,
By all are justly reckoned wise.

CXXIII. Marks of a virtuous man.

Mahâbhârata v. 1088.

No ill the thoughtful man disturbs,
His hungry appetite who curbs,
In comfort all his household keeps,
Who toils immensely, little sleeps,
Who, not content to help his friends,
When asked, his help to foes extends.

CXXIV. Selfishness.

Mahâbhârata v. 1011.

Who more inhuman lives than he,
Of dainty food who eats the best,
In rich attire is always drest,
And stints his helpless family?

CXXV. "**If any provide not for his own, . . . he is worse than an infidel**" (1st Epistle to Timothy v. 8.)

Manu xi. 9.

Those men who ample gifts on strangers waste,
And leave their own to pine in want and woe,
Of goodness only earn the empty show :—
To poison turns the honied praise they taste.
The fools who thus to suffering doom their kin,
And costly rites fulfil to merit heaven,
From all the acts performed, and largess given,
No bliss shall find, but reap the fruit of sin.

CXXVI. **Disinterestedness**: "**Do good and lend, hoping for nothing again**" (St Luke vi. 34 f.)

Mahābhārata iii. 16796.

The good to others kindness show,
And from them no return exact :
The best and greatest men they know,
Thus ever nobly love to act.

CXXVII. **Do to others as ye would that they should do to you.**

Mahābhārata v. 1517 ; xii. 9248 b f. ; 9281 a ; xiii. 5571 f.

Whene'er thy acts the source must be
Of good or ill to other men,
Deal thou with them in all things then
As thou would'st have them deal with thee.

CXXVIII. Marks of a good man.

Mahâbhârata ii. 2424 and 2438 f.

The good kind actions recollect,
But base, injurious deeds forget;
On doing good to others set,
They never recompence expect.

CXXIX. The Same.

Mahâbhârata i. 6116, 6254; and iii. 13252.

Kind deeds are never thrown away
On men of real goodness,—such
Are not content to give as much,
As they have got, far more repay,
Nay, even a hundredfold bestow:
For here the gods no measure know.

CXXX. Beneficence a duty.

Mahâbhârata iii. 13745; xii. 3531[a].

A man should do with all his might
The good his heart has once designed.
Ne'er let him wrong with wrong requite,
But be to others ever kind.

CXXXI. The prosperity of others not to be envied.

Mahâbhârata xiii. 3880.

On thee to smile though fortune never deign,
Her favourites' happier lot with calmness bear;
For prudent men from wealth they do not share,
But others' own, enjoyment ever gain.

[The last two lines of this maxim are ambiguous, and may, perhaps, admit of an unfavourable interpretation; viz., that the unfortunuate may find means of benefiting by the wealth of others, by recommending themselves to their favour. See, however, the context, as given in the Appendix.]

CXXXII. The requiter, not equal to the doer, of good acts.

Mahâbhârata xii. 4993.

The man who manifold hath paid
  A kindness on himself conferred,
  Does less than he who, only stirred
By generous impulse, lent him aid.

CXXXIII. "This is the law and the prophets." (St Matthew vii. 12.)

Vikrama charita 158.

In one short verse I here express
The sum of tomes of sacred lore:
Beneficence is righteousness;
Oppression sin's malignant core.

CXXXIV. Do not to others what thou would'st not have done to thee.

Panchatantra iii. 104 (or 103, in another edition.)

Hear virtue's sum expressed in one
Brief maxim—lay it well to heart,
Ne'er do to others what, if done
To thee, would cause thee inward smart.

CXXXV. "If ye love them which love you what reward have ye?" (St Matthew v. 46.)

Panchatantra i. 277 (or 247 in another edition.)

His action no applause invites,
Who simply good with good repays:
He only justly merits praise
Who wrongful deeds with kind requites.

CXXXVI. The highest worship of the Deity.

Bhâgavata Purâṇa viii. 7, 44.

To scatter joy throughout thy whole
Surrounding world; to still men's grief:—
Such is the worship best and chief
Of God, the Universal Soul.

CXXXVII. The proper aim of life.

Bhâgavata Purâṇa x. 22, 35.

He only does not live in vain
Who all the means within his reach
Employs, his wealth, his thought, his speech,
T' advance the weal of other men.

CXXXVIII. The means of attaining to final liberation.

Vṛiddha Châṇakya xv. 1.

Those men alone the secret know
Which final liberation brings,
Whose hearts with pity overflow
To even the meanest living things:—
Not those a beggar's garb who wear,
With ashes smeared, with matted hair.

CXXXIX. "Overcome evil with good." (Epistle to the Romans xii. 21.)

Mahâbhârata iii. 13253; v. 1518; xii. 9972.

With meekness conquer wrath, and ill with ruth,
By giving niggards vanquish, lies with truth.

CXL. "Who when he was reviled, reviled not again." (1st Epistle of Peter ii. 2, 3; iii. 9.)

Mahâbhârata v. 1270; xii. 11008.

Reviling meet with patience; ne'er
To men malignant malice bear.
Harsh tones and wrathful language greet
With gentle speech and accents sweet.
When struck return not thou the blow.
Even gods their admiration shew
Of men who thus entreat a foe.

CXLI. "If thine enemy hunger, feed him." (Proverbs xxv. v. 21 f.; Epistle to the Romans xii. 20.)

Mahâbhârata xii. 5528.

That foe repel not with a frown
  Who claims thy hospitable aid;
  A tree refuses not its shade
To him who comes to hew it down.

CXLII. Forgiveness of Injuries.

Subhâshitârṇava, 274.

A hero hates not even the foe
Whose deadly bow is 'gainst him bent;
The sandal-tree with fragrant scent
Imbues the axe which lays it low.

CXLIII. Suppliants not to be sent empty away.

Mahâbhârata xiii. 3212.

Let none with scorn a suppliant meet,
  Or from the door untended spurn;
A dog, an outcast, kindly treat,
  And so shalt thou be blest in turn.

CXLIV. The same.

Hitopadeśa i. 55 (or 33).

The good extend their loving care
  To men, however mean or vile;
E'en base Châṇḍâlas' * dwellings share
  Th' impartial moonbeam's silvery smile.

CXLV. Narrow and large heartedness.

Panchatantra v. 38.

Small souls enquire "belongs this man
To our own race, or class, or clan"?
But larger-hearted men embrace
As brothers all the human race.

CXLVI. Compassion should be shown to all men.

Râmâyaṇa vi. 115, 41.

To bad as well as good, to all,
  A generous man compassion shows.
  On earth no mortal lives, he knows,
Who does not oft through weakness fall.

---

* Châṇḍâla has the same sense as Pariah, a man of the lowest, or of no, caste.

CXLVII. A man may learn from the humblest, &c.

Manu, ii. 238, and *Śarṅgadhara's Paddhati, Nīti*, 34.

From whomsoever got, the wise
Accept with joy the pearl they prize.
To them the mean may knowledge teach,
The lowliest lofty virtue preach.
Such men will wed, nor view with scorn,
A lovely bride, though humbly born.

When sunlight fails, and all is gloom,
A lamp can well the house illume.

CXLVIII. Good may be gained from everything.

Mahābhārata, v. 1125.

From madmen's ravings even, the wise,
And children's prattlings, good may gain:
As workmen skilled extract the vein
Of gold in rocks that bedded lies.

(Compare xii. 11812. (See above, No. lxxviii. p. 65.)

CXLIX. Men are formed by their associates.

Mahābhārata, v. 1272; vii. 5961; xii. 11023.

As cloth is tinged by any dye
In which it long time plunged may lie;
So those with whom he loves to live
To every man his colour give.

CL. Evil men to be avoided.

Mahâbhârata, v. 1164 ; xii. 2797.

Let good men ne'er with bad themselves ally ;
Whene'er a friendly bond the two unites,
The guiltless share the doom the knaves that smites.
Moist wood takes fire, and burns, when mixed with dry.

CLI. How the wise and foolish respectively are affected by Society.

Mahâbhârata, i. 3077.

The fool who listens day by day
To all that men around him say,
Whate'er is worst drinks in with greed,
As pigs on garbage love to feed.
But hearing others talk, the wise
The precious choose, the vile despise ;
Just so do swans, with innate tact,
From milk and water, milk extract.

CLII. Effects of good and bad company.

Mahâbhârata, iii. 25 (compare ii. 223, 251).

To herd with fools, delusion breeds,
To error, vice, and misery leads ;
While those who wait upon the wise
On virtue's ladder ever rise.
Let men who covet calm of mind
The old, the sage, the righteous find ;
From such the way of duty learn ;
Thus aided, truth and right discern.
Such men's example, influence, looks,
Teach better far than many books.

CLIII. Undiscerning men's praise worthless.

Mahâbhârata, xii. 4217.

What boots the censure or applause
Which undiscerning men bestow?
Who ever heeds the senseless crow
That in the forest harshly caws?

CLIV. "The tongue can no man tame." (James iii. 8.)

Mahâbhârata, v. 1170.

'Tis very hard to curb the tongue,
Yet all this needful power should seek ;
For who much useful truth can speak,
Or charm with brilliant converse long ?

CLV. "Casting pearls before swine."

Hitopadeśa, iv. 10.

He only threshes chaff who schools
With patient kindness thoughtless fools.
He writes on shifting sand who fain
By favours worthless men would gain.

CLVI. Hopelessness of reclaiming the bad.

Bhaminîvilâsa, i. 93.

Whoe'er the bad by kindness tries
To gain,—but vainly ploughs the skies,
The viewless wind with water laves,
And paints a picture on the waves.

CLVII. Good advice not to be wasted on fools.

Mahâbhârata, v. 3290 f.

When good advice is not more prized than ill,
What man of sense has any words to spare
For thoughtless fools? Does any minstrel care
On deaf men's ears to waste his tuneful skill?

CLVIII. Ability necessary for acquiring knowledge.

Mahâbhârata, ii. 2485; x. 178 f.; ii. 1945.

No teaching e'er a blockhead shows
What's right, what's wrong, or makes him sage;
No child in understanding grows
Mature in sense, with growing age.
The wise who proffer learning's boon
To stupid men, their labour waste:
Though filled with juices sweet, a spoon
Their pleasant flavour cannot taste.
But able men, though taught in haste
Truth, right, and wrong, can quickly learn.
The feeling tongue and palate taste,
And flavours sweet and sour discern.

CLIX. The pain inflicted by harsh words.

Mahâbhârata, xiii. 4985 f. = v. 1172 f.

The wound a foeman's trenchant steel
Inflicts, in time again will heal;
The tree a woodman's axe o'erthrows
Soon sprouts again, and freshly grows;
But never more those wounds are closed,
Which harsh and cutting words have caused.

The shafts men's flesh which pierce and gall,—
A leech's skill draws out them all.
No power extracts the sharp word-dart,
Which rankles, bedded in the heart.

CLX. The same.

Mahābhārata, xiii. 4986; v. 1266.

The tongue discharges shafts of speech,
Which cut and torture those they reach.
They light on none but tender parts,
They burn men's vitals, bones, and hearts:
Let none shoot forth those cruel darts.

CLXI. Harsh speech.

Mahābhārata, i. 3559; v. 1267.

Of all men him most luckless deem
With thorns of speech who others tears,
Who on his lips, with taunts that teem,
Destruction's cursing Goddess bears.

[Compare the expressions in Psalms li. 2; lv. 21; lvii. 4; and lxiv. 3, 4.]

CLXII. Disregard of good advice.

Mahābhārata, v. 4348; compare v. 4143 ff.

That self-willed man his foes delights,
Who, ill advised, the counsel slights
Of those sage friends who wish him well,
And how to help him, best can tell.

Or,

Whoe'er the prudent counsel slights,
Of honest friends who wish him well,
And best the safest course can tell,—
That fool his foeman's hearts delights.

CLXIII. The same.

Mahâbhârata x. 234.

Whene'er a man wise counsel scorns,
Which friends impress, but he dislikes;
And such a man misfortune strikes,
He then too late, his folly mourns.

CLXIV. The claims and duties of friendship.

Mahâbhârata v. 3317.

That mortal sages heartless call
Who does not help his friends in need,
Who does not kindly warn and lead,
Whene'er they seem about to fall.

He merits praise, who, urged by care
His friend from folly back to hold,
Should use all means, and waxing bold,
Should even seize him by the hair.

CLXV. A real friend.

Mahâhbârata, xii. 2998 f.; xii. 6284 ff.

He is a genuine friend who, free
From every taint of jealousy,
Regards with constant joy and pride
Thy fortune's ever-rising tide;—
Whose heart, again, within him sinks
Whene'er of ills of thine he thinks.

The man whose sympathising heart
In all thy joys and woes takes part,
Who as his own misfortunes treats
Thy woes, reverses, wrongs, defeats,
In him with perfect faith confide,
As in a father, brother, guide.

CLXVI. Broken friendships never thoroughly cemented.

Mahâbhârata xii. 4167.

Things well compact are hard to crack,
And broken things are hard to mend;
So shattered friendships, patched up, lack
The love that marked the former friend.

CLXVII. Honest advice.

Mahâbhârata v. 1348; compare v. 1097; ii. 2136;—
Manu iv. 138.

Bland courtly men are found with ease,
Who utter what they know will please;
But honest men are far to seek,
Who bitter truths and wholesome speak.
So, too, those thoughtful men are rare
Who blunt and sound advice can bear.

A prince's best ally is he,—
The man from servile truckling free,
Who faithful counsel gives, nor fears
With truth to wound his patron's ears;
Not he who spares him present pain
At certain cost of future bane.

CLXVIII. Dishonest eulogists and secret detractors.

Mahábhárata xii. 4221.

The men who praise you, bland and bright,
Before you,—rail behind your back,
Are dogs that dread a front attack,
But slink behind your heels to bite.

CLXIX. Evil of revengefulness.

Mahábhárata xii. 4225.

The injured man who weakly longs
To pay base slanderers back their wrongs,
Is like the ass which loves to lie
And roll in ashes dirtily.

CLXX. Results of foresight and courage and their contraries.

Mahábhárata i. 8404 f.

The prudent man, alive, awake,
To all the turns events may take,
The vigorous man, prepared to brave
All strokes of fate,* however grave,
Is never taken by surprise,
When ills assail and troubles rise.
Though laid by rude misfortune low,
He does not faint beneath the blow,
But soon recovering strength, is fain
To fight life's battle o'er again.
His manly spirit nought dismays,
He strives and hopes for better days.

* The word "fate" is used by me here merely in the sense of calamity.

But thoughtless men, who never see
Th' approach of dire calamity,—
Of yawning ruin never think,
Until they stand upon its brink,—
When trouble comes, oppressed and scared,
For struggling 'gainst it unprepared,
Succumb beneath the blows of fate,
And rise no more to high estate.

CLXXI. Conditions of success.

Mahābhārata xii. 4889 and 4908.

Whoe'er for future chance provides,
Or promptly meets whate'er betides,
Ensures success; while he goes wrong
In act who is not prompt and strong.

CLXXII. Boldness necessary to success.

Mahābhārata i. 5613.

No man gains good who is not bold,
And ready danger to confront;
But if he dares, and bears its brunt,
And lives,—he then shall good behold.

CLXXIII. Self-respect essential to success.

Mahābhārata iii. 1259.

A man should ne'er himself despise:
Who weakly thus himself contemns,
The flowing tide of fortune stems,
And ne'er to high estate can rise.

CLXXIV. What energy can effect.

Vṛiddha Chāṇakya MS., p. 32.

Mount Meru's peak to scale is not too high,
Nor Hades' lowest depth to reach too deep,
Nor any sea too broad to overleap,
For men of dauntless, fiery, energy.

CLXXV. Fearlessness.

Mahābhārata v. 1513.

The truly brave, however tried,
In all events the test abide.
The gloom of woods, the wild beasts' haunt,
Their manly spirits cannot daunt.

Amid alarms, distress and woe
They ne'er lose heart, no fear they know.
When swords are swung, or, thick as hail
The arrows fly, they never quail.

CLXXVI. Procrastination.

Mahābhārata vi. 2008.

Events have onward sped too fast;
The time to change thy course is past.
A dam thou rear'st the streams to stay
Which have already flowed away!
Thy house is burned; the flames to quell
For water now thou digg'st a well.*

* Compare Rāmāyaṇa, ii. 18, 23, "Thou in vain desirest to construct a dam when the water is gone." Bhartṛihari, iii. 76, "A wise man should strenuously strive after his own wellbeing whilst his body is in health, whilst decay is far off, whilst his strength is unbroken, and there is no decline of life: when the house is in flames, what is the use of making an effort to dig a well?"

CLXXVII. Evil of indecision.

Mahābhārata xii. 3814 ; ii. 164.

The dilatory men who let
The time for action pass away,
Though long they seek, can seldom get
Another opportunity.

CLXXVIII. Promptitude necessary.

Mahābhārata xi. 36.

While yet the hours for action last
A man should strive his ends to gain,
That so he may not mourn in vain
The chance away for ever past.

CLXXIX. Study beforehand the consequences of action.

Mahābhārata v. 1112.

If I now take this step, what next ensues ?
Should I forbear, what must I then expect ?
Thus, e'er he acts, a man should well reflect,
And weighing both the sides, his course should choose.

CLXXX. The best remedy for grief.

Mahābhārata xi. 184[b], f.

Nor valour, wealth, nor yet a band
Of friends can bring such sure relief
To mortals overwhelmed with grief,
As strong and steadfast self-command.

CLXXXI. The cure for grief.

Mahâbhârata iii. 14079 (= xi. 76ᵇ, f.; xii. 12494).

With drugs the body's pains are healed;
But wisdom mental anguish quells;
Such wholesome power in knowledge dwells.
To grief, then, never weakly yield.

CLXXXII. The wise superior to circumstances.

Mahâbhârata iii. 62; xi. 67; xii. 751; 6497ᵇ, f.; 12483.

No day arrives, but as it flies,
Of fear a hundred sources brings,
Of grief a thousand bitter springs,
To vex the fool,—but not the wise.

CLXXXIII. Marks of a wise man.

Mahâbhârata v. 993.

The men, too high who never aim,
For things once lost who never mourn,
By troubles ne'er are overborne,—
Such men the praise of wisdom claim.

CLXXXIV. Appearances not always to be trusted.

Mahâbhârata xii. 4148 f.

A bounded vault the æther seems;
With fire the firefly seems to shine;
And yet no bounds the sky confine;
'Tis not with fire the firefly gleams.

So other sense-perceptions too,
Which else might cheat, should first be tried,
And those which every test abide,
Should only then be deemed as true.

CLXXXV. Content, and final blessedness.
Mahābhārata iii. 14085.

What gain can discontent allay?
Contentment makes men truly blest.
He who has travelled wisdom's way
With gladness hails th' approaching day,
When he in bliss supreme shall rest.

CLXXXVI. The foolish discontented; the wise content.
Mahābhārata xi. 75.

Though proudly swells their fortune's tide,
Though evermore their hoards augment,
Unthinking men are ne'er content:
But wise men soon are satisfied.

CLXXXVII. Discontent.
Subhāshitārṇava, 110.

Most men the things they have, despise,
And others which they have not, prize;
In winter wish for summer's glow,
In summer long for winter's snow.

CLXXXVIII. No perfect happiness in the world.
Mahābhārata xii. 6712; comp. iii. 15382b.

Some men by circumstance of birth
Are happier, others more distrest;
But any man completely blest
I nowhere yet have seen on earth.

[This verse in the original immediately precedes the next No.

CLXXXIX. Desire insatiable.

Mahâbhârata xii. 6713; comp. xii. 514—522.

When men grow rich, for something else they pine,
They would be kings; * were kingly rank attained,
They fain would gods become; were godship gained,
They'd long to rule o'er all the race divine.

But shouldst thou wealth and royal power acquire,
And soaring higher yet, become a god,
Yea rule all Svarga† by thy sovereign nod,
Ev'n then unsated, thou wouldst more desire.

CXC. The same.

Mahâbhârata i. 3174 and 3513; iii. 80 ff., 6715; xii. 513 ff.; xii. 6609 ff.; xii. 9925.

Renewed enjoyment never tames,
But rather more excites desire.
The more by oil or wood a fire
Is fed, the more it fiercely flames.

Fools find it hard to quell this pest,—
This plague, which lasts out all man's days,
Which grows not old as he decays:—
Who cures it, he alone is blest.

---

* Compare the Phœnissæ of Euripides, 503 ff., where Eteocles says: "For I, o mother, will declare, concealing nothing; I would go to the place where the stars, and the sun rise, and beneath the earth,—if I were able to do these things,—in order to possess regal power, the greatest of the deities."—Compare Mbh. v. 4567 (see below in the story of "Sanjaya and Vidulâ.")

† The Hindu paradise, the abode of Indra.

Rule, then, thyself; desire abate:
Earth, all the gems her caverns hold,
With women, cattle, stores of gold,—
All fails one greedy man to sate.

CXCI. Evils of wealth: praise of contentment.

Mahâbhârata iii. 84.

As fire consumes the wood from which it springs,
So inborn greed to mortals ruin brings.
The rich in constant dread of rulers live,
Of water, fire, thieves, kinsmen crying "Give."
Ev'n wealth itself to some men proves a bane;
Who dotes on it, no lasting bliss can gain.
As flesh by denizens of earth, sea, air,—
Beasts, fishes, birds,—is seized as dainty fare,
So too the rich are preyed on everywhere.
Increasing wealth to greed and folly leads,
And meanness, pride, and fear, and sorrow breeds.
In getting, keeping, losing wealth, what pain
Do men endure! They others kill for gain.
The vain desires of mortals never rest;
Contentment only makes them truly blest.
Life, beauty, youth, gold, power, we cannot keep;
The loss of those we love we soon must weep.
On such-like things, from which he soon must part,
The thoughtful man will never set his heart.
In hoarding gold no more thy days expend;
Or else endure the ills that wealth attend.
Ev'n men who wealth for pious uses win,
Would better act, if none they sought to gain:
'Tis wiser not with mud to soil the skin,
Then first to soil, and then wash off the stain.

CXCII. A man's aims vary with his time of life.

Mahâbhârata x. 115.

In youth a man is led away
By other thoughts, ideas, aims,
Than those his middle life which sway:
In age yet other schemes he frames.

CXCIII. Wealth and poverty.

Mahâbhârata xii. 213, ff.

Amassing wealth with care and pains,
A man the means of action gains.
From wealth a stream of virtuous deeds,—
As copious rills from hills,—proceeds.
But action halts when affluence fails,
As brooks dry up when drought prevails.
Wealth every earthly good procures,
And heavenly bliss itself insures.
For rich men gold, with hand profuse,
Can spend for every pious use.*

The wealthy man has troops of friends;
A flattering crowd before him bends;
With ardour men his kinship claim;
With honour all pronounce his name;
They call him noble, learned, wise,
And all his words as maxims prize.

Men in the lap of affluence nurst
Look down upon the poor as curst.
The world deems want a crime; like bad
And guilty men, the poor are sad.

---

* There is nothing in the original corresponding to these two lines; but I assume that their substance is intimated in what precedes; and this is confirmed by what is afterwards said of the poor man.

A needy man is viewed with scorn,*
As base and vile, though nobly born;
On earth his lot is joyless, hard,
To him the gates of heaven are barred;
The rites which open wide that gate,
The needy cannot celebrate.

He merits most the name of lean
Who cattle lacks, whose garb is mean,
On whom no crowd of servants waits,
Whose food no hungry strangers sates:—
That hapless man is truly lean,
Not he whose frame is spare and thin.

CXCIV. Wealth often injurious.

Mahâbhârata xii. 6575.

The unthinking man with whom, too kind,
The goddess Fortune ever dwells,
Becomes the victim of her spells;
As autumn's clouds the wind impels,
She sweeps away his better mind.
Pride, born of viewing stores of gold,
Conceit of beauty, birth, invade
His empty soul; he is not made,
He deems, like men of vulgar mould.
He knits his brows, his lip he bites,
At poorer men he looks askance,
With proud contempt and angry glance,
With threatening words their souls affrights.

---

* Nil habet infelix paupertas durius in se
Quam quod ridiculos homines facit.
Juvenal, *Sat.* i. 3. 152.

"For unhappy poverty has in it nothing harder than this, than that it makes men the objects of ridicule."

How, how could any mortal brook
On such a hateful wretch to look,
Even though he owned the godlike power
On men all envied boons to shower?

CXCV. The same.

Sāhityadarpaṇa, 322.

A wealthy man not drunk with pride,
A youth who fickle folly flees,
A ruler scorning careless ease,
Among the great enrolled abide.

CXCVI. What will not men do to get wealth?

Śārṅgadhara's Paddhati, Dhanaprasaṃśā 12.

For gold what will not mortals dare?
What efforts, struggles, labours spare?
The hostile warrior's sword they brave,
And plunge beneath the ocean wave.

CXCVII. The same.

Mahābhārata iii. 15398.

On seas, in forests wild, the bold
Will risk their precious lives for gold.

CXCVIII. The rich hath many friends.

Mahābhārata xii. 12131.

A rich man's kinsfolk, while he thrives,
The part of kinsmen gladly play:
The poor man's kindred die away
Long e'er his day of death arrives.

CXCIX. The same.

Panchatantra i. 15.

A wealthy man ev'n strangers treat
As if they were his kinsmen born :
The poor man's kindred all with scorn
His claim to kinship basely meet.

CC. Heirs of the rich often spendthrifts.

Subāhshitārṇava, 64.

How many foolish heirs make haste
The wealth their fathers saved to waste !
Who does not guard with care the pelf
He long has toiled to hoard himself ?

CCI. Self-exaltation, and censure of others condemned.

Mahābhārata xii. 10576.

Himself in men's esteem to raise
On other's faults let no one dwell ;
But rather let a man excel
All other men in doing well,
And thus command the meed of praise.
Oft worthless men, in blind conceit,
Their own superior merits vaunt,
And better men with failings taunt :
Reproof themselves with scorn they meet.
By blameless acts alone the wise,
Although they ne'er themselves exalt,
Nor yet with other men find fault,
To high esteem and honour rise.
The odour sweet of virtuous deeds,
Though voiceless, far and wide will fly :

To tell his presence in the sky
The noonday sun no herald needs.
By self-applause a fool in vain
From others glory seeks to gain;
But nought a wise man's light confines:
Though sunk within a pit it shines.

CCII. **Bad men pleased to hear ill, not good, of others.**

Mahâbhârata v. 1380; xii. 11014.

Of others' ill to hear makes bad men glad;
To hear of others' virtues makes them sad.

CCIII. **The bad like, the good dislike, to censure others.**

Mahâbhârata i. 3079.

In censuring others wicked men delight:
With all good men 'tis just the opposite.

CCIV. **Men of merit alone can appreciate merit.**

Mahâbhârata viii. 1817.

No man can others' merits know
When he himself has none to show.

CCV. **Censoriousness and self-deception.**

Mahâbhârata viii. 2116; v. 1007.

All men are very quick to spy
Their neighbours' faults, but very slow
To note their own; when these they know,
With self-deluding art they eye.

CCVI. Men see other's faults, but are blind to their own.

Subhāshitārṇava, 275.

Men soon the faults of others learn:
A few their virtues, too, find out;
But is there one—I have a doubt—
Who can his own defects discern.

CCVII. "Why beholdest thou the mote that is in thy brother's eye?" &c.

(Matthew vii. 3 f.)

Mahābhārata i. 3069.

Thou mark'st the faults of other men,
Although as mustard seeds minute;
Thine own escape thy partial ken,
Though each in size a Bilva fruit.

CCVIII. Want of self-knowledge.

Mahābhārata i. 3074.

Until the ugly man has scanned
His form, as in a mirror shown,
He deems, in fond conceit, his own
The fairest face in all the land.
But when the faithful glass reveals
How every grace and charm it wants,
At once are silenced all his vaunts—
The galling truth he sadly feels.

CCIX. Conceit difficult to cure.

Panchatantra i. 314, or 357.

Declare what power the born conceit
Can drive from any creature's mind.

---

* The Bilva is the Bel, or Aegle Marmelos.

See yonder bird, its back reclined
On earth, throws up its little feet,
While there it sleeps, the sky to prop,
Which else to earth might downward drop.

CCX. **To give advice easy; to act well difficult.**

Hitopadeśa i. 98, or 107.

Whoe'er will others seeking light, advise,
His task is easy—here all men are wise;
But urged themselves to virtue, most no more
The wisdom show they seemed to have before.

CCXI. **To boast easy; to act difficult.**

Rāmāyaṇa vi. 67, 10 (Gorresio's Edition.)

In words to carry out a plan,
Is easy work for any man;
But those who vigour join with skill
Alone hard tasks in act fulfil.

CCXII. **Union is strength.**

Mahābhārata v. 1321 ff.; iii. 1333; i. 5915 f.

The forest tree that stands alone,
Though huge, and strong, and rooted fast,
Unable long to brave the blast,
By furious gusts is overthrown;

While trees that, growing side by side,
A mass compact together form,
Each sheltering each, defy the storm,
And green from age to age abide.

So too the man alone who stands,
However brave himself, and wise,
But lacking aid from stout allies,
Falls, smitten soon by hostile hands.

But those sage kinsmen ever thrive,
Like lotus flowers in blooming pride,
Who firmly each in each confide,
And each from each support derive.

CCXIII. The same.

Mahābhārata v. 1318.

Long threads, if all alike they be,
And many, even if thin, sustain,
Unbroken, many a heavy strain :
Of good men here an emblem see.

CCXIV. The same.

Mahābhārata v. 1319.

Would kinsmen deal a deadly stroke,
They all the common cause must aid,
When sundered, firebrands only smoke,
But blaze whene'er in contact laid.

CCXV. Mutual help.

Mahābhārata v. 863.

By woods unsheltered, tigers fall
Beneath the hunter-troop's attacks :
And stripped of tigers, forests tall
Soon sink before the woodman's axe.
Let tigers, therefore, woods defend,
And woods to tigers shelter lend.

CCXVI. Weak foes not to be despised.

Mahābhārata i. 5553 (compare i. 5627), xii. 4390.

Let none a feeble foe despise :
If but a little fire should seize
One out of many forest trees,
Soon low the wood in ashes lies.

CCXVII. Caution in dealing with a foe.

Mahâbhârata xii. 5315 ; v. 1405.

When with a crafty foe thou wagest war,
Ne'er rest secure because he dwells afar ;
For know, the arms of such a man are long,
When stretched to wreak his wrath on those who've done him wrong.

CCXVIII. The same.

Mahâbhârata xii. 3501 (compare v. 1389.)

If thou hast chanced to wrong a powerful foe,
Ne'er rest secure, though far he dwell away :
His arm with sudden stroke may lay thee low,
As hawks, down swooping, smite their helpless prey.

CCXIX. Machiavellian counsel.

Mahâbhârata i. 5563 ; xii. 5264.

Whilst thou dost watch thy chance,—with seeming care
Thy mortal foe upon thy shoulder bear ;
Then down to earth thy hated burden dash,
As men against the rocks an earthen vessel smash.

CCXX. How women ought to gain and keep their husbands' affections.

A free translation of portions of the section of the Mahâbhârata, entitled, the conversation of Draupadî with Satyabhâmâ, Book iii., verses 14649–14721 *of the Calcutta Edition.*

[Of the two ladies who figure in the following dialogue, the first is Satyabhâmâ, the wife of the renowned Kṛishṇâ, the ally of the Pâṇḍava princes ; while the second is Draupadî (as she is most commonly called by her patronymic, as the daughter of Drupada, although her proper name was Kṛishṇā), the wife of the five Pāṇḍava princes, Yudhishthira and his brothers. Here we have a case of polyandry, which the Mahābhārata, in accommodation to later ideas, explains as apparently originating in accident, but as pre-arranged in a former birth, although the custom is allowed by some of the personages who appear in the poem, to have been one immemorially practised. (See my paper in the "Indian Antiquary" for September last, and Professor M. Williams's "Indian Epic Poetry," pp. 99 f.) Some indications of its, at least, occasional occurrence in the Punjab, in ancient times, are found in two passages adduced in a paper recently communicated by me to the "Indian Antiquary." It is worthy of remark that Satyabhāmā is represented in the passage before us as seeking to bring her husband, Kṛishṇā, under subjection by some of the philtres which she supposes Draupadī to have found effectual with the Pāṇḍavas, although Kṛishṇā was, either at the time when this section of the Mahābhārata was composed, or somewhat later, regarded as an incarnation of Vishṇu, or of Brahma (the supreme Spirit), and (unless his deification was a later event, or unless his higher was not supposed always to permeate his human nature), might have been supposed, by his divine omniscience, to be incapable of deception by the wiles of his wife. I may add that, at the time when the dialogue is related to have occurred, the Pāṇḍavas were living in the forests, in pursuance of an engagement to exile themselves from their kingdom for a certain period. (See Williams's "Indian Epic Poetry," pp. 23 and 103.) The passage before us may, doubtless, be held to prove that, in ancient days, the women of India were in the habit of employing philtres of various kinds to gain, or keep, their husbands' affections. In other respects, and irrespectively of the dutiful, though exaggerated, sentiments which the second speaker expresses, it may possess some interest as a picture of ancient Indian manners.]

Two ladies fair, of high estate,
Long parted, now again had met.

The one herself could justly pride
On being noble Kṛishṇā's bride;
The other ruled five princes' hearts
With loving sway, by honest arts.
Rejoiced each other now to see,
They laughed and chatted, full of glee.
In thought o'er all the past they ranged,
And ancient memories interchanged.
When this at length had found an end,
The former thus addressed her friend.

SATYABHAMA.

"How is it, dearest Kṛishṇā,* say,
That thou thy husbands so can'st sway,—
Those godlike princes, youthful, bold,
Strong-limbed, and proud, and uncontrolled,—
Who ever watch thy looks, to find
What thoughts are passing in thy mind,
And ne'er against thy rule rebel?
Reveal, I pray, thy potent spell.
By what devices, what finesse,
Canst thou their proud self-will repress,
And make them all thy power confess?
Where lies thy strength? What philtres rare
Avail to gain thine end? declare.
Do rites, oblations, prayers, conduce
To work thy will, or lore abstruse?
Or is thy grand success the fruit
Of any drug, or herb, or root?
What art is thine, which fame ensures,
And full connubial bliss secures?

---

* Draupadi's proper name. See the prose introduction.

For I, too, seek to rule my lord :
Thy methods tell ; thy help afford."

These words when noble Kṛishṇā heard,
She spake, with grief and sorrow stirred.

KRISHNA (DRAUPADI).

" Such questions vain befit not thee,
A dame esteemed so sage to be.
For all but heartless wives eschew
Those wicked arts thou hast in view.
Could any female merit praise
For acts so shameful, schemes so base ?

Whene'er a hapless husband knows
His foolish wife is one of those
Who ply their lords with drugs and charms,
His soul is racked by dire alarms,
As any one is ill at ease
Who in his house a serpent sees.
How can he lead a happy life
Who lives in dread of such a wife ?
How many men whose wives thus sin,—
Who seek by drugs their lords to win,—
To fell diseases fall a prey,
Grow dropsied, leprous, pine away
In sad and premature decay !
Such madness could'st thou dare to share ?
For thine own lord such ills prepare ?
No wife has e'er, by drugs or charms,
Won back a husband to her arms.

Now, calmly hear how I proceed,
Avoiding every tortuous deed.

I seek to win my husbands' hearts
By none but open, honest arts.
And so their willing hearts I rule :
I ne'er cajole them, or befool,
Nor e'er on charms or drugs depend,
Their independent wills to bend.
From anger, pride, and passion free,
I serve my lords most zealously.
Without parade of fondness, still,
Submissive, I their wish fulfil.
By fitting gestures, gentle speech,
And mien, and acts, my goal I reach.
Those lords, whose glance alone could kill,
I please with all my might and skill.
Though they are never harsh nor rude,
But always kind, and mild, and good,
I act as if constrained by awe,
And treat their slightest hint as law.
No other object draws my love,
On earth beneath, or heaven above.
No handsome, wealthy, jewelled youth,
No god, could shake my plighted troth.
For no delight or joy I care,
Unless my lords the pleasure share.
Whene'er their home they chance to leave,
Dejected, pale, I fast and grieve.
Their homeward safe return I greet
With sparkling eyes, and welcome meet.
Till all their wants are well supplied,
I never for my own provide.
At meal times, I, without delay,
The food they love before them lay,
Served up in golden platters fair,
All burnished bright with constant care.
My house is clean, and fairly swept,
Well stocked and ordered, neatly kept.

As friends I own, and talk with, none
But virtuous women : bad I shun.*
From all such words and acts I shrink
As wellbred dames unseemly think.
Loud laughter, foolish jests I hate.
And constant loitering at the gate.
My lords' behests I all observe,
From these I could not bear to swerve.
Just issued from the bath, and bright
In fair attire, with jewels dight,
Before my lords' appearing, I
Delight their eyes to gratify.

Whatever usage, rule or rite,
Whatever courtly forms polite,
My husbands' sires observed of old,
And they themselves in honour hold,
All these with never-ceasing care
I carry out; no toil I spare.

---

* Compare the Troades of Euripides, 647 ff., where Andromache says of herself—

"πρῶτον μέν, ἔνθα κἂν προσῇ κἂν μὴ προσῇ
ψόγος γυναιξὶν, αὐτο τουτ' ἐφέλκεται
κακῶς ἀκούειν, ἥτις οὐκ ἔνδον μένει,
τούτου παρεῖσα πόθον ἔμιμνον ἐν δομοις,
εἴσω τε μελάθρων κομψὰ θηλειῶν ἔπη
οὐκ εἰσεφρούμην, τὸν δὲ νοῦν διδάσκαλον
οἴκοθεν ἔχουσα χρηστὸν ἐξήρκουν ἐμοί.

"In the first place, where (whether a slur already attaches to women or not,) this very conduct is sure to bring ill repute in its train, when one does not keep (literally, to her who does not keep) at home; giving up the desire of this, I used to stay within the house, and did not bring into it the clever sayings of women (*i.e.*, their gossip and romantic notions); but having my mind a good teacher by its own instinct, I was content with myself."—*Paley.*

And here the way their mother shows,
Who all the past exactly knows.
Her will I follow; her revere;
And hold the noble woman dear.

By constant care, alertness, zeal,
I strive to work my husbands' weal.

Base women's wicked arts I shun;
By nobler means my ends are won.

In happier days,* at sumptuous feasts
We entertained eight thousand priests.
Those Brahmans learn'd and grave, in state
Their food from golden platters ate.
And many other guests beside
Were every day with food supplied.
Whate'er within our household passed,
Was known to me from first to last.
I knew the servants, one by one,
And all they did or left undone.
My husbands' hordes of gold I knew,
Their income, all their outlay too.
To me they left all household cares,—
A mass of manifold affairs.
On me this burthen all was thrown;
This load I bore without a groan,
And sacrificed my rest and ease,
My task to end, my lords to please.
I rose the first by dawn's faint light,
Retired the last to rest at night.

* That is while the Pāṇḍavas were at home, and in possession of their dominions. Some of the preceding details also, though expressed in the present tense, should,—if the story is to be regarded as self-consistent, be referred to this earlier period.

Such are the philtres, such the spells,
Whose power my husbands' love compels.
To please her lord a virtuous wife
Should deem the object of her life.
To him her thoughts should ever turn;
With love to him her heart should burn;
Her hope is he, her refuge, god;*
And all her acts should wait his nod.
 In vain by ease is pleasure sought;
By pains and toil alone 'tis bought.
Strive, then, thy lord's esteem to win;
A new career of love begin.
Whene'er his step without the gate
Is heard, start up, and on him wait.
With cheerful tact his wishes meet,
His palate please with viands sweet,
His every sense with pleasure sate;
Within thy home a heaven create.
So doing, thou shalt make it clear
That he to thee is very dear;
And then thy love perceiving, he
With answering love will cherish thee.
This course will bring thee high renown,
Thy life with bliss connubial crown.

Compare the story of Śāṇḍilī in Mahabharata xiii. 5864 ff.; and see the passages in praise of women, Nos. ccxxii. ff.

CCXXI. A Kshatriya heroine's exhortation to her son.

Mahābhārata v. 4494—4637.

There lived a Kshatriya queen of old,
Well known to fame, far-sighted, bold,
Who sate in councils, heard debate
Proceed on grave affairs of state,

* *Mahābhārata* xiii. 6783, 6799.

Who, studying much and long, a store
Possessed of rich and varied lore.
She dwelt with joy 'mid war's alarms,
And loved to hear of feats of arms,
How Kshatriya's power the proud subdued,
And blessed the subject multitude.
It chanced, a foe's superior might
Once overcame her son in fight;
And all his host dispersing, drove
The prince in foreign lands to rove.
There, stunned by fortune's crushing blow,
He lived, and pined, in want and woe.
Desponding, sad, he deemed it vain
To seek to raise his head again.
His spirit seeing so depressed,
The mother thus her son addressed.

VIDULA.

"Of all thy friends the grief and bane,
Of all thy foes the joy and gain,—
No real son art thou of mine,
No scion of the kingly line,
A Kshatriya thou wast never born;
Of every warrior thou the scorn.
Whence spring'st thou? from what outcast race?
All nobler sires thou would'st disgrace.
Who can of thee with honour speak?—
In spirit faint, in act so weak.
Desponding thus, hast thou no care
Thy shattered fortunes to repair?
Contemn thyself no longer; rise,
Awake to deeds of high emprize.
Why liest thou prone, as if the dread
Forked bolt of heaven had struck thee dead?

Start up, aspire to high renown;
By knightly deeds regain thy crown.

By force of will respect command;
Blaze fiercely like a glowing brand.*
Like smouldering chaff, that only smokes,
A weakling men's contempt provokes.
Whoever strikes a manly blow,
And strives to lay his foeman low,
Has done his duty; though he fail,
That failure let him ne'er bewail.
For duty wage a constant strife;
Than this, what other use has life?

Thy pious acts have borne no fruit;
And cut is now thy welfare's root.
If all thy hopes of good are gone,
In life why should'st thou linger on?

Though hardly pressed, a warrior ne'er
Should yield to sad and weak despair.
Though fell'd to earth, a man should seize
With deadly grasp his foeman's knees,
Should drag him down with main and might,
And smiting, end the deadly fight.

The sons who earn no honoured name,
Can bring their mothers only shame.
Whoe'er in splendour, valour, lore,
Stands forth all other men before,
He justly claims,—no other can,—
The high and noble name of man.
He's falsely called a man, whose heart
Is weak, who plays a woman's part.

---

* Compare *Mahâbhârata* xii. 5265; and No. ccxiv. above, p. 112.

On this our sad condition think :
We stand on utter ruin's brink,
From home and country driven, laid low,
Of joy bereft, and plunged in woe.
And wilt thou, nerveless, thus lie low,
Nor dare to strike another blow ?

I called thee son, but now I see
I bore the Kali age in thee.*
May woman never bear again
A son so base, so dire a bane !

Submission, meekness, ne'er can raise
The sunk, or bring them happier days.
Fierce, energetic, strife alone
Can win thee back thy father's throne.
Ambition only, restless, proud,
Can lift a man above the crowd.
Steel, then, thy heart :—a hero grown,
From haughty foes wrest back thy own."

SANJAYA.

" What worth has earth, its wealth, its joys,
Its power, its state, its glittering toys,

---

* The Kali, which is the present Yuga, is the last of the four immense periods into which the Indian system of cosmogony divides the duration of the existing creation. The first, or Satya, Yuga, was the age of perfection ; and during those which have followed, the world is conceived to have been undergoing a gradual course of deterioration to the extent of one-fourth in each succeeding Yuga. In the Kali age corruption and calamity are thus regarded as attaining their climax. The word Kali as used in the text may thus be considered as denoting an impersonation or incarnation of all evils.

What worth has even life—for thee,
My mother, if thou hast not me?
Then urge me not to peril life,
In fruitless, bootless, desperate strife."

VIDULA.

"Their lot is base, who once were great,
But now have fallen from high estate;
Who, masters once, dependent now,
To others' wills must humbly bow,
Whom none regards, and who, by need
Constrained, on others' bounty feed.
To such a servile life as now
Thou lead'st, my son, no longer bow.
Win back those days,—alert and brave,—
When thou wast lord and not a slave,
When all men watched thy kingly nod,
And bent before thee as a god.*
Like heavenly bliss is kingly sway,
Like hell their lot who must obey.†
The prince whose arm his rule assures,
And well his kinsfolks' weal secures,—
He during life enjoys renown,
And earns at length a heavenly crown.

Yet thou continuest faint of heart,
And wilt not act a hero's part.
But know, whene'er from love of life,
A Kshatriya shrinks from battle's strife,
With no fierce warlike ardour burns,—
His tribe that recreant soldier spurns.

---

* Compare *Manu* vii. 8.

† This line, which has nothing corresponding to it in the original, is given as a counterpart to the preceding.

Yet why should I my speech prolong ?
No pleas of mine, however strong,
Can sway, poor youth, thy wavering mind,
To all bold action disinclined.
Just so, no drugs his death can stay,
Whose life is ebbing fast away.

Yet hear another reason why
Thou still in war thy chance should'st try.
The foe who now usurps thy throne
The people's love has never known.
Too weak to rise,—with none to guide,
They watch the turn of fortune's tide.
But if men saw thee bent on war,
Allies would flock from near and far.
With these combined, thy plans prepare,
Thy standard raise, and war declare.

Thy foe is mortal, bears no charm
To guard his life from deadly harm.
Go forward then ; to battle stride ;
Successes yet thine arms abide.
Thy name is Victor ; * prove thy right
To bear it : triumph now in fight.

Whilst thou wast but a child, of old
A Brahman seer thy lot foretold,
That after dire reverses, thou
Once more in pride should'st rear thy brow.
The sage's word remembering, I
Expect thy coming victory.

But what a life is this we lead,
Starvation dreading, sunk in need !

---

* His name "Sanjaya" means "victorious," or "victory."

What sad vicissitudes I've seen !
A princess born, a wedded queen,
Resplendent once with jewels bright,
My husband's joy, my friends' delight,
In splendour nursed, I knew no care ;
And now !—but yet I'll not despair.

Should'st thou continue still to see
Thus plunged in woe thy spouse and me,
What joy could life then have for thee ?

Our servants, all attached and good,
Have left us, forced by lack of food.
Our honoured teachers, Brahman priests,
Enjoy no more their former feasts.
What comfort have I yet in store ?
Shall glad bright mornings dawn no more ?
It rends my heart, augments my woe,
To say a needy Brahman "no."
In happier days my spouse and I
A Brahman's suit could ne'er deny.
We stand before a trackless sea,
We have no raft, no guide but thee.
Be thou our pilot, steer us o'er
And land us on a happier shore.
A dying life is this we live ;
Do thou full life and vigour give.

What joy have I, if thou disgrace
By shrinking fear thy father's race ?
I could not bear to see thee act
A flatterer's part with servile tact.
A manly Kshatriya, highly born,
All base unworthy acts should scorn ;
By fawning, cringing aspect meek
For others' grace should never seek.

Think what our race's law requires,—
A law observed by all our sires,
On all their hearts inscribed, divine,
And why not too, engraved on thine ?
A Kshatriya bold, with lofty brow,
To lower men should never bow,
But always grandly stand erect
With conscious, noble, self-respect.
And even when nought can doom forefend,
Defiant let him meet his end;
By force be broken,—never bend.

To duty, Brahmans, gods above,
A Kshatriya bows with reverent love:
To these alone he homage pays;
All humbler men he lord-like sways."

SANJAYA.

" Thou hast a hard, an iron heart,
And play'st no loving mothers' part,—
True daughter of a warrior line;
A fierce unbending soul is thine.
To all thy Kshatriya instincts true,
Thou dost not yield to love its due;
Nor seek to guard me as thy one
Supreme delight, thine only son!
But spurr'st me on, devoid of ruth,—
As if I were an alien youth,—
To join again in hopeless strife,
And all in vain to peril life.
What worth would earth, its wealth, its joys,
Its power, its state, its glittering toys,—

What worth would life—possess for thee,
My mother, if thou hadst not me?" *

VIDULA.

"Life has two aims,—with zeal pursued
By thoughtful men,—the right, the good.†
These worthy ends of life to gain
I've urged thee on, as yet in vain.
The time has come, the favoured day
For action,—long it may not stay;—
Improve it e'er it pass away:
Thy fame is perilled by delay.
Should I to warn thee now decline,
I'd show a fondness asinine. ‡

Thou cravest love, then prove thy right
To be indeed my heart's delight.
When thou shalt play the hero's part,
I then will clasp thee to my heart.

The Kshatriya race was formed for fight,
In martial deeds should take delight;
And heaven is earned by warriors all,
By those who conquer, those who fall."

SANJAYA.

"I lack all means, have no allies
To aid my hostile enterprise.

---

* In the original these ideas are repeated here.

† *Dharma* and *Artha*, or Duty, and Prosperity.

‡ This follows the original: "Were I not to address thee, when thou art affected by infamy, this would be the weak, causeless, fondness of a she-ass."

From home and empire rudely driven,
My forces into fragments riven,—
How can I face my conquering foe,
Or think, unhelped, to lay him low?
Alone, could even a giant hope
With fierce embattled hosts to cope?
But thou art fertile in resource;
Do thou direct and shape my course.
Thou bidd'st me now the strife renew;
What thou commandest, I will do."

VIDULA.

"Let not thine ancient ill success
In war, my son, thy soul depress.
To self-distrust no longer yield;
Once more thy sceptre hope to wield.
Misfortune lasts not always long;
The strong grow weak, the weak grow strong.*

---

* Compare Sophocles, *Electra*, 916—

ἀλλ', ὦ φίλη, θάρσυνε. τοῖς αὐτοῖσί τοι
οὐχ αὑτὸς αἰεὶ δαιμόνων παραστατεῖ.

"But, oh, dear [sister], be of good courage: the same deity does not always attend on the same persons."

And Euripides, *Hercules Furens*, 101—

κάμνουσι γάρ τοι καὶ βροτῶν αἱ συμφοραί,
καὶ πνεύματ' ἀνέμων οὐκ αἰεὶ ῥώμην ἔχει,
[οἵ τ' εὐτυχοῦντες διὰ τέλους οὐκ εὐτυχεῖς].
ἐξίσταται γὰρ πάντ' ἀπ' ἀλλήλων δίχα.
οὗτος δ' ἀνὴρ ἄριστος ὅστις ἐλπίσι
πέποιθεν ἀεί. τὸ δ' ἀπορεῖν ἀνδρὸς κακοῦ.

"For the calamities of mortals too cease; and the blasts of the winds have not always the same strength, [and the prosperous do not prosper in the end]. For all things separate themselves from each other. But he is the best man who always trusts in hope; while despair is a quality of a weak man."

But trust not chance ; by strife alone,
And toil, canst thou regain thine own.

Heroic men, awake, alert,
Spring up, and all their force exert.
Resolved to win, with stubborn will,
Despising risk, and braving ill,
They never rest, but struggle on
Till all the good they seek is won.

A well-starred prince, religious, wise,
To high estate must surely rise.
On such Śrī * smiles, benignly bright,
As rising suns the Orient light.

But listen yet, while I reveal
How thou with other men should'st deal ;
How thou with art, and tact, and skill,
May'st always mould them to thy will,
By varying means may'st all persuade,
Thy will to work, thy schemes to aid.
Men's several natures sharply note,
The various loves on which they dote,
Gold, splendour, pleasure, honour, fame,
Revenge, and every other aim ;—
These mark, indulge, to these give scope :
And swaying all by fear and hope,
Their passions use to serve thine ends,
To thwart thy foes, attach thy friends.
By such means, too, the wise man knows
To sow dissension 'mong his foes.
And, never, son, evince alarm,
Whate'er may rise to threaten harm.
A ruler fear should never know,
Or, if he feels, should never show ;

* The goddess of good fortune.

For if he shows he danger dreads,
O'er all his host a panic spreads.

I've shown thee how, if thou wilt dare,
Thou may'st thy losses yet repair.
I've stirred thee up to flee from shame,
To gain thyself a glorious name.
I've sought thy soul with hope t' inspire,
With martial glow thy breast to fire.
I've told thee how, though now forlorn,
Thou wast for future glory born.
And now, my son, at length arise,
Arise, and snatch the envied prize.

Now, last of all, my secret hear,
That thou no more may'st doubt or fear.
We yet possess, to thee unknown,
Large treasures, known to me alone.
And many hundred friends remain,
Good friends, who've borne misfortune's strain,
Whom no reverse of our's could shake,
Who common cause with us will make ;—
They surely will not leave us now,
When fortune comes to crown thy brow.
What need for more, my son, what need?
So on to fight, and victory speed !"

SANJAYA.

"O thou, thy race's joy and pride,
Heroic mother, sagest guide,
Fond prophetess of coming good,
How thou hast roused my timid mood !
Whilst thou didst strive, in long discourse,
My languid soul to nerve with force,

In war of words I strove in vain
O'er thee the mastery to gain.
For thou couldst all my pleas refute,
And leave me stunned, abashed, and mute.
With thee to lead, sustain, and cheer,
How can I longer shrink or fear?
Drunk with the nectar of thy word,
To superhuman valour stirred,
I must, with thee to show the way,
Impossibilities essay.
I will not see the ocean whelm *
My own, my dear, paternal realm,
But lift it high above the wave,
Yea death itself with joy will brave
My cherished heritage to save."

Thus by his mother's tauntings stung,
By these her exhortations fired,
Away the youth his weakness flung,
And snatched the prize her soul desired.

[The women of Rājputāna, as represented by Colonel Tod in his "Annals and Antiquities of Rajasthan" (see chapter xxiii. pp. 607, ff.), maintain in more recent times the character of heroism ascribed to Vidulā in his passage of the Mahābhārata. I give a few extracts. Vol. i. p. 607, f. "C'est aux hommes à

* The original verse (4634), literally translated, runs thus :—"This earth must be supported in the water. I must die, (plunging) down into an abyss, or precipice." This is thus explained by the Commentator: "This land, my paternal kingdom, sinking as it were in the water, . . . must be supported by me, or the sunken kingdom must be raised; or I must die in the gulf called battle; and not thus remain inactive." Supposing the word "earth" to stand for the world, the phrase might perhaps be understood of a superhuman effort, as I have done in the lines which precede.

faire des grandes choses ; c'est aux femmes à les inspirer," is a maxim to which every Rajpoot cavalier would subscribe, with whom the age of chivalry is not fled, though ages of oppression have passed over him. He knows there is no retreat into which the report of a gallant action will not penetrate, and set fair hearts in motion to be the objects of his search." P. 610. "Like the ancient Germans or Scandinavians, the Rajpoot consults her in every transaction; from her ordinary actions he draws the omens of success, and he appends to her name the epithet of *devī*, or godlike." P. 613. "Nor will the annals of any nation afford more numerous or more sublime instances of female devotion, than those of the Rajpoots; and such would never have been recorded, were not the incentive likely to be revered and followed." P. 614. "The annals of no nation on earth record a more ennobling or more magnanimous instance of female loyalty than that exemplified by Dewuldé, mother of the Binafur brothers," &c. P. 617. "Dewuldé says, would that the gods had made me barren, that I had never borne sons who thus abandon the paths of the Rajpoots, and refuse to succour their prince in danger." P. 625. "Were we called upon to give a pendant for Lucretia, it would be found in the queen of Ganore," who the story tells, clothed her enemy, the Khan who sought to marry her, in poisoned garments, which caused him to die in great agony, and then threw herself from the battlements of the fortress. P. 633. "The Rajpoot mother claims her full share in the glory of her son, who imbibes at the maternal fount the first rudiments of chivalry; and the importance of this parental instruction cannot be better illustrated than in the ever recurring simile, make thy mother's milk resplendent," &c.]

CCXXII. Praise of women.

Mahābhārata i. 3027 ff. See xiii. 6781 ff.; xii. 5561 ff; iii. 13661 ff.

[These lines have been partially and differently versified in my "Religious and Moral Sentiments metrically rendered from Sanskrit Writers," p. 65.]

That dame deserves the name of wife
Whose husband is her breath of life,

Who, versed in all indoor affairs,
Her lord relieves of household cares;
Who fills his house, a mother proud,
With children bright, a merry crowd.
  A wife is half the man, transcends
In value far all other friends.
She every earthly blessing brings,
And even redemption from her springs.
Who on him ever fondly dotes,
To him her being all devotes;
The men possessed of virtuous wives
Can lead at home religious lives.
They need not to the woods repair,
And merit seek through hardships there.*
A happy, joyful life they lead;
Their undertakings all succeed.
  In lonely hours, companions bright,
These charming women give delight;
Like fathers wise, in duty tried,
To virtuous acts they prompt and guide.
Whene'er we suffer pain and grief,
Like mothers kind they bring relief.†

The weary man whom toils oppress,
When travelling through life's wilderness,

---

* Four stages in the religious life of a Brahman, viz., those of the student, householder, anchorite, and mendicant, are recognised by Indian writers, and the last are generally regarded as representing an advance in perfection. In two passages, however, of the Mahābhārata xii. 343 ff., 652 ff., preference is given to the householder's life, as more excellent than all the others; and an abandonment of domestic life is characterised as folly. I have introduced this sentiment here, although it is not expressed in the original of the passage translated.

† "When pain and anguish wring the brow,
A veritable angel thou."—SIR WALTER SCOTT.

Finds in his spouse a place of rest,
And there abides, refreshed and blest.

When men at length this life forsake,
And other forms of being take,
Then too do faithful wives pursue
Their husbands all their wanderings through.
The wife who first departs, awaits
Her lord's approach at Hades' gates;
When he dies first, the faithful wife
To join her spouse, resigns her life.

The following is another translation of part of one of the same passages.

Mahābhārata i. 3028.

Our love these sweetly-speaking women gain;
When men are all alone, companions bright,
In duty, wise to judge and guide aright,
Kind tender mothers in distress and pain.

The wife is half the man, his priceless friend;
Of pleasure, virtue, wealth, his constant source;
A help and stay along his earthly course;
Through life unchanging, yea, beyond its end.

CCXXIII. The same.

Mahābhārata xii. 5497 ff.

Although with children bright it teems,
And full of light and gladness seems,
A man's abode, without a wife,
Is empty, lacks its real life.
The housewife makes the house; bereft
Of her, a gloomy waste 'tis left.

That man is truly blest whose wife,
With ever sympathetic heart,
Shares all his weal and woe; takes part
In all th' events that stir his life;
Is filled with joy when he is glad,
And plunged in grief when he is sad,
Laments whene'er his home he leaves,
His safe return with joy perceives,
With gentle words his anger stills,
And all her tasks with love fulfils.

Her husband's chiefest treasure, friend,
And comrade to his journey's end,—
A wife in duty aids her lord,
With gold she helps to swell his hoard;
Assists in all his hours of joy,
And seeks to spare him all annoy.

A spouse devoted, tender, kind,
Bears all her husband's wants in mind,
Consults his ease, his wishes meets,
With smiles his advent ever greets.
He knows, when forced abroad to roam,
That all is safe, with her at home.
In doubt, in fear, in want, in grief,
He turns to her, and finds relief.

When racked by pain, by sickness worn,
By outrage stung, by anguish torn,
Disturbed, perplexed, oppressed, forlorn,
Men find their spouses' love and skill
The surest cure for every ill.
The luckless wight who lacks a wife,
And leads a doleful single life,
Should leave his home, and cheerless dwell
In some secluded forest dell,

And there should spend his days and nights
In fasting, penance, painful rites,—
For now, without a helpmate dear,
His house is but a desert drear.
Who then would live without a wife—
His house's joy and light and life?
With her the poorest hut will please,
And want and toil be borne with ease.
Without her spacious gilded halls
Possess no charm,—all splendour palls.

CCXXIV. **The bachelor only half a man.**

Brāhma Dharma ii. 2, 1.

A man is only half a man, his life
Is not a whole, until he finds a wife.
His house is like a graveyard, sad and still,
Till gleeful children all its chambers fill.

CCXXV. **The best cure for misfortune.**

Mahābhārata iii. 2325.

Thou sayest right;—for all the ills of life
No cure exists, my fair one, like a wife.

CCXXVI. **Reward of a wife's devotion.**

Rāmāyaṇa ii. 24, 26 (Bomb. ed.) *Mahābhārata* xiii. 2496; iii. 13649[b] f.

That wife to bliss celestial soars,
Whose loving care her lord delights,
Although she shuns all holy rites,
And never any god adores.

CCXXVII. Women naturally pandits.

Mrichchhakaṭikâ, Act iv.

Men, seeking knowledge, long must strive,
And over many volumes pore:
But favoured women all their lore,
Unsought, from nature's grace derive.

CCXXVIII. Women's wiles.

Mahâbhârata xiii. 2236 ff.

[I have above and elsewhere quoted from this great poem passages in which the fair sex is cordially eulogized, directly or indirectly. The following picture, though in some respects it is flattering to women, as testifying to their great cleverness and powers of allurement, is otherwise far from laudatory. The fair sex, however, need not be vindicated against this representation. As the names of the Indian sophists referred to in these lines are not familiar to the English reader, I have substituted that of Macchiavelli.]

Deep steeped in Macchiavellian wiles,
With those that smile a woman smiles,
With those that weep dissolves in tears,
The sad with words of comfort cheers,
By loving tones the hostile gains,
And thus firm hold on men attains,—
Her action suiting well to all
Th' occasions that can e'er befall.
As words of truth she praises lies,
As arrant falsehood truth decries,
And, mistress of deceptive sleight,
Treats right as wrong, and wrong as right.
All powers which wizard demons old,
Of whom such wondrous tales are told,
Displayed the gods themselves to cheat,

To blind, elude, and so defeat,—
Such fascinating powers we find
In artful women all combined.
So skilfully they men deceive,
So well their viewless nets can weave,
That few whom once these syrens clasp,
Can soon escape their magic grasp.
Yet, once their earlier ardour cooled,
They jilt the men they've thus befooled;
And fickly newer objects seek
To suit their changing passion's freak.
Such charmers well to guide and guard,
For men must prove a task too hard.

CCXXIX. A spell to promote concord in a family.

Atharva Veda iii. 30. 1.

Within this house, by this my spell,
  I concord, union, peace, create;
  That none may more another hate;
But all in love together dwell.
  Let these, the sons, their sire obey,
  And ne'er their mother's word gainsay.
Let this fair wife, with aspect bright,
  And honied words her lord delight.
Let brothers mutual rancour shun,
  And sister sister kindly treat,
  Let each the rest with accents sweet
Address, and all in heart be one.

CCXXX. Description of a good king.

Mahābhārata xii. 3450, &c. (*see* Appendix).

That man alone a crown should wear
Who's skilled his land to rule and shield;
For princely power is hard to wield—
A load which few can fitly bear.

That king his duty comprehends
Who well the poor and helpless tends,
Who wipes away the orphan's tears,
Who gently calms the widow's fears,
Who, like a father, joy imparts,
And peace, to all his people's hearts;
On vicious men and women frowns,
The learn'd and wise with honour crowns;
Who well and wisely gifts on those
Whose merits claim reward, bestows;
His people rightly guides and schools,
On all impressing virtue's rules;
Who day by day the gods adores,
With offerings meet their grace implores,
Whose vigorous arm his realm protects,
And all insulting foes subjects;
Who yet the laws of war observes,
And ne'er from knightly honour swerves.

CCXXXI. Self-conquest must precede other conquests.

Mahābhārata ii. 194; v. 1150 ff.; 1157; 1162; 4332 ff.; xii. 2599 f.; *Manu* vii. 44.

The king who long aspires to rule,
Must all his lawless passions school.
Whoever these neglects to sway
Soon sees his empire pass away;
While he who well himself commands
Can wisely govern all his lands.
For lust and anger men delude,
And draw them from proper good.
But he who these two foes enchains,
A world-wide empire surely gains.
This lofty rank, this envied state,
This power to fix each subject's fate,

Usurped by base and wicked kings,
On men dire woe and ruin brings.

Whoe'er would ample wealth amass,—
In virtue other men surpass,—
In check must all his senses hold;
When these are ever well controlled,
In strength the understanding grows,
As fire by fuel brightly glows.

But men whom lawless passions sway
To swift destruction fall a prey,
As steeds uncurbed, in wild career
Dash down to earth their charioteer.

The prince who fails himself to school
His ministers can never rule;
And he his foes can ne'er defeat
His ministers who has not beat.

A monarch first himself must school,
Then seek his court and camp to rule;
Must first subdue himself in fight,
And then march forth his foes to smite.
For who can other men subject
Who has not first his passions checked?

Kind fortune on that monarch waits
Who first his fierce desires abates,
Who rules his ministers, and wields
The rod which good from bad men shields,
Who first investigates the facts,
And then deliberately acts.

CCXXXII. Mercy should be shown to ignorant offenders.

Mahābhārata iii. 1055.

When men from want of knowledge sin,
A prince to such should mercy show;
For skill the right and wrong to know
For simple men is hard to win.

CCXXXIII. A king's best treasures and castles.

Mahābhārata ii. 2020.

Though other treasures kings may boast,—
Of gems and gold a glittering hoard,—
The richest far is he, the lord
Of stalwart men, a numerous host.

Amid impending war's alarms,
Though round us lofty castles rise,
The fort that best assault defies
Is formed by manly warriors' arms.

CCXXXIV. "Vixere fortes ante Agamemnona," &c.

Bilhana in Śārngadhara's Paddhati, Sāmānyakavi-praśamśā 13 (12).

Without a bard his deeds to sing
Can any prince be known to fame?
Of old lived many a valiant king
Of whom we know not even the name!

CCXXXV. Love of home.

Panchatantra v. 49; iii. 92 (Bombay Edition).

Not such is even the bliss of heaven
As that which fills the breast of men

To whom, long absent, now 'tis given
Their country once to see again,
Their childhood's home, their natal place,
However poor, or mean, or base.

CCXXXVI. Untravelled men's horizon contracted.

Panchatantra i. 21.

Th' incurious men at home who dwell,
And foreign realms, with all their store
Of various wonders, ne'er explore,
Are simply frogs within a well.

CCXXXVII. "The wolf also shall dwell with the lamb."

(Isaiah xi. 6.)

Mahābhārata xiii. 651.

With serpents weasels kindly play,
And harmless tigers sport with deer;
The hermit's holy presence near
Turns hate to love,—drives fear away.

CCXXXVIII. The saint should patiently await the hour of his departure.

Manu vi. 45; *Mahābhārata* xii. 8929.

Let not the hermit long for death,
Nor cling to this terrestrial state:
Their lords' behests as servants wait,
So let him, called, resign his breath.

CCXXXIX. What is injurious, though dear, is to be abandoned.

(*St. Matthew* xviii. 8 f.)

Bhāgavata Purāna vii. 5, 37.

That alien man who blessings brings,
The wise with love parental greet;
But like a dire disease will treat
The son from whom destruction springs.

Thy limb unsound, although with pain,
Lop off, remove the noxious taint
Which renders all thy body faint,
That thus the whole may strength regain.

CCXL. "A prophet has no honour in his own country."

Dṛishṭānta Śataka, 76.

A man in whom his kindred see
One like themselves, of common mould,
May yet by thoughtful strangers be
Among the great and wise enrolled.
In Vishṇu clowns a herdsman saw,
Gods viewed the lord of all with awe.

CCXLI. Asita and Buddha; or the Indian Simeon.*

(*Lalita Vistara, in Bibliotheca Indica*, p. 115 ff.)

In the Lalita Vistara—a legendary history in prose and verse of the life of Buddha, the great Indian Saint, and founder of the religion which bears his name—it is related that a Ṛishi, or inspired sage, named Asita, who dwelt on the skirts of the Himâlaya mountains, became informed, by the occurrence of a variety of portents, of the birth of the future lawgiver, as the son of King Śuddhôdana, in the city of Kapilavastu, in Northern India, and went to pay his homage to the infant. I have tried to reproduce the legend in the following verses. The similarity of some of the incidents to portions of the narrative in the second chapter of St Luke's Gospel, verses 25, ff., will strike the reader.

I may mention that the Buddhist books speak also of earlier Buddhas, that the word means "the enlightened," or, "the intelligent," and that Buddha also bore the appellations of Gautama, and of Śâkyasinha, and Śâkyamuni—*i.e.*, the lion, and the devotee, of the tribe of the Śâkyas, to which he belonged.

That I have not at all exaggerated the expressions in the text which speak of Buddha as a deliverer or redeemer, or assimilated his character more than was justifiable to the Christian conception of a saviour, will be clear to any one who can examine the original for himself. Kumârila Bhaṭṭa, a renowned Brahmanical opponent of the Buddhists, while charging Buddha with presumption and transgression of the rules of his caste in assuming the functions of a religious teacher (with which, as belonging to the Kshatriya, and not to the Brahmanical, class, he had no right to interfere), ascribes to him these words—"Let all the evils (or sins) flowing from the corruption of the Kali age" (the fourth, or most degenerate, age of the world) "fall upon me; but let the world be redeemed!" If we might judge from this passage, it would seem that the character of a vicarious redeemer was claimed

* This, and the next piece, are reprinted from my "Original Sanskrit Texts," &c., Vol. ii., pp. 494 ff.

by, or at least ascribed to, Buddha. I am informed by Mr R. C. Childers, however, that in his opinion the idea of Buddha's having suffered vicariously for the sins of men is foreign to Buddhism, and indeed, opposed to the whole spirit and tendency of the system.

Another valued correspondent, Professor E. B. Cowell, is unable to think that the sentiment ascribed to Buddha by Kumârila is foreign to his system, as it is thoroughly in accordance with the idea of the six pâramitas. He does not understand it as implying any theological notion of vicarious atonement, but rather the enthusiastic utterance of highly-strung moral sympathy and charity; and would compare it with St Paul's words in Romans ix. 3, and explain each in just the same way as, he thinks, Chrysostom does. He further refers to the existence of numerous Buddhist stories in the Kathâsarit-sâgara, among which is one from lvi. 153, viz., the story of the disobedient son with a red-hot iron wheel on his head, and he says—

"Pâpino 'nye 'pi (vi?) muchyantâm pṛithvyām tat-pâtakair api. â pâpa-kshayam etad me chakram bhrâmyatu mûrdhani." "Let other sinners on earth be freed from their sins; and until the removal of [their] sin let this wheel turn round upon my head." In either case it is only a wish, and it is not pretended that it really had, or ever could have, any effect on other men. It only expresses a perfection of charity. The same idea (borrowed, as Dr Cowell supposes, from Buddha), occurs in the Bhâgavata Purâṇa, ix. ch. 21. The "immortal word" (*amṛitam vachaḥ*) contained in the 12th verse, and ascribed to the pious and benevolent King Rantideva,—who himself endured hunger and thirst to relieve others,—is as follows: *na kāmaye 'ham gatim īśvarāt parām ashṭarddhi-yuktām apunar-bhavam vā. ārtim prapadye 'khila-dehabhājām antaḥ-sthito yena bhavanty aduḥkhāḥ.* "I desire not from God that highest state which is attended with the eight perfections; nor do I ask to be exempted from future births. I seek to live within all corporeal beings, and endure their pains, that so they may be freed from suffering." On this the commentator annotates thus: *Para-duḥkhāsahishṇutayā sarveshām duḥkham svayam bhoktum āśāste. . . . "akhila-dehabhājām ārtim" duḥkham tat-tad-bhoktṛi-rūpeṇa "antaḥsthitaḥ" sann aham "prapadye" prāpnuyām ity evam kāmaye.* "Being unable (in thought) to endure the sufferings of others, he desires himself to endure the sufferings of all. . . . I desire, in the form of each sufferer, living within him, to undergo the sufferings of them all."

On Himālaya's lonely steep
  There lived of old a holy sage,
  Of shrivelled form, and bent with age,
Inured to meditation deep.

He—when great Buddha had been born,
  The glory of the Śākya race,
  Endowed with every holy grace,
To save the suffering world forlorn—

Beheld strange potents, signs which taught
  The wise that that auspicious time
  Had witnessed some event sublime,
With universal blessing fraught.

The sky with hosts of gods was thronged:
  He heard their voices Buddha's name
  Resounding loud with glad acclaim,
And clear exulting shouts prolonged.

The cause, exploring, far and wide
  The sage's vision ranged; with awe
  Within a cradle laid he saw
Far off the babe, the Śākyas' pride.

With longing seized this child to view
  At hand, and clasp, and homage pay,
  Athwart the sky he took his way,
By magic art, and swan-like flew;

And came to King Śuddhôdan's gates,
  And entrance craved—"Go, royal page,
  And tell thy lord an ancient sage
To see the king permission waits."

The page obeyed, and joined his hands
  Before the prince, and said—"A sage,
  Of shrivelled form, and bowed with age
Before the gate, my sovereign, stands,

"And humbly asks to see the king."
  To whom Śuddhôdan cried—"We greet
  All such with joy; with honour meet
The holy man before us bring."

The saint beside the monarch stood,
  And spake his blessing—"Thine be health,
  With length of life, and might, and wealth;
And ever seek thy people's good."

With all due forms, and meet respect,
  The king received the holy man,
  And made him sit; and then began—
"Great sage, I do not recollect

"That I thy venerable face
  Have ever seen before; allow
  Me then to ask what brings thee now
From thy far-distant dwelling place."

"To see thy babe," the saint replies,
  "I come from Himālaya's steeps."
  The king rejoined—"My infant sleeps;
A moment wait until he rise."

"Such great ones ne'er," the Rishi spake,
  "In torpor long their senses steep,
  Nor softly love luxurious sleep;
The infant prince will soon awake."

The wondrous child, alert to rise,
  At will his slumbers light dispelled.
  His father's arms the infant held
Before the sage's longing eyes.

The babe beholding, passing bright,
  More glorious than the race divine.
  And marked with every noble sign,*
The saint was whelmed with deep delight;

And crying—" Lo! an infant graced
  With every charm of form I greet!
  He fell before the Buddha's feet,
With fingers joined, and round him paced.†

Next round the babe his arms he wound,
  And "One," he said, "of two careers
  Of fame awaits in coming years
The child in whom these signs are found.

"If such an one at home abide,
  He shall become a king, whose sway
  Supreme a mighty arm'd array
On earth shall stablish far and wide.

---

* Certain corporeal marks are supposed by Indian writers to indicate the future greatness of these children in whom they appear. Of these, thirty-two primary, and eighty secondary, marks, are referred to in the original as being visible on Buddha's person.

† The word here, imperfectly translated, means, according to Professor H. H. Wilson's Dictionary, "reverential salutation, by circumambulating a person or object, keeping the right side towards them."

" If, spurning worldly pomp as vain,
He choose to lead a joyless life,
And wander forth from home and wife,
He then a Buddha's rank shall gain."

He spoke, and on the infant gazed,
When tears suffused his aged eyes;
His bosom heaved with heavy sighs ;
When King Śuddhôdan asked, amazed —

" Say, holy man, what makes thee weep,
And deeply sigh ? Does any fate
Malign the royal child await ?
May heavenly powers my infant keep !"

" For thy fair infant's weal no fears
Disturb me, king," the Ṛishi cried ;
" No ill can such a child betide ;
My own sad lot commands my tears.

" In every grace complete, thy son,
Of truth shall perfect insight* gain,
And far sublimer fame attain
Than ever lawgiver has won.

" He such a wheel† of sacred lore
Shall speed on earth to roll, as yet

---

* The term here translated " insight " is derived from the same root as the word " Buddha," and means " intelligence," or " enlightenment."

† The term thus rendered, *dharmachakra*, expresses a somewhat singular figure. It literally denotes the " wheel of the law," or the " wheel of righteousness," or the " wheel of religion." See, however, on the sense of *dhammachakka*, Mr Childers's Pali Dictionary. He renders it " dominion of the law." In Böhtlingk and Roth's Sanskrit Lexicon, one of the senses assigned to *chakra* (wheel) is the "wheel of the monarch rolling over the lands ; dominion."

Hath never been in motion set
By priest, or sage, or god before.

" The world of men and gods to bless,
The way of rest and peace to teach,
A holy law thy son shall preach—
A law of stainless righteousness.

" By him shall suffering men be freed
From weakness, sickness, pain, and grief,
From all the ills shall find relief
Which hatred, love, illusion breed.

" His hand shall loose the chains of all
Who groan in fleshly bonds confined;
With healing touch the wounds shall bind
Of those whom pain's sharp arrows gall.

" His potent words shall put to flight
The dull array of leaden clouds
Which helpless mortals' vision shrouds,
And clear their intellectual sight.

" By him shall men who, now untaught,
In devious paths of error stray,
Be led to find a perfect way—
To final calm* at last be brought.

---

* The word in the original is *nirvâṇa*, a term of which the sense is disputed—some scholars esteeming it to mean absolute annihilation; others explaining it as the extinction of passion, the attainment of perfect dispassion. Mr Childers informs me that he considers *nirvâṇa* to signify active bliss on earth for a brief period, followed (upon death) by total annihilation. See a letter from him on this subject in No. 62 of Trübner's Literary Record for October 1870, p. 27. See also the long article in his Pali Dictionary on the word *nibbânam*, the Pali form for *nirvâṇam*.

"But once, O king, in many years,
The figtree* somewhere flowers perhaps;
So after countless ages' lapse,
A Buddha once on earth appears.

"And now, at length, this blessed time
Has come; for he who cradled lies
An infant there before thine eyes
Shall be a Buddha in his prime.

"Full, perfect insight gaining, he
Shall rescue endless myriads tost
On life's rough ocean waves, and lost,
"And grant them immortality.†

"But I am old, and frail, and worn,
I shall not live the day to see
When this thy wondrous child shall free
From woe the suffering world forlorn.

"'Tis this mine own unhappy fate
Which bids me mourn, and weep, and sigh;
The Buddha's triumph now is nigh,
But ah! for me it comes too late!"

When thus the aged saint, inspired,
Had all the infant's greatness told,
The king his wondrous son extolled,
And sang, with pious ardour fired—

---

* The tree referred to in the original is the Udumbara, the *Ficus glomerata*.

† The word so rendered is in the original *amṛita*, commonly understood as translated. The Pali form is *amata*, which Mr Childers, in his Dictionary, *s.v.*, says means *nirvāṇa*. See the preceding note.

"Thee, child, th' immortals worship all,
  The great physician, born to cure
  All ills that hapless men endure;
I, too, before thee, prostrate fall."

And now—his errand done—the sage
  Dismissed with gifts, and honour due,
  Athwart the æther swan-like flew,
And reached again his hermitage.

CCXLII. Ravana and Vedavati.

The Râmâyaṇa, as is well known to students of Indian literature, relates the adventures of Rāma, son of the king of Ayodhyā (Oude), who, in consequence of a domestic intrigue, became an exile from his country, and wandered about the southern regions of India, in company with his brother Lakshmaṇa and his wife Sītā. Sītā was carried off by Rāvaṇa, king of the Rākshasas (demons or goblins), to his capital, Lankā, in the island of Ceylon. Ultimately, Rāvaṇa was slain in battle by Rāma, who (according, at least, to the poem in its existing, and perhaps interpolated, form) was an incarnation of the supreme god Vishṇu, and Sītā was rescued. Rāma returned to Ayodhyā after his father's death, and succeeded him on the throne. The legend now freely translated is taken from the supplementary book of the Rāmayāṇa, the Uttara Kāṇḍa, chapter 17, and relates a passage in the earlier life of Rāvaṇa. Vedavatī, the heroine of the story, agreeably to the Indian theory of the transmigration of souls, was subsequently re-born in the form of Sītā.

Where, clothed in everlasting snow,
  Himālay's giant peaks arise
  Against the ambient azure skies ;
And bright as molten silver glow—
While, far beneath, the solitudes
Are green with Devadāru* woods—

It chanced that once the demon lord
  Who ruled in Lankā's isle afar,
  And, mounted on his airy car,
These northern tracts sublime explored,
Alighted there upon the ground
And roamed those forests wild around.

* *Pinus devadāru* which signifies the "divine tree;" the Deodar, a magnificent tree, both in height and girth.

And, lo, he saw a maiden, fair
And brilliant as a goddess, clad
In garb ascetic, rude and sad,
Deform with squalid matted hair:
And all at once with passion fired,
The damsel's secret thus inquired:

"How is it, tell me, lovely maid—
Whose virgin charms subdue the heart,
Whose form with every grace of art
In gold and gems should be arrayed—
Thou dost this doleful garb assume,
Which ill beseems thy youthful bloom?

"Whose daughter art thou? What hath led
Thy choice to such a life austere?
O blest were he whom, lady dear
And beauteous, thou should'st deign to wed!'
Him, duly honoured as a guest,
The fair ascetic thus addressed:

"My father was a holy sage:
From him I sprang as, calm, and dead
To earthly aims and joys, he read
Th' eternal Veda's hallowed page:
The Voice which spoke within the book
In me a form corporeal took.

"The gods, enamoured, all aspired
The honour of my hand to gain;
Their ardent pleas were urged in vain;
A loftier aim my father fired;
For he had vowed, with lawful pride,
I could be only Vishṇu's bride.

"Incensed at his rejection, one
   Among the suitors, proud but base,
   The chieftain of the Daitya race,*
Avenged the slight the sage had shown:
By night he nigh my father crept,
And vilely slew him while he slept.

"That I my sire's high aim may gain,
   And win great Vishṇu for my lord,
   I lead this life, by thee abhorred,
Of hard austerity and pain;
And, till the god himself impart,
I wed his image in my heart.

"I know thee, Rāvan, who thou art;
   By virtue of this life austere,
   All secret things to me are clear;
I bid thee hence; avaunt, depart!"
But by the maiden's charms subdued,
The demon still his suit pursued.

"Proud art thou, lady fair, whose soul
   So high aspires; but such sublime
   Devotion suits not well thy prime,
Nor stern and painful self-control.
The old may so their days employ;
But thou should'st live for love and joy.

"I am the lord of Lankā's isle;
   Thy peerless charms my bosom fire:
   If thou wilt crown my heart's desire,
And ever on me sweetly smile,
Then thou, my favoured queen, shalt know
The bliss that power and wealth bestow.

* The Daityas in character correspond with the Titans of the Greeks.

" And who is Vishṇu, pray, declare,
Whose form thy fancy paints so bright?
Can he in prowess, grandeur, might,
And magic gifts with me compare?
A phantom vain no longer chase,
The offer of my love embrace."

To whom the holy maid replied—
" Presumptuous fiend, thy boast is loud.
No voice but thine, profanely proud,
Hath ever Vishṇu's might defied;
Heaven, earth, and hell, all own him lord—
By all their hosts and powers adored."

She spake; the fiend with rage was fired:
The damsel's hair he rudely grasped;
Thus by his hated fingers clasped,
She tore her locks, and cried, inspired—
" This insult I may not survive:
I enter now this fire, alive.

" Yet though I die, I once again
Shall live to recompense this wrong.
And though my vengeance slumber long.
My pious works their meed shall gain,
And I shall reappear on earth,
A virgin fair of royal birth."

She ceased. With fixed resolve to die,
The fire she entered, calm, elate;
When all at once, to celebrate
This deed heroic, from the sky
There fell a shower of fragrant flowers,
Rained down by gods from heavenly bowers.

Nor was this maid's prediction vain.
  Attaining all her heart's desire,
As Sītā she was born again,
  The daughter of a royal sire,
And won great Rāma for her lord,
Whom men as Vishṇu's Self adored.

And now the demon-king profane,
  Whose coming doom had been foretold
  By that insulted maid of old,
By Rāma's hand in fight was slain.
For how could hellish power withstand
Incarnate Vishṇu's murderous brand?

SKETCHES OF DIFFERENT DEITIES AS REPRESENTED IN THE HYMNS OF THE RIGVEDA.*

CCXLIII. Varuna.

Lo, reared of old by hands divine,
High towers in heaven a palace fair;
Its roof a thousand columns bear:
A thousand portals round it shine.

Within, enthroned in god-like state,
Sits Varuṇa, in golden sheen:
To work his will, with reverent mien,
His angel hosts around him wait.

When I beheld this vision bright,
I deemed the god was clad in flame,
Such radiance from his presence came,
And overpowered my aching sight.

Each morn when Ushas starts from sleep,
He mounts his car, which gleams with gold:
All worlds before him lie unrolled,
As o'er the sky his coursers sweep.

The righteous lord the sceptre wields,
Supreme, of universal sway;
His law both men and gods obey:
To his decree the haughtiest yields.

He spread the earth and watery waste;
He reared the sky; he bade the sun

* These sketches are reprinted from the fifth volume of my "Original Sanskrit Texts," &c.

His shining circuit daily run :
In him the worlds are all embraced.

By his decree the radiant moon
Moves through the nightly sky serene,
And planets sparkle round their queen ; *
But whither have they fled at noon !

The rivers flow at his request ;
And yet—admire his wondrous skill—
The ocean-bed they never fill,
Although their currents never rest.

The path of ships across the sea,
The soaring eagle's flight he knows ; †
The course of every wind that blows,
And all that was or is to be.

Descending, ceaseless, from the sky,
His angels glide this world around :
As far as earth's remotest bound,
All-scanning, range their thousand eyes.

This mighty lord who rules on high,
Though closely veiled from mortal gaze,
All men's most secret acts surveys :
He, ever far, is ever nigh.

---

* In Indian mythology the moon is a god, not a goddess ; but I have in this line adhered to the customary English poetical phraseology.

† Compare Proverbs xxx. 18—"There be three things which are too wonderful for me ; yea, four which I know not : 19. The way of an eagle in the air ; the way of a serpent upon a rock ; the way of a ship in the midst of the sea ;" &c.

Two think they are not overheard,
  Who sit and plot as if alone;
  Their fancied secrets all are known;
Unseen, the god is there, a third.

Whoe'er should think his way to wing,
  And lurk unknown beyond the sky;
  Yet could not there elude the eye,
And grasp, of Varuṇa, the king.

For all within the vast expanse
  Of air that heaven and earth divides,
  Whate'er above the heaven abides,
Lies open to his piercing glance.

The ceaseless winkings all he sees,
  And counts, of every mortal's eyes;
  In vain to move a creature tries,
Unless the god the power decrees.

To thoughtful men, who truth discern,
  And deeply things divine explore,
  The god reveals his hidden lore;
But fools his secrets may not learn.

He marks the good and ill within
  The hearts of men;—the false and true
  Discerns with never-erring view:
He hates deceit, chastises sin.

His viewless bonds, than cords and gyves
  More hard to burst, the wicked bind;
  In vain, within their folds confined,
To cast them off the sinner strives.

And yet the god will not refuse
  His grace to one who inly moans,
  When fetter-bound, his errors owns,
And for forgiveness meekly sues.

But where is, lord, thy friendship now ?*
  Thine ancient kindness, O restore ;
  May we, so dear to thee of yore,
No longer dread thy frowning brow.

Thine ire we did not madly brave,
  Nor break thy laws in wanton mood ;
  We fell by wrath, dice, wine, subdued,
Forgive us, gracious lord, and save.

Absolve us from the guilt, we pray,
  Of all the sins our fathers wrought,†
  And sins which we commit in thought,
And speech, and act, from day to day.

From dire disease preserve us free,
  Nor doom us to the house of clay
  Before our shrivelling frames decay :
A good old age yet let us see.

In vain shall hostile shafts assail
  The man thy shielding arm defends :
  Secure, no wrong he apprehends,
Safe as if cased in iron mail.

As mother birds their pinions spread
  To guard from harm their cowering brood ;
  Do thou, O lord, most great and good,
Preserve from all the ills we dread.

---

* Compare Psalms lxxxix. 49 ; xxv. 6 ; and lxxxv. 5.

† See Exodus xx. 5 ; Deuteronomy v. 9 ; and Ezekiel xviii. 1 ff.

Many of the ideas in the preceding sketch are derived from the following hymn:—

Atharva veda, iv. 16.

The mighty lord on high our deeds, as if at hand, espies;
The gods know all men do, though men would fain their acts disguise:
Whoever stands, whoever moves, or steals from place to place,
Or hides him in his secret cell,—the gods his movements trace.
Wherever two together plot, and deem they are alone,
King Varuṇa is there, a third, and all their schemes are known.
This earth is his, to him belong those vast and boundless skies;
Both seas within him rest, and yet in that small pool he lies.
Whoever far beyond the sky should think his way to wing,
He could not there elude the grasp of Varuṇa the king.
His spies, descending from the skies, glide all this world around;
Their thousand eyes all-scanning sweep to earth's remotest bound.
Whate'er exists in heaven and earth, whate'er beyond the skies,
Before the eyes of Varuṇa, the king, unfolded lies.
The ceaseless winkings all he counts of every mortal's eyes,
He wields this universal frame as gamester throws his dice.
Those knotted nooses which thou fling'st, O god, the bad to snare,
All liars let them overtake, but all the truthful spare.

CCXLIV. Indra.

i. *Invitation of Indra to the Sacrifice.*

Hear, Indra, mighty thunderer, hear,
Great regent of the middle sphere:
List, while we sweetly sing thy praise,
In new and well-constructed lays,
Hymns deftly framed by poet skilled,
As artizans a chariot build.
Come, Indra, come, thou much invoked;
Our potent hymn thy steeds has yoked;
Thy golden car already waits
Thy pleasure at thy palace gates.
Friend Indra, from the sky descend,
Thy course propitious hither bend;
Come straight, and let no rival priest
Prevail to draw thee from our feast.
Let no one catch thee unawares,
Like bird the artful fowler snares.
All is prepared; the soma draught
Is sweet as thou hast ever quaffed:
And we will feed with corn, and tend,
Thy coursers at their journey's end.
But, Indra, though of us thou thinkest,
And our oblations gladly drinkest,
We, mortal men, can only share
A humble portion of thy care.
We know how many potent ties
Enchain thee in thy paradise.
Thou hast at home a lovely wife,
The joy and solace of thy life;
Thou hast a ceaseless round of joys
Which all thy circling hours employs,
Joys such as gods immortal know,
Unguessed by mortals here below.

But, brother Indra, come, benign,
Accept our gifts, thou friend divine.
Come, Indra, come in eager haste,
Our hymns to hear, our food to taste,
Like lover lured by female charms,
Who rushes to his dear one's arms.
Accept our sweet and grateful song,
Come, we will not detain thee long.

ii. *Indra's Birth.*

Hear, Indra, while thy birth we sing,
Thy deeds, thy greatness, glorious king.
Old father Sky* and mother Earth,
Both quaked, confounded, at thy birth.
The Sky exclaimed, at that great sight,
"Thy father was a stalwart wight;
Of most consummate skill was he,
The god whose genius fashioned thee."
This infant, of unrivalled force,
Sprang forth from a transcendant source.
A blessed mother bore the child,
And fondly on her offspring smiled;
Foretelling then, with pride and joy,
The might and glory of the boy.
He needed not a tedious length
Of autumns to mature his strength.
His force he felt as soon as born,
And laughed all hostile powers to scorn.
Grasping his deadly shafts, in pride
Of prowess, thus the infant cried:
"Where, mother, dwell those warriors fierce,
Whose haughty hearts these bolts must pierce?"
And when thy father proved thy foe,
Thy fury, Indra, laid him low.

---

* Dyaus = Ζεύς.

Who vainly sought thy life to take,
Then thou didst sleep, when thou didst wake?
Who, Indra, in his vengeful mood,
Thy mother doomed to widowhood?
What god stood by, thy wrath to fire,
When seizing by the foot thy sire,
Thou smot'st him dead, in youthful ire?

iii. *Indra's Arrival.*

Fulfilling now our ardent prayer,
The god approaches through the air.
On, on, he comes, majestic, bright;
Our longed-for friend appears in sight.
His brilliant form, beheld afar,
Towers stately on his golden car.
Fair sun-like lustre, god-like grace,
And martial fire, illume his face.
Yet not one form alone he bears;
But various shapes of glory wears,
His aspects, changing at his will,
Transmuted, yet resplendent still.
In war-like semblance see him stand,
Red lightnings wielding in his hand.
The heavenly steeds, his shining team,
With all the peacock's colours gleam.
Resistless, snorting, on they fly,
As swift as thought, across the sky;
And soon bring nigh their mighty lord,
To us, his friends, a friend adored.
Now Indra from the sky descends;
Yes, yes, to us his way he wends,
Although we see him not, we know
He now is present here below.
Within our hallowed precincts placed,
He longs our grateful feast to taste.

iv. *Indra Invited to Drink the Soma Draught.*

Thou, Indra, oft of old hast quaffed,
With keen delight, our Soma draught.
All gods delicious Soma love ;
But thou, all other gods above.
Thy mother knew how well this juice
Was fitted for her infant's use.
Into a cup she crushed the sap,
Which thou didst sip upon her lap.
Yes, Indra, on thy natal morn,
The very hour that thou wast born,
Thou didst those jovial tastes display,
Which still survive in strength to-day.
And once, thou prince of genial souls,
Men say thou drained'st thirty bowls.
To thee the Soma-draughts proceed,
As streamlets to the lake they feed,
Or rivers to the ocean speed.
Our cup is foaming to the brim,
With Soma pressed to sound of hymn.
Come, drink, thy utmost craving slake,
Like thirsty stag in forest lake,
Or bull that roams in arid waste,
And burns the cooling brook to taste.
Indulge thy taste, and quaff at will ;
Drink, drink again, profusely swill ;
Drink, thy capacious stomach fill.

v. *Praise of Soma.*

This Soma is a god ; he cures
The sharpest ills that man endures.
He heals the sick, the sad he cheers,
He nerves the weak, dispels their fears,
The faint with martial ardour fires,
With lofty thoughts the bard inspires,

The soul from earth to heaven he lifts—
So great and wondrous are his gifts.
Men feel the god within their veins,
And cry in loud exulting strains :
" We've quaffed the Soma bright,
And are immortal grown ;
We've entered into light,
And all the gods have known.
Nought mortal now can harm,
Or foeman vex us more ?
Through thee beyond alarm,
Immortal god, we soar."
The gods themselves with pleasure feel
King Soma's influence o'er them steal ;
And Indra once, as bards have told,
Thus sung in merry mood of old.

vi. *Indra's Drinking Song*.

Yes, yes, I will be generous now,
And grant the bard a horse and cow ;
For haven't I quaffed the Soma draught ?
These draughts impel me with the force
Of blasts that sweep in furious course ;
For haven't I quaffed the Soma draught ?
They drive me like a car that speeds,
Then whirled along by flying steeds.
These hymns approach me fondly now,
As hastes to calf the mother cow.
I turn them over, as I muse,
As carpenter the log he hews.
The tribes of men, the nations all,
I count as something very small.
Both worlds, how vast soe'er they be,
Don't equal even the half of me.

The heaven in greatness I surpass,
And this broad earth, though vast her mass.
Come, let me as a plaything seize,
And toss her wheresoe'er I please.
Come, let me smite with vigorous blow,
And send her flying too and fro.
My half is in the heavenly sphere ;
I've drawn the other half down here.
How great my glory and my power !
Aloft into the skies I tower.
I'm ready now to mount in air,
Oblations to the gods to bear :
For haven't I quaffed the Soma draught ?

vii. *Indra Drinks the Libation.*

And not in vain the mortal prays,
For nothing loth the god obeys :
The proffered bowl he takes.
Well trained the generous juice to drain,
He quaffs it once, he quaffs again,
Till all his thirst he slakes.
And soon its power the Soma shows,
Through Indra's veins the influence flows,
With fervour flushed he stands;
His forehead glows, his eyes are fired,
His mighty frame with force inspired,
His towering form expands.
He straightway calls his brave allies,
To valorous deeds exhorts, and cries :—
"Stride, Vishṇu, forward stride.
Come, Maruts, forth with me to war,
See yonder Vṛitra * stands afar,

* The demon who personifies drought—called also Śushṇa and Ahi.

And waits the coming of my car:
We soon shall crush his pride."

viii. *Indra, attended by the Maruts, sets out to encounter Vṛitra.*

Amid the plaudits long and loud,
Which burst from all the heavenly crowd,
Charmed by the sweet and magic sound
Of hymns pronounced by bards renowned,
Viewed by admiring troops of friends,
The valiant god his car ascends.
Swept by his fervid, bounding steeds,
Athwart the sky the hero speeds.
The Marut hosts his escort form,
Impetuous spirits of the storm.
On flashing lightning-cars they ride,
And gleam in warlike pomp and pride:
Each head a golden helmet crests,
And glittering mail adorns their breasts.
Spears on their shoulders rest, their hands
Bear arrows, bows, and lightning brands.
Bright tinkling anklets deck their feet,
And thought than they is not more fleet.
Like lion's roar their voice of doom,
With iron force their teeth consume.
The hills, the earth itself, they shake;
All creatures at their coming quake.
Their headlong fury none can stay,
All obstacles are swept away.
The forest's leafy monarchs tall
Before their onset crashing fall,
As when, in fierce, destructive mood,
Wild elephants invade a wood.

ix. *Indra's Conflict with Vṛitra.*

Who is it that, without alarm,
Defies the might of Indra's arm;
That stands and sees without dismay
The approaching Maruts' dread array,
That does not shun in wild affright,
The terrors of the deadly fight?
'Tis Vṛitra; he whose magic powers
From earth withhold the genial showers,
Of mortal men the foe malign,
And rival of the race divine,
Whose demon hosts from age to age
With Indra war unceasing wage;
Who, times unnumbered, crushed and slain,
Is ever newly born again;
And evermore renews the strife
In which again he forfeits life.
Perched on a steep aerial height,
Shone Vṛitra's stately fortress bright.
Upon the wall, in martial mood,
The bold gigantic demon stood,
Confiding in his magic arts,
And armed with store of fiery darts.
And then was seen a dreadful sight,
When god and demon met in fight.
His sharpest missiles Vṛitra shot,
His thunderbolts and lightnings hot
He hurled as thick as rain.
The god his fiercest rage defied,
His blunted weapons glanced aside,
At Indra launched in vain.
When thus he long had vainly toiled,
When all his weapons had recoiled,
His final efforts had been foiled,
And all his force consumed,—
In gloomy and despairing mood,

The baffled demon helpless stood,
And knew his end was doomed.
The lightnings then began to flash,
The direful thunderbolts to crash,
By Indra proudly hurled.
The gods themselves with awe were stilled,
And stood aghast, and terror filled
The universal world.
Even Tvashṭṛi sage, whose master hand
Had forged the bolts his art had planned,
Who well their temper knew,—
Quailed when he heard the dreadful clang,
That through the quivering welkin rang,
As o'er the sky they flew.
And who the arrowy shower could stand
Discharged by Indra's red right hand,
The thunderbolts with hundred joints,
The iron shafts with thousand points,
Which blaze and hiss athwart the sky,
Swift to their mark unerring fly,
And lay the proudest foeman low,
With sudden and resistless blow,—
Whose very sound could put to flight
The fools who dare the thunderer's might ?
And soon the knell of Vṛitra's doom
Was sounded by the clang and boom
Of Indra's iron shower.
Pierced, cloven, crushed, with horrid yell,
The dying demon headlong fell
Down from his cloud-built tower.
Now, bound by Śushṇa's spell no more,
The clouds discharge their liquid store ;
And, long by torrid sunbeams baked,
The plains by copious showers are slaked.
The rivers swell, and seaward sweep
Their turbid torrents broad and deep.

The peasant views with deep delight,
And thankful heart, the auspicious sight.
His leafless fields so sere and sad,
Will soon with waving crops be clad;
And mother earth, now brown and bare,
A robe of brilliant green will wear.
And now the clouds disperse, the blue
Of heaven once more comes forth to view.
The sun shines out, all nature smiles,
Redeemed from Vṛitra's power and wiles.
The gods with gratulations meet,
And loud acclaim, the victor greet;
While Indra's mortal votaries sing
The praises of their friend and king.
The frogs, too, dormant long, awake,
And floating on the brimming lake,
In loud responsive croak unite,
And swell the chorus of delight.

x. *Indra's Greatness.*

What poet now, what sage of old,
The greatness of that god hath told,
Who from his body vast gave birth
To father sky and mother earth,
Who hung the heavens in empty space,
And gave the earth a stable base,
Who framed and lighted up the sun,
And made a path for him to run;
Whose power transcendent, since their birth
Asunder holds the heaven and earth,
As chariot wheels are kept apart
By axles framed by workman's art?
In greatness who with him can vie
Who fills the earth, the air, the sky;

Whose presence, unperceived, extends
Beyond the world's remotest ends?
A hundred earths, if such there be,
A hundred skies, fall short of thee;
A thousand suns would not outshine
The effulgence of thy light divine.
The worlds, which mortals boundless deem,
To thee but as a handful seem.
Thou, Indra, art without a peer,
On earth, in yonder heavenly sphere.
Thee, god, such matchless powers adorn,
That thou without a foe wast born.
Thou art the universal lord,
By gods revered, by men adored.
Should all the other gods conspire,
They could not frustrate thy desire.
The circling years, which wear away
All else, to thee bring no decay;
Thou bloomest on in youthful force,
While countless ages run their course.
Unvexed by cares, or fears, or strife,
In bliss serene flows on thy life.

xi. *Indra's relations to his Worshippers.*

Thou, Indra, art a friend, a brother,
A kinsman dear, a father, mother.
Though thou hast troops of friends, yet we
Can boast no other friend but thee.
With this our hymn thy skirt we grasp,
As boys their fathers' garments clasp;
Our ardent prayers thy form embrace,
As women's arms their lords enlace;
They round thee cling with gentle force,
Like saddle-girth about a horse.

With faith we claim thine aid divine,
For thou art ours, and we are thine.
Thou art not deaf; though far away,
Thou hearest all, whate'er we pray.
And be not like a lazy priest,
Who battens at the dainty feast,
Sits still in self-indulgent ease,
And only cares himself to please.
Come, dole not out with niggard hand
The brilliant boons at thy command.
Thy gracious hands are wont to grant
Profusely all thy servants want.
Why is it, then, thou sittest still,
And dost not now our hopes fulfil?
If I were thou, and thou wert I,
My suppliant should not vainly cry.
Wert thou a mortal, I divine,
In want I ne'er would let thee pine.
Had I, like thee, unbounded power,
I wealth on all my friends would shower.
Shed wealth, as trees, when shaken, rain
Their ripe fruit down upon the plain.
Thy strong right hand, great god, we hold
With eager grasp, imploring gold.
Thou canst our longings all fulfil,
If such shall only be thy will.
Like headlong bull's, thy matchless force
Strikes all things down that bar thy course.
Art thou to gracious deeds inclined?
Then who shall make thee change thy mind?
Abundant aids shoot forth from thee,
As leafy boughs from vigorous tree.
To wifeless men thou givest wives,
And joyful mak'st their joyless lives.
Thou givest sons, courageous, strong,
To guard their aged sires from wrong.

Lands, jewels, horses, herds of kine,—
All kinds of wealth are gifts of thine.
Thy friend is never slain; his might
Is never worsted in the fight.
Yes, those who in the battle's shock,
Thine aid, victorious god, invoke,
With force inspired, with deafening shout
Of triumph, put their foes to rout.
Thou blessest those thy praise who sing,
And plenteous gifts devoutly bring;
But thou chastisest all the proud,
The niggard, and the faithless crowd,
Who thine existence doubt, and cry
In scorn, "No Indra rules on high."
The rich can ne'er thy favourites be,
The rich who never think of thee.
When storms are lulled, and skies are bright,
Wine-swillers treat thee with despite.
When clouds collect, and thunders roar,
The scoffers tremble and adore.
No deed is done but thou dost see;
No word is said unheard by thee.
The fates of mortals thou dost wield,
To thy decree the strongest yield.
Thou dost the high and fierce abase,
The lowly raisest in their place.
But thy true friends secure repose,
By thee redeemed from all their woes,
From straits brought forth to ample room,
To glorious light from thickest gloom.
And thou dost view with special grace
The fair-complexioned Aryan race,
Who own the gods, their laws obey,
And pious homage duly pay.
Thou giv'st us horses, cattle, gold,
As thou didst give our sires of old.

Thou sweep'st away the dark-skinned brood,
Inhuman, lawless, senseless, rude,
Who know not Indra, hate his friends,
And spoil the race which he defends.
Chase far away, the robbers, chase,
Slay those barbarians, black and base;
And save us, Indra, from the spite
Of sprites that haunt us in the night,
Our rites disturb by contact vile,
Our hallowed offerings defile.
Preserve us, friend, dispel our fears,
And let us live a hundred years.
And when our earthly course we've run,
And gained the region of the Sun,
Then let us live in ceaseless glee,
Sweet nectar quaffing there with thee.

CCXLV. Parjanya, the Rain God.

Ṛigveda v. 83.

Parjanya laud with praises meet,
The fertilizing god extol,
And bless, of living things the soul,
Whose advent men, exulting, greet.

Like steeds a charioteer has spurred,
His watery scouts before him fly.
Far off, within the darkening sky,
The thundering lion's roar is heard.

Fierce blow the blasts, the lightnings flash,
Men, cattle, flee in wild affright.
Avenging bolts the wicked smite;
The guiltless quake to hear the crash.

Malignant demons stricken lie;
The forest's leafy monarchs tall
Convulsed, uprooted, prostrate fall,
Whene'er Parjanya passes by.

Speed on thy car, Parjanya, haste,
And, as thou sweepest o'er the sky,
Thine ample waterskins untie,
To slake with showers the thirsty waste.

Now forth let swollen streamlets burst,
And o'er the withered meadows flow;
Let plants their quickening influence know;
And pining cattle quench their thirst.

Thy wondrous might, O god, declare;
With verdure bright the earth adorn,
Clothe far and wide the fields with corn,
And food for all the world prepare.

But oh, we pray, Parjanya kind,
Since now our harvests, drenched with rain,
Bright sunbeams fain would see again,
Thy waterskins no more unbind.

CCXLVI. Vata or Vayu, the Wind God.

Ṛigveda x. 168.

King Vāta's car my hymn extols,
Which thundering, crashing, onward rolls.
Its bounding steeds now soaring high,—
With ruddy glow it tints the sky;
Again a lower path it keeps,
And clouds of dust before it sweeps.
As maidens after lovers haste,
By kindred hosts the god is chased;

While round him floats the impetuous throng,
His stately car is borne along.
Pursuing still his airy way,
He never rests on any day.
Primeval, changeless, old ally
Of waters streaming through the sky,
This god was born,—we know not where,—
Within the boundless realms of air.
No power may e'er this lord control,
Of other gods the breath, the soul,
Of all existing things the source,
Who, where he wills, directs his course.
His voice is heard in breeze and storm,
But who hath ever seen his form ?

CCXLVII. Surya, the Sun.

Ṛigveda i. 50.

By lustrous heralds led on high,
The omniscient Sun ascends the sky,
His glory drawing every eye.
All-seeing Sun, the stars so bright,
Which gleamed throughout the sombre night,
Now scared, like thieves, slink fast away,
Quenched by the splendour of thy ray.
Thy beams to men thy presence show ;
Like blazing fires they seem to glow.
Conspicuous, rapid, source of light,
Thou makest all the welkin bright.
In sight of gods and mortal eyes,
In sight of heaven, thou scal'st the skies.
Bright god, thou scann'st with searching ken,
The doings all of busy men.
Thou stridest o'er the sky ; thy rays
Create, and measure out, our days ;
Thine eye all living things surveys.

Seven lucid mares thy chariot bear,
Self-yoked, athwart the fields of air,
Bright Sūrya, god with flaming hair.
That glow above the darkness we
Beholding, upward soar to thee,
For there among the gods thy light
Supreme is seen, divinely bright.

CCXLVIII. Ushas, the Indian Aurora.

Ṛigveda i. 48; i. 92; i. 113.

Hail Ushas, daughter of the sky,
  Who, borne upon thy shining car
  By ruddy steeds from realms afar,
And ever lightening, drawest nigh:—

Thou sweetly smilest, goddess fair,
  Disclosing all thy youthful grace,
  Thy bosom bright, thy radiant face,
The lustre of thy golden hair:—

(So shines a fond and winning bride,
  Who robes her form in brilliant guise,
  And to her lord's admiring eyes
Displays her charms with conscious pride:—

Or virgin by her mother decked,
  Who, glorying in her beauty, shows
  In every glance, her power she knows
All eyes to fix, all hearts subject;—

Or actress, who, by skill in song
  And dance, and graceful gestures light,
  And many-coloured vesture bright,
Enchants the eager gazing throng:—

Or maid, who wont her limbs to lave
  In some cool stream among the woods,
  In deep surrounding solitudes,
Emerges fairer from the wave) :—

But closely by the amorous sun
  Pursued, and vanquished in the race,
  Thou soon art locked in his embrace,
And with him blendest into one.

Fair Ushas, though through years untold
  Thou hast lived on, yet thou art born
  Anew on each succeeding morn,
And so thou art both young and old.

As in thy fated ceaseless course
  Thou risest on us day by day,
  Thou wearest all our lives away
With silent, ever-wasting force.

Their round our generations run :
  The old depart, and in their place
  Springs ever up a younger race,
Whilst thou, immortal, lookest on.

All those who watched for thee of old
  Are gone, and now 'tis we who gaze
  On thy approach ; in future days
Shall other men thy beams behold.

But 'tis not thoughts so grave and sad
  Alone that thou dost with thee bring,
  A shadow o'er our hearts to fling ;—
Thy beams returning make us glad.

Thy sister, sad and sombre Night,
With stars that in the blue expanse
Like sleepless eyes mysterious glance,
At thy approach is quenched in light;—

And earthly forms, till now concealed
Behind her veil of dusky hue,
Once more come sharply out to view,
By thine illuming glow revealed.

Thou art the life of all that lives,
The breath of all that breathes; the sight
Of thee makes every countenance bright,
New strength to every spirit gives.

When thou dost pierce the murky gloom,
Birds flutter forth from every brake,
All sleepers as from death awake,
And men their myriad tasks resume.

Some, prosperous, wake in listless mood,
And others every nerve to strain
The goal of wealth or power to gain,
Or what they deem the highest good.

But some to holier thoughts aspire,
In hymns the gods immortal praise,
And light, on earthly hearths to blaze,
The heaven-born sacrificial fire.

And not alone do bard and priest
Awake;—the gods thy power confess
By starting into consciousness
When thy first rays suffuse the east;—

And hasting downward from the sky
They visit men devout and good,
Consume their consecrated food,
And all their longings satisfy.

Bright goddess, let thy genial rays
To us bring stores of envied wealth
In kine and steeds, and sons, with health,
And joy of heart, and length of days.

CCXLIX. Agni, the God of Fire.

Rigveda, passim.

Great Agni, though thine essence be but one,
Thy forms are three ; as fire thou blazest here,
As lightning flashest in the atmosphere,
In heaven thou flamest as the golden sun.

It was in heaven thou hadst thy primal birth ;
But thence of yore a holy sage benign
Conveyed thee down on human hearths to shine,
And thou abid'st a denizen of earth.

Sprung from the mystic pair,* by priestly hands
In wedlock joined, forth flashes Agni bright ;
But—O ye heaven and earth, I tell you right,—
The unnatural child devours the parent brands.

But Agni is a god : we must not deem
That he can err, or dare to reprehend
His acts, which far our reason's grasp transcend :
He best can judge what deeds a god beseem.

---

* The two pieces of fuel, by the attrition of which fire is produced, and which are represented as husband and wife.

And yet this orphaned god himself survives :
Although his hapless mother soon expires,
And cannot nurse the babe, as babe requires,
Great Agni, wondrous infant, grows and thrives.

Smoke-bannered Agni, god with crackling voice
And flaming hair, when thou dost pierce the gloom
At early morn, and all the world illume,
Both heaven and earth, and gods and men rejoice.

In every home thou art a welcome guest ;
The household's tutelary lord ; a son,
A father, mother, brother, all in one ;
A friend by whom thy faithful friends are blest.

A swift-winged messenger, thou callest down
From heaven, to crowd our hearths, the race divine,
To taste our food, our hymns to hear, benign,
And all our fondest aspirations crown.

Thou, Agni, art our priest, divinely wise,
In holy science versed ; thy skill detects
The faults that mar our rites, mistakes corrects,
And all our acts completes and sanctifies.

Thou art the cord that stretchest to the skies,
The bridge that spans the chasm, profound and vast,
Dividing earth from heaven, o'er which at last
The good shall safely pass to paradise.

But when, great god, thine awful anger glows,
And thou revealest thy destroying force,
All creatures flee before thy furious course,
As hosts are chased by overpowering foes.

Thou levellest all thou touchest; forests vast
Thou sheer'st like beards which barber's razor shaves,
Thy wind-driven flames roar loud as ocean-waves,
And all thy track is black when thou hast passed.

But thou, great Agni, dost not often wear
That direful form; thou rather lov'st to shine
Upon our hearths with milder flame benign,
And cheer the homes where thou art nursed with care.

Yes, thou delightest all those men to bless
Who toil, unwearied, to supply the food
Which thou so lovest, logs of well-dried wood,
And heaps of butter bring, thy favourite mess.

Though I no cow possess, and own no store
Of butter, nor an axe fresh wood to cleave,
Thou, gracious god, wilt my poor gift receive,
These few dry sticks I bring; I have no more.

Preserve us, lord, thy faithful servants save
From all the ills by which our bliss is marred;
Tower like an iron wall our homes to guard,
And all the boons bestow our hearts can crave.

And when away our brief existence wanes,
When we at length our earthly homes must quit,
And our freed souls to worlds unknown shall flit,
Do thou deal gently with our cold remains;

And then thy gracious form assuming, guide
Our unborn part across the dark abyss,
Aloft to realms serene of light and bliss,
Where righteous men among the gods abide.

CCL. Yama, and a future life.

Ṛigveda x. 14; x. 15; x. 16; and *Atharva Veda.*

To great king Yama homage pay,
Who was the first of men that died,
That crossed the mighty gulf, and spied
For mortals out the heavenly way.

No power can ever close the road
Which he to us laid open then,
By which, in long procession, men
Ascend to his sublime abode.

By it our fathers all have passed;
And that same path we too shall trace,
And every new succeeding race
Of mortal men, while time shall last.

The god assembles round his throne
A growing throng, the good and wise,—
All those whom, scanned with searching eyes,
He recognises as his own.

Departed mortal, speed from earth
By those old ways thy sires have trod;
Ascend, behold the expectant god
Who calls thee to a higher birth.

First must each several element
That joined to form thy living frame,
Flit to the region whence it came,
And with its parent source be blent.

Thine eye shall seek the solar orb,
Thy life-breath to the wind shall fly,
Thy part ethereal to the sky;
Thine earthy part shall earth absorb.

Thine unborn part shall Agni bright
With his beniguant rays illume,
And guide it through the trackless gloom
To yonder sphere of life and light.

On his resplendent pinions rise,
Or soar upon a car aloft,
By wind-gods fanned with breezes soft,
Until thou enterest paradise.

And calmly pass, without alarm,
The four-eyed hounds which guard the road
That leads to Yama's bright abode:
Their master's friends they dare not harm.

All imperfections leave behind:
Assume thine ancient frame once more,—
Each limb, and sense, thou hadst before,
From every earthly taint refined,

And now with heavenly glory bright,
With life intenser, nobler, blest,
With large capacity to taste
A fuller measure of delight.

Thou there once more each well-known face
Shalt see of those thou lovedst here:
Thy parents, wife, and children dear,
With rapture shalt thou then embrace.

The fathers, too, shalt thou behold,
The heroes who in battle died,
The saints and sages glorified,
The pious, bounteous kings of old.

The gods whom here in humble wise
Thou worshippedst with doubt and awe,
Shall there the impervious veil withdraw
Which hid their glory from thine eyes.

The good which thou on earth hast wrought,
Each sacrifice, each pious deed,
Shall there receive its ample meed :
No worthy act shall be forgot.

In those fair realms of cloudless day,
Where Yama every joy supplies,
And every longing satisfies,
Thy bliss shall never know decay.

CCLI. Nonentity, Entity, and the One.

Ṛigveda x. 129.

There then was neither Aught nor Nought, no air nor sky beyond.
What covered all ? Where rested all ? In watery gulf profound ?
Nor death was there, nor deathlessness, nor change of night and day.
That One breathed calmly, self-sustained : nor else beyond It lay.
Gloom hid in gloom existed first—one sea eluding view.
That One, a void in chaos wrapt, by inward fervour grew.
Within It first arose desire, the primal germ of mind,
Which nothing with existence links, as sages searching find.
The kindling ray that shot across the dark and drear abyss,—
Was it beneath ? Or high aloft ? What bard can answer this ?

There fecundating powers were found, and mighty
forces strove,
A self-supporting mass beneath, and energy above.
Who knows, whoe'er hath told, from whence this vast
creation rose?
No gods had then been born, who then can e'er the
truth disclose?
Whence sprang this world, and whether framed by hand
divine or no,
Its lord in heaven alone can tell,—if even he can
show.

CCLII. Aranyani, the Forest Goddess.

Ṛigveda x. 146.

Thou seemest, goddess, here to stray
Forlorn among these trackless woods,
These dark and dreary solitudes.
Why dost thou not enquire the way
That leads to cheerful human haunts?
Is there nought here thy spirit daunts?

Herself the goddess does not slay,
Although she nurtures murderous beasts.
On luscious fruits the traveller feasts,
Supplied by her, and goes his way.

Sweet-scented, fragrant, rich in flowers,
Her realm with various food is filled;
For though by hinds she is not tilled,
She drinks in sap from heavenly showers.

CCLIII. Men's various tastes.

Ṛigveda ix. 112.

Men's tastes and trades are multifarious ;
And so their ends and aims are various.
The smith seeks something cracked to mend ;
The leech could fain have sick to tend ;
The priest desires a devotee
From whom he may extract a fee.
Each craftsman makes and mends his ware,
And hopes the rich man's gold to share.
My sire's a leech, and I a bard ;
Corn grinds my mother, toiling hard.
All craving wealth, we each pursue
By different means, the end in view,
Like people running after cows,
Which too far off have strayed to brouse.
The draught-horse seeks an easy yoke,
The merry dearly love a joke,
Of pretty maidens men are fond,
And thirsty frogs desire a pond.

CCLIV. The gambler.

Ṛigveda x. 34.

These dice that roll upon the board
To me intense delight afford.
Sweet Soma-juice has not more power
To lure me in an evil hour.
To strife and wrangling disinclined,
My gentle wife was always kind ;
But I, absorbed in maddening play,
Have chased this tender spouse away.

She now, in turn, my person spurns;
Her mother's wrath against me burns.
Distressed and vexed, in vain I plead,
For none will help me in my need.
As wretched as a worn-out hack's,
A gamester's life all joyance lacks.
His means by play away are worn,
While gallants court his wife forlorn.
His father, mother, brothers shout,
"The madman bind, and drag him out."
At times,—the scorn of every friend,—
I try my foolish ways to mend,
Resolve no more my means to waste
On this infatuated taste:
But all in vain:—when, coming near,
The rattle of the dice I hear,
I rush, attracted by their charms
Like lady to her lover's arms.
As to his game the gambler hies,
Once more his hopes of winning rise;
And loss but more his ardour fires;
To tries his luck he never tires.
The dice their victims hook and tear,
Disturbing, torturing, false though fair.
The transient gains they yield to-day,
To-morrow all are swept away.
These sportive dice, a potent band,
The destinies of men command.
They laugh to scorn the fierce man's frown;
Before them doughty kings bow down.
They downward roll, they upward bound,
And handless, men with hands confound.
They scorch the heart like brands, these dice,
Although themselves as cold as ice.
The gambler's hapless wife is sad;
His mother mourns her wayward lad.

In want, at night he seeks relief
By graceless shifts, a trembling thief.
He groans to see his wretched wife,
And then the happy wives, and life,
Of others, free from care and strife.
His bad career, with morning light
Begun, in ruin ends by night.
To him, the Chief who leads your bands,
Ye Dice, I lift my suppliant hands:
"I hail thy gifts, when those art kind,
But crave thy leave to speak my mind.
Forgive me, King of all the Dice,
If thus I give my friend advice;
Abandon play, and till the soil;
For this shall better pay thy toil.
Well pleased with what thou hast, forbear
To crave of wealth an ampler share."
"Thy wife, thy kine;—in these rejoice;"
Thus cries a god with warning voice.
Be gracious, Dice, we now implore;
Bewitch us with your spells no more.
From us withdraw, to us be kind,
And others with your fetters bind.

CCLV. Praise of liberality.

Ṛigveda x. 107. 8 ff.

The liberal does not mourn or die;
No care or pain his life annoys;
The world is his with all its joys,
And future bliss beyond the sky.

He owns a princely palace bright,
And dwells in godlike pomp and pride;
A richly decked and winning bride
Sits fair and blooming by his side,
And fills his heart with love's delight.

With plenteous store of corn and wine
Supplied, a merry life he leads;
Swift o'er the plain his chariot speeds,
Whirled on by prancing, snorting steeds;
He smites his foes by aid divine.

CCLVI. The same.

Ṛigveda x. 117.

The gods have not ordained that we
Should die of want: the lean and weak
Are not death's only prey; the sleek
Themselves must soon his victims be.

The man endowed with ample pelf,
Who steels his heart, in selfish mood,
Against the poor who sue for food,
Shall no consoler find himself.

No friend is he who coldly spurns
Away his needy friend forlorn;
He thus repulsed, in wrath and scorn
To some more liberal stranger turns.

Relieve the poor while yet ye may;
Down future time's long vista look,
And try to read that darkling book;
Your riches soon may flit away.

Ye cannot trust their fickle grace.
As chariot wheels in ceaseless round
Now upward turn, now touch the ground,
So riches ever change their place.

The man whose friend receives no share
Of all his good, himself destroys:
Who thus alone his food enjoys
His sin alone shall also bear.

CCLVII. The frogs in autumn.

Ṛigveda vii. 103.

As Brahmans, who a vow fulfil,
The frogs had now a year been still.
Like dried and shrivelled skins they lay,
Faint, parched with heat, for many a day,
Expecting, long in vain, the showers
Withheld by Air's malignant powers.
But autumn comes: Parjanya rains
In copious streams, and floods the plains.
Clouds veil the sun, the air is cool,
The ponds, long empty, now are full.
There float the frogs, their bodies soak:
Afar is heard their merry croak.
Well drenched, they jump aloft in glee,
And join in noisy colloquy.
They leap upon each other's backs,
And each to t'other cries co-ax.
As teachers first call out a word,
Then boys repeat what they have heard,
Just so the frogs croak out once more
What other frogs had croaked before.
Sounds diverse issue from their throats,
Some low like cows, some bleat like goats,
Though one in name, of various sheen,
For one is brown, another green.
As Brahmans at a Soma-rite,
Around the bowl in talk unite,

This day the frogs their pond surround,
And make the air with noise resound.
These priests, the frogs, their voices raise,
And sing their annual hymn of praise.
As priests who sweated o'er a pot,
Soon quit the fire they find too hot,
The frogs so long oppressed with heat
Emerge in haste from their retreat.
From rules divine they never swerve,
But all the seasons' laws observe.
When autumn comes their sufferings cease,
From scorching heat they find release.
The frogs that bleat and those that low,
Brown, green, on men all wealth bestow.
The kine that on our pastures graze
We owe to them, with length of days.

CCLVIII. The warrior.

Ṛigveda vi. 75.

When, cased in mail, the warrior proud
Stalks on, defiant, to the front,
To bear the raging battle's brunt,
We seem to see a flashing cloud.
Bold warrior, may thine armour bright
Preserve thee scatheless in the fight.

May I the foeman's malice foil
With this my all subduing bow!
May I, triumphant, lay him low,
And all his goods and cattle spoil!
This bow our foes with ruin whelms,
And conquers all surrounding realms.

The bowstring to the bowman's ear
Approaches close, as if to speak:
Its twang is like a woman's shriek:
It guards the warrior's soul from fear.

See, yonder on the chariot stands
The dauntless charioteer, whose skill
His horses onward drives, whose will
Their movements to and fro commands.
The reins (their wondrous power extol !)
Although behind, the steeds control.

The impetuous coursers shrilly neigh,
As forward to the fight they rush :
Their trampling hoofs our foemen crush ;
They never shun the murderous fray.

APPENDIX.

I. *Atharva Veda* x. 8, 44. "Knowing that Soul, who is wise [or, calm], undecaying, young, free from desire, immortal, self-existent, satisfied with the essence [of good, or blessedness], and in no respect imperfect, a man does not dread death."

As the soul (*ātman*) is masculine in Sanskrit, I have ventured to put the relative pronoun following the word in that gender.

I am indebted to Professor Adolf Kägi, of Zürich, for recalling my attention to this verse, which I had quoted in my Original Sanskrit Texts, iv., p. 20.

II. *Śvetāśvatara Upanishad* iii. 19. "Without hands or feet, He grasps, and moves; without eyes He sees, without ears He hears. He knows whatever is knowable, but no one knows Him. Men call Him the great, primeval Purusha (Man or Spirit)."

I subjoin a portion of the context of this passage beginning at iii. 7: "Knowing that lord, the Brahma which is beyond that, the supreme, the vast, hidden in the bodies of all creatures, the one enveloper of the universe, men become immortal. 8. (= Vājasaneyi Śamhitā xxxi. 18). I know that grand Purusha (male or spirit), of sunlike lustre, beyond the darkness. It is by knowing him that a man overpasses death; there is no other road to go. 9. This whole universe is filled by this Purusha, to whom there is nothing superior, from whom there is nothing different, than whom there is nothing either minuter or vaster, who stands alone, fixed like a tree in the sky. 10. That which is above this world is formless, and free from suffering; they who know it become immortal; others encounter pain. . . . 12. Purusha is the great lord; he is the mover of existence ; he rules over this purest state (of blessedness ?), he is light, he is undecaying. . . . 19. Without hands and feet, he grasps, he moves, without eyes he sees, and hears without ears. He knows whatever is to be known ; and no one knows him; men call him the great primeval Purusha. 20. Minuter than the minutest, greater than the greatest, the soul dwells in the heart of this creature. He who is devoid of grief beholds by the favour of the creator this passionless (soul), this great one, this lord. 21. I know this undecaying, ancient one, the soul of all things, from his universal diffusion omni-present, whom the expounders of the Vedas declare to be incapable of birth, and eternal."

The following are two other passages from the same Upanishad :—iv. 19, "None hath grasped him above or across, or in the middle. There is no similitude of him, whose name is the great renown. 20. His form is not perceptible by vision; no one sees him with the eye. Those who through heart and mind know him abiding in the heart, become immortal."

Ibid. vi. 1, "Some wise men, deluded, speak of Nature, and others of Time (as the cause of all things) : but this great power of God (acting) in the world is that whereby this wheel of Brahma is made to revolve. 2. For he by whom the universe is eternally enveloped, who is the knower, who is the maker of time, who is possessed of excellent attributes, and omniscient :—ruled by him this creation, which is to be thought of as earth, water, fire, air, and ether, revolves. . . . 7. We know him who is the great and supreme lord of lords, the supreme deity of deities, the master of masters, the adorable god who is sovereign of the world. 8. There is in him no effect, or instrument (*i.e.*, he has no body, and no organ of sense : commentator). No one equal or superior to him is beheld. His supreme power is declared in Scripture to be various ; it is the natural action of his knowledge and force. 9. There is not in the world any one who is his master, or his ruler ; nor is there any (outward) indication of him. He is the cause, the lord of the lords of creation ; no one is the producer of him or his master. . . . 12. He is the one god hidden in all beings, all-pervading, the inner soul of all beings, the superintender of all acts, who dwells in all beings, the witness, the observer, the only one, and without qualities 12. (=Kaṭha Upanishad v. 12), the one who is independent among many inactive (souls), who develops in various manners the one seed. The wise who behold him abiding in themselves, and they alone, have eternal joy. 13. (=Kaṭha Upanishad v. 13) The eternal among the eternal (ones), the conscious among the conscious (ones), who alone among many dispenses the objects of desire—knowing that cause, the god who is to be apprehended through the Sānkhya and Yoga systems, a man is freed from all bonds. 14. (=Kaṭha Upanishad v. 15, and Muṇḍaka Upanishad ii. 2, 10), There to reveal him no sun shines, nor moon, nor stars, nor do these lightings gleam, much less this fire. It is through his shining that all else shines; by his lustre this universe is illuminated. . . . 16. He is the maker of all things, knows all things, is self-originated (or the soul and the source), the creator of time, endowed with (excellent) attributes, the lord of Pradhāna (rudimentary matter), of the embodied spirit and of the guṇas (three qualities), the cause of liberation from the world, of the world's continuance and (the) bondage (which it involves)."

III. *Vikramacharita*, 232. "Thou, even thou, art (my) mother, thou my father, thou (my) kinsman, thou (my) friend. Thou art knowledge, thou art riches. Thou art my all, O God of gods."

IV. *Raghuvanśa* x. 15 ff.—15. "Glory to Thee, who art first the creator of the universe, next its upholder, and finally its destroyer; glory to Thee in this threefold character. 16. As water falling from the sky, though having but one flavour, assumes different flavours in different bodies, so Thou, associated with the three qualities [Sattva, Rajas, and Tamas, or Goodness, Passion, and Darkness*], assumest [three] states [those of creator, preserver, and destroyer,—according to the commentator], though Thyself unchanged. 17. Immeasurable,

* See Wilson's *Vishṇu Purāṇa*, vol. i., p. 41 (Dr Hall's Edition), where Rajas is translated "activity," and not "passion."

Thou measurest the worlds; desiring nothing, Thou art the fulfiller of desires; unconquered, Thou art a conqueror; utterly indiscernible, Thou art the cause of all that is discerned. 18. Though one, Thou from one or another cause assumest this or that condition; Thy variations are compared to those which crystal undergoes from the contact of different colours. 19. Thou art known as abiding in [our] hearts, and yet as remote; as free from affection, as ascetic, merciful, untouched by sin, primeval, and imperishable. 20. Thou knowest all things, Thyself unknown; sprung from Thyself (or self-existent), Thou art the source of all things; Thou art the lord of all, Thyself without a master; though but one, Thou assumest all forms. 21. Thou art declared to be He who is celebrated in the seven Sâma-hymns, to be He who sleeps on the waters of the seven oceans, whose face is lighted up by the god of seven rays (Fire), and who is the one refuge of the seven worlds. 22. Knowledge which gains the four classes of fruit [virtue, pleasure, wealth, and final liberation], the division of time into four yugas [ages], the fourfold division of the people into castes,—all these things come from Thee, the four-faced. 23. Yogins (devoutly contemplative men) with minds subdued by exercise, recognise Thee, the luminous, abiding in their hearts; (and so attain) to liberation from earthly existence. 24. Who comprehends the truth regarding Thee, who art unborn, and yet becomest born; who art passionless, yet slayest thine enemies; who sleepest,* and yet art awake? 25. Thou art capable of enjoying sounds and other objects of sense, of practising severe austerity, of protecting thy creatures, and of living in indifference to all external things. 26. The roads leading to perfection, which vary according to the different revealed systems, all end in Thee, as the waves of the Ganges flow to the ocean. 27. For those passionless men whose hearts are fixed on Thee, who have committed to Thee their works, Thou art a refuge, so that they escape further mundane births. 28. Thy glory as manifested to the senses in the earth and other objects, is yet

---

* This, I presume, refers to the stories of Vishṇu sleeping on the ocean in the intervals between the dissolution of one world and the creation of the next.

incomprehensible: what shall be said of Thyself, who canst be proved only by the authority of scripture and by inference? 29. Seeing that the remembrance of Thee alone purifies a man,—the rewards of other mental acts also, when directed towards Thee, are thereby indicated. 30. As the waters exceed the ocean, and as the beams of light exceed the sun, so Thy acts transcend our praises. 31. There is nothing for Thee to attain which Thou hast not already attained: kindness to the world is the only motive for Thy birth and for Thy actions.* 32. If this our hymn now comes to a close after celebrating Thy greatness, the reason of this is our exhaustion or our inability to say more, not that there is any limit (*iyattâ*, so-muchness, quantitas = the Dutch *hoeveelheid*) to Thy attributes." These verses have not all been rendered metrically.

v. *M. Bh.* iii. 1124 ff. In this passage, the greater part of which has been translated by me in the "Indian Antiquary" for June 1874, Draupadî complains of the hard lot of her righteous husband Yudhishṭhira, and charges the Deity with injustice; but is answered by Yudhishṭhira. I give here the verses, which I have attempted to render metrically, as well as some others. 1138ᵇ. "God (Iśâna) the Disposer, allots to creatures everything—happiness and suffering, the agreeable and the disagreeable, darting radiance before Him. 1140. Just as the wooden figure of a woman moves its several limbs, according as it is adjusted, so too do these creatures. As a bird bound and confined by a string is not its own master, so a man must remain under the control of God; he is neither the lord of others nor of himself. Like a gem strung upon a thread, or a bull tied by a nose-rope, a man follows the command of the Disposer, to whom he belongs and on whom he depends. Not self-directing, a man yields to some conjuncture of time, like a tree which has fallen from a river bank, and has reached the middle of the current. Ignorant, and powerless

* Compare the *Bhagavad Gîtâ* iii. 22. "There is nothing which I am bound to do, nor anything unobtained which I have yet to obtain; and yet I continue to act. 25. As the ignorant, who are devoted to action, do, so let the wise man also do, seeking to promote the benefit of the world."

to command his own pleasures and sufferings, he must go to heaven or hell, according as he is impelled by God. 1145. As the tips of grass are swayed by the blasts of a strong wind, so, too, all beings are subject to the Disposer. Impelling to noble action, and again to sinful deeds, God pervades all creatures, and it is not perceived that He is there. . . . 1153. Acting according to His pleasure, this Lord, associating them, or dissociating them, plays with living creatures as with a child's toys. The Disposer does not treat His creatures like a father or a mother, but acts angrily, as any other being like ourselves. 1155. Seeing noble, virtuous, and modest men in want, and ignoble men happy, I am,* as it were, agitated with perplexity; and perceiving this adversity of thine, and the prosperity of Suyodhana, I blame the Disposer, who regards you with an unequal eye. Bestowing good fortune on him who transgresses the rules of conduct observed by noble men, who is cruel, greedy, and a perverter of justice, what good end does the Disposer gain?"

[The same sentiments are expressed in the following fragment of Sophocles, No. 94 (in the edition of Dindorf); Stobæus iv. 31 (Ed. Meineke).

Δεινόν γε τοὺς μὲν δυσσεβεῖς κακῶν τ᾽ ἄπο
βλαστόντας εἶτα τούσδε μὲν πράσσειν καλῶς,
τοὺς δ᾽ ὄντας ἐσθλοὺς ἔκ τε γενναίων ἅμα
γεγῶτας, εἶτα δυστυχεῖς πεφυκέναι.
οὐ χρῆν τάδ᾽ οὕτω δαίμονας θνητῶν πέρι
πράσσειν· ἐχρῆν γὰρ τοὺς μὲν εὐσεβεῖς βροτῶν
ἔχειν τι κέρδος ἐμφανὲς θεῶν πάρα,
τοὺς δ᾽ ὄντας ἀδίκους τοῖσδε τὴν ἐναντίαν
δίκην κακῶν τιμωρὸν ἐμφανῆ τίνειν,
κοὐδεὶς ἂν οὕτως εὐτύχει κακὸς γεγώς.

"It is strange that those who are impious, and descendants of wicked men, should fare prosperously, while those who are good, and sprung from noble men, should be unfortunate. It was not meet that the gods should deal thus with mortals.

* I am indebted to Professor Aufrecht for suggesting the reading which gives this sense, viz., *vihvalāmiva* for *vihvalān iva*, which the Calcutta text of the M. Bh. has.

Pious men ought to have obtained from the gods some manifest advantage, while the unjust should, on the contrary, have paid some evident penalty for their evil deeds; and thus no one who was wicked would have been prosperous."

With verses 1140 ff. compare also Euripides' Supplices, verses 734 ff.:—

> ὦ Ζεῦ, τί δῆτα τοὺς ταλαιπώρους βροτοὺς
> φρονεῖν λέγουσι; σοῦ γὰρ ἐξηρτήμεθα,
> δρῶμέν τε τοιαῦθ' ἂν σὺ τυγχάνῃς θέλων.

"O Zeus, why do they say that wretched mortals are wise? For we are dependent upon thee, and do whatever thou happenest to will."]

YUDHISHTHIRA *replies*:—

1160. "I have heard, Yājnasenī (=Draupadī), the charming and amiable discourse, full of sparkling phrases, which thou hast spoken; but thou utterest infidel sentiments (*nâstikya*). I do not act from a desire to gain the recompense of my works. I give what I ought to give, and perform the sacrificial rites which I am bound to celebrate. Whether reward accrues to me or not, I do to the best of my power what a man should do, as if he were living at home. [The speaker is represented as being at the time in the forests.] . . . 1164. It is on duty alone that my thoughts are fixed, and this, too, naturally. The man who seeks to make of righteousness a gainful merchandize is low,* and the meanest of those who speculate about righteousness. The man who seeks to milk righteousness (*i.e.*, to extract from it all the advantage that he can) does not obtain its reward. . . . I say it authoritatively: do not doubt about righteousness: he who does so is on the way to be born as a brute. . . . 1171. Vyâsa, Vasishṭha, Maitreya, Nârada, Lomaśa, Śuka, and other sages are all wise through righteousness. For thou plainly seest these saints distinguished by a celestial intuition (*yoga*), able both to curse and to bless, and more important even than the

* *M. Bh.* xiii. 7595. "Those men are mere traffickers in righteousness who live by it."

gods. These men . . . in the beginning declared that righteousness was continually to be practised. Thou oughtest not, therefore, O fair queen, with erring mind to censure and to doubt the Deity and righteousness. . . . 1183. Righteousness and nothing else is the boat which conveys those who are on their way to heaven : it only is a ship like those on which merchants seek to cross the ocean. If righteousness, when practised, were without reward, this world would be plunged in bottomless darkness ; men would not attain to final tranquillity (*nirvāṇa*), would lead the life of brutes, would not addict themselves to learning, nor would any one attain the object of his desire. If austerity, continence, sacrifice, sacred study, liberality, honesty—if all these things brought no reward, men now, and others succeeding them, would not practise righteousness. If works were followed by no rewards, this state of things would be an exceeding delusion. Ṛishis, deities, Gandharvas, Asuras, and Râkshasas,—why should these lordly beings have reverenced and practised righteousness?* But knowing that the Deity was a bestower of rewards, unalterably attached to goodness, they practised righteousness; for that is the source of eternal blessedness. 1194. The award of recompense to works which are declared by revelation to be holy, and to such as are wicked, as well as the production and dissolution of the world,—these things are secrets of the gods. . . . 1196. These (secrets) of the gods are to be guarded; for the wonder-working power of the deities is mysterious. Brâhmans who have formed the desire, who are devoted to religious observances, whose sins have been burnt up by austerities, and who have a clear mental intuition, perceive these (secrets). No doubts must be entertained regarding righteousness, or the gods, merely because the recompense of works is not visible. . . . 1199. Wherefore let all thy doubts vanish as a vapour. . . . 1200. Be certain that all (this) is (so): abandon the state of disbelief (*nāstikya*). Do not censure God, the creator of living beings.

* This and what immediately precedes appears to be scarcely reconcilable with the indifference to the recompense of works which is inculcated in the earlier part of Yudhishṭhira's discourse.

Learn (to know) Him: reverence Him: let not thy opinion be such (as thou hast declared it). Do not contemn that most exalted (or, most excellent) Deity, through whose favour the mortal who is devoted to him attains to immortality." [Compare Æschylus, fragment 369 (Dindorf):—

Ἀνδρῶν γάρ ἐστιν ἐνδίκων τε καὶ σοφῶν
ἐν τοῖς κακοῖσι μὴ τεθυμῶσθαι θεοῖς.

"For it is the part of just and wise men when suffering misfortune not to be incensed against the gods."

In the Ion of Euripides, 1619 ff., the following sentiments are found:—

ὦ Διὸς Λητοῦς τ' Ἄπολλον, χαῖρ'· ὅτῳ δ' ἐλαύνεται
συμφοραῖς οἶκος, σέβοντα δαίμονας θαρσεῖν χρεών·
ἐς τέλος γὰρ οἱ μὲν ἐσθλοὶ τυγχάνουσιν ἀξίων,
οἱ κακοὶ δ', ὥσπερ πεφύκασ', οὔποτ' εὖ πράξειαν ἄν.

"Oh Apollo, son of Zeus and Leto, hail! And it becomes the man whose house is vexed with misfortunes to adore the gods, and take courage. For in the end the good obtain their due; but the wicked, as their nature requires, can never prosper."

In the Supplices of the same poet, verses 195 ff., Theseus is introduced as affirming the preponderance of good over evil in human life, as apparent both in the gifts of reason and speech which distinguish man from the lower animals, and in the support afforded to him by the fruits of the earth, in the means which he has of protection from heat and cold, in the exchange of products procured by foreign commerce, and finally in the supernatural aids obtained by divination; and then as asking, 214 ff.:—

ἆρ' οὐ τρυφῶμεν, θεοῦ κατασκευὴν βίῳ
δόντος τοιαύτην, οἷσιν οὐκ ἀρκεῖ τάδε;
ἀλλ' ἡ φρόνησις τοῦ θεοῦ μεῖζον σθένειν
ζητεῖ, τὸ γαῦρον δ' ἐν φρεσὶν κεκτημένοι,
δοκοῦμεν εἶναι δαιμόνων σοφώτεροι.

"Are we not, then, too fastidious, when we are not satisfied with all this provision which a god has made for our life?

But our reason seeks to be stronger than the god, and being possessed in our minds by conceit, we fancy that we are wiser than the deities."

I introduce here a passage of the highest interest from Plato, which, after stating that, from the nature of things, evil must always continue, gives that great writer's idea of the Deity, and inculcates the duty of men to strive to become like Him.

Theaetetus, section 84—'Αλλ' οὔτ' ἀπολέσθαι τὰ κακὰ δυνατόν, ὦ Θεόδωρε· ὑπεναντίον γάρ τι τῷ ἀγαθῷ ἀεὶ εἶναι ἀνάγκη· οὔτ' ἐν θεοῖς αὐτὰ ἱδρύσθαι, τὴν δὲ θνητὴν φύσιν καὶ τόνδε τὸν τόπον περιπολεῖ ἐξ ἀνάγκης. διὸ καὶ πειρᾶσθαί χρὴ ἐνθένδε ἐκεῖσε φεύγειν ὅτι τάχιστα. φυγὴ δὲ ὁμοίωσις θεῷ κατὰ τὸ δυνατόν. ὁμοίωσις δε δίκαιον καὶ ὅσιον μετὰ φρονήσεως γενέσθαι . . . θέὸς οὐδαμῇ οὐδαμῶς ἄδικος, ἀλλ' ώς οἷόν τε δικαιότατος, καὶ ούκ ἔστιν αὐτῳ ὁμοιότερον οὐδὲν ἢ ὃς ἂν ἡμῶν αὖ γένηται ὅτι δικαιότατος.

"Evils, Theodorus, can never perish; for there must always remain something which is antagonistic to good. Of necessity they hover around this mortal sphere and the earthly sphere, having no place among the gods in heaven. Wherefore, also, we ought to fly away thither, and to fly thither is to become like God as far as this is possible; and to become like Him is to become holy and just and wise. . . . In God is no unrighteousness at all—he is altogether righteous; and there is nothing more like him than he of us, who is the most righteous."—Dr JOWETT'S *Translation*, Vol. III., p. 400. (Comp. the passages cited in Prof. L. Campbell's edition of the Theaetetus).

A further passage from the same author may also be cited:

Republic ii. 18—οὐκουν ἀγαθὸς ὅ γε θεὸς τῷ ὄντι τε καὶ λεκ·έον οὕτως; Τί μήν; . . . Οὐδ' ἄρα, ἦν δ' ἐγώ, ὁ θεός, ἐπειδὴ ἀγαθός, πάντων ἂν εἴη αἴτιος, ὡς οἱ πολλοὶ λέγουσιν, ἀλλ' ὀλίγων μὲν τοῖς ἀνθρώποις αἴτιος, πολλῶν δὲ ἀναίτιος· πολὺ γὰρ ἐλάττω τἀγαθὰ τῶν κακῶν ἡμῖν. καὶ τῶν μὲν ἀγαθῶν οὐδένα ἄλλον αἰτιατέον, τῶν δὲ κακῶν ἄλλ' ἄττα δεῖ ζητεῖν τα αἴτια ἀλλ' οὐ τὸν θεόν.

"And is he [God] not truly good? And must he not be represented as such? Certainly . . . Then God, if he be good, is not the author of all things, as the many assert, but he is the cause of a few things only, and not of most things that occur to men; for few are the goods of human life, and many are the evils, and the good only is to be attributed to him; of the evil, other causes have to be discovered."—JOWETT, II., 203 f.]

DRAUPADI *replies* :—

"1202. I do not scorn, or think lightly of, righteousness; and how should I contemn God, the Lord of creatures? In my distress, I talk thus idly; understand me so: and I shall yet further lament. Do thou, who art kind, comprehend me." She then goes on to pronounce a long discourse, in which she acknowledges and enforces the value of action and exertion; denounces dependence on fate or on chance, though she does not appear to deny the influence of these causes (verses 1233 ff.); and affirms that a man's lot is the result of his works, *i.e.*, including those performed in a former birth. The following are some of the verses: "1222. For God, the Disposer, also determines his own acts according to this or that reason, allotting to men the recompenses of their previous works. Whatever act, good or bad, a human being performs, know that that is the realization, fixed by the Disposer, of the recompense of previous works. This (present) body is the cause of the Deity's action. Just as He impels it, so it acts submissively.* For the great God ordains (the man) to do such and such acts: He constrains all creatures to act, and they are helpless." Here the man seems to be represented as a mere machine, but the next verse says: "Having first of all fixed in his mind the objects at which he shall aim, a man of himself afterwards attains them by action, preceded by design: of this man is the cause."

VI. *M. Bh.* v. 916 f. "The Disposer (of events) brings under his control the good, the bad, the child, the old man,

---

* The commentator translates these words thus: "The existing body is the cause of the Deity's action. As it impels Him, He acts submissively:" and remarks that God and the body are mutually dependent; it, as the result of previous works, necessitating Him to determine the man's present lot.

the weak, the strong. And the Lord gives learning to the child, and childishness to the learned man, darting radiance before him." The last phrase (*purastāch chhukram uchcharan*) occurs in *M. Bh.* iii. 1139 (see above p. 201); v. 2751. See also v. 1739. Verses v. 1737 ff. are as follows: "That radiance, that great and shining light, that great renown, is worshipped by the gods; by it the sun shines. 1738. Devotees behold this eternal lord. 1739. From radiance Brahma is produced; through radiance Brahma is augmented. Among the lights, that radiance burns, unburnt, and glowing. . . . 1747. His form is not to be beheld; no one perceives him with the eye. Those who know him by the intellect, the mind, and the heart, they become immortal." See St Matthew xi. 25, and Kathāsaritsāgara li. 34.

VII. *M. Bh.* xii. 7058[b] f. "Unlearned men conceal the sin which they have committed knowingly. Men do not see the man; but the dwellers in heaven (the gods) behold him." iii. 13754. "When he has committed sin, a man will think, 'It is not I;' but the gods behold him, and his own inner man."

VIII. *Manu* viii. 84. "The soul (or self, *ātman*) is its own witness; the soul is its own refuge. Disregard not thy soul, which is the best (or highest) witness of men. 85. Sinners think 'no one sees us;' but the gods behold them, and their own inner man." 91. "Though, good man, thou thinkest of thyself, 'I am alone?' this sage (*muni*) residing in thy heart is a beholder of virtuous and sinful acts."

M. Bh. i. 3015. "Thou thinkest 'I am alone;' thou knowest not the ancient sage (*muni*) seated in thy heart, who is cognizant of sinful acts. In his presence thou committest sin." 3018. "Yama, the son of Vivasvat, puts away the sin of that man, the soul (*kshetrajna*) seated in whose heart as the witness of his actions, is satisfied; (3019) but punishes that sinner whose soul is not satisfied." Comp. *M. Bh.* xiii. 2382 f. (where it is said that the seasons, and day and night, see the secret sinner), and *Rāmāyaṇa*, iv. 18.15 (Bombay Edition).

IX. and X. *M. Bh.* v. 1251[b] f. "The rent which is covered over with unjustly gotten gains, becomes uncovered, and another is opened up. 1252[b] f. A teacher corrects the intelligent; a king corrects the wicked; Yama, the son of Vivasvat, corrects secret sinners."

XI. *M. Bh.* xii. 2791. "When sin," says Kaśyapa, "is committed by wicked men, then, O Aila, this god Rudra is born. The wicked by their sins generate Rudra; and he then destroys both good and bad." 2792. Aila says: "Whence comes Rudra? Or of what nature is Rudra? A creature is seen to be slain by creatures. Declare to me all this, O Kaśyapa, from what this god Rudra is born." 2793. Kaśyapa answers: "The self in the heart of man is Rudra; it slays each its own and others' bodies. They declare that Rudra resembles the hurricane; his form is like the celestial (?) clouds" (*devair jīmūtaiḥ*).

In this passage we find a rationalistic account of the origin of Rudra the destroyer, who seems to be represented as nothing else than the natural and inevitable retribution which follows men's sins. See, however, the commentator's remarks quoted below. Another apparent instance of rationalizing, which may not, however, be seriously meant, occurs in Manu ix. 301 f., and Mahābhārata xii. 2674 ff., 2693, and 3408, where it is stated that the four Yugas or great mundane periods (which are represented as differing in regard to the physical and moral condition of the men who lived in each of them,—the first being the most highly blest in these respects, while the others undergo a gradual declension), are really only names for the better or worse character of the king, on which the welfare of his subjects depends. I translate the essential verses of the Mahābhārata xii. 2674: "Either the king causes the time, or the time causes the king. Doubt not as to this alternative; the king causes the time. When the king completely fulfils the duties of criminal justice, then the Kṛita Age, a product of time, exists." This principle is next applied to the other three Yugas (or ages). It is then said, v. 2693: "The king is the creator of the Kṛita, Tretā, and Dvāpara ages, and the cause of the fourth (the Kali)." The same idea is afterwards repeated in v. 3408 (= Manu ix. 301): "The Kṛita, the Tretā, the Dvāpara, and the Kali Yugas (ages), are modes of a king's action; for it is the king who is denoted by the word Yuga." The commentator on Manu ix. 302 says, however, that that verse (which declares that the king is one or other of the Yugas, according to the character of his action), is merely designed to intimate that a king ought to be intent upon the performance of his duties; and not to deny the real existence of the four Yugas (ages).

The commentator thus remarks on the verses before us: "'Rudra' means '*hinsra*,' 'destructive;' 'god' means 'king;' 'Rudra' (further on, in the accusative) means the 'Kali' age. To the question whence arises the king's destructive character (*Rudratva*), he replies in the words, 'The self,' &c. It is the self (or soul, '*ātman*'), the living principle (*jīva*), in the heart of men, which is (or becomes) Rudra, the destroyer. And just as the body of a person possessed by an evil spirit is not the property of the owner of that body, but at the time of the possession is the property of the spirit possessing it, just so at the time of his being possessed by Rudra, the king's body belongs to, or takes the character of, Rudra (*Raudram bhavati*). Then in reply to the enquiry whence is it that the tranquil self (or soul) takes the character of Rudra? he answers in the words, 'The hurricane,' &c. As the hurricane in the air drives hither and thither the cloud-goddess residing in the air, makes her thunder, and causes lightnings, thunderbolts, and rain-falls to be manifested from her, just so the passions of desire, anger, &c., which spring from the soul, impel the life (or spirit) springing from the soul, to commit every sort of destructive act."

XII. *M. Bh.* v. 1222. "The gods do not, like cattle-herds, guard men by carrying a club; but they endow with understanding him whom they wish to preserve." M. Bh. ii. 2679. (= v. 1175). "The man for whom the gods are preparing defeat, is deprived by them of understanding; he sees everything pervertedly. 2680. When his understanding has become dimmed, and destruction approaches, folly, taking the guise of prudence, does not depart from his heart; (2681) and hurtful things with the appearance of advantages, and advantages under the guise of hurtful things, rise up for his destruction: and this (delusion) pleases him. 2682. Time (destiny) does not lift up a staff and strike off anyone's head. The power of time is this, that it shows things in a perverted shape."

With verse 2679, compare the Latin adage: *Quos Deus vult perdere prius dementat.* "God deprives of reason those whom he wishes to destroy." The same thought is stated in the following Greek lines, quoted by Grotius in his "Annotationes" on the Epistle to the Romans xi. 8:—

ὅταν γὰρ ὀργὴ δαιμόνων βλάπτῃ τινά,
τούτῳ τὸ πρῶτον ἐξαφαιρεῖται φρενῶν
τὸν νοῦν τὸν ἐσθλόν, εἰς δὲ τὴν χείρω τρέπει
γνώμην, ἵν' εἰδῇ μηδὲν ὧν ἁμαρτάνει.

"For when the wrath of the deities smites a man, it first deprives his mind of its good understanding, and turns him to a worse way of thinking, that he may know nothing of the things in which he errs."

The two following passages are quoted by Dr A. Nauck in a note on the Œdipus Coloneus of Sophocles, v. 800 f.:

Iliad, xix. 137. ἀασάμην καί μευ φρένας ἐξέλετο Ζεύς.

"I acted foolishly, and Zeus deprived me of reason."

And from an anonymous writer:—

ὅταν δ' ὁ δαίμων ἀνδρὶ πορσύνῃ κακά,
τὸν νοῦν ἔβλαψε πρῶτον.

"But when the god brings evil upon a man, he first injures his understanding." Compare Epistle to the Romans xi. 8, and Exodus vii. 1 ff.: "And the LORD said unto Moses, . . . 3. And I will harden Pharaoh's heart, and multiply my signs and wonders in the land of Egypt. 4. But Pharaoh shall not hearken unto you, that I may lay mine hand upon Egypt, &c." See also 1 Samuel ii. 25: "Notwithstanding they (Eli's sons) hearkened not unto the voice of their father, because the LORD would slay them."

See also Odyssey, xxiii. 10 ff:

> Τὴν δ' αὖτε προσέειπε περίφρων Πηνελόπεια·
> μαῖα φίλη, μάργην σε θεοὶ θέσαν οἵ τε δύνανται
> ἄφρονα ποιῆσαι καὶ ἐπίφρονά περ μάλ' ἐόντα,
> καί τε χαλιφρονέοντα σαοφροσύνης ἐπέβησαν.
> οἵ σέ περ ἔβλαψαν· πρὶν δὲ φρένας αἰσίμη ἦσθα.

"Her again the wise Penelope addressed: 'Dear nurse, the gods have made thee mad,—they who are able to render foolish even one who is very wise, and have made reasonable one who was silly: they have deprived thee of reason; bnt formerly thou wast sound in mind.'"

XIII. *M. Bh.* v. 1451.—"That gain which brings loss is not to be highly esteemed; but the loss which brings gain is to be greatly valued, even though it be a loss. 1452. The loss which brings gain is no loss; but that acquisition which occasions great destruction is to be esteemed a loss."

Compare the fragment of Menander's Koniazomenai, page 102, Ed. Meineke.

> Ὥστε μηδεὶς πρὸς θεῶν
> πράττων κακῶς λίαν ἀθυμήσῃ ποτέ.
> ἴσως γὰρ ἀγαθοῦ τοῦτο πρόφασις γίνεται.

"So let no one despond too much, when evil is allotted to him by the gods; for perhaps this becomes an occasion of good."

Plato, Republic, x. 6:—*Λέγει που ὁ νόμος ὅτι κάλλιστον ὅτι μάλιστα ἡσυχίαν ἄγειν ἐν ταῖς ξυμφοραῖς καὶ μὴ ἀγανακτεῖν, ὡς οὔτε δήλου ὄντος τοῦ ἀγαθοῦ τε καὶ κακοῦ τῶν τοιούτων, οὔτε εἰς τὸ πρόσθεν οὐδὲν προβαῖνον τῷ χαλεπῶς φέροντι, οὔ τέ τι τῶν ἀνθρωπίνων ἄξιον ὂν μεγάλης σπουδῆς, ὅ τε δεῖ ἐν αὐτοῖς ὅτι τάχιστα παραγίγνεσθαι ἡμῖν, τούτῳ ἐμποδὼν γιγνόμενον τὸ λυπεῖσθαι.*

"The law would say that to be patient under suffering is best, and that we should not give way to impatience, as there is no knowing whether such things are good or evil; and nothing is gained by impatience; also, because no human thing is of serious importance, and grief stands in the way of that which, at the moment, is most required."—*Jowett*, Vol. II., p. 446.

I quote here a passage from the Phaedrus of the same author, section 147:—Ὦ φίλε Πάν τε καὶ ἄλλοι ὅσοι τῇδε θεοί δοίητέ μοι καλῷ γενέσθαι τἄνδοθεν· ἔξωθεν δὲ ὅσα ἔχω, τοῖς ἐντὸς εἶναί μοι φίλια. πλούσιον δὲ νομίζοιμι τὸν σοφόν. τὸ δὲ χρυσοῦ πλῆθος εἴη μοι ὅσον μήτε φέρειν μήτε ἄγειν δύναιτ' ἄλλος ἢ σώφρων.

"Beloved Pan, and all ye other gods who haunt this place, give me beauty in the inward soul; and may the outward and inward man be at one. May I reckon the wise to be the wealthy, and may I have such a quantity of gold as none but the temperate man can carry."—*Jowett*, Vol. I., p. 615.

In the Phoenissæ of Euripides the following sentiment occurs (vv. 555 ff.); which I cite for its excellence, though there is nothing corresponding to it in the Sanskrit passage.

Οὔτοι τὰ χρήματ' ἴδια κέκτηνται βροτοί,
τὰ τῶν θεῶν δ' ἔχοντες ἐπιμελούμεθα.
ὅταν δὲ χρῄζωσ', αὔτ' ἀφαιροῦνται πάλιν.

"For mortals possess no goods of their own, but we hold as stewards things which belong to the gods; and when they require them, they take them away again."

XIV. *M. Bh.* iii. 87.—"Wealth brings loss to some men; and the man devoted to the good derived from wealth does not find good." xii. 3885.—"Hurtful things take the appearance of advantages, and advantages of things hurtful; for in the case of some men the loss of wealth is a benefit." The first part of this maxim appears also in M. Bh., ii. 2681.

Compare the hymn of Kleanthes to Zeus, vv. 18 ff.:—

Ἀλλὰ σὺ καὶ τὰ περισσὰ ἐπίστασαι ἄρτια θεῖναι,
καὶ κοσμεῖν τὰ ἄκοσμα καὶ οὐ φίλα σοὶ φίλα ἐστίν·
ὧδε γὰρ εἰς ἓν πάντα συνήρμοκας ἐσθλὰ κακοῖσιν,
ὥσθ' ἕνα γίγνεσθαι πάντων λόγον αἰὲν ἐόντων.—κ. τ. λ.

"But thou knowest also to make even the things that are uneven, and to order what is disordered; and the things that are not dear are dear to thee. For so hast thou combined all good things into one with the bad, that there is but one reason [or, account, to be given] of all things ever existing, &c."

XV. *M. Bh.* v. 1155.—"Considering loss as gain, and gain as loss, a foolish man, whose senses are not subdued, regards as happiness what is his great misery."

XVI. *M. Bh.* vii. 429.—"When men are ripe for slaughter, even straws turn into thunderbolts."

XVII. *M. Bh.* xiii. 7607.—"A man whose time of death has not yet come, does not die, though pierced by hundreds of arrows; while he whose time has arrived, if touched only with the point of a straw, does not live." *Mārkaṇḍeya Purāṇa*, ii. 49 f.—"The life of a man, whether he is keeping out of the way, or fighting, endures so long as Providence has ordained before, not so long as he desires in his mind. Some die in their houses, others when flying, others when eating food and drinking water; others in the midst of health and enjoyment, and wounded by no weapons, are overcome by the King of the dead. Others devoted to austerities are carried off by his servants. Others bent upon contemplation have not attained exemption from death."

Compare Æschylus, fragment 299 (Ed., Dindorf):

> *'Αλλ' οὔτε πολλὰ τραύματ' ἐν στέρνοις λαβὼν*
> *θνήσκει τις, εἰ μὴ τέρμα συντρέχοι βίου,*
> *οὔτ' ἐν στέγῃ τις ἥμενος παρ' ἑστίᾳ*
> *φεύγει τι μᾶλλον τὸν πεπρωμένον μόρον.*

"For neither does any one die, although he has received many wounds in his breast, unless the end of his life coincides; nor does any one sitting in his house by the hearth, on that account any more escape his allotted fate."

XVIII. *Hitopadeśa* i. 171 (or 189).* "He by whom swans are made white, and parrots green, and peacocks variegated, will provide thy subsistence."

Compare Matthew vi. 25 ff.

XIX. *Vṛiddha Chāṇakya* x. 17. "What fear is there for my life if the all-nourishing Vishṇu is hymned? otherwise, how

* When here and elsewhere alternative figures are given, different editions are referred to.

has he provided for the life of the infant the milk of its mother? So reflecting continually, O Lord of the Yadus, and husband of Lakshmī, I ever spend my time in doing homage to thy lotus-feet."

Hitopadeśa i. 170 (or 188). "Let no one labour overmuch for his livelihood; for this is furnished by the Creator. When the child has left the womb, its mother's breasts flow (with milk)."

The same idea occurs elsewhere.

Śārṅgadharaś Paddhati, Santoshapraśansā 6. "Shall he who, while I was in the womb, prepared milk for my support, be asleep or dead in providing for my future support?"

Kavitaratnākara 101. "Let a wise man think on his duty, not on his sustenance; for the sustenance of men is born with their birth."

XX. *M. Bh.* iii. 13461 ff., 13463ᵇ. "Neither this world, nor the next, nor happiness, is the portion of the doubter. Old men possessed of knowledge have said that faith is the sign of final liberation. . . . Forsaking fruitless reasonings, resort to the Veda (*Śruti*) and the Smṛiti."

But it is allowed that the Veda does not regulate everything; *M. Bh.* xii. 4035 (compare viii. 3455 ff.) *Śrutir dharmaḥ iti hy eke nety āhur apare janāh: nacha tat pratyasuyāmo na hi sarvam vidhīyate.* "The Veda (declares what) is duty: so say some; 'not so,' say others; and we do not find fault with that, for everything is not prescribed (in it)."

XXI. *M. Bh.* xii. 6736 ff. "I was a would-be Pandit, (learned man) a rationalist, a contemner of the Vedas (Indian scriptures considered inspired), fond of logic, the useless science of reasoning, an utterer of reasoned propositions, a propounder of arguments in assemblies, a reviler and abuser of Brahmans in theological discussions, an unbeliever, an universal doubter, a fool, who plumed myself on being a Pandit (learned man). The recompence which I have earned by this career is that I have been born as a jackal. But perhaps it may yet happen that, hundreds of days and nights hence, I shall be born again as a man; and then contented and alert, devoted to the practice of sacrifice, of liberality, and of self-restraint, I shall seek to know (only) what is to be known, and avoid all that is to be avoided."

It will be seen from the preceding verses that the requirements of Indian orthodoxy are no less stringent than those of some other religions. The words are part of an address of the god Indra, who had taken the form of a jackal, to the sage Kāśyapa, in which various topics, not all very closely connected with each other, are touched upon, and which concludes with the jackal giving the account of himself which I quote. At the end of the address the sage is struck with the wisdom of the speaker, and by supernatural intuition discovers that it is Indra who has been talking to him; and if the story is part of a consecutive speech of Indra, it might seem that, in consonance with the recognised doctrine of transmigrations, the god had first been a man, and then, in consequence of his infidelity, had been reborn as a jackal, as a punishment. This, however, may not be so, and in any case the introduction of Indra makes no difference as to the lesson sought to be conveyed, which is meant as a warning to men.

XXII. *M. Bh.* xiii. 2194 ff; xii. 2980. "The opinion that the Vedas possess no authority, the transgression of the Śāstras, and an universal lawlessness—(these things) are the destruction of a man's self. The Brahman who fancies himself a Pandit (learned man), and who reviles the Vedas, who is devoted to the science of reasoning, useless logic, who utters argumentative speeches among good men, who is a victorious wrangler, who continually insults and abuses Brahmans, who is an universal sceptic and deluded—such a man, however sharp in his speech, is to be regarded as a child. He is looked upon as a dog. Just as a dog assails to bark and to kill, so such a man aims at talking, and at destroying all the Śāstras (scriptures)."

Whatever conclusion might have been drawn from such passages as the preceding, it is a fact that the Brahmans of old were by no means indisposed to argumentative discussions; but, on the contrary, seem to have made a practice of indulging in them on important occasions when they met in large numbers. This is shown by two passages from the Rāmāyaṇa, i. 14, 19 (Bombay edition), and the Mahābhārata, xiv. 2536, where it is said, in similar terms, that during the Aśvamedhas (horse-sacrifices) celebrated, in the one case by Daśaratha, and in the other by Yudhishṭhira, "wise and eloquent Brahmans, eager for victory, engaged in argumentative discussions about the reasons of things."

It was only when the authority of the Vedas was called in question, or anything decidedly heretical, or adverse to their own high caste pretensions (though in this last respect the Mahābhārata itself is often unorthodox), was asserted, that the Brahmans took the alarm, and sought to silence argument.]

XXIII. *Naishadha Charita* xvii. 45.—These words form part of the speech of a Chārvāka, or Materialistic Atheist, who is represented as addressing Indra and other gods on their return to heaven from Damayantī's Svayamvara. He assails the authority of the Vedas when they affirm that sacrifice is followed by any rewards, denies that men's good and bad actions are recompensed in another world; recommends unbridled sensual indulgence; says that adultery has the example of the gods in its favour; and throws ridicule on the orthodox Indian doctrines. The following are the verses which have been metrically rendered. 45. "The Veda teaches that when men die, pains result from their sin, and pleasures from their holy acts. The very reverse, however, is, manifestly, the immediate consequence of those deeds. Declare, therefore, the strong and weak points (in this controversy)." 77. "If there is an omniscient and merciful God, who never speaks in vain, why does he not by the mere expenditure of a word satisfy the desires of us his suppliants? 78. By causing living creatures to suffer pain, though it be the result of their own works, God would be our causeless enemy, whilst all our other enemies have some reason or other for their enmity." 74. "When the Vedantists say that in our mundane existence both a man's self and Brahma exist, but that after final emancipation, Brahma alone remains, and when they thus define that state as the extinction of one's self; is this not a great piece of cleverness?"

The Chārvāka is briefly answered by the four Deities, Indra, Agni, Yama, and Varuṇa.

For an account of the Chārvāka system, see Prof. Cowell's edition of Mr Colebrooke's Essays, Vol. I., pp. 426 ff., and 456 ff.

XXIV. *Rāmāyaṇa* ii. 108. 1. "When Rāma who understood duty, had thus consoled Bharata, Jābāli the eminent Brahman addressed to him these immoral words:—Well, descendant of Raghu, do not thou, who art noble in sentiments and austere in character, entertain, like a common man, this useless idea. What man is a kinsman of any other? What relationship has any one with another? A man is born alone and dies alone. Hence he who is attached to any one as his father or his mother is to be regarded as if he were insane, for no one belongs to another. 5. Just as a man going to another village abides outside, and next day leaving that abode proceeds on his journey; so father, mother, home, property, are only men's resting places. Good men are not attached to them. Thou oughtest not to abandon thy father's kingdom and stay (here) in a sad and miserable abode attended with many trials. Cause thyself to be inaugurated king in the wealthy Ayodhyā. That city, with its hair in one braid (as a sign of mourning for thine absence) expects thee. Tasting excellent royal enjoyments, take thy pleasure in Ayodhyā, as Śakra (Indra) in heaven. 10. Daśaratha is nothing to thee, or thou to him; the king is one, and thou another; do, therefore what is said. . . . 12. The king has gone whither he had to go. Such is the course of creatures' lives, but thou art wrongly ruined. I pity those men, and them alone who are devoted to (wealth* and?) righteousness; for they suffer here, and after death they perish. Men offer oblations to the Manes on prescribed days; but see what a waste of food! for

* The reading of the Bombay edition is *artha-dharma-paraḥ*, of which it is not easy to make any sense. Gorresio's edition has *atha* 'now,' in place of *artha*, 'wealth.'

what can a dead man eat? 15. If what is eaten by one here enters into the body of another, let Śrâddhas be offered to those who are travelling; they need not get food to eat on their journey." [This idea is repeated in verses quoted in the Sarva-darśana-sangraha, p. 6, Bibl. Ind.; and the further question is asked:—"Since men in heaven are satiated by these offerings, why are they not given (by those below) to people upon the roof of the house?"] 16. "These books (which enjoin men to) sacrifice, give, consecrate themselves, practise austerities, and forsake the world, are composed by clever men to induce others to bestow gifts." [*Vishṇu Purāṇa*, iii. 18.30. "Authoritative words do not, O great Asuras, fall from heaven. Let me, and others like yourselves, embrace whatever assertion is supported by reason." See Dr Hall's edition of Wilson's Vishṇu Purāṇa, Vol. iii., pp. 205-213.] "Believe, O wise Râma, that there is no hereafter. Adhere to what is apparent to the senses, and reject what is invisible." . . . . "This world is the next world; do thou therefore enjoy pleasure, for every virtuous man does not gain it. Virtuous men are greatly distressed, while the unrighteous are seen to be happy."* [The next lines are from the Sarva-darśana-sangraha, p. 6:—"While a man lives, let him live happily; let him borrow money and drink clarified butter; there is no return of the body when once it has been reduced to ashes."]

ii. 109. 1. "Hearing these words of Jābâli, Râma, who was strong by truth, uttered excellent words in a contrary sense:—The words which you have addressed to me, though they recommend what seems to be right and salutary, advise in fact the contrary. The sinful transgressor, who lives according to the rules of heretical systems, obtains no esteem from good men. It is good conduct that marks a man to be noble, or ignoble, heroic, or a pretender to manliness, as pure or impure. 5. But ignoble men look like noble, impure look like pure, men without good characteristics, as if they possessed them, bad men as good. If under the garb of virtue I were to practise vice, occasioning confusion of classes,

* These last bracketed lines are from Gorresio's Edition.

forsaking what is good, and acting contrary to rule, what sensible man who knows right and wrong would hold me in much esteem, when I was wicked in conduct and a corrupter of mankind? Following such a course and departing from my promise, whose conduct should I imitate (?) or how should I attain to heaven? The whole world devoted to pleasure follows in train. (?) Such as is the conduct of kings, the same is that of their subjects. 10. Truth and mercy are immemorial characteristics of a king's conduct. Hence royal rule is in its essence truth; on truth the world is based. Both ṛishis (sages) and gods have esteemed truth. The man who speaks truth in this world attains the highest imperishable state. Men shrink with fear and horror from a liar, as from a serpent. In this world the chief element in virtue is truth; it is called the basis of everything. Truth is lord in the world; virtue always rests on truth. All things are founded on truth; nothing is higher than it. Gifts, sacrifices, oblations, self-inflicted pains, and austerities, the Vedas, are founded on truth; wherefore a man should be devoted to truth. 15. A man singly protects the world, singly he protects his family, singly he is plunged into hell, and singly he is glorified in heaven. Why then should I not be true to my promise, and faithfully observe the truthful injunction given by my father? Neither through covetousness, nor delusion, nor ignorance, will I, overpowered by darkness, break through the barrier of truth, but remain true to my promise to my father. . . , . 24. How shall I, having promised to him that I would thus reside in the forest, transgress his injunction, and do what Bharata recommends?" After Rāma had added more, Jābāli rejoins:—38. "I do not utter infidel words, nor am I an infidel, nor does nothing exist. Regarding the fit time, I have again become a believer; and at a suitable time I shall again become an atheist. And this time has now gradually arrived: just as infidel sentiments were uttered by me on thine account to stop (thine intention), I have said this to appease thee."

XXV. *Rāmāyaṇa* vi. 83, 14 ff. (Bombay ed. and vi. 62, 15 ff. Gorr.) "Useless virtue cannot, my noble brother, deliver thee from misfortunes, though thou walkest in a hallowed path, and controllest thy senses. 15. Virtue is not visible, as are created things, whether stationary or moving: hence my opinion is that it has no existence. . . . 17. Did unrighteousness really exist, Rāvaṇa would sink to hell; and thou, who art righteous, wouldst not suffer calamity. 18. But since he suffers no evil, whilst thou art afflicted by calamity, it results that righteousness and unrighteousness mutually conflict, *i.e.* (according to the commentator), are in their fruits opposed (to what is revealed regarding them)." [The corresponding verse in Gorresio's edition is clearer. "Since he suffers no evil, whilst thou art involved in calamity, by righteousness I understand unrighteousness, and by unrighteousness righteousness]." . . . 21. "Inasmuch as those men who are settled in unrighteousness increase in prosperity, whilst the virtuous are afflicted, virtue and vice have no effect (or, as Gorresio's edition has it, virtue is useless). (21. Gorresio's edition.—If men pure in their acts are smitten by unrighteousness, then righteousness is smitten by unrighteousness, and, being smitten, what can it do?) . . . 43. Arise, thou man-tiger, long-armed, resolute in purpose. Why dost thou not recognise thyself as high-souled?"

XXVI. *M. Bh.* iii. 17402. "Reasoning has no proper basis; Vedic texts are at variance with each other; there is no one muni (sage) whose doctrine is authoritative; the essence of virtue is enveloped in mystery; the (proper) path is that which the many follow."

XXVII. *M. Bh.* xii. 12078. "Before thou art carried away dead to the Ender, by the royal command of Yama, by his dreadful (messengers), strive after rectitude. Before the impassive lord Yama, whom none can oppose, snatches away thy life with its roots and kinships; 12080. Before the wind which precedes him blows, before thou art carried away, practise preparation for death. Before this destroying wind blows upon thee, before the four quarters of the sky whirl round, when great fears come upon thee, and before thy hearing is closed, as thou goest away, confounded, practise the most perfect contemplation. Before thou recollectest with anguish thy former good and bad deeds full of folly, appropriate the only treasure. Before decay wears away thy body, and carries off thy strength, thy limbs and thy beauty, appropriate the only treasure. 12085. Before Death, conveyed by his charioteer Disease, violently dissolves thy body, and ends thy life, practise great austerity. Before the fearful wolves which dwell in men's bodies rush on thee from every side, strive after holiness. Before, all alone, thou beholdest the darkness, make haste, before thou seest the golden trees on the mountain summit. Before evil associates and foes that look like friends, pervert thy views, seek what is highest. 12089. Amass that wealth which has nothing to fear from kings or thieves, and which does not desert thee in death. 12090. (See also v. 12101). There there is no division of goods according to each person's deeds; everyone enjoys his own individual property. Give that by which men live in the next world; amass thyself that wealth which is imperishable. (Do not delay?) until the pottage of the multitude is cooked; while it is yet uncooked, make haste before thou diest. Neither mother, nor children, nor kinsmen, nor dear familiar friends follow a man in his straits; he departs alone. The deeds alone, good or bad, which he has formerly done, are his fellow-travellers when he goes to the next world. 12095. The collections of gold and gems which he has made, by good or evil means, do not help him when his body is dissolved. When thou goest thither there is no witness of the deeds which thou hast or hast not done, equal to thine own self. . . . 12100[b]. (On the road) where there are many enemies, and where there are dreadful insects, guard thine own works. A man's works accompany the doer. 12102. As the bands of Apsarases (celestial nymphs) obtain as a reward enjoyment along with the great sages, so do men gain the fruits of their works, moving about at will on celestial cars. On the bridges of the duties of householders they attain the highest condition, and reside in the same world as Prajāpati, as Vṛihaspati, as Indra. 12106. Thy twenty-fourth year has passed, thou art certainly twenty-five years old; amass righteousness; for thy life is passing away."

With verse 12089 above, compare what Cicero says, Paradox. vi. 3.—"Quanti est estimanda virtus, quæ nec eripi, nec surripi potest unquam; neque naufragio, neque incendio amittitur; nec tempestatum, nec temporum permutatione mutatur? Qua prædití qui sunt, soli sunt divites." "At what a rate ought virtue to be esteemed, which can neither be taken away nor stolen; nor can we lose it by shipwreck or fire; nor is it to be changed by the change of seasons or of time? Those who possess it alone are rich." Ramage's beautiful thoughts from Latin authors, p. 49. Partly quoted also in Wuestemann's Promptuarium Sententiarum, p. 88, and Hartung's Sententiarum Liber, p. 189.

XXVIII. *Manu* viii. 17; and iv. 239 ff.—These verses have been already metrically translated in my Orig. Sanskrit Texts, i. 380; and are thus rendered by Sir W. Jones, viii. 17; "The only firm friend who follows men even after death is justice; all others are extinct with the body." iv. 239 ff. "For in his passage to the next world, neither his father nor his mother, nor his wife, nor his son, nor his kinsman, will remain in his company—his virtue alone will adhere to him. 240. Single is each man born; single he dies;* single he receives the reward of his good, and single the punishment of his evil deeds. 241. When he leaves † his corse, like a log or a lump of clay, on the ground, his kindred retire with averted faces; but his virtue accompanies his soul. 242. Continually, therefore, by degrees, let him collect virtue, for the sake of securing an inseparable companion; since with virtue for his guide he will traverse a gloom, how hard to be traversed!"

The same idea is repeated in the 13th book of the Mahabharata vv. 5405 ff., and is briefly alluded to in the Mārkaṇḍeya Purāṇa, i. 7. 28. See also Mbh. i. 654; v. 1547 ff.

My attention has been drawn by Professor E. B. Cowell to two passages—the one in Sophocles and the other in Euripides

---

* Je mourrai seul.—*Pascal.*

† This should be rendered: "Leaving his corse," &c., "his kindred retire," &c.

—the first of which, if the text be genuine, appears to convey the same idea as in Manu. It is in the Philoctetes, 1443:—

ἡ γὰρ εὐσέβεια συνθνήσκει βροτοῖς,
κἂν ζῶσι κἂν θάνωσιν, οὐκ ἀπόλλυται.

"For piety dies with men; and whether they live or die, it does not perish." The first only of these lines is retained as it stands, in the text, by Wunder. Dindorf has put both, along with a preceding line, within brackets as spurious. Nauck considers these two lines as spurious, as he thinks that a negative is required in the first of them to make it coincide in sense with the second; and in support of this view he quotes the passage about to be cited from Euripides. If the words of the first line, as they stand, are genuine, they seem to give the same sense as Manu, that piety accompanies men in death. In Professor Lewis Campbell's metrical translation, the two lines, with the one preceding them, are rendered as follows:—

"For our great Father counteth piety
Far above all. This follows men in death,
And faileth not when they resign their breath."

The passage of Euripides is, in Dindorf's Edition, fragment No. 1 of the Temenidae:—

Ἀρετὴ δὲ κἂν θάνῃ τις, οὐκ ἀπόλλυται,
ζῇ δ' οὐκέτ' ὄντος σώματος· κακοῖσι δὲ
ἅπαντα φροῦδα συνθανόνθ' ὑπὸ χθονός.

"But virtue does not perish even if a man dies, but lives, though the body no longer exists; but to the bad all things disappear, dying with them, beneath the earth."

XXIX. *M. Bh.* xii. 12047. Vyāsa says to his son.—"Follow righteousness, my son, holding thy senses always under control, vanquish sharp cold and heat, hunger and thirst and wind. 12048. Maintain, according to rule, truth, rectitude, patience, an unenvious temper, self-restraint, austerity; and abstain from destroying life and from cruelty. . . . 12050. Seeing that thy spirit abides like a bird in a body which resembles mere foam, why sleepest thou, my son, in this dear abode, which is so transitory? 12051. When thy foes are awake and alert, and continually observant, and seeking some assailable point in thee, art thou not watchful, thou foolish youth? 12052. Since thy days are being numbered, and thine age is wearing away, and thy life is being written down, dost thou not rise and flee? 12053. Men cling to this world's bonds of flesh and blood, and are asleep as regards the concerns of the next world, and very infidels. 12054. That man suffers distress who follows those who hate righteousness, who are deluded, and pursue a wrong road. 12055. Attend upon, and enquire of, those great and powerful men who delight to follow the scriptures, and who have entered on the path of righteousness. 12056. Pondering the opinion of the wise who have an intuition into righteousness, control with thy best intelligence thy disposition to go astray. 12057. Foolish men who are fearless, because they regard to-day only and think to-morrow is far off, eating everything, do not perceive the opportunity of performing good works. Standing upon the ladder of righteousness, mount up by degrees. Thou dost not perceive that thou art enveloping thyself like a silk-worm.* 12059 (= 12118). Confidently cast aside, like a reed rooted out, the infidel who breaks down all barriers, and who is as the degrader of his race. 12060. Cross over the evils of existence, which are hard to overpass, over desire, anger, death, the river whose waters are the five senses, having constructed the boat of patience (compare v. 8623 bf.) 12061. The world being smitten by death, and distressed by decay, and the unfailing (nights) ever succeeding, cross over on the bark of righteousness. 12062. Since death hastens after the man who is standing and him who is lying, being suddenly destroyed by it, from what can he obtain happiness? 12063 (= 12505). Death carries him off as a wolf a sheep, when he is gathering, and is unsatisfied with, the objects of his desire. 12064. Hold firmly fast the lamp of the knowledge of righteousness, whose

---

* See v. 12449 f., where the same image is more fully stated. "Dost thou not perceive that thou art through delusion enveloping thyself in many threads coming out of thyself, wrapping thyself round like a silkworm? Farewell to all attachments, for attachment is faulty; the silkworm is bound by what it throws round itself." See also Bhâg. Pur. vi. i. 52.

flames have been gradually gathered; for thou must enter into the darkness."

xii. 12453. "Family, children, and wife, body, and amassed wealth,—all these things are strange to us. What is our own? Our good and bad deeds. 12454. Since thou must abandon all and depart without power of resistance, why art thou attached to that which is valueless, and dost not seek thine own proper good? 12455. How shalt thou travel alone that road through the wilderness of gloom, where thou shalt find no repose, no support, no provisions, and no guide? 12456. No one shall walk behind thee when thou hast set out; thy good and thy evil deeds shall follow thee as thou goest.

XXX. *M. Bh.* xi. 116.—"Deluded by avarice, anger, fear, a man does not understand himself. He plumes himself upon his high birth, contemning those who are not well born; and overcome by the pride of wealth, he reviles the poor. He calls others fools and does not look to himself. He blames the faults of others, but does not govern himself. When the wise and the foolish, the rich and the poor, the noble and the ignoble, the proud and the humble, have departed to the cemetery and all sleep there, their troubles at an end, and their bodies are stripped of flesh, little else than bones, united by tendons, other men then perceive no difference between them, (anything) whereby they could recognise a distinction of birth or of form. Seeing that all sleep, deposited together in the earth, why do men (now) foolishly seek to treat each other injuriously? He who, after hearing this admonition, acts in conformity therewith from his birth onwards, shall attain the highest blessedness."

XXXI. *M. Bh.* xii. 3892.—"Either, O king, a man must needs leave his wealth, or his wealth must leave a man. What wise man would lament this?"

XXXII. *M. Bh.* xii. 6526 ff (=9932 ff.*); 8307 ff.—The son asks: "What should a wise man, who knows (the proper course

* The second of these two passages is nearly, but not entirely, a repetition of the first.

of action), do? for the life of men quickly passes away; tell me, O father, correctly and in order, how I should practise duty. The father replies: after reading the Vedas, my son, as a student, then seek for sons to hallow the fathers. Then kindle the fires, and offer the proper sacrifices; and at last entering the forests, seek to become a Muni. Son: When the world is so smitten, and on every side distressed, and when the unfailing ones ever recur, dost thou speak like a wise man? Father: How is the world smitten and on every side distressed? Who are the unfailing ones? Why dost thou seem to alarm me? Son: 6530(=9936). The world is smitten by death, and distressed by decay: the days and nights recur. How dost thou not comprehend? The unfailing nights constantly come and go; when I know that death never stays, how should I wait expectantly, as if enveloped by ignorance? When, as every night passes, life becomes shorter, then the intelligent man will comprehend that the day is vain. How then can any one find happiness, when he is like a fish in shallow water? Death assails a man* when he has not obtained the objects of his desire, and when his mind is turned in another direction, like one gathering flowers. 6535 (=9946).

---

* Some of these verses were rendered as follows in "Moral and Religious Sentiments," &c., p. 49:—

Death comes, and makes a man his prey,
  A man whose powers are yet unspent,
  Like one on gathering flowers intent,
Whose thoughts are turned another way.

Begin betimes to practise good,
  Lest fate surprise thee unawares
  Amid thy round of schemes and cares;
To-morrow's task to-day conclude.

For ruthless death will never stay
  To notice whether thou hast done
  Or not, the work thou hadst begun;
But haste to bear thy life away,
As wolves and tigers snatch their prey.

And none can tell how things may chance,
  And who may all this day survive.
  While yet a stripling, therefore, strive,—
On virtue's arduous path advance.

Death carries a man off as a wolf takes a sheep. Do to-day what is good, let not this time pass away from thee. Death tears away a man before he has done the things which he purposed to do. (= 12,116). Do to-day the work of to-morrow, and in the forenoon the work of the afternoon. For death does not wait (to see) whether a man's work is done or not done. Who knows whose time of death will come to-day? Let a man be virtuous even while yet a youth; for life is transitory. If duty be performed, a good name will be obtained here, and after death happiness. For being filled with delusion, a man exerts himself, both by proper and improper acts for the benefit of his children and his wife, and procures for them maintenance. 6540. The man who possesses children and cattle, and whose mind is devoted to them, is carried off by death as a sleeping deer by a tiger. Death bears off the man who by himself is amassing (wealth) and is not satiated with enjoyments, as a tiger carries off another animal. Death makes himself master of the man who is striving, and has effected this, and not yet effected that, and has another third thing partly done and partly undone. Death carries off the man who has not obtained the fruit of his labours, and who is bent on effecting other objects, and while he is engaged with the field, the shop, or the house. Death takes away the weak and the strong, the hero and the timorous, the fool and the wise man, who have not obtained the objects of their desires. 6545. When death, decay, disease, and suffering from many causes are inseparable from the body, why dost thou live as if thou wert well? Death and decay follow a man from his birth to his end: things both motionless and moving are subject to these two things. The attachments of a man dwelling in the village are death's delight (or death's home according to the reading of v. 9952[b]); whilst, according to the scripture, the forest is the abode of the gods. The virtuous sever the fettering rope of the attachments of the man who dwells in the village, and depart; whilst the vicious do not sever it. . . . 6550. No one can by force arrest the approaching army of death; truth only (not falsehood and the like) can do this; for immortality is founded on truth. Immortality and death both lodge in the body; death results from delusion; immortality is attained by truth. I, being innoxious, truth-seeking, abandoning desire and anger, regarding pain and pleasure as equal, and peaceful, shall escape death, as if I were immortal. I, a sage, tranquil, loving composure as my sacrifice, practising Vedic study (or contemplation of Brahma) as my sacrifice, and taking word, thought, and deed as my sacrifice, shall follow the sun's northward course. 6555. How can an intelligent man, such as I am, offer destructive animal sacrifices, which are, as it were, temporary (in their effects), or a warrior's sacrifices, like a fiend? Being born in myself, and by myself, and resting on myself, though without offspring, I shall exist in myself (or be my own sacrifice, according to the reading in verse 9961[a]): offspring does not deliver me. * 6560. What hast thou, o Brahman, who shalt die, to do with riches, or relatives, or a wife? Search out thy self which has entered into the heart. Whither have thy forefathers and thy father gone?"

XXXIII. *Bhagavad Gitâ* xvi. (= *M. Bh.* vi. 1403 ff.), 6.—"Two creations of beings exist in this world, the divine and the devilish: the former has been described at length. [I have left out the enumeration of the virtues ascribed to this class in vv. 1-3.] Hear (the account of) the other from me. These devilish men are equally ignorant of action, and cessation from action; they are distinguished neither by purity, nor by right conduct, nor by truth. . . . . . 10. Yielding to insatiable desire, full of hypocrisy, arrogance, and conceit, impure in their practices, and governed by delusion, they snatch at wrongful gains. 11. Entertaining boundless anticipations extending to the end of all things, esteeming enjoyment the main thing, and the only thing, bound in a hundred chains of hope, the slaves of lust and anger, for the sake of gratifying their passions, they strive to amass wealth by unjust means. 'This has been gained by me to-day; that object of desire I shall obtain; † I have this

---

* Connected with v. 6527 (= 9933), this seems to intimate that in the writer's opinion Śrâddhas (oblations to ancestors) are worthless.

† To these exclamations of self-congratulation and security the commentator Râmânuja gives the special sense of boastings that the speaker had gained all these advantages by his own power, unassisted by destiny and other causes supposed to influence human welfare.

property, and that further wealth I shall acquire. That enemy has been slain by me, and I shall slay the others also. I am lord; I enjoy pleasure, I am complete, powerful, happy; I am opulent, of noble birth; who else is like me? I will sacrifice and bestow largesses, I will rejoice.' Thus speaking, deluded by ignorance, carried away by many imaginations, enveloped in the net of illusion, and abandoned to gratifications, they fall into an impure hell."

This passage is one of those adduced by Dr Lorinser (see the introduction to this volume) as exhibiting the influence of the New Testament. See Luke xii. verses 17 ff. The parallel of one part with these verses is striking; but the passage of the Bhagavad Gītā has various traits which are not found in the Gospel.

XXXIV. Compare Ps. xxxvii.; Job xx. 5, and xxvii. 13 ff. *Manu* iv. 170.—The following is Sir W. Jones's rendering of this passage:—"Even here below an unjust man attains no felicity; nor he whose wealth proceeds from giving false evidence;" (or from falsehood, or wrong generally,—J. M.), "nor he who constantly takes delight in mischief. 171. Though oppressed by penury in consequence of his righteous dealings, let him never give his mind to unrighteousness; for he may observe the speedy overthrow of iniquitous and sinful men. 172. (M. Bh. i. 3333 f.) Iniquity, committed in this world, produces not fruit immediately, (but) like the earth, (in due season); and advancing by little and little, it eradicates the man who committed it. 173. Yes, iniquity, once committed, fails not of producing fruit to him who wrought it; if not in his own person, yet in his son's; or, if not in his son's, yet in his grandson's. 174. He grows rich for a while through unrighteousness; then he beholds good things; then it is that he vanquishes his foes; but he perishes at length from his whole root upwards." In the metrical version I have altered the order of verses 173 and 174. Compare M. Bh. iii. 8489 ff.

XXXV. *M. Bh.* xii. 2798.—See the preceding verses which introduce this, about the sufferings of the good; and compare v. 776, 778. "Aila says: The earth now supports the good and the bad, and the sun warms both. So too the wind blows on the good and the bad, and the waters purify them. 2799. Kaśyapa replies: So is it in this world, but not so in the next; after death there shall be a wide distinction between him who practises virtue, and him who practises vice. 2800. In the world of the righteous, there is a centre of immortality, sweet, with a bright glow, and golden splendour. There after death the man of restrained passions dwells in blessedness; there, is neither death, nor decay, nor suffering. 2801. The abode of the wicked is a dismal hell with continual suffering, and great grief. There for many years the sinner bewails his fate, falling downwards (into a) bottomless (abyss)."

XXXVI. *M. Bh.* xiv. 2784.—"The gate of heaven, which is very small, is not seen by men owing to their delusion. The bolt of (the door of) heaven is created by (*lit.* has its root in) covetousness, guarded by passion, and difficult (to draw aside). 2785. But men who have conquered anger and subdued their senses, Brahmans practising austerity, and liberal according to their power, behold it. 2786. A man who could bestow a thousand, and gives a hundred, he who could give a hundred, and gives ten, and he who gives water according to his power,—all these receive an equal reward. 2787. For poor king Rantideva bestowed water with a pure mind, and thence ascended to heaven. 2788. Righteousness is not so much pleased with presents conferring large advantages, as with small gifts (given out of wealth) justly obtained, and purified by faith. 2789. King Nṛiga gave thousands of largesses of cows to Brahmans; but because he gave away one belonging to another person, he went to hell." 2790. "By giving his own flesh the devoted King Śivi Auśīnara has obtained the realms earned by virtue, and rejoices in the sky. . . . 2793. A reward equal to thine is not gained by offering many Rājasūya sacrifices with large gifts, or many Aśvamedhas. By bestowing the measure of meal thou hast conquered the eternal world of Brahmā." With verses 2786 and 2787 compare Matthew x. 42. In the Taittirīya Brāhmaṇa, iii. 12, 4, 7, It is said, "These are the five doors of heaven. . . . Austerity guards the first, faith the second, truth the third, mind the fourth, and good conduct the fifth." 7 doors of heaven are mentioned in *M. Bh.* i. 3621.

The following parallel passages are referred to in Kuinoel's Commentary on the Gospel of Matthew, vii. 13 f.:

Cebetis Tabula, cap. 12.—Ὁρᾷς, ἔφη, ἄνω τόπον τινὰ ἐκεῖνον, ὅπου οὐδεὶς ἐπικατοικεῖ, ἀλλ' ἔρημος δοκεῖ εἶναι; Ὁρῶ. Οὐκοῦν καὶ θύραν τινὰ μικρὰν, καὶ ὁδόν τινα πρὸ τῆς θύρας, ἥτις οὐ πολὺ ὀχλεῖται, ἀλλὰ πάνυ ὀλίγοι πορεύονται, ὥσπερ δι' ἀνοδίας τινὸς καὶ τραχείας καὶ πετρώδους εἶναι δοκούσης; Καὶ μάλα, ἔφην. Οὐκοῦν καὶ βουνός τις ὑψηλὸς δοκεῖ εἶναι, καὶ ἀνάβασις στενὴ πάνυ, καὶ κρημνοὺς ἔχουσα ἔνθεν κἀκεῖθεν βαθεῖς; Ὁρω. Αὕτη τοίνυν ἐστὶν ἡ ὁδὸς, ἔφη, ἡ ἄγουσα πρὸς τὴν ἀληθινὴν παιδείαν. "Dost thou see," said the old man, "yonder a certain place where no one dwells, but it appears to be deserted?" "I see it," said the stranger. "Do you then see," continued the old man, "a certain little door, and a road in front of the door which is not much frequented, but very few pass along it, as it seems to be, in fact, no road at all, but rough and rocky?" "I do, certainly," replied the other. "And does there not appear to be a certain high hill, and a very narrow ascent, with deep precipices on either side?" "I see it all." "This, then, is the way which leads to true education." "And," said the stranger, "it looks very difficult." Diodorus Siculus, p. 296 B. κατάντης ἡ πρὸς τὸ χεῖρον ὁδὸς, ῥαδίαν ἔχουσα τὴν ὁδοιπορίαν. "The way to what is bad slopes downward, and it is very easy to traverse." . . . . Vitringa (Obss. Sacr. 3, p. 199), has explained a famous passage in the Gemara Berachoth, c. 4, sect. 11, about the two roads leading, the one to the Garden of Eden, the other to Gehenna."

XXXVII. *Kathâ-sarit-sâgara* lv. 110. "The streams of rivers, the flowers of trees, the phases of the moon, disappear, but return again; not so the youth of embodied beings."

Compare Euripides, Hercules Furens, 655 ff.:

εἰ δὲ θεοῖς ἦν ξύνεσις καὶ σοφία κατ' ἄνδρας,
δίδυμον ἂν ἥβαν ἔφερον
φανερὸν χαρακτῆρ'
ἀρετᾶς ὅσοισιν

μέτα, κατθανόντες τ'
εἰς αὐγὰς πάλιν ἁλίου
δισσοὺς ἂν ἔβαν διαύλους,
ἁ δυσγένεια δ' ἁπλᾶν ἂν
εἶχε ζωᾶς βιοτάν,
καὶ τῷδ' ἦν τούς τε κακοὺς ἂν
γνῶναι καὶ τοὺς αγαθούς.—κ. τ. λ.

"But if the gods had intelligence and wisdom according to man (*i.e.*, according to the standards of human wisdom), they (the gods) would bring them a second youth, as a visible stamp of prowess, to those who possess it, and so, when dead, they would be again restored to the light of the sun, and would have run a double course; while ignobleness would have a single term of life, and by that it would be possible to know both the bad and the good," &c. Paley.

And in the Supplices of Euripides, 1080 ff., Iphis says:—

οἴμοι· τί δὴ βροτοῖσιν οὐκ ἔστιν τόδε
νέους δὶς εἶναι καὶ γέροντας αὖ πάλιν:
ἀλλ' ἐν νόμοις μὲν ἤν τι μὴ καλῶς ἔχῃ,
γνώμαισιν ὑστέραισιν ἐξορθούμεθα,
αἰῶνα δ' οὐκ ἔξεστιν. εἰ δ' ἦμεν νέοι
δὶς καὶ γέροντες, εἴ τις ἐξημάρτανε,
διπλοῦ βίου τυχόντες ἐξωρθούμεθ' ἄν.

"Alas! Why is it not granted to men to be twice young, and again old? But if there be anything in the laws which is not as it should be, we amend it by our subsequent decisions, but we cannot do this in regard to our life; while, if we were both young and old twice, and any one made a mistake, we could rectify it, if we had a double life."

XXXVIII. *Subhâshitârṇava*, 255. "Again the morning (dawns), again the night (arrives). Again the moon rises, again the sun. As time passes away, life too goes; yet who regards his own welfare?" (The word for welfare in the original is *hitam*, and the epithet "final," given in the metrical version is absent.)

XXXIX. *M. Bh.* iii. 17401. "Day after day men proceed hence to the abode of Yama (the ruler of the dead); and yet those who remain long for a state of permanence (here); what is more wonderful than this?"

XL. *Dampati-śikshá*, 26. "Who, now, are destitute of sight? Those who do not perceive the future world. Say, say, who are the deafest? Those who do not listen to good advice."

Praśnottara-málá, 15. "Who is blind? He who is bent on doing what he should not. Who is deaf? He who does not listen to what is beneficial. Who is dumb? He who does not know how to say kind things at the proper time."

XLI. *Śántiśataka*, 35. "When thou hast heard that in an adjoining house some trifling article of property has been stolen, thou guardest thine own house;—it is right to do so. Dost thou not fear death, which every day carries off men from every house? Be wakeful, O men!"

XLII. *Manu* xi. 228 (compare *M. Bh.* iii. 13751; xiii. 5534). "In proportion as a man, who has committed a sin, shall truly and voluntarily confess it, so far he is disengaged from that offence, like a snake from his slough. 229. And in proportion as his heart sincerely loathes his evil deed, so far shall his vital spirit be freed from the taint of it. 230. If he commit sin, and actually repent, that sin shall be removed from him; but if he merely say, 'I will sin thus no more,' he can only be released by an actual abstinence from guilt." (Sir W. Jones's translation).

XLIII. *M. Bh.* v. 1474. "Since life is uncertain, let not a man do at first an act by which, when reclining on his bed, he would be distressed." See also xii. 10599 bf.

XLIV. *Subháshitárṇava*, 163. "Men in distress bow down before the gods; the sick practise austerity; the poor man is humble; an old woman is devoted to her husband."

Vṛiddha-Cháṇakya, 17, 6. "A man who is powerless will be virtuous; a poor man continent; a sick man devout; an old woman devoted to her husband."

XLV. *Subhāshitārṇava* 43. "Men desire the fruits of virtue; virtue itself they do not desire. They do not desire the fruits of sin; but practise sin laboriously." Compare Juvenal Sat. x. 140. Tanto major famæ sitis est quam Virtutis. Quis enim virtutem amplectitur ipsam Præmia si tollas. "So much more do men thirst after reputation than after virtue. For who embraces virtue itself, if you take away its rewards?" Also Horace Epist. i. 16, 52. Oderunt peccare boni virtutis amore. "The good, from love of virtue, hate to sin."

XLVI. *M. Bh.* v. 1242. "Sin, committed again and again, destroys the understanding; and a man who hast lost his understanding constantly practises sin only. 1243. Virtue (or holiness, *puṇya*), practised again and again, augments the understanding; and he whose understanding is augmented does continually only what is good (or holy)."

XLVII. *Vṛiddha-Chāṇakya* xiv. 6. "If those sentiments which men experience when duty is expounded to them, or in a cemetery, or when they are sick, were abiding, who would not be delivered from bondage?"

XLVIII. *Panchatantra* ii. 127 (or 117). "The man seeking for final emancipation (*moksha*), would obtain it by (undergoing) a hundredth part of the sufferings which the foolish man endures in the pursuit of riches."

XLIX. *M. Bh.* v. 1248. "Let a man so act by day, that he may live happily at night. 1249. Let him for eight months so act, that he may live happily during the rainy season. In early life let him so act that he may enjoy happiness in his old age. All his life let him so act that he may enjoy happiness in the next world."

L. *Sārṇgadhara's Paddhati Nīti* 2. "Let a man every day examine his conduct, (enquiring thus,) 'What is common to me with the brutes, and what with noble men?'"

LI. *Sārṇgadhara's Paddhati*, p. 4. "Constantly rising up, a man should reflect [and ask himself], 'What good thing have I done to-day?' The setting sun will carry with it a portion of my life."

LII. *Hitopadeśa* ii. 44. "As a stone is rolled up a hill by great exertions, but is easily thrown down, so it is with ourselves in respect of meritorious acts and faults." Comp. Hesiod, Opera et Dies:—

> *Τὴν μέν τοι κακότητα καὶ ἰλαδὸν ἔστιν ἑλέσθαι*
> *ῥηϊδίως· λείη μὲν ὁδὸς, μάλα δ' ἐγγύθι ναίει.*
> *τῆς δ' ἀρετῆς ἱδρῶτα θεοὶ προπάροιθεν ἔθηκαν*
> *ἀθάνατοι· μακρὸς δὲ καὶ ὄρθιος οἶμος ἐς αὐτὴν*
> *καὶ τρηχὺς το πρῶτον· ἐπὴν δ' εἰς ἄκρον ἵκηται,*
> *ῥηϊδίη δὴ ἔπειτα πέλει, χαλεπή περ ἐοῦσα.*

"Men may easily choose wickedness even in abundance; for the road is smooth and is near at hand. But the immortal gods have placed sweat in front of virtue, and the road to it is long and steep, and rough at first, but when the summit is reached, it then becomes easy, though difficult." Seneca takes a different view. He says (De Ira, 2, 13, 2,):—Non ut quibusdam visum est, arduum in virtutes et asperum iter est: plano adeuntur . . . Facilis est ad beatam vitam via; inite modo bonis auspiciis ipsisque dis bene juvantibus. "The road to the virtues is not, as has appeared to some, difficult and rough; they are reached by a level (path) . . . The road to a happy life is easy, provided only you enter upon it under good auspices, and with the gods themselves for your helpers." Wuestemann's Promptuarium Sententiarum, p. 89. Other writers agree with Hesiod; see the same work, p. 89 f., and Hartung's Sententiarum Liber, p. 188.

LIII. *Vriddha Chāṇakya* xii. 22. "A jar is gradually filled by the falling of water-drops. The same rule holds good in regard to all sciences, to virtue, and to wealth."

LIV. *M. Bh.* v. 1537. "How can the man who loves ease obtain knowledge? The seeker of knowledge can have no ease. Either let the lover of ease give up knowledge, or the lover of knowledge relinquish ease."

LV. *Chāṇakya*, 5. "That jewel knowledge, which is not plundered by kinsmen, nor carried off by thieves, which does not decrease by giving, is great riches." In two other similar maxims, kings are mentioned among those who carry off a man's wealth.

LVI. *Vṛiddha Chāṇakya* xv. 10. "Books are endless, the sciences are many, time is very short, and there are many obstacles: a man should therefore seek for that which is the essence, as a swan seeks to extract the milk which is mixed with water."

Subhāshitārṇava, 92. "There are many books, the Vedas, &c.; life is very short, and there are millions of obstacles; let a man therefore seek to discover the essence, as the swan finds the milk in water."

LVII. *Rāmāyaṇa* ii. 105, 16 ff. "All collections end in dissolutions; high heapings end in falls; unions in separations; and life in death. As fruits when ripe have only to fear falling, so men when born have only to fear death. As a house resting on firm pillars, when (they) become worn out, sinks; so men sink, subdued by decay and death. The night which passes never returns; the Jumna flows to the ocean, which is a full receptacle of waters. The days and nights of all creatures move on and wear away their lives, as the sun's rays dry up water in the summer. . . . 22. Death walks with men; death sits with them; and having travelled a long journey, death returns with them. . . . 24. Men delight when the sun rises, they delight when it sets; but they do not perceive the consumption of their own lives. Men rejoice when they behold the beginning of each new season as it arrives; and with the revolution of the seasons the life of creatures is curtailed. As two logs of wood meet on the great ocean, and after a time part again, so wives, sons, relatives, and riches, having come into contact with men, hasten away again; separation from them is certain . . . 29. As any one standing on the road says to a company of people moving onward, 'I too will follow behind you;' so the road which has been traversed by fathers and ancestors, preceding us, is certain (to be trodden by us also); and having entered on it, why should any one lament, since it cannot be avoided."

LVIII. *M. Bh.* xii. 854; iii. 13,850 ff.; xii. 12,521 ff.—"And physicians become sick, and strong men weak . . .; such are the strange vicissitudes of time. 855. High birth, heroism, health, beauty, good fortune, and enjoyment, aregained through destiny. The poor, who do not desire them, have many sons, while the rich have none: such is the wonderful action of fate! Creatures have to suffer from pain, fire, water, weapons, hunger, calamities, poison, fever, death, and falls from elevated positions. . . . 859[b]. A rich man is noticed to die while he is quite young; (860) while a poor man lives for a hundred years distressed and worn out. Poor men are seen who are long-lived, while those who are born in a wealthy family perish like moths. (= v. 1145). For the most part the rich have no power of enjoyment (iii. 13857[b] f.,* and those who have food to eat are unable to eat it, owing to disease in the intestines), whilst poor men's sticks even are eaten. . . . 863. Hunting, dice, women, drinking, are attachments blamed by the wise; but even very learned men are addicted to them. . . . 866. Cold, heat, and rain come in turn through the lapse of time. 867. So, too, neither herbs, nor sacred texts, nor oblations, nor recitations, (868) deliver

---

* Some of these verses were rendered in "Religious and Moral Sentiments," p. 57:

Some men decrepit, poor, distrest,
  Survive to life's extremest stage,
While some by fortune richly blest
  Are seized by death in early age;
And few of those with splendour graced
Enjoy the bliss they hoped to taste.

xii. 859.—"For a wealthy man is observed to perish while he is young; and a poor distressed man to attain to a hundred years and to decrepitude . . . and for the most part prosperous men lack the power to enjoy." Compare Job xxi. 23 ff.

Stobæus quotes the following lines from Antiphanes:—

οὐ πώποτ' ἐζήλωσα πλουτοῦντα σφόδρα
ἄνθρωπον ἀπολαύοντα μηδὲν ὧν ἔχει.

"I never envied the very wealthy man who enjoys nothing of all that he possesses."

the man who is assailed by death and decay. (= xii. 6471; and Rāmāyaṇa ii. 105, 26). Just as two logs of wood meet upon the ocean (869) and again separate, such also is the manner in which living creatures meet. Time is equally the agent in the lot of men who have wives, and enjoy singing and music; (870) and of orphans who eat the bread of strangers. Thousands of fathers and mothers, and hundreds of sons and wives, are perceived to exist in the world—(871) to whom do they—to whom do we—belong? No one belongs to this man, nor does this man belong to any one. 872. This meeting with wives, relations, friends, has occurred on the way. Where am I? whither shall I go? who am I? and why standing here? 873. Why should I mourn anything? So let a man resolve. In this transitory world, with its dear unions, revolving like a wheel, (874) we have met upon our road brothers, mothers, fathers, friends. . . . 877[b]. Many medical men, the readers of medical books alone, (878) are seen to be overcome with sicknesses, along with their dependants. Drinking decoctions and various preparations of butter, (879) they cannot overpass death, as the ocean cannot overpass its shores. And men who are acquainted with elixirs, and who have skilfully applied them, (880) are seen to be broken down by decrepitude, like trees crushed by powerful elephants. So, too, ascetics devoted to sacred study, (881) liberal, practising sacrifice, cannot escape decay and death. Neither the days, nor the months, nor the years, (882) nor the half-months, nor the nights of born creatures return. Transient, dependent, man, under the influence of time, (883) travels over the long and everlasting road traversed by all creatures. Either a living man's body passes away from him, or his life passes from his body. 884. He has met his wife and other connections by the way; here there is no perpetual association with any one, (885) not even with one's own body, how much less with any one else. Where now, O king, is thy father? Where are thy ancestors? 886. Thou beholdest them not now; nor do they behold thee." (Repeated in xii. 3864.)

LIX. *M. Bh.* iii. 13846.—"Whatever act, good or bad, a man

performs, of it he necessarily receives the recompense. When an unwise man falls into an unfavourable condition, he greatly reviles the gods (comp. xii. 3877), and does not recognise the faults of his own action. A fool, a bad, and an unstable man invariably experiences reverses of fortune.* Neither wisdom, nor prudence, nor energy, delivers a man. He would gain at will whatever object of desire he sought, (13850) if the rewards of energy in action were not dependent (on something else). Self-restrained, able, and intelligent men, are seen to receive no rewards for their works; while some other being, who is constantly employed in injuring others, and in deceiving the world, lives always happily. The goddess of prosperity (Śrī) attends upon some who sit inactive; whilst others who act do not attain the object of their desires. To poor men who sacrifice to the gods, who practise austerity, desiring to have offspring, sons who are a disgrace to their family are born, after being carried for ten months in the womb. Others are born with wealth, with stores of grain, with many sources of enjoyment collected by their fathers. . . . For there is no doubt that men's diseases spring from their works (done in a previous existence). And they are harassed by diseases as the smaller wild animals are by huntsmen. And these diseases † are not stopped by skilful physicians, with all their collections of drugs, as wild animals are by huntsmen. And those who have food which they might enjoy, are distressed by a disorder of the intestines, and are disabled from enjoying it. Many other men who are strong of arm live in distress, (13859) and with difficulty obtain food. . . . 13860[b]. Men would not die, nor decay, but would enjoy all they desired, and experience nothing unpleasant, if they were their own masters. Every one seeks to rise higher and higher in the world, and strives according to his power, but things do not turn out so (as he had desired). . . 13864. According to the Veda the life (soul) is eternal, (13865) but the body of all creatures is perishable. When the body is destroyed, . . . the soul departs elsewhere, being fettered by the bonds of works."

* This is rather opposed to the general tenor of the passage.

† See the passages quoted under No. lviii. and xii. 12540 ff.

LX. *Bhartṛihari*, and *Subhāshitārṇava*, 28, 313. "In one place (is heard) the sound of the lute; in another lamentation and weeping. In one place (is found) an assemblage of learned men; in another (is heard) the wrangling of drunkards. In one place (is seen) an enchanting woman; in another a dame whose body is worn out by decay. I know not whether the essence of this world is ambrosia or poison."

LXI. *M. Bh.* xii. 831; xii. 6486[b] f.—"Friends do not suffice for happiness, nor foes for suffering. Intelligence does not suffice to bring wealth, nor wealth to bring enjoyment."

LXII. *M. Bh.* v. 1430.—Compare xiii. 7597 ff. "Intelligence does not (always lead) to the acquirement of wealth; nor stupidity to poverty. The wise man, and no other, knows the course of events in the world."

LXIII. *M. Bh.* v. 1144 f.—"Poor men eat more excellent food (than the) rich; for hunger gives it sweetness; and this is very rarely to be found among the rich."

LXIV. 77. *Vishṇu Purāṇa* iv. 24, 48 (compare *Mbh.* xii. 8260 ff.; and *Rāmāyaṇa* (Gorresio's edit.), ii. 116, 28 ff.).—The passage, a small part of which I have versified, may be found in Professor H. H. Wilson's translation of this Purāṇa, vol. iv., of Dr Hall's edition, pp. 237 ff. I subjoin my own version of the lines which I have reproduced in verse. 50, 51. "These and other kings who, blinded by delusion, and possessed of perishable bodies, claimed this imperishable earth as their own, (saying), distressed by anxiety, 'How [shall] this female [become] mine, and my son's, and my descendants' property,'—these have all come to their end. 52. So, too, others who preceded, and those who followed them, and those who are to come, and others who again are to succeed them, shall (all) depart. 53. Beholding princes eager to march and strive for the subjugation of herself,* the Earth, smiling with

* Professor Wilson renders the words which I have so translated, as follows: "Kings unable to effect the subjugation of themselves;" and Dr Hall would substitute "harassed with the enterprise of self-con-

flowers in autumn, appears to laugh. . . . The Earth once said: 55. 'How does this delusion exist in kings, even in the intelligent, through which, although in their nature (as transient) as foam, they are filled with confidence? . . . 57. We shall thus at length (they say) conquer the Earth with her oceans; but while their thoughts are thus fixed, they do not perceive death, which is close at hand. . . . 60. On my account, wars arise between fathers, sons, and brothers, whose hearts, through exceeding delusion, are seized by selfish ambition. . . . 62. How is it that ambition, directed towards me, finds a place in the heart of the descendant who has seen his ancestor, whose soul was possessed by the same desire, following the road to death, and leaving me behind?' . . . 72. Prithu—who, unconquered, traversed all the regions, whose chariot-wheels tore to pieces his enemies—he, smitten by the blast of time, has perished, like the down of the Śālmali tree when thrown into the fire. 73. Kārtavīrya, who invaded and possessed all the zones of the earth, shattering the chariot-wheels of his foes, and who is celebrated in narrative tales, is (now merely) a subject for affirmation and denial.* 74. Out upon the royal splendour of Daśānana (Rāvaṇa) Avīkshita, and Rāghava (Rāma), who illuminated the face of all the quarters of the globe! how has it not been turned to ashes in a moment by the frown of Death? (Or, according to the commentator, the second half of this verse may be alternatively rendered: "How has it not even been turned to ashes,—how have not even ashes been left of it,—by the frown of Death?") 75. Seeing that Māndhātṛi, who was an emperor upon earth, has now his only embodiment in a story,—what good man, even if slow of understanding, would indulge in selfish desire? 76. Did Bhagīratha, Sagara, Kākutstha.

quest." But on comparing the parallel verse in the Bhāgavata Purāṇa xii. 3, 1, which, as explained by the commentator, means, "Beholding kings eager to conquer herself, this earth laughs," it appears to me that the word *ātman* in the line of the Vishṇu P. also must be rendered "herself," not "themselves."

* Professor Wilson quotes as a parallel to this the concluding lines of the well-known passage of Juvenal (x. 147) about Hannibal:

"I, demens, et sævas curre per Alpes,
Ut pueris placeas, et declamatio fias."

Daśānana, Rāghava, Lakshmaṇa, Yudhishṭhira, and the rest exist in truth, or only in imagination? And where are they? We do not know."

I introduce here a sentence from Plato:—*Ἧι οὖν ὑπάρχει διανοίᾳ μεγαλοπρέπεια καὶ θεωρία παντὸς μὲν χρόνου, πάσης δὲ οὐσίας, οἷόν τε οἴει τούτῳ μέγα τι δοκεῖν εἶναι τὸν ἀνθρώπινον βίον;*—*Republic*, vi. 2.

"And do you think that a spirit full of lofty thoughts, and privileged to contemplate all time, and all existence, can possibly attach any great importance to this life?"—Messrs DAVIES and VAUGHAN'S *Translation*, 1852.

"Can the soul then, which has magnificence of conception, and is the spectator of all time and all existence, think much of human life?"—Prof. JOWETT'S *Translation*, 1871.

A soul whose flight so far extends—
A soul whose unrestricted range
Embraces Time with all its change—
All Being's limits comprehends—
Can such a soul the life of man
Deem worth a thought,—this petty span?

LXV. *M. Bh.* i. 3176 f.; xii. 781 ff.; 6508^{b} ff.—"When a man never sins against any creature, either in act, in thought, or in word, then he attains to Brahma. When he does not fear, and when no one is afraid of him; when he neither loves nor hates, then he attains to Brahma" (xii. 783). "When he has overcome pride and illusion, and is freed from many attachments, then the good man, self-resplendent, attains to final tranquillity (*nirvāṇa*)" (xii. 6508^{b} f.). "When it suppresses all desires, as a tortoise draws in its limbs, then this soul beholds its own glory in itself."

LXVI. *M. Bh.* v. 1382.—"He whose soul has ceased from sin, and is fixed upon goodness,—he understands this universe, both its primal substance (*Prakriti*) and its developments."

LXVII. *M. Bh.* xii. 7447.—"Knowledge is generated in a man by the decay of sinful action; and then, as in a clear mirror, he beholds the soul in himself (or himself in the soul)."

LXVIII. In *M. Bh.* xii. 8957, Vyāsa discourses to his son Śuka as follows :—" Repressing all desires, let the man fix his mind on the reality (*sattva*); and having done so, he will annihilate time. Through clearness (or calmness) of spirit, the Yati (ascetic) relinquishes good and evil. With an untroubled soul abiding in himself, he enjoys extreme happiness. This tranquillity may be characterised as resembling sweet sleep, or a lamp which in calm air burns without flickering. So, as time goes on, fixing his soul on itself, eating little, inwardly purified, he sees the soul in himself. This lore, my son, is the esoteric essence of all the Vedas, independent of tradition or of scripture, a self-evidencing doctrine. All the substance which is to be found in religious narratives, in true tales, the ambrosia yielded by churning ten thousand Ṛik-verses, is (here) extracted. As butter is drawn out of milk, or fire out of wood, so has this knowledge possessed by the wise been extracted for my son. . . . This doctrine should not be communicated to any one who is not composed, calm, and ascetic, to one who is ignorant of the Veda, is not submissive (*upagata*), is envious, dishonest, who does not obey the instructions he receives, to one who has been burnt by logical books, or who is cruel. . . . This esoteric lore is to be communicated to a dear son, to an obedient disciple, and to no other. This instruction is better than the gift of this whole earth filled with jewels would be."

The phenomenon described by Professor Reuss, alluded to in the text (p. 49, note), is related in 1 Samuel xix. 20 ff. In verse 23 we read:—"And he (Saul) went thither to Naioth in Ramah; and the Spirit of God was upon him also, and he went on, and prophesied, until he came to Naioth in Ramah. 24. And he stripped off his clothes also, and prophesied before Samuel in like manner, and lay down naked all that day and all that night. Wherefore they say, Is Saul also among the prophets?" The following note is in explanation of verse 24.

"This is the sequel of the fact just mentioned. If Saul experienced the effects of the inspiration even before arriving at the spot, his transports only became stronger when he arrived in the midst of the assembly. He not only took off his (upper) garments, as the others did: but he found himself for a time in such a state of enthusiasm and ecstasy, that as a consequence of that over-excitement, he experienced an utter prostration of strength for twenty-four hours. Such a phenomenon has not only nothing in it that is inexplicable, but must have been frequent everywhere that the prophetic excitement attained a degree of intensity which disturbed the intellectual faculties. (See my explanation of the Glossolaly, 1 Corinthians xiv., and Jeremiah xxix. 26; 2 Kings ix. 11.)"

LXIX. *M. Bh.* xii. 12064.—"With effort hold fast the great lamp, formed by the comprehension of righteousness, whose flames have been gradually collected; seeing that thou must enter into the darkness."

LXX. *M. Bh.* xii. 529, 6641, and 9917.—This saying, ascribed to Janaka, King of Videha, occurs in all the three passages here specified: "Boundless, verily, is my wealth, though I possess nothing. If Mithila [his capital] were burnt up, nothing of mine would be consumed." In verse 9917 the words, "Most happily, verily, do I live," are substituted for "Boundless, verily, is my wealth." In the last passage the saying is expanded. See also xii. 7981. Κλεάνθης ἐρωτώμενος πῶς ἄν τις εἴη πλούσιος, εἶπεν "εἰ τῶν ἐπιθυμιῶν εἴη πένης."—Stobæus Floril. ii. 196 (Teubner's Edn.). "Cleanthes, when asked how a man could be rich, said, If he were poor in desires." Compare Valerius Maximus, 4, 4, 1:—Omnia habet qui nihil concupiscit: ("He who lusts after nothing, has all things"); and Cicero, Parad. 6, 3: "Contentum suis rebus esse, maximæ sunt certissimæque divitiæ: ("To be content with what one has, is the greatest and surest riches").

LXXI. *Śatapatha Brāhmaṇa* x. 5, 4, 15.—"This (soul) is without desires, but possesses all objects of desire; for it has no desire for anything. On this subject there is this verse:—

'By knowledge mortals thither soar
Where all desires have passed away;
Gifts, penance, cannot there convey
The man who lacks this holy lore.'

That is, the man who does not possess this knowledge, does not attain to that world by largesses, or by austerities; those only who have that knowledge attain to it."

LXXII. *M. Bh.* xii. 12121.—"Men who possess knowledge do not die when they are separated from their bodies; nor do they perish when they have carefully kept to the (proper) path. For he who increases (his) righteousness is an instructed man; whilst he who falls away from righteousness is deluded."

LXXIII. *M. Bh.* xii. 530; xii. 5623. Compare iii. 14789.—"Mounted on the palace of wisdom, a man (beholds) others grieving for those who are not objects of commiseration, as one who is standing on a hill beholds those standing on the plain; but the dull man does not perceive this."

LXXIV. The dialogue of which a portion is here rendered occurs, with some variations, in two places of the Bṛihad Araṇyaka Upanishad, viz., ii. 4, 1 ff., and iv. 5, 1 ff. (according to Dr Roer's numeration). The introductory sentence is found only in the latter place. "Yājnavalkya had two wives,* Maitreyī and Kātyāyanī. Of these two, Maitreyī was acquainted with theology, while Kātyāyanī had only that understanding which is common among women. Yājnavalkya was bent upon commencing another stage of life (than that of a householder); 2. And said to Maitreyī, "I am about to leave this place, and begin the life of a wandering mendicant; come, let me divide my property between thee and Kātyāyanī." 3. Maitreyī replied: "O reverend lord, if this entire earth, filled with riches, were mine, should I thereby become immortal, or not?" "No," said Yājnavalkya, "in that case thy life would be such as is that of the opulent; but there is no hope of thy gaining immortality by means of wealth." 4. Maitreyī rejoined: "What could I do with that which would not make me immortal? Declare to me, O reverend sir,

* On the existence of polygamy in India in early times, see my Original Sanskrit Texts, v. pp. 457 f.

whatever thou knowest (regarding the means of attaining that end)." 5. Yājnavalkya said: "Being (already) dear to me thou hast now (by this speech) increased my affection, [or done more than ever what is pleasing to me]. I shall therefore explain this (which thou askest of me); do thou seek to ponder my explanation." The discourse of some length which follows may be found rendered in Dr Roer's translation of this Upanishad in the Bibliotheca Indica (Calcutta, 1856), pp. 242 ff., in Professor Max Müller's "History of Ancient Sanskrit Literature" (London, 1859), pp. 22-25; and in the same author's Hibbert Lectures, pp. 327 ff. Yājnavalkya begins: 6. "It is not from affection to the husband that the husband is dear (to his wife); but it is from her affection to the Self or Soul (*ātman**) that he is dear to her. It is not from affection for the wife that she is dear (to her husband), but from his affection for the Soul that she is dear (to him)." After saying the same of children, of wealth, of the gods, &c., the speaker proceeds:—"It is not from affection for the totality of things that it is dear (to any one), but it is dear from affection for the Soul. The Soul is to be seen, to be heard, to be thought, to be pondered. O Maitreyī, when the Soul is seen, heard, thought, and known, this entire universe is known. 7. . . . This universe should reject the man who regards the universe as other than the Soul. The Brahmanical class, the Kshatriya class, these gods, these Vedas, all these creatures, all this universe, is nothing else than this Soul." 13.† "As a lump of salt is without an interior or an exterior, but is all a mass of flavour; so this Soul has no

---

* This word is rendered by Professor Müller "the Divine Spirit," or "the Divine Self."

† The first half of this paragraph runs as follows in the parallel passage in the earlier part of the Upanishad: "12. Just as a lump of sea salt, when thrown into the sea, will be dissolved into it, and no one will be able to take it out again (as a lump); but from whatever place you take water it will be salt; so this great Being is infinite, boundless, a totality of knowledge." The same illustration is employed in the Chhāndogya Upanishad, vi. 13, 1 ff. Uddālaka there says to his son Svetaketu, "'Throw this salt into water, and come to me in the morning.' He did so. U. said: 'Take out the salt which Thou didst put into the water in the evening.' By touch he could not discover it. (U. said): 'Since it is dissolved, taste the water at (one) end.' 'How

interior or exterior, but is one mass of knowledge. Arising out of these elements, it enters into them again. After death there is no consciousness (of separate individuality)." 14. Maitreyī replied: "Thou hast brought me into a state of bewilderment by saying that after death there is no consciousness. I do not know this soul." He replied: "I do not speak what should cause bewilderment. This Soul is imperishable, and by nature indestructible. 15. When a state of duality appears to exist, then one sees another, . . . addresses another, hears another . . . but if the Soul is the whole of this, then whom [what other] can he see . . . or address, or hear, and by whom? . . . by whom can he know him by whom he knows this universe? He is not this or that.[?] The Soul is unseizable, for he is not seized; indissoluble, for he is not dissolved; free from attachment, for he is not attached; unbound, he is not subject to pain or injury. How could he know the knower? Thus hast thou been instructed, O Maitreyī. Such is immortality." Having thus spoken, Yājnavalkya wandered forth. The story leaves us in ignorance whether the sage was moved when he set out, or whether he departed with Stoical insensibility.

The doctrine which Maitreyī was taught by her husband does not at first sight appear to be of the most comforting character. See the Chārvākas' estimate of the Vedantic redemption above, No. xxiii., pp. 13 f. and 217 f. But see the remarks of Professor Müller in the next page. I give a note by Professor Cowell in the Supplementary Appendix, p. 352.

The expression *na pretya sanjṇā sti*, which I have rendered above by the words "after death there is consciousness (of separate individuality," is thus explained by the commentator on ii., 4.12 (p. 467 of text of the *Upanishad* in the Bibliotheca Indica). "There is no consciousness of a distinction of this character that I am such a person, such a one's son, happy,

---

is it?' 'Salt.' 'Taste (some) from the middle.' 'How is it?' 'Salt.' 'Take (some) from the (other) end.' 'How is it?' 'Salt.' 'Having thus tasted it,' (said U.) 'wait upon me.' S. did so, and said, 'It (the salt) continues to exist.' U. replied: 'That Reality is here (in this body) though thou dost not perceive it. That atom,—it forms the essence of this universe,—that is the Truth, that is the Soul. That art thou, O Svetaketu.'"

unhappy, &c.; since it (such a consciousness) is caused by ignorance. And since the science of Brahma (or divine knowledge) utterly destroys ignorance, how should such consciousness of distinctness arise in one who has acquired such knowledge? Such consciousness of distinctness is inconceivable in a man who has attained to the state of oneness (*kaivalya*), even though he is still in the body. How much less can it subsist in one who is entirely freed from effects and instruments (*kārya-karaṇa-vimuktasya*)."

The Commentator then explains Maitreyī's perplexity as arising from the apparent contradiction between Yājnavalkya having declared that the soul was compact of knowledge, and then affirmed it to have no consciousness or knowledge.

In regard to this doctrine, the reader may consult what Professor Müller says in his Hibbert Lectures, pp. 358, 361 f. He there states: "And yet they did not believe in the annihilation of their own self." "Here we see that annihilation was certainly not the last and highest goal to which the philosophy or the religion of the Indian dwellers in the forest looked forward. The true self was to remain after it had recovered himself. We cease to be what we seemed to be; we are what we know ourselves to be," &c.

In the *M. Bh.* xii. 7931, however, king Janaka expresses his doubts in regard to this doctrine thus: "Venerable sir, if no one has any consciousness after death, of what consequence will ignorance or knowledge be in that case? 7932. And see, O most excellent of Brahmans, everything will end in annihilation. What difference will it then make whether a man is thoughtful or deluded? 7933. If there is either no connection then with living beings, or, a connection only with such as perish, what certainty can then be entertained, or realised, of any future reward?"

After a discourse of some length, beginning (verse 7935) with the words, "Here neither is annihilation the end, nor, on the other hand, is individual existence the end;" Panchaśikha arrives at the conclusion (verses 7971 ff.); "This being so, what annihilation can there be, or on the other hand, how can any individual be eternal? since all things naturally exist by their cause [ignorance]. Just as all rivers, when they reach the ocean lose their individualities and their names, and the larger rivers swallow up the smaller, so are beings absorbed. Such being the case, how can there again be any consciousness after death, the individual lives being collected from every quarter and absorbed [by soul]? And he who possesses this comprehension of liberation, and calmly seeks after the self, is not implicated in the undesired fruits of works, as the leaf of the lotus when sprinkled with water (is not wetted). Freed from many rigid bonds arising from offspring and deities, when he abandons pleasure and pain, then, being liberated, he reaches the highest state without a subtle body. Without fear of decay or death he rests, with the blessings of the scriptures, founded upon the authority of the Vedas. And both holiness and sin having become exhausted, and the fruits resulting from them having ceased, when they have ascended to the ether, which has no stain or mark, they behold it without any attachment to the mundane understanding (*buddhi*). As a revolving spider when its web is exhausted remains thrown down, so when freed, the man abandons suffering, and dissolves as a clod dashed against a rock. Just as a deer leaving its old horn, or a serpent its skin, departs, without regarding them, so he abandons suffering; or as a bird deserting a tree which is falling into the water, flies away, indifferent to it; so having abandoned pleasure and pain, and liberated, he attains the highest state without a subtle body."

The preceding story of Maitreyī is interesting as one of the instances in which women are recorded in the Indian books as receiving scholastic instruction.

As an additional case of the same kind, I may refer to another female student of theology mentioned in the same Upanishad, iii. 6. 1, and iii. 8. 1 (pp. 198 and 203 of the English translation), viz., Gārgī Vachaknavī (the daughter of Vachaknu), who puts questions to Yājnavalkya. In the Grihya Sūtras of Aśvalāyana, she is mentioned along with Vadavā Prātitheyī (daughter of Pratithi) and Sulabhā Maitreyī (the daughter of Maitri),* in company with various famous teachers,

* See also Professor Weber's Indische Studien, x. 118 f. The Brihad Aranyaka, viii. 4, 17 (p. 1086 Bibl. Ind.)=Satapatha Brāhmana, xiv. 9.4. 16, has a passage prescribing a certain rite for the man.

to the spirits of all of whom, men and women, oblations are enjoined to be offered. In a formula quoted in Mr Colebrooke's Essays, Vol. I., p. 162 (Professor Cowell's edition) the names of Vaijavāpī, Hūhū, Lokākshī, Maitrāyaṇī, and Aindrayaṇī, are mentioned in a similar connection. If by the Sulabhā Maitreyī above referred to, the wife of Yājnavalkya is meant, her story is different from the Sulabhā whose name occurs in the Mahābhārata xii. 11854—12043, who was a king's daughter, and never was married, but embraced the life of a mendicant (verses 11858 and 12033 f.) She came, assuming a form of youthful beauty, to see and to prove King Janaka (see above, No. lxx., p. 245), who was renowned as a royal sage (11856 ff.) A long conversation ensues between them. Janaka declares that, while retaining his kingly position, he lives happily in a state of indifference to all objects of sense (11888), asks why, if ascetics attain to a state of liberation (or redemption) by knowledge, kings should not be able to gain the same end by the same means? (11893) urges that ascetics too, in finding fault with, and abandoning, one state of life and embracing another, are not free from attachment to external things (11895), and that it is knowledge, and not a man's particular condition of life, which is the cause of liberation (11897 ff.) He, himself, he says, "has cut through the chains formed by royalty,—whose binding power consists in attachment,—by the sword of abnegation, sharpened on the whetstone of knowledge" (11903). He then goes on to find fault with her for doubting that he has attained perfection, charges her with meditating the offence of confusion of castes

---

who wishes to have a learned daughter born to him (*atha yaḥ ichhed duhitā me paṇḍitā jāyeta, &c.*) On this the commentator on the *Upanishad* explains that the learning of a daughter has reference only to domestic matters, as women are not empowered to study the Veda (*duhituḥ pāṇḍityam gṛiha-tantra-vishayam eva vede nādhikārāt*). And the commentator on the Brāhmaṇa similarly says: That a daughter's learning is skill in the domestic activity proper to women, and has no reference to the Vedas, as women have no power to engage in such study (*duhituḥ pāṇḍityam strīṇām uchite gṛiha-karmaṇi kauśalam na tu vedādi-vishayam strīṇām tatrānadhikārāt*). Professor Eggeling has sent me a list of females to whom hymns of the Rigveda are ascribed by tradition as the authoresses.

by seeking to marry him, and calls upon her to tell who she is, and all about herself. Sulabhā replies at great length (vv. 11930—12042), asking if he does not perceive his oneness with all other beings, and if he does, how he can inquire who she is? (11978) but how, she proceeds, can a king who recognises such relations as those of friend, enemy, &c., be in a state of liberation? (11981) then goes on to describe the distractions of a king's life (11990 ff.), says he must have listened in vain to the instructions of the sage whose pupil he claimed to be, and continues in bondage to things of sense, like an ordinary man (12017 f.), stating her opinion that he neither continued in the state of a householder, nor had attained to final liberation, but remained somewhere between the two (verse 12027), and concludes by vindicating her own conduct,—with the result that Janaka makes no reply.

LXXV. *Taittirīya Araṇyaka* iii. 11, 8, 1.—"Desiring reward. Vājaśravasa, bestowed all his property (at a sacrifice). He had a son called Nachiketas. Into him, being a boy, faith (a rigorous sense of duty) entered, as the presents were being brought. He said, 'Father, to whom wilt thou give me?' (This he did) a second, and a third time. Being angry (his father) said to him, 'I give thee to Death.' When he arose a Voice addressed him (2), the descendant of Gotama: 'He (thy father) hath said: go to the abode of Death; I have given thee to him. She then said: Thou shalt go when he (Death) is absent; remain three days in his house without eating. If (when he comes) he asks thee: Boy, how many nights hast thou abode (here), reply, three. If he asks what didst thou eat the first night, answer (3); Thy sons: What didst thou eat the second, say, thy cattle; what didst thou eat the third, say, thy good deeds.' He (accordingly) went when he (Death) was absent; and remained three nights in his house without food. He (Death) came to him and asked: Boy, how many nights hast thou stayed? He replied, three. (4) What didst thou eat the first night? Thy sons. What, the second? Thy cattle. What, the third? Thy good deeds. (Death then) said: Obeisance to thee, O reverend: choose a boon: May I return alive to my father; choose a second: Command that (the fruits of) my sacrifices and oblations may be imperishable: He bestowed on him this Nāchiketa fire. Hence his sacrifices and oblations do not lose their effect. . . . He (Death) then said, choose a third (boon). Command that I may again overcome death. (The commentator explains that command to mean, death as the result of a subsequent birth). He gave him this Nāchiketa fire; whereby he again overcame death. . . ." The story in the Brāhmaṇa ends here; the interesting dialogue contained in the Kaṭha Upanishad being altogether wanting in it. *Kaṭha Upanishad.* Omitting the earlier part of this Upanishad, I take it up at Vallī i. 20. Having been asked to choose a third boon, Nachiketas replies: 20. "In answer to the doubt as to a man's state after death, some say that he exists, others that he does not. The third boon which I ask is that, being instructed by thee, I may know [what is the truth] regarding this. (Death answers) 21. Even the gods have of old been in doubt on this subject; for it is not easy to know. The question is one of a subtle character. Choose another boon, Nachiketas, do not press me; give this up. 22. (Nachiketas rejoins): Thou tellest me that the gods have of old been in doubt regarding this; and as for what thou sayest that it is difficult to know, no one can be found so capable as thou art to declare it; and no other boon is equal to this. 23. (Death replies): Choose sons and grandsons who shall live a hundred years, much cattle, elephants, gold, horses; choose a wide domain of land, and live thyself as many autumns as thou desirest. 24. Or, if thou regardest any (other) boon as equal to this, choose it, with wealth and long life; be (lord) over a great kingdom; I grant thee the fulfilment of all thy desires. 25. Ask at will all those enjoyments which cannot be obtained in the world of mortals, those enchantresses with their cars and musical instruments; for such as they cannot be gained by men. Be waited upon by them after I have given them to thee; but do not, O Nachiketas, enquire about death. 26. (Nachiketas says): "These, O Death, which are things of the morrow,*

---

* *Śvobhāvāḥ*, "Things, the existence of which to-morrow is doubtful" (commentary). "Equivalent to, cares for the morrow," Böhtlingk and Roth, s.v. "Ephemeral" (Regnaud).

wear out the vigour of all a man's senses. An entire life, too, is but short. Thine be the cars, and the dancing and singing. 27. A man cannot be satisfied with wealth. Shall we obtain wealth if we have seen thee? We shall live only so long as thou shalt rule.* The boon I will choose is the one I have said. 28. What decaying mortal, living here below on earth,† but attaining to the undecaying state of the immortals, yet knowing (the reality), and reflecting on the enjoyments springing from beauty and love, would take delight in a very long life? 29. Tell us, Death, that about which they doubt regarding the great future. Nachiketas chooses no other than this boon regarding the question which is involved in mystery. ii. Vallī. 1. 1. (Death speaks): "One thing is the good, another the pleasant. Both objects, though varying, enchain man. It is well with him who of these two embraces the good; but he who chooses the pleasant misses the (highest) end. 2. The good and the pleasant present themselves to man. The wise man considering them, distinguishes them, and chooses the good in preference to the pleasant; but the unthinking man prefers the pleasant as consisting in (present) enjoyment. 3. But thou, O Nachiketas, pondering them, hast abandoned enjoyments which are pleasant and lovely, not following the road of wealth on which many men fall. 4. Far apart and divergent are these two things, ignorance, and what is known as knowledge. I regard thee, Nachiketas, as desiring knowledge; many pleasures did not allure thee. 5. Fools living enveloped in ignorance, wise in their own conceit, regarding themselves as instructed, go wandering about like blind men led by a blind man. 6. The means of attaining future felicity are not apparent to the unthinking and careless man deluded by

---

* Dr Roer (Bibliotheca Indica, vol. xv., p. 102), renders this: "If we should obtain wealth, and behold thee, we would (only) live as long as thou shalt say." In Windischmann's "Philosophie im Fortgang der Weltgeschichte, page 1709, the words are rendered: "Shall we strive after riches when we have beheld thee? We shall live so long as thou commandest." (Sollen wir nach Reichthum streben, wenn wir dich gesehen? wir werden leben so lange du befiehlst).

† There is another reading in place of the word *kvadhaḥsthaḥ* so rendered; but it is not necessary to refer further to it.

riches. Fancying that this world and no other exists, he again and again becomes subjected to my sway. 7. Wonderful is he who declares, skilful is he who attains, wonderful is he who, instructed by a skilful teacher, knows that (the Soul), which many can never hear of, which many who hear of it, cannot comprehend. 8. This (Soul) when declared by an inferior man, is not easy to comprehend, being regarded in various ways. But when it is declared by one who beholds no duality, there is no doubt as to it.* It is more minute than an atom, and transcends reasoning. 9. This recognition is not to be gained by reasoning. It can be well known when declared by another. 12. The wise man, recognising by spiritual contemplation, the primeval divine (Soul), invisible, and enveloped in mystery, seated in the heart, dwelling in the cavity, abandons joy and grief. 18. The omniscient (soul) is not born, and does not die. If it did not spring from aught, nor was any one (produced) from it. It is unborn, perpetual, eternal, and primeval. It is not slain when the body is slain. 19. If the smiter thinks that he kills, or the smitten thinks himself slain, both of them are ignorant: the one does not slay, nor is the other slain. 20. The Soul, which is, minuter than the minutest, and greater than the greatest, dwells in the heart of this living being. The man who is free from desire, and exempt from grief, beholds this greatness of the Soul by the grace of the creator.† 21. Resting, it travels afar; sleep-

---

* The words *ananya-prokte gatir atra nâsti* are differently rendered by different translators. Dr Roer renders: "(but) when it is declared by a teacher who beholds no difference, there is no doubt concerning it." Mr Gough, in the *Calcutta Review*, translates: "There is no dissenting about it when it is explained by one that recognises nought but it." M. Regnaud (Matériaux pour servir à l'histoire de la philosophie de l'Inde, p. 173) renders: "On ne saurait y atteindre si elle n'est pas transmise par un maitre qui ne voit point de différences (pour qui tout est l'Âtman);" and Windischmann, p. 1711. "Ist er von einem wahrhaften Lehrer verkundet, so kan keine Meinung (keine Verschiedenheit der Ansicht) mehr darin sein." Can the real reading be *ananyâprokte* and the sense, "when it is *not* taught by one who recognises no duality, there is no attaining to it?"

† Dr Roer, following the commentator, renders the last words "by the tranquillity of his senses;" and Mr Gough "through the limpid

ing, it moves everywhere. Who but I (the wise man, Comm.) should know this god who rejoices, and does not rejoice? 22. Regarding the soul as bodiless in bodies, as unchanging in changing things, as vast, and all pervading, the wise man does not mourn. 23. This soul is not attainable by teaching, nor by the understanding, nor by much Vedic learning. It is attainable by him whom it chooses; that man's body the soul chooses as its own.* 24. The man who has not ceased from evil deeds, who is not tranquil, meditative, and calm in spirit, cannot attain that soul by knowledge."

LXXVI. *M. Bh.* xiii. 2160. "By the victorious power of the Brahmans the Asuras lie prostrate on the ocean, by the Brahmans' favour the gods dwell in heaven. The æther could not be created, the Himalaya mountain cannot be shaken, the Ganges cannot be stemmed by an embankment. The Brahmans cannot be conquered on earth. The earth cannot be governed in opposition to the Brahmans, for they are the gods of the gods. Honour them always with gifts and service, if thou desirest to possess this earth which is girdled by the ocean. xiii. 7163. The might of the Brahmans could destroy even

---

clearness of his faculties." Windischmann translates: "durch die Gnade des Schoepfers." The commentator on Śvet. Upan. iii. 20 (see p. 198 above), renders "by the favour of the Creator."

* This verse occurs also in the Muṇḍa Upanishad iii. 2, 2. Dr Roer, who, in his translation of that passage, in his text renders the words according to the commentator's interpretation, states in a note (p. 163), that it appears to him at variance with the strict sense of the words, and he would prefer the following rendering:—"It (the supreme soul) can be obtained by him (the individual soul) whom it chooses; it (the supreme soul) chooses as its own the body of him (of the individual soul)." The same words have been rendered as follows by Professor Max Müller (Anc. Sansk. Lit., p. 320): "That divine self," the poet says, "is not to be grasped by tradition, nor by understanding, nor by all revelation: by him whom He himself chooses, by him alone is He to be grasped; that self chooses his body as his own." Mr Gough translates: "This spiritual reality is not attainable by learning, by memory, by much spiritual study; but if he choose this reality, it may be reached by him; to him the soul unfolds its own essence." And Windischmann, p. 1713, renders thus: "Welchen jener sich erwaehlt, von dem ist er erlangbar, für diesen erwaehlt, er einen eigenen Leib." "Whomsoever that one chooses for himself, by him is he attainable; for this (man) he chooses a body of his own."

the gods.* . . . 7164[b]. They are to be honoured and reverenced, and men ought to act the part of sons towards them, for these wise men support all these worlds. The Brahmans are the barriers of righteousness in all worlds; they delight in parting with riches, and control their speech. They are amiable, the supporters of creatures. . . . 7167. Austerities are ever their riches, and their word is great power. . . . They are skilled in duty and have nicety of perception. . . . 7170. They ever bear the heavy load handed down from fathers and ancestors,† and like stout oxen never sink under the load, though the road be uneven. 1771[b]. They are a lamp to all the people, the eye of those who have eyes, rich in instruction and in scriptural knowledge, skilful, perceiving the way of redemption, understanding the course of all men, ponderers of the path to the highest spiritual goal. 7175. Sandal wood and mud, food or no food, are the same to them. Their clothing may be silk, or sackcloth, of linen cloth, or skins. . . . 7177. They can make what is not divine divine, or what is divine not divine. If incensed, they could create other worlds and other rulers of worlds. The curse of these mighty ones rendered the ocean undrinkable, and the fire kindled by their anger in the Daṇḍaka forest is not even now extinguished. They are the gods of the gods, the cause of the cause, the authority of authority. What wise man can overcome them? They all, whether young or old, deserve respect; but by eminence in learning and austerities they honour [or, confer honour on] each other. An ignorant Brahman is a god, honourable, and a great source of purity. A learned Brahman is still more a god, like a full ocean. . . . . 7183. Just as even in a cemetery fire is not soiled, it shines duly in the sacrifice with butter, and in the house;

* If the proper sense is here assigned to the words *brāhmaṇānām paribhavaḥ* (and it is confirmed by the use of the words in xiii. 2160—see above), the metrical rendering in lines 9—12 of p. 62 would appear to be wrong, as the *overthrow* of the *deities* by the *victorious power* of the *Brahmans* seems to be the idea contemplated.

† The same expressions occur in xiii. 377, and xiv. 25. Ancestral rites and usages must be intended. The exact idea is not reproduced in the metrical rendering, lines 15 ff. of p. 63.

so too a Brahman, though he engages in all sorts of undesirable occupations, is in all cases to be respected."

LXXVII. *M.Bh.* xiii. 2092 ff. The following is a literal rendering of this passage, though the sense is not always clear: 2092. "Even violent men regard them with dread, since they have great qualities; (some are) like wells covered over with grass; whilst others resemble the clear sky. 2093. Some are violent in action; some others are mild as cotton; some of them are exceedingly knavish; others are austere in their lives. 2094. Some practise agriculture, or tend cattle; others pursue begging, others are thieves, others are liars, others are actors and dancers. 2095. Other Brahmans dare all kinds of acts, and in other regions (?) are possessed of various forms. 2096. Let a man always celebrate the knowledge of righteousness possessed by these good men, who are attached to, and live by, many and various occupations."

Instead of understanding these verses as descriptive of the variety of occupations and characters among contemporary Brahmans, the commentator explains as follows, the various epithets which they contain, as referring to the early Brahmanical sages who figure in the legends: 2092. "Even the violent, those who do things which they ought not to do, are afraid of them: how much more, then, men of discrimination? 'Covered over' (or 'concealed'), *i.e.*, some like Jaḍabharata *; 'others,' like Vaśishṭha. 2093. 'Violent in action;' he refers to Durvāsas and others: 'mild,' Gautama and others, who fearing lest they should inflict injury on creatures, even by walking on foot, placed eyes in their feet, and so got the name of Akshapāda,† *i.e.*, eye-footed. 'Exceedingly knavish': *i.e.*, Agastya and others, who in order to devour Vātāpi, showed themselves very greedy of flesh. 2094. 'Practising agriculture': Uddālaka, Guru, and others; 'tending cattle'; Upamanyu and others, on their teacher's account; 'begging': Dattātreya and others; 'thieves': Vālmīki, Viśvāmitra, and others; 'liars,' fond of wrangling: Nārada and others;

* Whose story is told in the Bhāgavata Purāṇa, Book v., Section 9 and 10.

† A name of Gautama.

'actors and dancers': Bhărăta* and others. 2095. 'Venturing upon, or daring, all acts;' even equal to the drying up of the ocean and such like acts; 'various occupations;' perpetrating even forbidden acts in order to conceal their own forms, or for the protection of the world; but in reality knowing their duty: the praise of such men should always be celebrated."

This view of the sense of these verses, however, cannot be correct, and must be dictated by a desire to save the honour, and veil the faults, of the commentator's own class.

In fact, such an interpretation is quite inconsistent with other passages in this same book of the Mahābhārata (See verses 1583 ff. and 4273 ff. of book xiii.), and in Manu iii. 150 ff. (See Sir W. Jones's translation). In these texts the Brahmans characterised in the Mahābhārata, xiii. 4374, 4293, and 4309, as those who are ornaments to their class, and those who disgrace it, (*panktipāvana* and *panktidūsha*, or *apānkteya*), who in the one case are fit, and in the other unfit, to be invited to Śrāddhas (celebrations and feasts in honour of deceased ancestors), are respectively described. A variety of physical blemishes and infirmities, unsuitable occupations, and offences against morality are enumerated, which render many Brahmans unfit to be so entertained. Among those disqualified persons are mentioned thieves (*stena*), gamblers (*kitava*), dancers (*kuśīlava*, *nartaka*), singers (*gāyana*), tumblers (*plavaka*), drinkers of intoxicating liquors (*madyapa*), hypocrites (*dāmbhika*), unbelievers, (*nāstikavritti*), revilers of the Vedas (*vedanindaka*), incendiaries (*agāradāhin*), fanciers of dogs (*śvakrīdin*), &c. Some of the offences specified are merely infractions of caste rules (such as sacrificing for Śūdras (*hotāro vṛishalānām*), teaching, or being taught by Śūdras (*vṛishalādhyāpaka*, *vṛishalaśishya*), teaching, or being taught for hire (*anuyoktṛi* and *anuyukta*, or *bhṛitakādhyāpaka* and *bhṛitakādhyāpita*.) The disparaging opinions cited above from Manu and the Mahābhārata in regard to all Brahmans who came forward as singers, dancers, and tumblers, may, however, perhaps be extended to all

---

* Bharata is the reputed originator of dramatic literature.

members of the sacerdotal class who appeared in any capacity as professional performers for the public amusement.

I subjoin a translation of some other verses in the same book of the Mahābhārata xiii. 2154 ff.

"I esteem their power greater, like that of a king who practises austerity. And they are dangerous to approach, fiery, fierce, impetuous (or quick), in action. Some of them have the nature of lions, others of tigers, others of boars, or deer, or fishes. The touch of some is like that of serpents, of others like that of sea-monsters (*makara*). Some kill by bitter words, others by their glance. Some are like poisonous serpents, others are sluggish;—such are the various characters of Brahmans."

On this the commentator merely remarks thus: "greater," &c.: though they possess the faults of being fiery, &c., they deserve respect.

In the Mahābhārata xii. 2655, it is enjoined upon a king that actors and dancers, wrestlers and jugglers, should give lustre and pleasing amusement to his city.

In the preface to his "Select Specimens from the Theatre of the Hindus," Prof. H. H. Wilson remarks in regard to these Indian actors: "Companies of actors in India must have been common at an early date, and must have been reputable, for the inductions (introductions?) often refer to the poets as their personal friends, and a poet of tolerable merit in India under the ancient regime, was the friend and associate of sages and kings. The Hindu actors were never apparently classed with vagabonds and menials, and were never reduced to contemplate a badge of servitude as a mark of distinction."]

LXXVIII. *M. Bh.* xii. 11811. Yājnavalkya is the speaker. "From knowledge springs final liberation; it is not attainable without knowledge; so they (the wise) declare. Wherefore a man should seek after true knowledge, whereby he may deliver himself from birth and death. Constantly obtaining knowledge from a Brāhman, a Kshatriya, Vaiśya, or a lowly Śūdra, a man should always practise faith; birth and death do not affect him who has faith. All castes are Brahmanical and sprung from Brahmā, and they all constantly utter the sacred word (*brahma*). Having an understanding of this sacred word, I declare to thee the reality, the scripture;—this entire universe is Brahma. The Brāhman sprang from (Brahmā's) mouth, the Kshatriyas from his arms, the Vaiśyas from his navel, the Śūdras from his feet: all the castes are to be understood as having no other origin. From ignorance men adopt this or that source of action, (*karma-yoni*), and as they proceed into non-existence (? *abhāva*), so the castes, destitute of knowledge fall, from dire ignorance, into a net of natural births (? *prākṛitam yoni-jālam*). Wherefore knowledge is to be sought everywhere, wherever existing, as I have told thee. The Brāhman or whosoever else stands on (appropriates) it has, they declare, eternal redemption."

LXXIX. *M. Bh.* xii. 6939. "There is no distinction of castes: this entire world, having been by Brahmā originally created Brahmanical (or in the image and of the essence of Brahmā), became separated into castes in consequence of (the diversity of men's) works." The characteristic qualities of the Kshatriyas, Vaisyas, and Śūdras are then described. It will be observed that the verse which I have quoted goes further than the preceding passage (xii. 11811 ff.), by ignoring the common statement adopted there in verse 11814, (unless that is an interpolation) of the different castes having sprung from different parts of Brahmā's body.

M. Bh. xiii. 6612. "For pure acts a pure-minded Śūdra who subdues his senses, should be honoured as a Brahman:—Such is the doctrine revealed by Brahmā (or in the Scripture). 6613. The Śūdra in whom a virtuous nature and virtuous actions are found, is to be esteemed more excellent than a Brāhman. Such is my opinion." (Mahādeva is the speaker.) "6614. Neither birth, nor initiation, nor learning, nor progeny, (descent?) are the causes of Brahmanhood: good conduct alone creates it. 6615. All this class of Brāhmans in the world is only constituted such by virtuous conduct; and a Śūdra who continues to conduct himself virtuously attains to Brahman hood.* 6616. I consider that the Brahmanical nature (or the nature derived from Brahmā: see *Mahābhārata* xii. 6939, quoted above in p. 261) is the same everywhere (*i.e.*, in whomsoever it is found). He in whom the pure Brahma, devoid of qualities (goodness, passion, darkness), resides, is a Brāhman."

The passage in which these lines occur forms a long reply by Mahādeva to a question of his wife Umā, who had enquired how men of one caste are, in another birth born as members of another class, higher or lower, than the one they had previously belonged to. Mahādeva begins by saying that Brahmanhood was difficult to attain; and that Brāhmans, Kshatriyas, Vaisyas, and Śūdras were all such by nature, and either retained or lost their former caste, or were raised to a higher caste, according to their works. In the verses which I have last quoted, however (unless it be the second half of verse 6615), the idea is different. It is that the real essence of Brahmanhood is, or depends upon, conduct, or on participation in the nature of Brahma, and so may be common to men of all classes who possess that character.

LXXX. *M.Bh.* xii. 8801. "Even a man of low caste, and a woman solicitous of righteousness, may attain to the highest state by following this path."

xiv. 592. "The eternal Brahma is the highest state, in whom a man, after leaving his body, attains to immortality, and is ever blessed. Following this course, even people of low birth, women, Vaiśyas, and Śūdras arrive at the highest condition; how much more, then, learned Brahmans and Kshatriyas, devoted to their duties, and seeking after the world of Brahma."

LXXXI. *M.Bh.* xiii. 2610. "A man of high rank (jyāyāmsam) is not to be honoured if devoid of good qualities, while even a Śūdra is to be honoured if acquainted with duty and virtuous in conduct."

---

* *Niyachhati*, the reading of the word so rendered, is alleged in Böhtlingk and Roth's Lexicon (vol. v. column 1370) *s.v.*, *gam* + *ni*, to be wrong, the correct reading being regarded as *niyachhati*.

LXXXII. *M. Bh.* xii. 10931. "Let no one destroy himself although he be destitute of enjoyments. Manhood (*i.e.*, man's nature) is altogether noble, even in the state of a Chāṇḍāla."

LXXXIII. *M. Bh.* xii. 8752. "The wise look with an equal eye on a learned Brahman of good birth, on a cow, an elephant, a dog, an outcast. For in all creatures, moving and stationary, dwells that one great Spirit by whom the universe is stretched out. Brahma is then attained when an embodied being perceives himself in all beings, and all beings in himself."

LXXXIV. *M. Bh.* v. 1492. "He who, whether of low or high birth, does not transgress law, but regards virtue, and is mild and modest, is better than a hundred high-born men." iii. 12531. "Truth, self-restraint, austerity, liberality, abstinence from cruelty, continual adherence to duty,—these qualities always constitute perfect men, and not caste or birth."

LXXXV. *M. Bh.* xii. 9667. "The gods call that man a Brahman by whom all this universe is comprehended, both rudimental nature (Prakṛiti) and its mutations (Vikṛiti), and who knows the course of all beings."

LXXXVI. *M. Bh.* xii. 8925. "He by whom, though alone, the ether (ākāśa) is, as it were, always filled, and by whom (by whose absence) it becomes empty, though crowded with men, is called by the gods a Brahman."

LXXXVII. *M. Bh.* iii. 17392. "A Yaksha (ghost or spirit) asks:—In what does Brahmanhood consist, O king, in birth, in conduct, in study, in Vedic learning? declare this distinctly. Yudhishṭhira replies:—Hear, Yaksha, neither birth, nor study, nor Vedic learning are the causes of Brahmanhood; the cause is conduct alone, without a doubt. Good conduct is to be carefully adhered to, by a Brahman especially. He who is not destitute in respect of conduct is not destitute, but he who is ruined in conduct is ruined. Readers and teachers and other people who are interested in the Śāstras are (only) devoted fools; he who acts is wise. The man whose conduct is bad, though he knows the four Vedas, exceeds (is worse than) a Śūdra; he who zealously offers the Agnihotra and is calm in spirit is called a Brahman." iii. 12470. "He in whom truth, liberality, patience, a good disposition, freedom from cruelty, are seen, is a Brahman, so (says) the Smṛiti."

LXXXVIII. *M.Bh.* iii. 14075. "The Brahman who practises vicious acts which occasion loss of caste, who is hypocritical, skilled in evil, is on the level of a Śūdra, while I regard the Śūdra who is constantly active in self-command, in truth, in duty, as a Brahman, for he is such in conduct."

LXXXIX. *M. Bh.* xii. 2363. "He who is self-controlled, a drinker of soma, of noble disposition, compassionate, all-enduring, free from desire, honest, mild, innocent, patient, is a Brahman, and not any other man whose acts are sinful."

XC. *M. Bh.* xiii. 1542. "Kaśyapa says:—All the Vedas with the six Angas (appendages), the Sānkhya (philosophy), the Purāṇas, and high birth, all these things do not save the Brahman who is destitute of good character. 1543. Agni says:—The man who studies and thinks himself learned, but who by his knowledge injures the reputation of others, he falls, he does not practise truth; the worlds (future states of happiness) which he gains are temporary."

XCI. *M. Bh.* xci. "But whosoever gives gold, jewels, cows, or horses to those who go about this earth praising righteousness, but not practising it, bent on causing a confusion of castes,—he abides in hell for ten years, eating ordure."

XCII. *M. Bh.* xiii. 3082[b], f. "It is a misfortune to a Brahman to possess great stores of riches. Constant association with Fortune will puff up, and delude, a man. And when Brahmans become deluded, righteousness is sure to perish."

XCIII. *Manu* ii. 162. "A Brahman should ever shrink from

honour, as from poison; and ever desire disrespect, as he would nectar. 163. Though treated with disrespect he sleeps sweetly, and sweetly awakes; but his despiser perishes." *Mahābhārata* xii. 8449. "A man who knows the reality will enjoy disrespect as he would nectar; and the wise man will ever shrink from honour as from poison. Though treated with disrespect, he sleeps sweetly, and being liberated from all faults, he is free from fear both here and hereafter; but the contemner perishes." Ibid 9064. "He will not love scents, or well flavoured things, or pleasure, nor receive the ornaments of this or that (person?). He will not desire honour, fame, or reputation. Such is the practice of a Brahman who sees." Ibid. 11016. "Let not a wise man abuse the unwise with reviling or contempt; and so let him not elevate another and injure himself. 11017. Let the wise man enjoy disrespect as he would nectar. Treated with disrespect he sweetly sleeps, but he who so treats him perishes." Ibid. v. 1168. "The foolish afflict the wise with reviling and abuse; the speaker incurs sin, while the endurer is freed."

XCIV. *M. Bh.* iii. 13448. "They who do not in thought, speech, act, or intention (buddhi) commit sin,—these great men practise austerity. It is not the maceration of the body." *Ibid.* xii. 343. "The wise say of the four stages of life (āśramas) when placed in the balance, that the other three together occupy the one scale, and that of the householder alone occupies the other. This is the path trodden by great sages, this is the course of men who know the worlds, when they regard in the scale pleasure and heaven. [The sense of this is not very clear.] He who acts thus is the ascetic, not he who leaves his home and goes to forest, like a madman." Ibid. 2929. "Avoidance of injury, truth-speaking, austerity (tapas) and compassion,—these things the thoughtful regard as austerity (tapas), and not the maceration of the body."

XCV. *M. Bh.* xii. 12126. "Those who are born in forest hermitages, and who die there, have less merit, since they have no experience of the enjoyment of pleasure. But he who abandons enjoyments and practises bodily austerity, by him nothing is unattained; this I regard as a great reward."

XCVI. *M. Bh.* xii. 5961. 'What need has either a self-subduing man, or one who is not such, of (retiring to) the forest? The place where the self-subduing man dwells, is a forest, is an hermitage." Ibid v. 1680. "A muni (sage) is not so called from remaining silent (*maunât*), nor from living in a forest. He is called the most excellent muni who knows his own character."

XCVII. *M. Bh.* xii. 293. "It is enjoined as fitting that men should abandon the world in the time of calamity, or when worn out by decay, or overcome by enemies. 294. Wherefore the wise do not approve of abandonment of the world, and the keen-eyed regard it as a transgression of duty. . . . 296. This untrue conception of the Vedas, which has only a semblance of justice, has received currency from needy infidels unblessed by fortune. 297. A man who has adopted this condition of a shaveling, who maintains himself alone, and assumes the guise of holiness, cannot (truly) live, but only sink. 298. He may indeed live happily in the forests alone, without supporting his sons and grandsons, the divine ṛishis, guests, or ancestors. 299. Neither these deer, nor boars, nor birds conquer heaven [by their forest life]. . . . 300. If any one could gain perfection by abandoning the world, the hills and trees would soon attain it; 301, for these are seen to practise constant retirement from the world, free from distresses, free from family attachments, and leading the life of religious students. 302. Now, if a man attains happiness through his own successes, not through those of others, he must therefore act; no good fortune results from inaction. 304. Behold how people are actively engaged each in their own occupations. Act, therefore, for no success results from inaction."

XCVIII. *M. Bh.* xii. 4094. "If my birth is mean, good birth arises from good character. I seek those acts by which reputation is spread. If I dwell in a cemetery, hear about my contemplation. It is the soul which produces actions; a hermitage does not confer righteousness. If a man slay a Brahman in an hermitage, is that no sin? and if he bestows a cow in a place other than a hermitage, is the gift fruitless?"

XCIX. *M.Bh.* v. 1623. "Dhṛitarāshṭra asks: Is the man who knows the Ṛig-, the Yajur-, and the Sāma- Vedas, and commits sin, polluted by that sin or not? Sanatsujāta answers: Texts of the Sāma-, Ṛig-, or Yajur- Vedas, do not deliver the ignorant man from his sinful action; this I tell thee truly. 1635. (=v. 1224). Vedic texts do not deliver from sin the guileful man living in guile. They abandon him at the time of his end, as birds whose wings are grown leave their nests." (compare Isaiah i. 11 ff., lviii. 6; Hosea vi. 6.) Vṛiddha Chāṇakya, xi. 7.—"A man who is inwardly depraved is not cleansed by bathing at a hundred Tīrthas (holy places); just as a pitcher holding intoxicating liquor, even though burnt (is not rendered pure)." Subhāshitārṇava, 267. As a vessel which has held intoxicating liquor does not become clean though washed with river water, so, too, a living being defiled by falsehood and other sins is not purified by bathing. *Ibid.*, 96. Liberality, worship, austerity, visiting holy places, learning—all these things avail nothing to the man whose heart is not pure."

C. *M. Bh.* iii. 13445. "The carrying of the triple staff, silence, a load of matted locks, shaving, a garb of bark or skin, religious observances, consecration, the agnihotra offering, abode in a forest, the drying up of the body—all these things will be worthless if the disposition is not pure. . . . 13448[b]. Those high-souled men who sin not in thought, word, deed, or intention—they practise austerity which does not consist in drying up the body. . . . 13450[b]. A sage living at home, always clean and adorned, who throughout his life is merciful—he is freed from his sins. Sinful deeds are not cleansed by abstinence from food and so forth. 13454. It is not from eating roots and fruits, nor from silence, nor from fasting (*lit.* eating air), nor by shaving the head, nor by sitting in a hut, nor by wearing matted hair, nor sleeping on the bare ground, nor constant abstinence, nor by tending fire, nor by entering into water, nor sleeping on the ground, nor by knowledge (?), nor by rites, that decay, death, and diseases are averted, and the highest condition is attained. As seeds burned by fire do not sprout again, so the soul again is never associated with sufferings which have been burnt up by knowledge." *M. Bh.* xii. 2979.—"Austerity is superior to sacrifice—this is the highest doctrine of the Veda. I shall describe this austerity. Hear from me what it is. Abstinence from injury and cruelty, truth, austerity, pity—this is what the wise regard as austerity, and not the maceration of the body."

CI. *M. Bh.* i. 3095, repeated in xii. 6002, and xiii. 3650ᵇ ff. "Let a thousand Aśvamedhas (immolations of a horse) and truth be weighed in the balance—truth exceeds the thousand aśvamedhas.

CII. xiii. 1544. "Let a thousand Aśvamedhas and truth be weighed against each other—I know not if the sacrifices would weigh half so much as truth." Comp. xiii. 6073.

CIII. This is a prose passage from the Śatapatha Brāhmaṇa, ii. 2, 2, 19: "As fire is kindled into brilliancy when clarified butter is shed upon it, so the man who speaks truth acquires ever greater glory, and becomes daily more prosperous; whilst he who utters falsehood declines continually in glory, and becomes every day more wretched, as fire is extinguished when water is poured upon it. Wherefore a man should speak nothing but truth." *Ibid.* iii. 1, 2, 10: "A man becomes impure by uttering falsehood."

CIV. This passage also is from a prose work, the Taittirīya Araṇyaka x. 9, and was pointed out to me by Professor R. von Roth of Tübingen: "As the odour of a tree in full flower is wafted from a distance, so, too, the odour of a holy act is wafted from afar. As a man who steps upon the edge of a sword placed over a pit (cries out),* 'I shall slip, I shall fall into the pit:' so let a man guard himself from falsehood

* Professor Roth observes that the text here appears not to be quite correct, though the sense is not thereby affected.

(or sin)." (The commentator on the passage remarks that reference is here made to a man expert in performing various difficult feats, and engaged in exhibiting his skill for the amusement of a king and his court.)

CV. *M. Bh.* v. 1289. "Let a man maintain good conduct. Riches come and go. He whose wealth only is lost suffers no loss; but he who loses his good conduct is indeed lost."

CVI. *M. Bh.* v. 1381. "Let him who desires great prosperity in respect of wealth, first practise righteousness; for prosperity does not depart from righteousness, as ambrosia does not depart from heaven." *Ibid.* 1223. "Just as a man sets his heart on what is good, all the objects which he has in view are attained; of this there is no doubt." *Ibid.* 4158. "Let him who seeks pleasure and riches first practise righteousness; for riches and pleasure never depart from righteousness."

CVII. *M. Bh.* xii. 9810 (incorrectly quoted in p. 78 as xii. 910). "In wealth there is a small portion of enjoyment; but the highest enjoyment is found in righteousness."

CVIII. *Vâyu Purâṇa* viii. 190 (see Original Sanskrit Texts, i. 98 f.) "The Vedas, with their appendages, sacrifices, fasts, and ceremonies, avail not to a depraved man when his disposition has become corrupted. All external rites are fruitless to one who is inwardly debased, however energetically he may perform them. A man who bestows even the whole of his substance with a defiled heart will thereby acquire no merit—of which a good disposition is the only cause."

CIX. *M. Bh.* iii. 13747. "They who think there is no such thing as righteousness, who have no faith in it, and who deride the pure, undoubtedly perish. The sinner is ever like a great inflated skin. The imaginations of conceited fools are baseless." [The reference to the passage from which the last four lines of the metrical passage have been derived has been lost.]

M. Bh. xii. 2317. "A man who has faith, and who

has subdued his senses, kindles the sacrificial fire whether the sun has risen or not: faith is the great cause (of well-doing). That which he spills is the first; and what he does not spill is the last. There are many forms of sacrifice, and various rewards of works. The Brahman who knows these, who has acquired certain knowledge, and is possessed by faith—he ought to sacrifice. 2320. They declare to be good that man who desires to sacrifice, though he be a thief or a sinner, or the worst of sinners. The rishis applaud him —and this is certainly good; it is a settled point that the castes should in every way and always sacrifice. There is nothing in the three worlds equal to sacrifice; wherefore they say that a man should sacrifice ungrudgingly, according to his power and will."

CX. *M.Bh.* xiv. 2835. "The sinful, hypocritical Brahman, the worst of men, who, possessed by passion and illusion, and unbridled in conduct, has acquired riches by sinful acts, and in order to make men trust him [or believe him virtuous], bestows gifts on Brahmans, he comes to a miserable end. Bent also upon gathering (money), enslaved by avarice and illusion, he torments living creatures by sin, springing from impure intention (?) He who, having so gained wealth by delusion, bestows it, or sacrifices, does not in the next world enjoy the reward of these acts, owing to his sinful acquisition of riches. But those righteous men who according to their means give gifts, gleanings of grain, roots, fruits, vegetables, a vessel of water, go to heaven." *Ibid.* xiii. 5544[b].—"Excellent food, rightfully gained, is to be given to Brahmans."

This passage, it will be noticed, is very freely rendered in the metrical version.

CXI. *Mbh.* xiii. 7594 (wrongly quoted in p. 80 as xiii. 7574), 7595[b].—"A man should worship the gods with sincerity, should serve his guru (teacher) honestly, and lay up treasure in the next world.' 7594. Let him practise righteousness alone, and not make mere pretences to it."

CXII. *M.Bh.* xiv. 2788.—"Righteousness is not so delighted by the bestowal of abundant gifts, as it is pleased by small gifts (derived from means) gained justly, and purified by faith." *Ibid.* xii. 10788.—" A gift bestowed with contempt, and without faith, is declared by munis, who state the truth, to be the worst of gifts." Compare Proverbs xv. 8, " The sacrifice of the wicked is an abomination to the Lord; but the prayer of the upright is his delight." Ecclesiasticus xxxiv. 19, " The Most High is not pleased with the offerings of the wicked; neither is he pacified for sin by the multitude of sacrifices. Whoso bringeth an offering of the goods of the poor, doeth as one that killeth the son before his father's eyes." *Ibid.* xxxv. 7, " The sacrifice of a just man is acceptable, and the memorial thereof shall never be forgotten."

Euripides, fragment of his *Danae*:—*ἐγὼ δὲ πολλάκις σοφωτέρους πένητας ἄνδρας εἰσορῶ τῶν πλουσίων, καὶ θεοῖσι μικρὰ χειρὶ θύοντας τέλη τῶν βουθυτούντων ὄντας εὐσεβεστέρους.*

" But I often perceive poor men to be wiser than the rich; and those who present with their hands small offerings to the gods, to be more pious than those who sacrifice oxen."

Euripides, fragment (940) in Nauck's Edition:—*εὖ ἴσθ', ὅταν τις εὐσεβῶν θύῃ θεοῖς, κἂν μικρὰ θύῃ, τυγχάνει σωτηρίας.*

" Know this well, that when any pious man sacrifices to the gods, even if his offering be small, he obtains safety."

CXIII. *M. Bh.* v. 1028. " These two men, O king, abide above in heaven, a master who is patient, and a poor man who is liberal."

CXIV. *M. Bh.* xii. 795. "They (the wise) declare that riches should be bestowed, not enjoyed or hoarded. What is the use of hoarding money, when a higher employment of it exists?" This direction as to the use of wealth has been somewhat modified in the translation.

CXV. *M. Bh.* xii. 5906. " These men do not practise righteousness for the sake of wealth or reputation, but because it must necessarily be practised; and so of bodily acts." *Ibid.* 1328: " Let not a righteous man bestow gifts for reputation, nor from fear, or upon a benefactor," &c., &c.

CXVI. *M. Bh.* vii. 5960. " They say that noble deeds are

easily practised by a noble man; but ignoble deeds are perpetrated by him with the greatest difficulty."

CXVII. *M. Bh.* v. 3313. "If striving according to his power for a righteous end, a man does not gain it, he undoubtedly attains the merit of it."

CXVIII. *M. Bh.* v. 3314. "If a man who has in thought meditated sin does not seek to carry out his intention, he does not receive its punishment; so moralists think."

CXIX. *M. Bh.* xii. 7063. "The wise say that the righteousness of all creatures is seated in the mind; let every one therefore seek in his mind the good of all creatures."

CXX. *M. Bh.* xii. 7064. "Let a man practise righteousness alone (*i.e.*, by himself). In doing so he has no helper. Having only ascertained the rule, what can a helper do?"

CXXI. *M. Bh.* xiii. 3010. "He who gives, and who does, what is (dear) pleasing, receives (dear) pleasant things. He is dear to (all) creatures, here and hereafter. But he who from haughtiness does not honour according to his power a poor helpless (?) suppliant is cruel. He who shows kindness even to a poor enemy who takes refuge with him in his misfortune, is an excellent man."

CXXII. *M. Bh.* v. 1010. "He who has acquired great wealth, or knowledge, or regal power, and yet displays no arrogance, is called a wise man."

CXXIII. *M. Bh.* v. 1088. "Misfortunes do not visit the excellent man who eats moderately, meting out support to those who depend upon him, who sleeps moderately after doing an immense amount of work, and who when asked gives to his enemies."

CXXIV. *M. Bh.* v. 1011. "Who is more cruel than the man who alone eats of the best, and wears fine garments, but does not (properly) support those who depend upon him."

CXXV. *Manu* xi. 9 f. The following is Sir Wm. Jones's translation of these verses, 9. "He who bestows gifts on strangers (with a view to worldly fame), while he suffers his family to live in distress, though he has power (to support them), touches his lips with honey, but swallows poison; such virtue is counterfeit. 10. Even what he does for the sake of his future spiritual body, to the injury of those whom he is bound to maintain, shall bring him ultimate misery both in this life and in the next." The words placed by Jones at the beginning of verse 10 are explained by the commentator Kullūka as "gifts and so forth given from a feeling of duty in reference to the next world."

CXXVI. *M. Bh.* iii. 16796. "Knowing that such is the conduct in which noble men delight, the good, when they promote the welfare of others, expect no reciprocity."

CXXVII. *M. Bh.* v. 1517[b] f. (= xiii. 5571). "Let no man do to another what would be repugnant to himself. This is duty in summary. Any other rule is according to inclination." *Ibid.* xiii. 5572. "In refusing, in bestowing, in regard to pleasure and pain, to what is agreeable and disagreeable, a man obtains the proper rule by considering the case as like his own." *Ibid.* xii. 9248[b] f. "Let no man do to others any action which he would not wish to be done by others to himself," knowing that it is displeasing to himself. 9250[b]. How can any one who himself desires to live slay another? 9251 (wrongly printed 9281 in p. 84). "What a man wishes for himself let him also meditate for another."

In the 8th vol. of the "Bijbel voor Jongelieden," being the 2d vol. of the Apokriefe Boeken, p. 168, Professor Oort refers to the following as a saying of Hillel: "Wat uzelven onaangenaam zou zijn, doe dat ook uwen naaste niet aan; ziedaar de gansche Wet; al het overige is hiervan slechts de verklaring;" i.e., *Do not to your neighbour what would be disagreeable to yourself; see in this the whole law; all the rest is only the explanation of this.*

CXXVIII. *M. Bh.* ii. 2442. "The good recollect only benefits, and not hostile acts, though done to them, being grateful that confidence has been placed in them." [Compare *Ibid.* verse 2424.] *Ibid.* 2438. "They who do not recognise any hostilities, who look to good qualities, not bad, who do not enter upon quarrels, are most excellent men. 2439. The good recollect only benefits and not hostile acts though done to them; and doing what is beneficial to others, they expect no return."

CXXIX. *M. Bh.* i. 6116 (= 6254b f.) "He only is a complete man, a (good) deed done to whom is not lost and who does more" ["many times more," in verse 6255] "for another, than another has done for him." *Ibid.* iii. 13252. "Let a man do a hundredfold what has been done to him. Among the gods there is nothing fixed (in regard to this)."

CXXX. *M. Bh.* iii. 13745 (=xii. 3531b.) "Let a man set himself to do the good which he may design. Let him not reward evil for evil, but be always good."

CXXXI. *M. Bh.* xii. 3880. I give this verse with its context from the *Mahābhārata* xii. 3877 ff. "A foolish man who is unfortunate from of old, in consequence of what has gone before, constantly reviles the Disposer of events, (comp. iii. 13847). He cannot endure those who are successful, (3878) and regards prosperous men as undeserving. From this cause this (his) suffering continually recurs. 3879. Those who fancy themselves heroes, are full of envy and haughtiness. Be not thou thus envious, O king. 3880. Endure thou the prosperity of others, although thyself unprosperous. Discreet men always enjoy good fortune, though it is found elsewhere. 3881. For prosperity, though abiding with an enemy, flows away to a man. And righteous men who are thoughtful and (3882) practised in contemplation, voluntarily abandon prosperity, and quit their sons and grandsons, perceiving, as they do, that the love (of gain) and wealth, occasion much pain. 3883. Other men, too, abandon (the pursuit of) wealth, thinking it to be very difficult of acquisition."

CXXXII. *M. Bh.* xii. 4993. "A man who repays very largely a benefit conferred on himself is not equal to the first benefactor. He only acts in requital of what has been done for him; the other acts without (this) motive."

CXXXIII. *Vikrama Charita*, 158. "Hear the sum of duty which is declared in a million of books. Helping others is to be esteemed as righteousness, oppression of others as sin."

CXXXIV. *Panchatantra* iii. 103 (Bombay ed.) "Hear the sum of righteousness, and when thou hast heard, learn (or ponder) it. Do not to others what would be repugnant to thyself."

CXXXV. *Panchatantra* 247 (Bombay ed.), 227 (Kosegarten's ed.) "What merit is there in the goodness of the man who is good to his benefactors; he only who is good to those who do him wrong, is called good by the virtuous."

CXXXVI. *Bhāgavata Purāṇa* viii. 7-44. "Good men are generally distressed by the distresses of mankind; such (sympathy) is the highest worship of Purusha, the Soul of all things."

Bahudarśana, 122. "That the wise man should in whatever manner (he can) promote the satisfaction of every embodied creature—this is the worship of Vishṇu." Compare Kāmandakīya-nīti-sāra, iii. 34 ff.; Rājatarangiṇī, i. 227; Agni Purāṇa, &c.

CXXXVII. *Bhāgavata Purāna* x. 22. 35. "What constitutes the birth of embodied creatures in this world completely fruitful is this, that they should with their life, with their means, with their understanding, and with their speech, always seek to promote the welfare of other creatures in this world." Panchatantra, iii. 96 (Bomb. ed.). "He whose days come and go devoid of righteousness,—he, like the bellows of a blacksmith, though breathing, does not live."

CXXXVIII. *Vṛiddha Chāṇakya* xv. 1. "The man whose heart melts with pity to all creatures, has knowledge, and gains final liberation (*moksha*); which are not attained by matted hair, ashes, and the garb of a mendicant."

CXXXIX. *M.Bh.* iii. 13,235. "Let a man conquer a niggard by generosity, a liar by truth, a cruel man by patience, and a bad man by goodness." *Ibid.* v. 1518. "Let a man conquer anger with calmness, a bad man by goodness, a niggard by generosity, and falsehood by truth." (This maxim occurs also as verse 223, in the Buddhist Dhammapada, written in the Pali language.) A very different maxim is found in *M. Bh.* xii. 4052. "To act towards any man as he has acted to any other, is righteousness. Deceitful conduct is to be quelled by deceit; and kindly conduct is to be requitted with kindness."

CXL. *M. Bh.* v. 1270. "The gods regard with delight the man who does not utter opprobrious language, or cause it to be uttered; who when struck does not strike again, or cause (his smiter) to be struck; and who does not desire to smite the wicked man." *Ibid.* xii. 11008. "He who when reviled does not say anything either bitter or pleasing, who, through patience, when smitten does not smite again, nor wish any evil to his smiter, in him the gods constantly delight." Instead of "delight in," Dr Böhtlingk here renders "envy." In *M. Bh.* xii. 9968 ff., it is said, among other things, of a man who in pursuit of final emancipation has renounced the world, and adopted a mendicant and ascetic life, v. 9972: "Let him endure reviling with patience; let him desire nothing; when he is angrily addressed, let him speak kindly; when reviled, let him reply benevolently."

CXLI. *M. Bh.* xii. 5528. "Suitable hospitality should be shown even to an enemy when he comes to one's house. A tree does not withdraw its shade even from him who comes to cut it down." (These words are said in the poem to be addressed by a bird to a fowler.)

M. Bh. ii. 189. "Dost thou cherish as a son an enemy who has resorted to thee from fear, or who has fallen into decay, or who has been conquered in battle?" This is one of a series of questions on duty proposed by Nārada to Yudhishṭhira, ii. 151 ff.

M. Bh. xiii. 3012. "He is a most excellent man who befriends in his calamity even an enemy in distress who takes refuge with him."

xiii. 6657. "Those friendly men go to heaven who, when they meet with them, treat with the same disposition foes and friends."

CXLII. *Subhâshitârṇava*, 274; and quoted in the preface of Halhed's Gentoo Code. "A good man who regards the welfare of others does not show enmity even when he is being destroyed. Even when it is being cut down, the Sandal tree imparts fragrance to the edge of the axe."

CXLIII. *Mahâbhârata* xiii. 3212. "Let no one contemn a person who comes to his house, or send him away (empty). A gift bestowed even on an outcast or a dog is not thrown away."

The sentiment in verse 3216 is not so good. "He who has committed a very sinful act, and gives food to a suppliant, especially to a Brahman, does not suffer for his sin."

CXLIV. *Hitopadeśa* i. 55 (or 63). "The good show compassion even to worthless creatures. The moon does not withdraw its light from the house of the Chânḍâla."

CXLV. *Panchatantra* v. 38 (Bombay edition). "To consider, Is this man one of our own or an alien? is a mark of little-minded persons; but the whole earth is of kin to the generous hearted." Compare St Luke x. 29 ff, "And who is my neighbour?"

Bhâgavata Purâṇa x. 72, 19. "Who is an alien to men who look upon all with an equal eye?" Compare Euripides, fragment 19, of an uncertain author:

Ἅπας μὲν ἀὴρ αἰετῷ περάσιμος,
ἅπασα δὲ χθὼν ἀνδρὶ γενναίῳ πατρίς.

"The entire air can be crossed by an eagle; the entire earth is the native country of the noble man."

CXLVI. *Râmâyaṇa* vi. 115, 41. "A noble man should show mercy to men whether virtuous or wicked, or even deserving of death; there is no one who does not offend."

CXLVII. *Manu* ii. 238. "Let a man accept with faith valuable knowledge even from a person of low degree, (a knowledge of) the highest duty even from a humble man, and a jewel of a wife even from an ignoble family. 239. Nectar may be drawn even from poison; good words even from a child; (a lesson of) good conduct even from an enemy, and gold rom what is unclean. 240. Women, gems, knowledge, righteousness, purity, good words, and various arts are to be received from all quarters. 241. In time of calamity, it is prescribed that a student may read with one who is not a Brahman." Compare Mahābhārata xii. 6071 f., which corresponds nearly with the first of the two preceding verses: the last clause of verse 6072 runs thus: "For women, gems, and water from their nature cannot be spoiled." *Śārṅgadhara's Paddhati, Nīti*, 34. "A wise sentiment should be received even from a child. In the absence of the sun, does not even a lamp illuminate a house?" Similarly in the Hitopadeśa ii. 77 (or 78). See No. lxxviii. above.

CXLVIII. *M. Bh.* v. 1125. "Let a man take from all quarters what is valuable, even from a raving madman and a chattering child, as he extracts gold from stones."

CXLIX. *M. Bh.* v. 1272; xii. 11,023. "A man becomes such as those are with whom he dwells, and as those whose society he loves; and such as he desires to become. Whether he associates with a good man or a bad, with a thief, or an ascetic, he undergoes their influence, as cloth does that of the dye (with which it is brought into contact)." vii. 5961. "A man quickly acquires the character of those among whom he lives, and the places to which he resorts: this, (O Pārtha), is seen in thee." Compare 1 Corinthians xv. 33 (from Menander). "Evil communications corrupt good manners."

CL. *M. Bh.* v. 1164 = xii. 2797. "From not abandoning the wicked, those who themselves are not evil are, from the contact, smitten with a similar punishment. Moist wood, from being mixed with dry, is burnt. Do not, therefore, ally thyself with the wicked."

CLI. *M. Bh.* i. 3077. "For a fool when he hears the words, good and bad, of men who are talking, takes in what is bad, as a pig does garbage. But a wise man similarly circumstanced embraces what is good, as a swan extracts milk from water."

CLII. *M. Bh.* iii. 25. "The source of the net of delusion is association with fools; whilst daily association with the good is the source of righteousness. Wherefore, those who seek after tranquillity of spirit should cultivate the society of the wise, the aged, the sweet-dispositioned, the ascetic, the virtuous. A man should seek those in whom knowledge, birth, and action are found unexceptionable; to consort with them is better than studying books."

CLIII. *M. Bh.* xii. 4217. "Of what avail is the praise or the censure of one of the vulgar, who makes a useless noise like a senseless crow in the forest?"

CLIV. *M.Bh.* v. 1170. "To abstain from speaking is regarded as very difficult. It is not possible to say much that is valuable and striking."

CLV. *Hitopadeśa* iv. 10. "To address a judicious remark to a thoughtless man is a mere threshing of chaff. And beneficence shown to mean men is, O king, nothing better than writing on sand." Compare M.Bh. v. 1009. "He who teaches one who cannot be taught, or who waits upon a man who has nothing, or who court. a stingy man, is called a fool."

CLVI. *Bhāminīvilāsa* i. 93. "Whoever kindly treats a bad man, ploughs the sky, paints a picture on water, and bathes the wind with water." Compare Proverbs ix. 7: "He that reproveth a scorner getteth to himself shame; and he that reproveth a wicked man *getteth himself* a blot. 8. Reprove not a scorner, lest he hate thee; rebuke a wise man, and he will love thee." xiv. 6: "A scorner seeketh wisdom, and *findeth* it not; but knowledge *is* easy unto him that understandeth." xv. 12: "A scorner loveth not one that reproveth him; neither will he go unto the wise." xxvii. 22: Though thou shouldest bray a fool in a mortar among wheat with a pestle, *yet* will not his foolishness depart from him." Jeremiah xiii. 23: "Can the Ethiopian change his skin, or the leopard his spots? *then* may ye also do good that are accustomed (Heb., *taught*) to do evil." Matthew vii. 6: "Give not that which is holy unto the dogs, neither cast ye your pearls before swine, lest they trample them under their feet, and turn again and rend you." Titus iii. 10: "A man that is an heretic after the first and second admonition, reject; 11.

knowing that he that is such is subverted, and sinneth, being condemned of himself." Second Epistle of Peter ii. 22: "But it has happened unto them according to the true proverb, 'The dog is turned to his own vomit again; and the sow that was washed to her wallowing in the mire.'"

CLVII. *M. Bh.* v. 3290 f. "Let not a wise man speak (in a company) where good and bad words are equally esteemed; he would be like a singer to deaf men."

CLVIII. *M. Bh.* ii. 2485. "Instruction does not teach a fool what is good or the reverse. A child in understanding will never become mature (literally, aged)." *Ibid.* 1945: "He who has no understanding of his own, but is merely learned, does not learn the sense of books, as a spoon does not taste the flavour of broth." *Ibid.* x. 178: "A brave man (*śūraḥ*) if very stupid, though he long waits upon a learned man, does not discern what is duty, as a spoon does not taste the flavour of broth: but an intelligent man who has attended on the learned man but for a short time, quickly discerns duty, as the tongue tastes the flavour of broth."

CLIX. *M. Bh.* v. 1172 (xiii. 4987). "A wound inflicted by arrows heals; a wood cut down by an axe grows; but harsh words are hateful; a wound inflicted by them does not heal. Arrows of different sorts can be extracted from the body; but a word-dart cannot be drawn out, for it is seated in the heart."

CLX. *M. Bh.* xiii. 4986. "Word-arrows fly from the mouth; whoever is smitten by them mourns night and day. They alight only on vital parts; let not a wise man discharge them against others." v. 1266: "Harsh words burn the vital parts, the bones, the heart, the breath of men; the man who loves righteousness ought therefore to avoid burning and harsh words."

CLXI. *M. Bh.* i. 3559. "He should be regarded as the most luckless of men and as carrying Nirṛiti (the goddess of destruction) fastened to his mouth, who is sharp in speech, who wounds men and smites them with his word-arrows."

CLXII. *M. Bh.* v. 4348. "He who does not abide by the instructions of friends who desire his welfare, and who are wise and learned, is the delight of his enemies." Compare *Ibid.* 4143—5.

CLXIII. *M. Bh.* x. 234[b], f. "He who does not listen to the disagreeable but wholesome words of friends, laments when he falls into misfortune, as I, who have disregarded these two."

CLXIV. *M. Bh.* v. 3317. "Wise men regard him as cruel who does not come to the help of a friend distressed by calamity, and console him according to his power. He who, seeking to restrain his friend from an improper act, shall even seize him by the hair, can incur blame from no one, since he makes every effort in his power."

CLXV. *M. Bh.* xii. 2998 f. "They say that this is the best mark of a friend, that he should never be content with (his friend's) prosperity (*i.e.*, should always wish it greater); and should be sad at his decline. Confide, as in a father, in the man of whom one thinks that to him 'my loss (or death) will be his loss (or death).'" In xii. 6284: Among the marks of good men is stated that, "they are devoted to promoting the objects of their friends, even though they distress themselves in doing so."

CLXVI. *M. Bh.* xii. 4167. "What is broken is with difficulty united; and what is whole is with difficulty broken. But the friendship which has been broken and again cemented, does not continue to be affectionate."

CLXVII. *M. Bh.* v. 1348. "Men are easily found who always say what is agreeable; but one who speaks, and one who listens to, what is disagreeable but wholesome, are difficult to find. 1349 (= ii. 2137): He who adhering to duty, and disregarding what is agreeable or disagreeable to his master, utters disagreeable but wholesome things,—in him a king finds an ally." *Ibid.* ii. 2136: "A wicked man who utters agreeable things is (easily) found in this world." The next half verse corresponds to the second half of v. 1348. *Manu* iv. 138 is not so uncompromising: "A man should speak what is true, and what is agreeable, but not a disagreeable truth, nor an agreeable falsehood; this is the eternal law."

CLXVIII. *M. Bh.* xii. 4224. "The man who in your presence praises your virtue and reviles you behind your back, is a dog in the world." I am not clear as to the sense of the last clause of the verse. The explanation given of the similarity between the man and the dog in the third and fourth lines of the metrical translation is not found in the original.

CLXIX. *M.Bh.* xii. 4224. "For a bad man, uttering censure in public, proclaims faults, as a serpent displays its expanded hood. He who seeks to retaliate on this man who is performing his own natural part, (literally, his own acts, *sva-karmāṇi*), is like a senseless ass which plunges into a heap of ashes, into dirt."

CLXX. *M. Bh.* i. 8404. "An intelligent man is awake before the time of calamity; and when it arrives he suffers no vexation. But the foolish man who does not perceive that calamity has arrived, is distressed when it has overtaken him, and does not attain to great prosperity." The metrical version, it will be observed, greatly expands the original.

CLXXI. *M. Bh.* xii. 4889 and 4908. "He who provides for contingencies not yet arrived, and he who has presence of mind, these two prosper, whilst the procrastinator perishes."

CLXXII. *M. Bh.* i. 5613. "The man who does not encounter risks, never sees good; but he who faces risks, if he lives, sees (good)."

CLXXIII. iii. 1259. "A man should never despise himself; for brilliant success never attends on the man who is contemned by himself." *Ibid.* v. 4500: "Do not despise thyself, or set a low value on thyself." 4605: "My son, a man should not despise himself on account of his former ill successes. Things previously non-existent spring up, whilst others which have existed disappear." *Manu* iv. 137: "Let not a man despise himself on account of previous ill successes: until his death let him seek after prosperity, and not regard it as unattainable." The other extreme, of self-satisfaction, is condemned by Plautus. Trin. 2, 2, 40.

> Qui ipsus sibi satis placet, nec probus est nec frugi bonæ;
> Qui ipsus se contemnit, in eo est indoles industriæ.
>
> "The man who is satisfied with himself is neither virtuous nor excellent;
> He who contemns himself has a disposition for industry."

CLXXIV. *Vṛiddha Chāṇakya* (Berlin MS., 32). "The summit of Meru is not very lofty, nor the infernal world very profound, nor the ocean very far to cross, for men who have energy on their side."

CLXXV. *M.Bh.* v. 1513[b], f. "Men of spirit are never terrified in forests, in impervious woods, in hard calamities, in alarms, or when weapons are uplifted."

CLXXVI. *M.Bh.* vi. 2008. "Thy intention is like the construction of an embankment in a place whence the water has flowed away; or like the digging of a well when the house has been burnt." Compare Rāmāyaṇa, ii. 18, 23 (Bombay ed.) "Thou in vain desirest to construct a dam when the water is gone." Bhartṛihari iii. 76. "A wise man should strenuously strive after his own wellbeing whilst his body is in health, whilst decay is far off, whilst his strength is unbroken, and there is no decay of life: when the house is in flames, what is the use of making an effort to dig a well?"

CLXXVII. *M.Bh.* xii. 3814. "The opportunity which passes away from a man seeking for an opportunity can hardly be obtained by him again, when he wishes to act."

CLXXVIII. *Mbh.* xi. 36. "A man should at first act with all his might, that he may not afterwards lament the loss of an object which has passed away from him."

CLXXIX. *Mbh.* v. 1112. "What shall happen to me if I do this? What shall happen to me if I do not do it? Reflecting thus on acts, let a man do or not perform them."

CLXXX. *Mbh.* xi. 184[b] f. "Neither valour, nor wealth, nor friends, have such power to rescue a man from grief, as a resolute self-commanding spirit."

CLXXXI. *Mbh.* iii. 14079 (=xi. 76[b] f.; xii. 12494). "Let a man quell mental suffering by wisdom, bodily by medicines: such is the power of knowledge; let not a man place himself on an equality with children," or "with others" (xi. 77).

CLXXXII. *Mbh.* iii. 62; xi. 67; xii. 751; 6497[b] f.; 12483. "Thousands of occasions of grief, and hundreds of occasions of fear" ("joy" in xii. 751) "every day assail the fool, but not the wise man."

CLXXXIII. *Mbh.* v. 993. "Those men are wise who do not desire the unattainable, who do not love to mourn over what is lost, and are not overwhelmed by calamities."

CLXXXIV. *Mbh.* 4148 f. "The sky seems to have a boundary; a firefly looks like fire: yet the sky has no boundary, and there is no fire in a firefly. Therefore an object which looks (thus or thus) to the sense, should be examined. He who after examining things, makes them known, is not afterwards vexed."

CLXXXV. *Mbh.* iii. 14085. "There is no end to discontent, but contentment is the highest happiness. Those who have traversed the road (of life or of knowledge) do not lament, beholding the highest goal (in view)."

CLXXXVI. *Mbh.* xi. 75[b] f. "Men, after attaining to one distinguished condition of wealth after another, remain unsatisfied and deluded; but the wise attain contentment."

CLXXXVII. *Subhâshitârṇava,* 110. "Men long after what they have not got, and are indifferent to what they have. In winter they long for heat, and so in summer again for frost."

CLXXXVIII. *Mbh.* xii. 6712. "Some men by their birth have more enjoyment, others are very distressed, but I do not see that anywhere in this world any one has perfect enjoyment."

The word *jātyā*, which I have translated "by their birth," is explained in Böthlingk and Roth's Dictionary, vol. v., column 1441, under the word *jāti*, as meaning "from the beginning," "altogether:" (*von Anfang an, von Haus aus*].

CLXXXIX. *Mbh.* xii. 6713. "Men, after obtaining riches, desire royal power; after getting kingly power, they desire godhead; after obtaining that, they desire the rank of Indra. Thou art wealthy, but neither a king nor a god; but even shouldst thou attain to godhead, and to the rank of Indra, thou wouldst not be content."

CXC. *Mbh.* i. 3174 f.; 3511 f.; compare xii. 13 ff.: 6609 ff.; 9917 ff. "Desire is never satiated by the enjoyment of the desired objects, just as a fire increases the more by the butter (which is thrown into it). The earth, filled with jewels, gold, cattle, women,—all these things do not suffice for one man. Understanding this, a man should practise quietude and indifference." i. 3513 (iii. 82; xii. 9925). "Happiness is enjoyed by him who abandons that lifelong disease, desire, which the wicked cannot abandon, and which does not decay as men decay."

CXCI. *Mbh.* iii. 84. "As wood is consumed by the fire which springs from it, so a foolish man is ruined by his own innate greediness. The rich live in constant dread of kings, water, fire, thieves, their own kindred, as living creatures live in dread of death. The wealthy man is everywhere preyed upon, as flesh is by birds in the sky, by wild beasts on earth, and by fish in the water. Wealth brings injury to some men; he who is devoted to the good derived from it does not find (real) good. Wherefore all augmentations of wealth increase avarice and folly: stinginess, pride, fear, and anxiety are considered by the wise to spring from wealth; these are the griefs of embodied beings. And in the acquisition and preservation of wealth, as well as from the decay of it, they endure great suffering; and they even kill others for the sake of it." 91. "Fools are addicted to discontent; wise men attain contentment. There is no end of covetousness. Contentment is the highest enjoyment, and it is therefore regarded by wise men as the highest thing. Youth, beauty, life, and accumulated jewels, royal power, and the society of those we love, are all transitory; the wise man will not eagerly covet them. Even he who seeks wealth for pious purposes had better not seek it; for it is better for men not to touch dirt than to wash it off."

CXCII. *Mbh.* x. 115. "In youth a man is deluded by other ideas than those which delude him in middle life; and again in his decay he embraces yet different ideas."

CXCIII. *Mbh.* xii. 213. "What is called righteousness (pious action) proceeds from wealth. A man is robbed of his righteousness when his wealth is taken from him. For when this is taken away, for what have we power? Men call the poor man standing beside them cursed. Poverty is a sin in this world, and is not to be praised. A man fallen from virtue, and a poor man, both are sorrowful. I perceive no difference between a poor man and a low man." 216b. "For from wealth increased and collected from all quarters, all actions proceed, as streams from hills. From wealth come righteousness, pleasure, and heaven. Men's life does not prosper without wealth. The acts of an unintelligent man destitute of wealth are cut off, like small streams in the hot season. He who has wealth has friends, has relatives; he (is esteemed) a man in the world, and wise. The poor man, seeking to attain an object, cannot attain it though he strive after it. Riches (or desired objects) are attained by riches, as elephants are captured by elephants. Virtue, pleasure, joy, patience, anger, learning, pride,—all these things spring from riches; from riches springs high birth, and by riches virtue is augmented. The poor man has neither this world nor the next for his portion. The poor man does not properly perform pious acts. From wealth springs righteousness, as a river from a hill. That man is lean who is meagre as regards horses, cattle, servants, and guests; not he whose bodily frame is meagre."

CXCIV. *Mbh.* xii. 6571. (The metrical translation begins at verse 6575.) "I weighed against each other poverty and royal power. Poverty was found to excel even royal power, being superior in its excellences. 6572. The great difference of the two states is this, that the rich man lives in constant trouble, like one who is in the mouth of death. 6573. But when a man has abandoned wealth, and is free, and without desire, then neither fire, nor ill fortune, nor death, nor robbers can prevail over him. 6574. The gods applaud the man who wanders where he will, who sleeps without bedding, resting upon his arm, and tranquil. 6575. The rich man is filled with anger and avarice, deprived of understanding, glances askew, has a withered face, is wicked, knits his eyebrows, (6576) bites his under lip, is irascible, and speaks cruel words. Who would like to look upon him, (even) if he wished to bestow as a gift the (whole) earth? 6577 (= xiii. 3082 f.; iii. 12518). Continual union with fortune deludes the unwary man, and sweeps away his understanding, as the autumnal wind the clouds. 6578. Then pride of beauty and pride of wealth take possession of him; (he thinks) 'I am of noble birth, I am pure, I am no mere man.' 6579. From these three causes his understanding becomes disordered. Being devoted to pleasure, he squanders the means of enjoyment amassed by his father; 6580. and becoming impoverished, he thinks it a good thing to lay hold of the property of others. When he has transgressed all bounds, and plunders on every side (6581), then he is driven away by the rulers, as a deer is (driven) by the hunter with his arrows. . . . 6583. Without abandoning everything, a man can gain no happiness, nor what is highest, nor sleep without fear. Abandoning all, then, be happy."

CXCV. *Sâhityadarpaṇa*, 322.—"Rich men who are not intoxicated (by prosperity), young men who are not unsteady, and rulers who are not careless and thoughtless, these are truly great." Compare No. cxxii.

CXCVI. *Sârṅgadhara's Paddhati, Dhanapraśaṁsâ*, 12.—"What suffering do not men undergo in their pursuit of wealth? They run on the point of the sword, they enter the ocean."

CXCVII. *M. Bh.* iii. 15398.—"Abandoning their dear lives, men boldly plunge into the sea, or enter the forests, for the sake of wealth."

CXCVIII. *M. Bh.* xii. 12131.—"In this world the kinsmen of the rich act like kinsmen; but the kinsmen of the poor die away even while the poor themselves live."

CXCIX. The above is varied as follows in the *Panchatantra* i. 15.—"For in this world even a stranger turns himself into a relation of the rich. The relations of the poor straightway act like bad men."

Compare Proverbs xiv. 20. "The poor is hated even of his own neighbour; but the rich *hath* many friends." xix. 4—"Wealth maketh many friends; but the poor is separated from his neighbour. All the brethren of the poor do hate him; how much more do his friends go far from him? He pursueth *them with* words, *yet* they *are* wanting *to him.*"

The following are parallel passages from the classical authors:—

Euripides, Bressai (quoted by Stobæus)—

> *Ἐπίσταμαι δὲ καὶ πεπείραμαι λίαν,*
> *ὡς τῶν ἐχόντον πάντες ἄνθρωποι φίλοι.*

"I know, and have well experienced, that all men are friends to those who have wealth."

Euripides, Electra (1131)—

> *Πένητας οὐδεὶς βούλεται κτᾶσθαι φίλους.*

"No one wishes to gain the poor for friends."

Sophocles (fragment 109, Dindorf)—

> *Τὰ χρήματ' ἀνθρώποισιν εὑρίσκει φίλους.*

"Wealth obtains friends for men."

Euripides, Danae—

> *Φιλοῦσι γάρ τοι τῶν μὲν ὀλβίων βροτοὶ*
> *σοφοὺς τίθεσθαι τοὺς λόγους, ὅταν δέ τις*
> *λεπτῶν ἀπ' οἴκων εὖ λέγῃ πένης ἀνὴρ,*
> *γελᾶν. ἐγὼ δὲ πολλάκις σοφωτέρους, κ. τ. λ.*

"Men are accustomed to esteem the words of the rich as

wise ; but when any poor man of an insignificant family speaks well, to laugh."

The sequel of this passage is quoted under No. cxii.

CC. *Subhāshitārṇava*, 64.—"Who is not ready to enjoy, and to give away, the wealth which has been earned by his father? But those are rarely to be found who enjoy, or give away, the wealth earned by their own arms."

CCI. *M. Bh.* xii. 10576[b].—"Let no man seek to exalt himself by censuring others ; but let him endeavour, by his own virtues, to become more distinguished than they. Men devoid of merit, but thinking highly of themselves, frequently, through a lack of virtue, reproach others who are virtuous, with faults ; and even when admonished, they, under the influence of conceit, esteem themselves more excellent than the mass of men. A man who is wise and virtuous attains great renown, though he never finds fault with any one, nor gives expression to any self-worship. The pure and fragrant savour of the wise is wafted without speech (10581) ; so, too, the spotless sun shines in the firmament without uttering any voice (to announce its glory). In the same way many other objects which are devoid of intelligence, and utter no sound, shine with renown in the world. A fool attains no lustre among men merely through praising himself, whilst a man who has knowledge shines, even though concealed in a pit. An evil sentiment, though uttered aloud, ceases to be heard ; but an excellent saying, even if uttered in a low tone, attains to distinction. The abundant, empty, talk of proud fools shows what is in them, as the rays of the sun reveal its fiery character."

Compare M. Bh. iii. 13748[b] f. ; iv. 1556.—"Fire burns without speaking ; the sun shines silently : silently the earth supports all creatures moving and stationary."

Compare Xenophon's Memorabilia, i. 7, 1 :—*Ἐπισκεψώμεθα δὲ εἰ καὶ ἀλαζονείας ἀποτρέπων τοὺς συνόντας ἀρετῆς ἐπιμελεῖσθαι προέτρεπεν. ἀεὶ γὰρ ἔλεγεν ὡς οὐκ εἴη καλλίων ὁδὸς ἐπ' εὐδοξίαν ἢ δι' ἧς ἄν τις ἀγαθὸς τοῦτο γένοιτο ὃ καὶ δοκεῖν βούλοιτο.*

"But let us enquire if by turning men away from boasting, he (Sokrates) also disposed them to study virtue ; for he was always wont to say that there was no better way to reputation than for a good man to be that which he wished to appear."

Aeschylus, Septem adversus Thebas, 591 f., gives the following character to Amphiaraus :—*σῆμα δ' οὐκ ἐπῆν κύκλῳ. οὐ γὰρ δοκεῖν ἄριστος, ἀλλ' εἶναι θέλει. κ. τ. λ.*

"But he had no device upon his shield. For he does not desire to appear, but to be, most excellent," &c.

Sallust, Cataline, 54. Esse quam videri bonus malebat. "He sought to be, rather than to appear, good."

CCII. *Mbh.* v. 1380.—"Evil men do not so much like to learn the good qualities of others as their want of virtues." xii. 11014. "Detractors (or censorious men) do not so much like to speak of a man's good qualities, as of his lack of virtues."

CCIII. *M. Bh.* i. 3079.—"A bad man is as much pleased, as a good man is distressed, to speak ill of others."

CCIV. *M. Bh.* viii. 1817.—"A man of merit alone, not one destitute of it, can know (or appreciate) the merits of the meritorious; but how canst thou, who hast no good qualities, know what is good or bad?"

CCV. *M. Bh.* viii. 2116; v. 1007. "All men are always clever in detecting the faults of others; but they do not know their own; and even if they do, they are deluded in regard to them." v. 1007. "Who is a greater fool than he who reproaches another for a fault, which he himself commits; or than he who is angry while he has no power?"

CCVI. *Subhāshitārṇava,* 275.—"Innumerable are the men who know the faults of others; a few, too, know their merits. But it is doubtful if any one knows his own faults."

CCVII. *M. Bh.* i. 3069.—"O king, thou perceivest the weak points of others, although only as large as mustard seeds; but seeing, thou seest not, thine own, although as great as Bilva fruits." Compare lines 9 f. of No. xxx. above, p. 27; and the prose version of the same in p. 226.

CCVIII. *M. Bh.* i. 3074.—"Until the ugly man has beheld his face in a mirror, he regards himself as handsomer than others. But when he beholds his deformed visage in the glass, he then discovers the difference between himself and them."

CCIX. *Panchatantra* i. 357 (Kosegarten's ed.), i. 314 (Bombay ed.).—"How can the conceit engendered in any one's heart be quelled? The Ṭiṭṭibha (a kind of bird) sleeps with its feet thrown upwards, from an apprehension that the sky may break down."

CCX. *Hitopadeśa* i. 98 (or 107 in another edition).—"Skill in advising others is easily attained by all men. But to practise righteousness themselves is what only a few great men succeed in doing."

Compare the fragment of Euripides, No. 182, in Dindorf's edition, Oxford, 1833; and 1029 in Nauck's Edition:—*ἅπαντές ἐσμεν εἰς τὸ νουθετεῖν σοφοί, αὐτοὶ δ' ὅταν σφαλῶμεν* [or, *δ' ἁμαρτάνοντες*] *οὐ γινώσκομεν.*

Terence, Heaut., 3. 1. 97:—

"Itan' comparatam esse hominum naturam omnium,
Aliena ut melius videant et dijudicent
Quam sua? an eo fit, quia in re nostrâ aut gaudio,
Sumus præpediti nimio, aut ægritudine?
Hic mihi nunc quanto plus sapit quam egomet mihi!"

"Is it that the nature of all is so constituted that they see, and judge of, the matters of other men better than their own? or does this happen because in an affair of our own we are hindered (from judging rightly) by excessive joy or sorrow? How much wiser is this man now on my behalf, than I am for myself!"

CCXI. *Rāmāyaṇa* vi. 67, 10ᵇ f.—"It is not difficult, O lowest of Rākshasas, for any one in words to carry out his designs; he who carries out his plans in act is wise."

CCXII. *M. Bh.* v. 1321.—"A tree, which stands by itself, though large, strong and well-rooted, can be overthrown by the wind, and with its trunk be broken down in a moment. But those well-rooted trees, which stand together in a clump, resist the fiercest winds, owing to their mutual support. So, too, the enemies of a single man, though he be possessed of good qualities, regard him as in their power to overwhelm, as the wind can overthrow a solitary tree. Through mutual support and dependence kinsmen flourish as lotuses in a pond." iii. 1333. "Even a powerful enemy can be destroyed by weak foes combined together, as a honey-gatherer is by bees." The following lines convey partly a different sentiment :—

M. Bh. i. 5915.—"He who has no wicked kinsmen, disgraces to their race, can live happily in the world, like a tree standing alone. For a tree which stands alone in a village, and has leaves and fruit, is sacred, and honoured, has no fellows, and is to be held in reverence. And those who have many kinsmen brave and virtuous, live happily in the world, and endure no distress. Men who support each other live powerful and prosperous, the delight of their friends and relatives, as trees which have grown in a forest."

CCXIII. *M. Bh.* v. 1318.—"Threads, though long and thin, if many and similar, can, from their number, always bear many strains; in this is found an emblem of the good."

CCXIV. *M. Bh.* v. 1319.—"Kinsmen resemble firebrands: separated they only smoke; united they blaze."

CCXV. *M. Bh.* v. 863. "A tiger without a wood (to shelter him) is killed; a wood without a tiger (to guard it) is cut down. Let, therefore, the tiger guard the wood, and the wood protect the tiger." Compare the preceding verse, 862, and verses 1378 f., and 1396 ff.

CCXVI. *M. Bh.* i. 5553.—"An enemy is in no way to be despised, though he be weak. A little fire burns up an entire forest, by gainings helter in it." Verse 5627. "An insignificant enemy disregarded strikes root like a palmyra tree; just as fire thrown into a thicket speedily extends." xii. 4389. "A little fire sprinkled with butter increases; and a single seed grows into a thousand shoots. Let no one, therefore, despise a little wealth, having learnt that it has many increases and diminutions. An enemy, who though youthful, is no child, but mature, can destroy a careless enemy. When an opportunity is gained, another may uproot him. He who discerns his opportunity is the best of kings."

CCXVII. *M. Bh.* v. 1405. — "When thou hast wronged a clever man, be not confident, (thinking) I am far away (from him). Long are the arms of a clever man, wherewith, when injured, he injures." xii. 5315 is of the same tenor: "Being at variance with an able man, be not confident," &c. v. 1389 runs thus: "When at feud with a man who is able to inflict great injury upon thee, be not confident," &c.

CCXVIII. *M. Bh.* xii. 3501.—"When thou hast wronged a powerful man, be not confident (thinking) 'I am far off (from him).' Such men swoop down, like hawks, on the careless."

CCXIX. *M. Bh.* i. 5563 (=xii. 5264).—"Let a man carry his enemy on his shoulder till times change; then, when the opportunity has arrived, let him be smashed like an earthen vessel against a rock."

[Many other Machiavellian maxims are to be found in the two passages where this verse occurs.]

CCXX. In *M. Bh.* iii. 14651 ff., Satyabhāmā, Kṛishṇa's wife, asks Draupadī, the wife of the Pāṇḍus, how she manages to keep her husbands in subjection and in good humour, and makes them look up to her (to be *mukhaprekshāḥ* v. 14654): Is it by religious observances, or by incantations and drugs, that she effects this? She asks this in order that she may understand how to keep her own husband Kṛishṇa under her control (v. 14656). Draupadī replies (vv. 14658 ff.): "Thou askest me about the practice of bad wives; . . . such a question, and such a doubt, do not become thee, the wise and dear queen of Kṛishṇa. If a husband should know that his wife was in the habit of employing incantations or roots, he would shrink from her, as from a serpent in the house. When he was thus disturbed, what tranquillity could he have?—and without tranquillity what happiness? A husband can never be subjected to his wife by incantations." She then points out the injurious or deadly effects of such practices, by which women have rendered their husbands "dropsical, leprous, grey-haired, ... stupid, blind, and deaf" (v. 14664), and describes her own mode of action (vv. 14667 ff.) "Avoiding pride, desire, and anger, I constantly serve the Pāṇḍus and their wives with activity. Suppressing familiarity, keeping myself within myself, obedient and humble, acting agreeably to the wishes of my husbands, fearing wrong words, wrong postures, wrong looks, wrong sitting positions, wrong movements, signs, and movements of the limbs, I wait upon the sons of Pṛithā, the charioteers who resemble the sun, and fire, and the moon; who smite with their looks; who are fiery in heroism and prowess. Neither god, nor man nor Gandharva, nor well-decorated youth, wealthy, or handsome—no other man is regarded by me. I never sit nor eat when my husband has not eaten, nor bathed, nor sat down . . . Rising, I welcome him when returned home from the field or forest, with a seat and with water. I clean all vessels; I give sweet food; I supply it at the proper time; I am self-restrained; and I preserve the grain. I sweep the house clean; I am not abusive in my talk; never associate with bad women; am always pleasant and active. I avoid joking,* laughing, and frequent standing at the door; . . . (14677) excessive laughter and anger; always seeking truth, and waiting on my husbands. The absence of my husband is always undesired by me, and when he is abroad on any family business, I fast, using no flowers or scents (sandal-wood) (or paint). Whatever my husband does not drink, or like, or eat, I avoid, and constantly follow his advice. I deck myself with ornaments, am cleanly in person, and submissively seek to please him. I observe whatever duties were formerly enjoined on me in the family or by my mother-in-law, almsgiving, &c. . . . 14685. For I regard adherence to her husband as the immemorial duty of a woman; he is her god, he only is her refuge. What woman would do anything displeasing to him? I never repose more than my husbands, or eat, or adorn myself more than they do; nor do I ever find fault with my mother-in-law, but am always submissive to her. By attention and constant activity, and by obedience

* Must we not read *anarmā* here instead of *anarma*, which, construed with *varjaye*, gives the sense, "I avoid not jesting?"

to my elders, I keep my husbands in subjection." She goes on to say (vv. 14690 ff.) that in the former days (of his prosperity) she used to superintend the large hospitalities of her husband Yudhishṭhira, and knew all about his 100,000 richly dressed female slaves, skilled in music and dancing; about the other branches of his establishment; about the income and outlay of the Pāṇḍus. She was entrusted with the charge of the household; and abandoning all ease, she undertook all this weight of duty, which occupied her day and night. She was the first to rise, and the last to lie down. These are the means by which she acts upon her husbands. By such procedure, she goes on to say, Satyabhāmā may separate her husband from the influence of other women (v. 14710). She adds (v. 14713) that happiness is not gained by ease, but that a virtuous woman acquires it by painful effort. When she hears her husband at the door, she is to rise and receive him with attention, to send away her female slave, and serve him herself (14715 f.).

CCXXI. I have not given any prose translations of the passage versified under this number.

CCXXII. *M. Bh.* i. 3027. "She is a wife who is clever in the house, who bears children, whose husband is her breath of life, and who is devoted to him. 3028.—A wife is the half of a man; a wife is his most excellent friend; a wife is the foundation of the three objects of life, *i.e.*, virtue, pleasure, and wealth; a wife is the foundation for him who seeks to be redeemed (from this world.) 3029. "Those who have wives fulfil religious rites, are householders, live happily and enjoy prosperity. 3030. These sweetly-speaking women are friends in solitude, they are fathers in matters of duty, they are mothers to those who are in distress. 3031. They are a repose to the traveller in the wilderness. He who has a wife is trustworthy: hence wives are the best refuge. 3032. The wife who is devoted to her husband always follows him when he dies and departs hence, when he is alone and in misfortune. 3033. The wife who dies first, after death expects the coming of her husband; and when he dies first, the good wife follows him (as a Satī). 3037. Men scorched by mental pains and suffering from diseases, are gladdened by their wives, as men distressed by heat are by water."

The following is another text on the same subject:—*M. Bh.* xiii. 6781 ff. "That woman fulfils her duty who is sweet in disposition, speech, action, appearance, who constantly regards the face of her husband as the face of a son, who is virtuous and well regulated in conduct, ... who regards duty as the chief thing, performs the same rites as her husband, who ever looks upon him as a god, obeying and serving him like a god, is obedient, kind in disposition, devoted, pleasant to behold, regarding her husband alone. She who when harshly addressed, or regarded with an angry eye, looks placidly on her husband, is a devoted wife. She who does not look upon the moon or sun or a tree which have masculine names, that handsome woman, deserving honour from her husband, is dutiful. She who waits upon her husband when poor, sick, sad, tired by a journey, as if he were a son, is dutiful. She who is active, clever, has sons, is devoted to her husband, regards him as her life, who obeys and serves him without displeasure, is pleased and submissive, is dutiful. She who ever supplies her family with food, who does not delight in pleasures, enjoyments, in power, or in ease, so much as in her husband, she is dutiful. She who, bent on domestic service, loves to rise with dawn, who sweeps the house clean, and smears the floor with cow-dung, who attends to the rites of Fire, and brings flowers and offerings, making provision, along with her husband, for the gods, guests, and servants, herself, according to right and rule eating the leavings of food, with all the people about her pleased and satiated, she is dutiful. She who gratifies the feet of her father and mother-in-law, full of good qualities, devoted to her father and mother, she is rich in self-denying merit. She who feeds Brahmans, the weak, orphans, the distressed and wretched, is a devoted wife. . . . . This is holiness, austere virtue, and eternal heaven, when a woman is good, regards her husband as her chief object, and is devoted to him. For a husband is a god to women, a kinsman, a refuge; there is no refuge or deity equal to him."

M. Bh. xii. 5562. A female dove is made to speak thus of her lost husband:—"I recollect nothing unkind ever done by thee, O beloved one. Every widow laments, though she have many sons. Bereaved of her husband and oppressed, she is to be bewailed by her relations. I was ever fondled by thee, and greatly honoured, with sweet and affectionate words, unforced (?) and pleasant. . . . . 5566[b]. For a father, a brother, a son, bestow but moderately. But what woman will not honour her husband who is a boundless giver? There is no master like a husband; no joy like a husband. Abandoning all riches a wife finds refuge in her husband. I have nothing to do with life without thee, my lord. What virtuous women would endure to live without her husband?"

In the first of the above passages reference is distinctly made to the custom long prevalent in India of women burning themselves on the funeral piles of their deceased husbands. This practice was foreign to Greek usage; but in the Supplices of Euripides, we find Evadne devoting herself to death with her husband, Kapaneus, whose body was one of those rescued for burial from the Thebans who were preventing their interment. The following verses, 1000 ff., intimate Evadne's determination:—

> *προσέβαν δρομὰς ἐξ ἐμῶν*
> *οἴκων ἐκβακχευσαμένα,*
> *πυρὸς φῶς τάφον τε*
> *ματεύουσα τὸν αὐτόν,*
> *ἐς Ἅιδαν καταλύσουσ' ἔμμοχθον*
> *βίοτον αἰῶνός τε πόνους.*
> *ἥδιστος γάρ τοι θάνατος*
> *συνθνῄσκειν θνῄσκουσι φίλοις,*
> *ἐι δαίμων ταδε κραίνοι.*
>
> . . . .
>
> *ὁρῶ δὴ τελευτάν,*
> *ἵν' ἕστακα· τύχα δέ μοι*
> *ξυνάπτει ποδός. ἀλλα τῆς*
> *εὐκλείας χάριν ἔνθεν ὁρ—*
> *μάσω τᾶσδ' απὸ πέτρας*
> *πηδήσασα πυρὸς ἔσω,*

σῶμα τ' αἴθοπι φλογμῷ
πόσει συμμίξασα φίλον,
χρῶτα χρωτὶ πέλας θεμένα
Περσεφονείας ἥξω θαλάμους,
σὲ τὸν θανόντ' οὔποτ' ἐμᾷ
προδοῦσα ψυχᾷ κατὰ γᾶς.
ἴτα φῶς γάμοι τε.

"I came running, in wild excitement from my home, seeking what is at once the light of the fire and a tomb, seeking to release to Hades my toil-worn life and the pains of my existence. For it is the sweetest of deaths to die with dying friends, if the deity will fulfil this (desire)" . . . v. 1012. "I see the end where I stand, and fortune guides my steps. But for the sake of renown, I will spring from this rock, leaping into the fire; and seeking to commingle my dear body with my husband in the shining flames, placing skin close to skin, I shall reach the chambers of Persephone, never with my life abandoning beneath the earth thee who art dead. Let the light depart and the nuptials."

Before she can carry out her design her father, Iphis, arrives, and states that he had come in search of his daughter, who, when she was no longer watched, had escaped from his house, as she longed to die with her husband. He inquires after her; and she addresses him from the top of the rock where she was standing, prepared to leap down into her husband's funeral pyre beneath. Verse 1045. *Evadne.* "Why dost thou enquire of these women? This is I who like a bird hover a sad hovering on the rock over the funeral pyre of Kapaneus, O, my father. *Iphis.* Child, what wind is this? what journey dost thou take? why overpassing the threshold of thy home, hast thou come to this land? *Evadne.* Thou wouldst be angry, didst thou learn my designs, but I do not wish thee to learn them, my father. *Iphis.* Why? Is it not right that thy father should know? *Evadne.* Thou wouldst not be a wise judge of my design. *Iphis.* But why dost thou adorn thyself in this array? *Evadne.* This garb means something new, my father. *Iphis.* Thou dost not look like one who mourns her husband. *Evadne.* For we are arrayed for something novel. *Iphis.* And dost thou then show thyself near the tomb and the funeral pyre? *Evadne.* (Yes); because I shall gain a brilliant triumph. *Iphis.* What sort of victory wilt thou gain? I wish to learn from thee. *Evadne.* I shall surpass all women whom the sun has beheld. *Iphis.* In the works of Athene, or in wisdom of counsel? *Evadne.* In valour; for I shall lie dead with my husband. *Iphis.* What dost thou say? what poor enigma dost thou utter? *Evadne.* I will leap into this funeral pyre of the dead Kapaneus. *Iphis.* O, daughter, wilt thou not tell a tale to many? *Evadne.* I desire this that all the Argives should hear. *Iphis.* But I will not permit thee to do this. *Evadne.* It is of no consequence, for thou shalt not be able to seize me by the hand. And now my body is being thrown down, an act not dear to thee, but to me and to the husband who is burned with me. *Chorus.* Thou, O woman, hast done a dreadful deed. *Iphis.* I, wretched man, am undone, O Argive maidens."

Mr Paley (Euripides, Vol. I., p. 433) quotes some lines on the subject of the Indian practice of suttee from Propertius, iv. 13—15.

CCXXIII. *M. Bh.* xii. 5497. "Though crowded in every part with sons, grandsons, daughters-in-law, and servants, without a wife a householder's house will be empty. 5498. It is not the house itself which is called a house; the housewife is declared to be the house. A house destitute of a housewife is regarded as a desert. . . . 5501. That man is happy on earth who possesses a wife who is glad when he is glad, and sorrowful when he is sorrowful, who is downcast when he goes away from home, who speaks sweet words when he is angry, (5502) who is devoted to her husband, who regards him as the centre of her life, who seeks after his interests, and promotes his gratification, . . . 5504[b]. Destitute of her a palace is a wilderness. 5505. The wife is the ally of her husband in matters of duty, wealth, and pleasure; and whenever he goes abroad, she affords him confidence. 5506. A wife is said to be her husband's greatest riches, the partner of his journey through the world, when he has no other comrade. 5507. And whenever he is overcome by sickness or fallen into trouble, there is no remedy equal to a wife. 5508. There is no relative like a wife; no refuge like a wife; there is no helper like a wife, in accumulating righteousness. 5509. He in whose house there is no virtuous and sweetly speaking wife, should depart to the forest; for his house is like a wilderness." With the close of verse 5501, compare Euripides, Troades, 649 ff., where, among other things, Andromache says of herself:—

> *Γλώσσης τε σιγὴν ὄμμα τ' ἥσυχον πόσει*
> *παρεῖχον· ᾔδειν δ' ἁμὲ χρῆν νικᾶν πόσιν,*
> *κείνῳ τε νίκην ὧν μ' ἐχρῆν παριέναι.*

"And I offered to my husband a silent tongue and a quiet eye. But I knew in what points I ought to gain the victory over him, and in what points I should yield the victory to him." Compare the description of a wife in Proverbs xxxi. 10 ff.

CCXXIV. *Brāhma Dharma* ii. 2. "Until he finds a wife, a man is only half (of a whole). The house which is not occupied by children is like a cemetery. Compare the Taittirīya Brāhmaṇa iii. 3, 3, 1. "A wife is half a man's self;" and Genesis ii. 24, "Therefore shall a man leave his father and his mother, and shall cleave unto his wife; and they shall be one flesh;" and the Epistle to the Ephesians v. 31. See also the Taittirīya Brāhmaṇa iii. 3, 10, 4. "By offspring a man is completed" (*prajayā hi manushyaḥ pūrṇaḥ*). See also the Aitareya Araṇyaka, p. 78. 'The trishṭubh verse is a male, and the anushṭubh a woman: they are a pair. Hence also a man getting a wife considers himself, as it were, more of a whole. (*Vṛishā vai trishṭub yoshā anushṭup tasmād api purusho jāyām vittvā kṛitsnataram iva ātmānam manyate*).

See also *Manu* ix. 49. "A man is then only complete when made up of his wife, himself, and his offspring." The commentator on that verse quotes the Vājasaneya Brāhmaṇa as follows: *Arddho ha vā esha ātmano yaj jāyā. Tasmād yāvaj jāyām na vindāte naitāvat prajāyate asarvo hi tāvad bhavati. atha yadaiva jāyām vindate'tha prajāyate tarhi sarvo bhavati.* "A wife is the half of a (man's) self. Hence, till he finds a wife, he has no offspring; and so long he continues incomplete. But when he finds a wife, he obtains offspring; and then he becomes complete."

CCXXV. *M. Bh.* iii. 2325 f. "There is no remedy for all sufferings regarded by physicians as equal to a wife. This I tell thee truly. Nala replies: It is even as thou sayest, O Damayantī with the elegant waist. There is no remedy for a distressed man, equal to a wife."

CCXXVI. *Rāmāyaṇa* ii. 24-25^b f. (Bombay ed.) "The woman who is (otherwise) most excellent, and practises rites and fastings, but does not wait upon her husband, shall have an evil end; while she who is without religion, and has abandoned the worship of the gods, attains to the highest heaven by serving her husband."

M. Bh. iii. 13649^b f. "It is not by any sacrificial acts, or funeral rites or fastings; but by serving her husband, that a woman conquers heaven." *Ibid.* xiii. 2496. Substantially the same.

CCXXVII. *Mṛichhakaṭika.* Act iv. "For these women are instructed by nature; but the learning of men is taught by books."

CCXXVIII. *M. Bh.* xiii. 2236. "For these enchanting women delude men; and no man who has fallen into their hands is delivered. Like cows seeking fresh grass, they are ever seeking some new (person or thing). They know all the wiles of Śambara, of Namuchi, of Bali, of Kumbhīnasi. They laugh with those that laugh; weep with those that weep; and as opportunity offers, they lay hold of the unfriendly with kindly words. No device (literally, scripture, *Śāstra*) known to Uśanas or Vṛihaspati surpasses the wits of women; how are they to be guarded by men? They call lies truth, and truth lies . . . I consider that the books prescribing rules of conduct were composed principally to promote (?) the understanding of women. When honoured by men they pervert their minds; and they do the same when rejected by them."

CCXXIX. *Atharva Véda* iii. 30, 1. "I impart to you con cord, with unity of mind, and freedom from hatred; delight in one another, as a cow in a calf which is born to her. 2. Let the son be obedient to his father, and of one mind with his mother; may the wife be affectionate, and speak to her husband honied words. 3. Let not brother hate brother, nor sister sister. Concordant, and in harmony, address one another with kindly speech."

CCXXX. *M. Bh.* xii. 3450. "An unskilful king is unable to protect his subjects; for regal power is a great burthen, and a function difficult to fulfil. 3340. To wipe away the tears of the poor, of orphans, of the aged, and so to impart joy to men,—such is declared to be the duty of a king. 3251. Let a king constantly promote the welfare, and provide for the sustenance, of the poor, of orphans, of the aged, and of widows. 3315. Harlots, and procuresses who abide in drinking shops, loose men, gamblers, and the like, are to be repressed by the king, for such persons ruin the country where they dwell, and vex good citizens. 3238. Let the king put an end to all offences in town and country. 3243. Let religious teachers, priests, and family priests, (be) actively assisted. 3245. Let the king honour the virtuous, and restrain the vicious. 3250. Let a king constantly offer sacrifices, and give gifts, without inflicting suffering. 3303. Let a king, devoted to righteousness, and seeking the good of his subjects, instruct them in proper places, and at proper times, according to his understanding and his power. 3436. When a king protects his dominions, when he repels robbers, when he is victorious in battle, he fulfils what is declared to be his duty. 3548. Wherefore Manu Svāyambhuva enjoined that a warrior should fight righteously (or fairly). 3549. The sinful Kshatriya, living by treachery, who engages to fight fairly (?), but who conquers his foe unfairly, kills himself."

CCXXXI. *M. Bh.* v. 4332.—"The man who does not control

his passions cannot long enjoy royal power: but the wise man who has conquered himself can promote the good of his empire. For desire and anger draw a man away from (the pursuit of) desirable objects; but when he overcomes these foes, a king conquers the earth. This great position, kingly power, the sway over men, which wicked men desire, cannot long be retained by them. He who seeks to effect great things in the way of prosperity or virtue, must control his passions. When he does this his understanding is augmented, as fire grows by fuel. For these passions, when uncontrolled, are sufficient to destroy a man, as unbroken and unchecked horses can destroy an unskilful charioteer on the road. He who seeks to conquer his ministers without conquering himself, or to vanquish his enemies without overcoming his ministers, is helpless, and is defeated. He who first conquers himself as if he were an enemy, does not then seek in vain to overcome his ministers and his foes. Good fortune assiduously waits on the wise man whose passions are controlled, who rules his ministers, who holds the rod over malefactors, and who acts after examination. Like two fish enclosed in a net with small apertures, desire and anger abiding in his body destroy a man's understanding."

CCXXXII. *M. Bh.* 1055.—"Those offenders who have erred through ignorance should be pardoned. For it is not easy for a man to be wise in every respect."

CCXXXIII. *M. Bh.* xii. 2020[b] f.—"A king has no treasure which is more excellent than a host of men; and of all the six kinds of forts which are described in books, men regard the bulwark composed of men as the most impregnable."

CCXXXIV. *Bilhana in Śārṅgadhara's Paddhati, Sāmānyakavipraśaṃsā.*—"How can the king who has not great poets beside him attain to renown? How many princes have lived on the earth, and no one knows even their names?" This verse forms a parallel to Horace's lines, Ode iv. 9, 25 ff.

Vixere fortes ante Agamemnona
Multi; sed omnes illacrimabiles
Urgentur ignotique longa
Nocte, carent quia vate sacro.

CCXXXV. *Panchatantra* v. 49 (Bombay Edition).—"The same pleasure is not to be enjoyed even in heaven, which is so delightful from the contact of celestial objects, as men find in the poor place where they were born."

Ditto, iii. 92.—"Embodied creatures do not enjoy the same bliss even in heaven as they do, even when they are poor, in their own country, or town, or house."

Compare with this, Odyssey, i. 57 :

αὐτὰρ Ὀδυσσεύς
ἱέμενος καὶ καπνὸν ἀποθρώσκοντα νοῆσαι
ἧς γαίης, θανέειν ἱμείρεται.

"But Ulysses, longing to see even the smoke rising from his native country, yearns to die."

CCXXXVI. *Panchatantra* i. 21 (Kosegarten's Edition).—"He who does not go forth and explore all the earth, which is full of many wonderful things, is a well-frog." Mahābhārata v. 5509 and 5554. "Dost thou, like a frog lying in a well, not perceive this royal army assembled?" xiii. 2180. "The earth swallows up these two, a king who is not a warrior, and a Brahman who does not travel abroad, just as a serpent devours creatures lying in a hole, . . . a Brahman is spoiled by living at home."

CCXXXVII. *M.Bh.* xiii. 651. — One of the characteristics of the saint Upamanyu's hermitage is thus described in this verse : "Weasels play with serpents, and tigers with deer, like friends, through the great power of those saints of brilliant austerity, from the proximity of those mighty ones." Weasels are well known in India to be the enemies of serpents, and frequently kill them. This verse is quoted as a parallel to Isaiah xi. 6.

CCXXXVIII. *Manu* vi. 45 : and *Mahābhārata* xii. 8929.—"Let him (the hermit) not long for death ; let him not long for life ; but let him await his appointed time, as a servant the command (of his master)."

CCXXXIX. *Bhāgavata Purāṇa* vii. 5, 37.—"Even an alien who

does (a man) good, like a medicine, is a son ; while even a son born of one's own body, if injurious, is like a disease. Let a man cut off the limb which is a source of harm to himself, and from the separation of which the remainder (of the body) lives in comfort."

CCXL. *Drishṭânta Śataka*, 76.—" By his own kindred a man is regarded as one like themselves; by strangers he is looked upon as a person of merit. Hari (*i.e.*, Vishṇu regarded as incarnate in Kṛishṇa) was regarded by cowherds as a cowherd, but by gods as the lord of the universe."

Châṇakya, 42.—" Wheresoever any one constantly goes and wherever he perpetually eats, he is there treated without respect, even though he be (one who is) like the god Indra." *See* Mark vi. 4, and John iv. 44.

CCXLI. *Lalita Vistara*, 7th Adhyāya, p. 115 (occasionally abridged). " At that time a great ṛishi called *Asita*, who knew the five (principles or points), together with his sister's son, Naradatta, lived on the side of (or near) the king of mountains, the Himavat. He, as soon as the Bodhisattva (Buddha) had been born, saw many wonderful portents ; and he beheld the sons of the gods in the sky moving about rejoicing, and pronouncing the word Buddha, and waving their garments. He thought, 'I must look into this.' Beholding by divine intuition the whole of Jambudvipa, he saw in the house of king Śuddhodana, in the great city called Kapilavastu, a boy who had been born, radiant with a hundred holy glories, honoured by all worlds, and distinguished by the thirty-two marks of a great man. Seeing this, he then called to the youth Naradatta: 'Know, youth, that in Jambudvîpa a great gem has been born ; in the house of King Śuddhodana, in the city of Kapilavastu, a boy has been born,' &c., as above. 'If he shall dwell at home, he shall become a king, an universal sovereign (*chakravartin*), with an army composed of the four branches, victorious, righteous, ... a great hero, possessed of the seven gems (chariots, elephants, horses, women, &c.), the father of a thousand sons . . . . he shall conquer and rule the circle of the earth girdled by the ocean, without punishments, without weapons, by the force of his own righteousness. But if he wander away from home on an ascetic life, he shall become a Tathāgata, an Arhat, perfectly wise (*sambuddha*), a leader, led by no other, a ruler. This, now, I shall go near to see.' Accordingly Asita, with Naradatta, mounting and springing up into the sky like a swan, proceeded on his way to Kapilavastu; and having arrived, he ceased to manifest his supernatural power; and entering the city on foot, he proceeded to King Śuddhodana's house and stood at the door. . . . . He then approached the doorkeeper, and said, 'Go, tell King Śuddhodana that a ṛishi waits at the door.' The porter accordingly went, and with joined hands said to the king, 'An old withered ṛishi stands at the door, and says he wishes to see the king.' King Śuddhodana then ordered a seat for the great ṛishi, Asita, and said, 'Let him enter.' The porter then went forth and told him to enter. He went accordingly and stood before the king, and said, 'Hail, hail, O king: mayest thou live long, and rule thy kingdom righteously.' After making an offering to the sage, and touching his feet, the king received him kindly, and invited him to be seated. He then said respectfully, 'I do not remember, ṛishi, to have seen thee before; with what object in view hast thou now come?' 'I have come,' replied the ṛishi, 'desiring to see the son who has been born to thee.' 'He sleeps,' said the king, 'wait a little until he arises.' 'Such great men do not sleep long,' rejoined the ṛishi, 'such saints are wakeful.' The mendicant Bodhisattva, from compassion to the great ṛishi Asita, gave a sign of waking. The king then taking affectionately in both arms the child, perfect as regarded every object of desire, brought him to the ṛishi. The ṛishi, beholding the Bodhisattva, and seeing him to be distinguished by the thirty-two marks of a great man, and marked on his body by the eighty secondary signs, with a form surpassing that of Śakra (Indra), Brahmā, and the Guardians of the world, with a hundred thousand times greater brightness, beautiful in every limb, expressed his joy.*

* This is the sense of the words *udānam udānayati* given in Böht. and Roth's Lexicon, Vol. I., column 918. In the rectifications in Vol.

'Wonderfully fair is this child which has appeared in the world;' and rising from his seat, with joined hands, he fell down at the feet of the Bodhisattva, and making a circuit round him, he took him in his arms, and stood meditating. He saw the thirty-two marks of a great man which the Bodhisattva had, the beautiful possessor of which has only one of two careers before him. If he remains at home, he becomes a king, ... if he wanders forth as a mendicant, he shall become a Tathāgata. . . . . Beholding him, he wept, and shedding tears, he sighed deeply. King Śuddhodana saw the great ṛishi, Asita, weeping and deeply sighing; and seeing this, he who had had his hair standing on end with delight, quickly became sad, and said to the ṛishi, 'Why dost thou weep and sigh deeply? May there be no doubt (or apprehension) in regard to the child!' The sage rejoined: 'I do not weep on his account, nor is there any fear for him. I weep for myself; for I am old and worn and decayed, whilst he is perfect in every object of desire, and shall of necessity attain to complete intelligence, and shall set in motion a perfect wheel of righteousness, such as has never before been set in motion in the world by Śramaṇa, or Brahman, or god, or demon (Māra), or any one else, with righteousness. For the good and for the happiness of the world and of the gods he shall teach righteousness. He shall proclaim blessedness in the beginning, in the middle, and at the end; continence profitable, clear, unique, complete, pure, perfect,—and in the end righteousness. Learning this our righteousness, beings subject to birth shall be delivered from birth (from being again born); and so freed from decay, disease, death, grief, lamentation, pain, sadness, suffering, fatigue. He shall gladden those who are burned by the fire of desire, hatred, and illusion, by raining upon them the waters of pure righteousness. He shall lead by a straight road to the goal of redemption (*nirvâṇa*) those beings who have become possessed by various false views, and have fallen, and who have travelled on a wrong road. He shall release from their bonds those

---

V., column 1172, the sense is said to be, "He said spontaneously—without being asked."

who have been shut up and fettered in the cage of the world, and bound with the bonds of suffering. He shall generate an intuition of knowledge in those whose eyes have been enveloped by the veil of the dark gloom of ignorance. He shall extract the arrows of pain from those who have been pierced by them. Sometimes, and somewhere in the world, O king, the udumbara tree flowers. So, too, sometimes and somewhere the divine Buddhas are born in the world after many hundreds of thousands of crores of years. And thus this child shall certainly attain to perfect intelligence; and having attained this, he shall convey across the ocean of the world hundreds of thousands of millions of crores of beings; and place them in a state of immortality.* But I shall not see this jewel Buddha. Hence it is, O king, that I weep, and being sad at heart, draw long sighs—because I shall not adore him. As it is recorded in our Mantras, Vedas, and scriptures, he who is perfect in respect to every object must not dwell at home, (but go forth as an ascetic). The reason given is that he has the thirty-two marks † of a great man, and the eighty minor signs, which are enumerated; and it is added that such thirty-two marks do not belong to monarchs, but to Bodhisattvas; and that he who possesses the eighty signs should not remain at home, but go forth as a mendicant. Having learnt from the great ṛishi, Asita, this description of the boy, King Śuddhodana was gladdened, enraptured, and transported, and filled with pleasure and satisfaction; and rising from his seat, he fell at the Bodhisattva's feet, and pronounced this gāthā:—

'The world's physician blest art thou,
Before thee gods with Indra bow;
By ṛishis too art thou adored,
I too before thee bend, O Lord.'

King Śuddhodana then satiated (with gifts, or food?) the ṛishi, Asita, with his nephew, Naradatta, who was like him

* See the explanation of the word amṛita given above in the note, p. 152.

† In a note on the Sanskrit text it is stated that only thirty marks are actually enumerated.

and devoted to him; and having done so and covered him (with garments?) he walked reverentially round him. Asita then by his supernatural power departed by the route of the sky to his own hermitage."

CCXLII. *Rāmāyaṇa, Uttara Kāṇḍa*, sec. 17. 1. "Now, O king, the great-armed Rāvaṇa, wandering over the earth, came to, and walked about in, the Himavat forest. 2. There he saw a maiden clad in a black skin, and wearing matted hair, after the fashion of a ṛishi, and bright as a goddess. 3. Seeing that beautiful and ascetic maiden, he was pierced by the passion of love, and smiling, asked her: 'How, good lady, dost thou live so, in a way inconsistent with thy youth? for such a costume does not beseem thy beauty. 4. Thy unequalled form, O lady, which maddens men with love, is not suited for an ascetic life. . . . . 5. What does this mean? Whose daughter and whose wife art thou? He who possesses thee is a man who has obtained the reward of his merits.' . . . . 7. Thus addressed, the ascetic maid (8) replied, after treating Rāvaṇa as a guest: 'My father was Kuśadhvaja, a Brahman sage of boundless lustre, son of Bṛihaspati, and equal to him in understanding. 9. To him, a constant student of the Veda, I was born, a vocal daughter, and called Vedavatī. 10. Gods, Gandharvas, Yakshas, Rākshasas, and Pannagas came to my father and sued for my hand; (11) but he did not bestow me on them, (12) because he had designed for his son-in-law Vishṇu, the lord of the gods and of the worlds; (13) and therefore he did not desire to give me to any other, but to him. Hearing this, the proud Śambhu, lord of the Daityas, became incensed, (14) and the wicked being smote my father by night while he slept. 15. In consequence my afflicted mother, embracing his body, entered into the fire.* 16. To fulfil my father's desire in regard to Nārāyaṇa (Vishṇu), I wed him in my heart. 17. Having formed this

---

* The metrical translation seems to have been made under the idea that Vedavatī was born without the intervention of the mother who is here referred to. Her subsequent birth is in verse 33 declared to be of this character.

resolution, I practise many austerities. . . . . 18. Nārāyaṇa and no other than (he) the supreme lord, is my husband. In the hope of gaining him I engage in fearful rites. 19. Thou art known to me, Rāvaṇa, depart. By the intuition of an ascetic I know all that passes in the three worlds.' 20. Descending from his car, pained by the arrows of Kandarpa (Cupid), Rāvaṇa again said to the ascetic maiden: 21. 'Thou art proud, O fair damsel, who so resolvest. To gather merit (by asceticism) beseems the old (not the young). 22. Possessed of all excellent qualities, thou shouldst not so speak. O fairest creature in the three worlds, thy youth is passing away. 23. I am Daśagrīva, lord of Lankā (Ceylon); become my wife, and enjoy pleasures according to thy desire. 24. And who is he, the Vishṇu of whom thou speakest? He whom thou desirest does not equal me in valour, in austerity, in the means of enjoyment, or in power.' 25. She replied: 'Say not so; say not so; (26.) what other than thou, if wise, would despise Vishṇu, the sovereign of the three worlds, and reverenced by all worlds?' 27. Being thus addressed by Vedavatī, Rāvaṇa seized the hair of her head with the tips of his fingers. 28. She being incensed, cut off her locks with her hand, which became a sword and severed them. 29. Blazing and burning, as it were, with anger, she addressed Rāvaṇa, after kindling a fire, in which she was about to destroy herself: 30. 'Since I have been rudely treated by thee, thou ignoble being, I have no longer any desire for life. I will therefore enter into the fire whilst thou art looking on. 31. And since I have been insulted by thee, thou sinful being, in the wood, I shall be born again to slay thee. 32. A wicked male cannot be slain by a female; and were I to curse thee, I should lose (the fruit of) my austerities. 33. But if I have done, given, or offered aught in sacrifice, I shall become the daughter—not born of the womb—of a righteous man.' 34. So saying, she entered the blazing fire; when there fell from the sky a divine shower of flowers on every side. 35. It is she who was born as the daughter of king Janaka, thy wife, O king [this is addressed to Rāma], for thou art the eternal Vishṇu. . . . . 38. She who formerly in the Kṛita age was Vedavatī, has been born when the Tretā age has arrived, in the family of Janaka, the great King of Mithilā, for the destruction of that Rākshasa."

CCXLIII.—Referring to the fifth volume of my "Original Sanskrit Texts," &c., for fuller information about the Vedic deities, I shall here, and under numbers CCXLIV. and CCLI., supply some particulars about Varuṇa, Indra, and Yama, prefixing a reference to the attributes ascribed in the hymns of the Veda to the gods generally.*

The gods can do whatever they will: no mortal, however hostile, can thwart their designs (Ṛig Veda viii. 28, 4, addressed to the Viśve devāḥ,† or the totality of the deities). The same thing is said of the Maruts (R. V. viii. 20, 17), and of Indra (viii. 50, 4, and viii. 55, 4). It is similarly declared in R. V. iii. 56, 1 (addressed to the Viśve devāḥ), that no one, however skilful (or skilled in magic arts), or however wise, can disturb the first or firm ordinances (or works) of the gods. They stand above all creatures (x. 65, 15, addressed to the same). In a refrain occurring at the close of each of the verses of R. V. iii. 55 (addressed to the same), it is said that their divine character (*asuratva*) is great and unique. In one passage (x. 33, 8 f., of which verse 1 is addressed to the Viśve devāḥ), a grateful priest exclaims, "Had I power over the immortals, or over mortals, my bountiful patron should live; but no one, though he had a hundredfold vitality, could survive beyond the term prescribed by the gods: so that he has been parted from his friend." In i. 89, 1 f., the gods are thus invoked:—"May auspicious forces come to us from every quarter, unchecked, uncontrolled, shooting forth; that the gods may always act so as to advance us, being our unwearied protectors day by day. 2.

---

* In regard to Varuṇa and Indra, the reader may consult Professor Ludwig's recently published work, "Die Mantralitteratur und das alte Indien," being the third volume of his Ṛigveda, and forming an introduction to his translation of the Hymns contained in the first two volumes. Dr Hillebrandt has published a Dissertation on Varuṇa and Mitra. Breslau, 1877.

† These two words sometimes denote *all the gods*, and at other times a particular class of gods. See Böhtlingk and Roth's Wörterbuch *s.v. viśva*, and Grassman's Wörterbuch *s.v. deva*.

The kindly goodwill of the gods (is shown) to the righteous: may the bounty of the gods rest upon us. We have obtained the friendship of the gods: may the gods prolong our time, that we may live." And in vv. 8 f., blessings are thus implored from them:—"May we hear with our ears what is good, O gods; may we see with our eyes that which is good, O adorable beings. May we, with firm limbs and bodies, having praised them, attain to the ages determined by the gods. A hundred autumns are before us, within which Ye have ordained the decay of our bodies (to take place), within which sons become fathers. Do not arrest our life in the middle of its course." In x. 117, 1, an advocate of liberality expresses his assurance that the gods have not ordained hunger to be the mode of (his own or of men's) death, as even the full fed are overtaken by various forms of death. Another poet cries (x. 64, 2,—the hymn is addressed to the Viśve devāḥ), that there is no other comforter than the gods; and that his wishes are directed towards them.

In viii. 29, 7, their abodes are thus referred to: In the realms where the gods live in bliss, Vishṇu took his three strides. In iii. 54, 5, the author of the hymn asks, Who truly knows, who here can declare, what road leads to the gods? their lowest seats only are beheld, which (yet are) in remote and hidden regions.

The gods are represented as perhaps somewhat selfishly delighting in the man who offers libations: they do not love sleep (viii. 2, 18). They are no friends to him who does not toil in their service (iv. 33, 11). They give ear to those who bring them offerings (i. 45, 2). The active man conquers, rules, enjoys abundance: the gods favour not the illiberal (vii. 32, 9). The chariot of the godly man rushes forward, like a hero, in every fight. The sacrificer who seeks to please the gods overcomes him who does not sacrifice. Thou dost not suffer evil, O sacrificer, O offerer of libations, O lover of the gods (viii. 31, 15).

In the *Śatapatha Brāhmaṇa*, i. 1, 1, 7, it is said:—"The gods know the mind of a man. They are aware, when he takes on himself this vow, that he will present his offering in the morning; so they all come to his house and abide there." (*Mano ha vai devāḥ manushyasya ājānanti. Te enam etad vratam upayantam viduḥ prâtar no yakshyate iti. Te asya viśve devâḥ gṛihân âgachhanti.*)

Varuṇa is one of the Âdityas, the sons of Aditi,* who are described in the Ṛig Veda as blameless, sinless, mighty, resistless, profound, sleepless, far-observing, fixed in their purpose. Distant things are near to them; they guard and uphold all things, both moving and stationary; they see the good and evil in men, and distinguish the honest man from the deceitful; they are holy and awful, haters of falsehood (*ghorâso anṛita-drishaḥ*), and punish sin: which they are entreated to forgive, averting from the worshipper the consequences of the transgressions of others,† as well as of his own (*mâ vo bhujema anyajâtam enaḥ*, vii. 52, 2), or transferring the penalties to the head of Trita Âptya. They are supplicated for various boons, for guidance, light, long life, offspring, &c. They are said to know how to protect men from the wicked, and are besought to extend their guardianship to their worshipper, as birds spread their wings (over their young). Their servants are embraced in, or shielded by, them, as fighting men encased in armour, and no shaft, however sharp or heavy, can strike them.

Varuṇa, who is often associated with Mitra, and less frequently with Aryaman, is the most important of the Âdityas. He is sometimes, at least, described as apparent to the eye of his worshippers. Thus, in one place, R. V. i. 25, 18, the poet says:—"May I behold him who is visible to all; may I behold his chariot upon the ground." In another hymn (vii. 88, 2) the author exclaims,—"When I obtained a vision of Varuṇa, I regarded his lustre as like that of Agni." Mighty and fixed in purpose, he sits in his abode, exercising sovereignty. He is arrayed in golden apparel, and surrounded by his messengers or angels (i. 25, 10, 13). His house, at which his worshippers are said to have arrived, has a thousand gates (vii. 88, 5). He is in other places described

* In regard to this goddess, see Sanskrit Texts v. 35 ff., and Dr Hillebrandt's Dissertation Ueber die Göttin Aditi.

† Further reference will be found to this idea below.

as occupying, along with Mitra, a lofty and stable palace,* supported by a thousand columns (ii. 41, 5; v. 66, 2).

Mounted on their car in the highest empyrean they behold all things in heaven and earth (v. 62, 4, 8; v. 63, 1).†

Varuṇa is frequently spoken of as a king, as king of all, both gods and men (ii. 27, 10), as king of the universe, of all that exists (v. 85, 3; vii. 87, 6); as an universal monarch, as an independent ruler (i. 25, 10; ii. 28, 6). The same epithets of king and universal monarch are elsewhere applied to him and Mitra conjointly. In vii. 61, 5, it is said of him and of Varuṇa, either that their secrets are not revealed to the foolish, or that nothing is hid from them.

The grandest cosmical functions are ascribed to Varuṇa. Possessed of illimitable knowledge (or resources), he has meted out (or fashioned), and upholds, heaven and earth: he dwells in all worlds as sovereign ruler (viii. 42, 1). He made the golden sun to shine in the firmament (vii. 87, 5; v. 85, 2). The wind which resounds through the atmosphere is his breath (vii. 87, 2). He has opened boundless paths for the sun, and hollowed out channels for the rivers, which flow at his command (i. 24, 8; ii. 28, 4; vii. 87, 1). By his wonderful and unresisted contrivance the rivers pour their waters into the one ocean, but never fill it (v. 85, 6). His ordinances are fixed and steadfast (iii. 54, 18); they rest on him, unshaken, as on a mountain (ii. 28, 8). Through their operation the moon walks in brightness, and the stars which appear in the nightly sky, mysteriously vanish in the light of

---

* Compare Isaiah vi. 1 ff.; and see Psalms xi. 4, and xviii. 7, where the word rendered "temple" in the English version is translated "palace" in the German and French versions of Hupfeld and Reuss: and Habakkuk ii. 20. See also Ovid, Met. ii. 1 ff.

† The verse v. 62, 8, is thus rendered by Grassmann:—"At the break of dawn, ye mount your gold-adorned throne (*garta*) on iron pillars: at sunrise, O Mitra and Varuṇa, ye survey that which is endless (*aditi*), that which is bounded." Ludwig translates:—"Ye, Mitra and Varuṇa, mount your car which is golden-coloured at the break of dawn, and which has iron pillars at the setting of the sun, and thence ye survey infinity and limitation." Compare Habakkuk iii. 8.

day (i. 24, 10). Neither the birds flying in the air,* nor the rivers in their sleepless flow, can attain a knowledge of his power or his wrath (i. 24, 6). His messengers (or angels) behold both worlds (vii. 87, 3). He knows the flight of birds in the air, the path of ships on the ocean, the course of the far-travelling wind, and beholds all secret things that have been, or shall be, done (i. 25, 7, 9, 11).

In the Atharva Veda iv. 16, the power and omniscience of Varuṇa are thus celebrated :—" 1. The Great One who rules over these worlds beholds as if he were near at hand. When any man thinks that he is moving by stealth, the gods know it all (comp. Psalm cxxxi. 1-4) ; (2.) (and they perceive) every one who stands, or walks, or totters, or goes to hide himself, or slips along. Whatever two persons, sitting together, secretly discourse (or devise), Varuṇa the king knows it, (being there as) a third (comp. St Matthew xviii. 20). 3. This earth, too, is King Varuṇa's, and that vast sky, whose ends are so remote. The two oceans (the aerial and the terrestrial, comp. Genesis i. 7, and Ps. cxlviii. 4) are Varuṇa's stomachs ; and he is absorbed in this small pool of water. 4. He who should flee far beyond the sky, would not there escape from Varuṇa the king. His angels (descending) from heaven, traverse this world; thousand-eyed, they look across the whole earth. 5. King Varuṇa perceives all that exists between heaven and earth, and all that is beyond. The winkings of men's eyes are counted by him. He watches (?) all things, as a gamester his dice."

Varuṇa is said to have a hundred, a thousand, remedies, and is supplicated to show a wide and deep benevolence, and to drive away evil and sin ; to untie, like a rope, and remove sin (i. 24, 9 ; ii. 28, 5). He is entreated not to steal away, but to prolong, life (i. 24, 11 ; i. 25, 12) ; and not to abandon to the destroyer the suppliant who daily transgresses his laws

* This verse is in the Anukramaṇī said to be addressed to Varuṇa, though other deities are invoked in the preceding verses, and Varuṇa is not named before verse 7. In R. V. x. 80, 5, it is said that not only do ṛishis invoke Agni with hymns, and men harassed in battle call upon him, but birds flying in the air also. (*Agnim ukthair ṛishayo vi hrayante Agnim naro yâmani bâdhitâsaḥ Agnim vayo antarikshe patantaḥ.*)

(i. 25, 12). In many places mention is made of the bonds, or nooses, with which he binds transgressors (i. 24, 15, &c.). In one passage (vii. 65, 3) Mitra and Varuṇa are conjointly spoken of as enchainers, furnished with many nooses, from whom the sinner cannot release himself; and in another place (vii. 84, 2) Indra and Varuṇa are said to bind with bonds not formed of rope. On the other hand Varuṇa is said to be gracious even to him who has committed sin (vii. 87, 7). He is the wise guardian of immortality (or the world of the immortals, viii. 42, 2); and a hope is held out that he and Yama reigning in blessedness shall be beheld in the next world by the righteous (x. 14, 7).

I add in a different version a portion of the first, and the whole of the second, of two hymns translated by Prof. Max Müller in his "Ancient Sanskrit Literature," pp. 540 f.; and again in his "Chips from a German Workshop," i. 39 ff.: Ṛ.V. vii. 86, 3, "Seeking to perceive that sin, I enquire; I resort to the wise to ask. The sages all tell me the same; it is this Varuṇa who is angry with thee. 4. What great sin was it, Varuṇa, for which thou seekest to slay thy worshipper and friend? Tell me, O unassailable and self-dependent God; and freed from sin, I shall speedily resort to thee with adoration. 5. Release us from the offences of our fathers,* from

* This idea of a man suffering for the sins of others (which is found in the Old Testament, in Exodus xx. 5, and Deuteronomy v. 9; but which was repugnant to the moral sense of Ezekiel,—see chapter xviii. 1 ff., and compare Jeremiah xxxi. 29), occurs in other passages of the R.V. also. Thus vi. 52, 7; and vii. 52, 2, it is said there: "May we not suffer (the penalty of) sin committed by others." In the Atharva-veda, v. 30, 4, we find the words: "I release and acquit thee from sin committed by thy mother, or thy father, in consequence of which thou liest (sick)." (*Yad enaso mātṛikṛitāt śeshe pitṛikṛitāch cha yat unmochana-pramochane ubhe vāchā vadāmi te*). Atharva-veda, vi. 115, 1. "Whatever sins we have done, knowing or unknowing, do ye, all ye gods, united, deliver us from them. 2. If, sleeping or waking, I have committed sin, let the past and the future release me from it, as from a stake (to which any one is bound). 3. Released, as from a stake, or as a man covered with sweat (is cleansed) from filth by bathing,—let all the gods purify me from sin, as an oblation is cleansed by the instrument of purification." In the Taittirīya Brāhmaṇa iii. 7, 12, 3 f. the prayer occurs: "May Agni (free) me from the sin which my mother

those which we have committed in our own persons. O king, release Vasishṭha like a thief who is seeking after cattle: release him like a calf from its tether. 6. It was not our own will, Varuṇa, but some seduction (which led us astray), wine, anger, dice or thoughtlessness. The elder falls into the fault of the younger. Even sleep occasions sin."

vii. 89. 1. "Let me not, O king Varuṇa, go to the house of earth. Be gracious, O mighty god, be gracious. 2. When, O thunderer, I go along, quivering like an inflated skin, be gracious, &c. 3. I have, from lack of understanding, done what is contrary (to thy will): be gracious, &c. 4. Thirst has overcome thy worshipper, standing in the midst of the waters: be gracious, &c. 5. Whatever offence this be, O Varuṇa, that we as men commit against the gods, in whatever way we have infringed thy ordinances, through thoughtlessness, do not seek to harm us for that transgression."

In another place (vii. 88, 4) the same ṛishi, Vasishṭha, alludes to his previous friendship with Varuṇa, and to the favours which the god had formerly conferred upon him, and asks why they had now ceased. 4. "Varuṇa placed Vasishṭha on his boat; the wise and skilful deity made him in an auspicious time a ṛishi to offer praise, that his days and dawns might be prolonged. 5. Whither have those friendly acts of us twain now gone,—the harmony which we enjoyed before? I have gone, O self-dependent Varuṇa, to thy vast abode with a hundred gates. 6. When any one, thy friend, being thine own dear kinsman, has committed offences against thee,—let us not, O avenger, though transgressors, reap the fruits (of our sin). Do thou who art a wise god, grant protection to him who praises thee."

---

or my father committed when I was in the womb." The context of this passage contains an enumeration of various sorts of sins. In R.V. x. 37, 12, the worshipper asks: "If, gods, we have committed against you any grievous offence with our tongues, or through thoughtlessness (*manasaḥ prayutī*), transfer, O bright deities, (the guilt of) that sin to the enemy who seeks to wrong us." Sâyana renders *manasaḥ prayutī*, in translating which I have followed Roth, by *manasaḥ prayogena*, "application of mind" or attention.

CCXLIV. Indra. In the hymns of the Ṛig Veda Indra is described as the creator, or generator, of heaven and earth (vi. 30, 5; viii. 36, 4); as having beautifully fashioned (*sumite*) their masses by his power and wisdom (x. 29, 6); as having generated from his own body the father and mother, by which heaven and earth seem to be intended (x. 54, 3: compare x. 88, 15); as sustaining and upholding them (iii. 32, 8, &c.); as grasping them like a handful (iii. 30, 5); as stretching them out like a hide (viii. 6, 5). He is elsewhere (vi. 30, 1) said to transcend heaven and earth, which are equalled by a half of the god; and they are described as following him as a chariot wheel a horse (viii. 6, 38); as bowing down before him (i. 131, 1); as trembling from fear of him (iv. 17, 2, &c.); as being driven away or asunder by him (vii. 23; 3); as subject to his dominion (x. 89, 10); and as doing homage to his irresistible force (viii. 82, 12).

The following are specimens of numerous other passages in which his greatness is celebrated (See Vol. iv. 99—108, and v. 99—102 of Original Sanskrit Texts.)

i. 7, 3. "Indra has exalted the sun in the sky to be seen from afar." (Compare Psalm lxxiv. 16).

i. 55, 1. "His vastness is extended even beyond the sky: even the earth is not comparable to Indra in greatness."

i. 61. 9. "His greatness transcends the sky and the earth, and surpasses the atmosphere."

i. 81. 5. He has filled the terrestrial region; he has fastened the luminaries in the sky. No one like thee, Indra, has been born, or shall be born: thou hast transcended the universe."

ii. 12, 2. "He who fixed the quivering earth, who gave stability to the agitated mountains, who meted out the vast atmosphere, who propped up the sky, he, O men, is Indra."

ii. 15, 2. "He propped up the vast sky in empty space."

iv. 30, 1. "There is none, Indra, higher than thou, or superior to thee, thou slayer of Vṛitra; neither is there any one like thee." (Psalms lxxxix. 8; xcvii. 19; Exod. xv. 11).

vi. 31, 2. "Through fear of thee, Indra, all the terrestrial regions, though unshaken, totter: heaven and earth, mountains, forests, everything that is fixed, are afraid at thy coming." (Psalm civ. 32).

viii. 21, 13. "Indra, by thy nature, thou art of old without a rival, without a fellow."

viii. 37, 3. "Thou (Indra) rulest, a sole monarch over this world."

viii. 59. 5. "If, Indra, thou hadst a hundred skies, and a hundred earths, a thousand suns could not equal thee, O thunderer, nor anything created, nor the two worlds."

viii. 67, 5. "Indra is not to be overcome: the powerful (god) is not to be overpowered. He hears and sees every thing."

viii. 82, 11. "Whoso command and empire, no one—whether god or impetuous mortal—can resist."

viii. 87, 2. "Thou, Indra, art the conqueror; thou hast caused the sun to shine; thou art great, the all-fashioning (*viśvakarman*), the god of all (gods).

x. 89, 4. "(Indra) who by his power holds asunder heaven and earth, as the two wheels of a chariot are kept apart by the axle. 10. Indra rules over the sky, Indra rules over the earth, Indra rules over the waters, and over the mountains."

Indra's relations to his worshippers are described in the Ṛig Veda as follows:—He is the friend, kinsman, and even the brother, of his present worshippers, as he was the friend of their forefathers (iii. 53, 5; vi. 21, 8; vi. 45, 1, 7; and many other passages). His friendship and guidance are sweet (viii. 57, 11). One poet prays that his ancient friendly relations with the god may not be dissolved (x. 23, 7). He chooses for his intimate the man who presents offerings, but desires no friendship with him who offers no libations (x. 42, 4). He is not only a friend, but a father, and the most fatherly of fathers* (iv. 17, 17; compare i. 1, 9, in reference to Agni); and as a father he is invoked by men (x. 48, 1). He is both father and mother (viii. 87, 11). In one place the adoring poet exclaims, "Thou art ours and we are thine"† (viii. 81,

* Compare Psalm ciii. 13, and Isaiah lxiii. 16.

† The commentator quotes here a short text from an Âraṇyaka, signifying, "Thou art all this: we are thine."

32; compare i. 57, 5; and see Psalm cxix. 94). His worshippers are said to be in him (or closely connected with him), ii. 11, 12; viii. 55, 13; (and the same expression is used in addressing the Adityas in viii. 47, 8, and Agni in x. 142, 1). He is the only consoler to whom his worshipper has recourse (viii. 69, 1). He is told that he alone among the gods has compassion on mortals (vii. 23, 5), and is the only comforter of his worshippers (viii. 55, 13, and i. 84, 19). All men have a share in him (viii. 54, 7). He is the deliverer and advocate (or comforter) of his servants (viii. 85, 20), and their strength (vii. 31, 5). He is prayed to be firm; he is a wall of defence (or fortress) (viii. 69, 7; compare Psalm xviii. 2, and other similar texts). His friend is never slain or conquered (x. 152, 1). He is strong, and is resorted to for the protection afforded by his high arms (vi. 47, 8; compare Psalm lxxxix. 13). This mighty and heroic deliverer is easy to be entreated (vi. 47, 11). His worshippers, though invoking him from afar, know that he is not deaf, but hears (viii. 45, 17). His right hand is grasped by suppliants for riches (x. 47, 1). Their hymns imploring blessings, uttered by their minds, their longing messengers, proceed to the god, and touch his heart (x. 47, 7). The poet with his most dulcet hymn seizes the skirts of the god (as he would a father's, iii. 53, 2). He is clasped by the ardent hymns of his votaries, as a husband is embraced by his loving wives (i. 62, 11; i. 186, 7; x. 43, 1). The hymns hasten to him, and lick him, as cows their calves (x. 119, 4; i. 186, 7). He is entreated not to be lazy like a priest (viii. 81, 30); and not to allow other worshippers to arrest his horses when conveying him to the abode of the suppliants,—who will satisfy him with soma-libations,—but to overleap the bonds by which other candidates for his favour seek to catch him, as fowlers to snare a bird, and to pass by them as he would over a desert (ii. 18, 3; iii. 25, 5; iii. 45, 1; x. 160, 1). He is the king of things moving, of men, and of all terrestrial things, and out of his abundance he bestows on the man who brings oblations to him (vii. 27, 3). Both his hands are full of riches (vii. 37, 3), He is a magazine replenished with wealth whom the worshipper should urge to liberality (x. 42, 2). Manifold aids shoot out from him as branches from a tree (vi. 24, 3). He is asked to shower helpful wealth on his adorers, as a man with a hook shakes down ripe fruit from a tree (iii. 45, 4). Neither gods nor men can arrest him in his course when he is bent on liberality, as a terrific bull cannot be stopped (viii. 70, 3). His friendship is everlasting. He is a cow to the man who desires one, and is prayed to be a horse to him who seeks a horse (vi. 45, 26). He gives wives to those who had none (v. 31, 2; iv. 17, 16). He protects and richly rewards those who praise him and bring him offerings (ii. 12, 14; ii. 19, 4; ii. 22, 3). The days will dawn beneficently on the man who says "Let us pour out libations to Indra" (v. 37, 1). The king, in whose house Indra drinks soma mixed with milk, suffers no evil, marches at the head of his warriors, slays his enemy, and lives happily at home in the enjoyment of renown (v. 37, 4). His friend is handsome, possesses horses and cows, rides in a chariot, enjoys strengthening food, and walks radiant into the assembly (viii. 4, 9). The god is prayed to deliver his worshippers on every to-day, and on every to-morrow, and on the next day, and to protect them on all days both by day and by night (viii. 50, 17). He is invoked, and libations offered to him, both by day and by night (viii. 53, 6). Sometimes the god is importuned to be more prompt in his liberality. "Gracious are thy hands, O Indra (the poet cries in iv. 21, 9), beneficent thy palms, bestowers of wealth upon thy worshippers: why, then, dost thou sit still?* why dost thou not enjoy thyself? why dost thou not delight in giving?" Again (in x. 42, 3) he is asked: "Why do they call thee generous, O opulent god? enrich me, for I hear that thou art a bestower. Let my hymn be productive, O powerful god; bring to us, Indra, prosperity producing riches." The god is even told that the poet, if in his place, and possessed of the ample resources which he alone commands, would show himself more bountiful, and would not abandon his worshipper to poverty, but would daily lavish on him cows and other property (vii. 32, 18; viii. 14, 1: Agni is similarly remonstrated with in viii. 19, 25;

---

* Compare Psalm lxxiv. 11, "Why withdrawest thou thy hand, even thy right hand? Pluck it out of thy bosom."

and viii. 44, 23). Indra is the enemy of the irreligious, whom he punishes and destroys. Thus, i. 131, 4: "Thou, Indra, hast punished the mortal who does not worship thee;" and viii. 14, 15: "Thou, Indra, a soma-drinker, who art above all, hast destroyed and scattered the assembly which offers no libations;" and iv. 25, 5 ff: "Dear is the righteous man, dear to Indra is the man who reveres him, dear is the zealous (worshipper), dear is the offerer of soma. 6. This impetuous and heroic Indra appropriates to himself the cooked oblation of the zealous soma-offerer. He is not the relation, or friend, or kinsman of the man who offers no oblations; he is the slayer of the prostrated undevout man. 7. Indra, the soma-drinker, approves not friendship with the wealthy niggard, who offers no oblations. He seizes his wealth, and smites him when he is stripped bare; whilst he is the exclusive favourer of the man who offers libations, and cooks sacrificial food." Various other passages to the same effect might be quoted (see Original Sanskrit Texts, vol. i. pp. 259 ff.). Indra controls the destinies of men at his pleasure, and acts arbitrarily (vi. 47, 15 ff.) "Who can praise him, who can satiate him, who can adore him, that the bountiful god may always protect the bold man? Like one moving (changing the positions of) his feet (in walking), Indra by his power puts now one, now another, man first or last. 16. This hero is renowned as subduing every fierce man, and as advancing now one and now another. The enemy of the flourishing* man, the king of both (worlds), Indra protects the men who are his subjects. 17. He abandons his friendships with (his) former (favourites), and consorts with others in turn." Indra is, more than any other god, invoked as the patron of the Aryas, and as their protector against their enemies the Dasyus regarded as earthly, or aerial enemies (i. 51, 8, i. 103, 3; i. 130, 8; ii. 11, 18; iii. 34, 9; iv. 26, 2; vi. 18, 3, &c.).

I may take this opportunity of referring to the differences in the religious conceptions which we meet in different

* Does this expression intimate the same idea of the gods being jealous of human prosperity as we find in Herodotus i. 32 (near the beginning of the section); iii. 40; vii. 10, and 46 (at the end)?

portions of the Ṛig Veda. In the Nirukta of Yāska, which furnishes some contributions towards the proper understanding and interpretation of the Veda, it is stated in one passage (vii. 4) that owing to the greatness of the Deity, the one Soul is celebrated in many forms, and that the different gods are members of the one Soul. (See Original Sanskrit Texts, iv. 159, and v. 350.) This, however, is the view of a man who lived at a period when reflection had long been exercised on the contents of the hymns, and when speculation had already made great advances. But the co-existence of a plurality of deities, as recognised in the older portions of the hymns, is inconsistent with the supposition that the writers in general had attained to any clear comprehension of the unity of the godhead, although the ascription of universal dominion to several of the gods no doubt indicates enlarged and sublime conceptions of the divine nature, and an advance towards the idea of one sovereign deity. The Ṛig Veda does, however, elsewhere appear to recognise the unity of the divine nature, though manifested in a multiplicity of forms. In the 46th verse of an abstruse and mystical hymn, i. 164, it is said: "They call him Indra, Mitra, Varuṇa, Agni; and (he is) the celestial well-winged Garutmat." Sages name variously that which is but one; they call it Agni, Yama, Mātariśvan.* And in A. V. xiii. 3, 13, it is said that "Agni becomes in the evening Varuṇa (the god of night), and rising in the morning he becomes Mitra. Becoming Savitṛi (the sun), he moves through the atmosphere, and becoming Indra, he burns along the middle of the sky." In A. V. xiii. 4, 1 ff., Savitṛi is identified with various other deities. The verse R. V. i. 89, 10 is pantheistic in its character: "Aditi is the sky; Aditi is the air; Aditi is mother, and father, and son; Aditi is all the gods, and the five classes of men; Aditi is whatever has been born; Aditi is whatever shall be born."

Indra, as we have seen, receives in one verse (R. V. viii. 87, 2) the epithet of *viśvakarman*, "the all-fashion-

* On this verse compare the late Professor Haug's "Vedische Räthselfragen und Räthselsprüche," p. 56.

ing," or "all-fabricating." The same characteristic is assigned to the god Sūrya, the sun, in x. 170, 4; and in iv. 53, 2 Savitṛi is called the supporter of the sky and the lord of creatures (*prajāpati*), and in v. 82, 7, he is styled *viśvadeva*, the all-god, or the all-divine. In the two hymns, R. V. x. 81 and x. 82, however, this word *viśvakarman* becomes the proper name of a god who is conceived as the creator of all things. The following are some of the verses of the first of these hymns (see Original Sanskrit Texts, iv. pp. 5 ff.), x. 81, 2 :—" What was the foundation, which (of what kind) was the source from which the all-seeing Viśvakarman produced the earth, and by his might disclosed the heaven ? 3. The one god, who has on every side eyes, on every side a face, on every side arms, on every side feet, when producing the heaven and the earth, welds them together with his arms and his wings. 4. What was the wood, what was the tree, out of which they fashioned heaven and earth ? Enquire mentally, ye sages, what that was on which he took his stand when upholding the worlds." In x. 121, the god called Hiraṇyagarbha is thus celebrated: "1. Hiraṇyagarbha arose in the beginning; as soon as born, he was the sole lord of things existing. He established the earth, and this heaven. To what god shall we offer our oblation ? 2. He who gives breath, who gives strength, whose command all, and the gods too, reverence, whose shadow is immortality, whose shadow is death ;—to what god shall we offer our oblation. 3. Who by his might became the sole king of the breathing and winking world, who rules over this two-footed and four-footed (creation) ;—to what god, &c. 4. Whose greatness these snowy mountains, and the ocean, with the river, declare, of whom these (different) quarters of the sky are the arms ;—to what god, &c. 5. By whom the sky is fiery and the earth firmly fixed, by whom the firmament and the heaven were established, who, in the atmosphere, is the measurer of the aerial space ;—to what god, &c. ?" The following pantheistic verses are from the hymn known as the Purusha Sūkta (R. V. x. 90) :—" 2. Purusha himself is this whole universe, whatever has been and whatever shall be. He is also the lord of immortality, which grows by food. 3. Of such extent is his greatness; and Purusha is superior to this. All existing (terrestrial?) things are a quarter of him; and that which is imperishable in the sky is three-quarters of him. 4. With three quarters Purusha mounted upwards; again a quarter of him was produced here below." Further on the mystical sacrifice of Purusha is referred to, and the production from him of various creatures, and the several parts of the universe.

In R. V. x. 129, we have the following interesting speculations and guesses about the creation: "There was then neither nonentity nor entity; there was no atmosphere, or sky above. What enveloped [all]? Where, in the receptable? of what [was it contained]? Was it water, the profound abyss? Death was not then, nor immortality; there was no distinction of day or night. That One breathed calmly, self-supported; there was nothing different from, or above, it. In the beginning darkness existed, enveloped in darkness. All this was undistinguishable water. That One which lay void, and wrapped in nothingness, was developed by the power of fervour. Desire first arose in It, which was the primal germ of mind; (and which) sages, searching with their intellect, have discovered in their heart to be the bond which unites entity with nonentity. The ray [or cord] which stretched across these [worlds?], was it beneath, or was it above? There were there impregnating powers and mighty forces; a self-supporting principle beneath, and energy above. Who knows, who here can declare, whence has sprung—whence, this creation? The gods are subsequent to the development of this [universe]; who then knows whence it arose? From what this creation arose; and whether [any one] made it, or not,—he who in the highest heaven is its ruler, he verily knows, or [even] he does not know." *

---

* I have copied this translation as it stands in the 5th volume of my Original Sanskrit Texts, p. 356, though some parts of it are of doubtful correctness. See the translations of Professor Max Muller, Ancient Sanskrit Literature, p. 584; Monier Williams, Indian Wisdom, p. 22; and the German versions of Ludwig, Grassmann and Geldner in the Sieben Zig Lieder des Rigveda.

The Vājasaneyi Sanhitā of the Yajur Veda (a collection of formulas and verses of more recent date than the Ṛig Veda) has the following verses relating to Purusha (xxxi. 18): "I know this great Purusha, resplendent as the sun above the darkness. Knowing him a man overpasses death. There is no other road to go." *Ibid*, xxxii. 2: "All winkings of the eye have sprung from Purusha. No one has grasped him above, or across, or in the middle." The Atharva Veda has the following lines about Brahma (x. 7, 32):—"Reverence to that greatest Brahma, of whom the earth is the measure, the atmosphere is the belly, and who made the sky his head;" (x. 8, 1) "Reverence to that greatest Brahma, who presides over the past, the future, the universe, and whose alone is the sky." Yet in A. V. x. 7, 36, this Brahma is said to have sprung from toil and austerity. A. V. x. 2 is a hymn in which the deity is conceived as the man or male (Purusha), and the poet speculates on the agencies by which the different portions of his body could have been constructed, and the source from which his various attributes could have been derived. Among other questions proposed are these (verse 9): "Whence does the glorious Purusha bring many things pleasant and unpleasant, sleep, distress, fatigue, and various kinds of enjoyments? How do suffering, distress, evil, poverty, as well as success and opulence, exist in Purusha?" In verse 25 it is said, "The earth was made, and Brahma is placed aloft as the sky. Brahma is the expanse of atmosphere, placed above and stretched across." A. V. x. 8 ends with the following verse (44):—"Knowing that soul which is unimpassioned, calm, undecaying, young, immortal, self-existent, satisfied with the essence, deficient in nothing, a man is not afraid of death." (See No. I. above, pp. 1 and 197).

In regard to the later developments of Indian theology, see the translations from the Upanishads given above under Nos. LXXIV. and LXXV.

In the hymns of the Ṛig Veda we meet with an idea which, if I mistake not, is foreign to the later Indian literature—viz., that the compositions of the writers were inspired by the gods. Referring to the first volume of my Original Sanskrit Texts for a fuller treatment of this question, and for a reference to those verses in which the Vedic poets appear to regard themselves as the unassisted authors of their hymns, I will here adduce some passages in which these productions are spoken of as inspired or created by the gods.

Thus in i. 37, 4, the hymn is spoken of as god-given. In x. 61, 7, and x. 88, 8, the gods are said to have generated prayer, or the hymn. In iii. 18, 3; iv. 43, 1; vii. 34, 1, 9; viii. 27, 13; x. 176, 2, the hymn is styled divine (*devī*). The goddess Aditi is in one place said to have generated a hymn of praise to Indra (viii. 12, 14). Poetical thoughts, mental products, and hymns are said (iv. 11, 3) to spring from Agni, who is also styled (*rishikṛit*) the creator or former of *ṛishis* or sages among men (i. 31, 16). Bṛihaspati is said (ii. 23, 2) to be the generator of all prayers. The Gandharva Viśvāvasu is prayed to communicate to the worshippers what is true, and what they do not know (x. 139, 5) (?) In vi. 18, 15 Indra is supplicated to generate a new hymn through the sacrifices; in vi. 47, 15 to make the intellect of the worshipper sharp like the edge of an iron instrument. In vii. 97, 3 the wish is expressed that the divine hymn may reach Indra, the king of the god-made prayer. In viii. 13, 7 he is prayed to generate hymns as of old; and to hear his worshipper's invocation. Indra and Vishṇu conjointly are called the generators of all hymns (vi. 69, 2). In the xi[th]. of the apocryphal additions to the Ṛig Veda, the Vālakhilyas, verse 6, Indra and Varuṇa are said to have given to the ṛishis or sages of old, wisdom and understanding of speech. The ancient pious sages are said in one place (vii. 76, 4) to have participated in the festivities of the gods. In x. 62, 1, it is said of the family of the Angirases, that sanctified (?) by sacrifice and gifts, they had attained to the friendship of Indra and immortality. In verse 4 of the same hymn they are designated as sons of the gods.* In verses 5 and 6, the Virūpas, sons of Angiras, are said to have sprung from Agni and from the sky (or Dyaus). In x. 67, 2 the Angirases are said to be the sons of the divine Dyaus (the sky); and in iii. 53, 7, the Virūpas, Angirases,

---

* See the opinions of Professors Roth and Grassman regarding the Angirases and Ribhus, as stated in their lexicons; and p. 332, below.

are similarly said to be sons of Dyaus. In vii. 33, 11, and 13 the sage Vasishṭha is said to be the son of Mitra and Varuṇa. In vii. 87, 4 the last named god is said to have made a communication to the same sage; in vii. 88, 4 to have placed him in a boat, and made him a ṛishi. In iii. 53, 9 Viśvāmitra, another ṛishi, is spoken of as a son of a god or the gods.

In the Ṛig Veda, piety, faith in the gods, and devotion to their service, are represented as the necessary conditions of enjoying their favour, and obtaining the blessings which they are able to confer. I cite the following texts:—

i. 55, 5. "Men have faith (*śrad dadhate*) in the fiery Indra when he hurls again and again his destroying thunderbolt."

i. 102, 2. "Sun and moon move alternately, O Indra, for us to behold, that we may have faith [in thee?]"

i. 103, 5. "Behold therefore this his great force; have faith in Indra's prowess."

i. 104, 6. "Do not, O Indra, destroy our valued enjoyment: we have put faith in thy great power. 7. I verily believe that faith has been reposed in thee; do thou, who art vigorous, advance us to great wealth."

i. 108, 6. "Since I said at first, when desiring you twain (Indra and Agni), this our Soma is to be sought after by the deities,—come now, regarding with favour this our true faith, and drink the poured-out Soma."

vi. 26, 6. "Thou, O Indra, gladdened by acts of faith, and by Soma draughts, didst, for the sake of Dabhīti, cast Chumuri into a sleep."*

vii. 32, 14. "Who, O Indra, can overcome the man whose wealth thou art? By faith in thee in the critical day (of conflict) the hero gains spoil."

In the following texts the reality of Indra's existence and power is asserted in opposition to sceptical doubts:—

ii. 12, 5. "That dreadful deity, of whom they ask 'where is he,' of whom they say 'he is not,'—he carries off the riches

* The commentator explains this as meaning that Indra was gladdened by rites performed with faith, for as he says, "the rite which is accompanied by faith has real worth;" and he quotes the Chhāndogya Upanishad, 1, 1, 10, where it is said, "whatever is done with knowledge, with faith, and with esoteric science, is more efficacious."

of the foe, as (a gamester) the stakes;* put faith in him, he, O men, is Indra."

vi. 18, 3. "Hast thou prowess, O Indra, or not? tell us truly. Thy strength, O thou strongest of beings, who art great by nature, is really existent."

viii. 89, 3. "Seeking after good, present a true hymn to Indra, if he truly exists. 'Indra does not exist,' says some one; 'who has seen him? whom shall we praise?' 4. 'Here am I, O worshipper' (exclaims Indra); 'behold me here; I surpass all creatures in greatness."

See also Ṛ.V. viii. 1, 31; x. 39, 5; x. 147, 1.

The following texts also express the pious emotions of the worshippers:—

i. 61, 2. "They polished their praises for Indra, their ancient lord, with heart, mind, and understanding."

vi. 28, 5. "These cows, O men, are Indra: I desire Indra with my heart and mind."

i. 93, 8. "Do ye, O Agni and Soma, regard the acts of the man who worships you with an oblation, with a mind directed to the gods (*devadrīchā manasā*), and with butter." (The same phrase occurs in i. 163, 12).

iv. 25, 1. "What man, a longing lover of the gods, hath enjoyed Indra's friendship to-day?"

x. 42, 9. "The self-dependent god provides with opulence that man who loves the gods, and does not withhold his wealth."

The same phrase, "lover of the gods," *deva-kāma*, occurs also in ii. 3, 9, and iii. 4, 9, and also in the following verse:—

x. 160, 3. "Indra does abandon the cattle of the man who loves the gods, and with a longing mind, and with his whole heart, pours out to him libations of Soma."

iv. 24, 6. "He bestows deliverance on the man who, with

---

* The words of the original are *vijaḥ iva āmināti*. *Vijaḥ* occurs in two passages, i. 92, 10, and ii. 12, 5, in each of which Sāyaṇa assigns to it a different sense, though it must have the same meaning in both. Roth in his Lexicon, *s.v.* only says that it appears to be a gaming expression. Benfey in his translation of i. 92, 10, gives it the signification of "dice," Orient and Occident, ii. p. 237 and note.

mind directed to him and unreluctantly pours out Soma to the longing Indra: he makes him a companion in his fights."

vii. 100, 1. "That mortal never repents who, seeking (for good), offers gifts to the wide-striding Vishṇu, who worships him with devoted mind, and seeks to gain so great a hero."

viii. 2, 37. "Worship, O Priyamedhas, with devoted mind Indra, who is really exhilarated with Soma."

ix. 77, 4. This Soma, knowing (our affairs) and lauded by many with devoted minds, will overcome our assailants."

v. 4, 10. "Give renown, O Jātavedas (Agni), to me, who, a mortal, constantly invoke thee, an immortal, with a laudatory heart (*hṛidā kīriṇā*): may I with (or through) my offspring attain immortality."

viii. 50, 9. "The man, whether learned or unlearned, who, devoted to thee, dedicates to thee a word, will delight thee."

Prosperous men are said to disregard Indra, until alarmed by the display of his might:—

viii. 21, 14. "Thou never choosest a rich man to be thy friend. Men intoxicated with wine are hostile to thee. When thou makest a sound, thou gatherest them together; then thou art called upon as a father."

In v. 44 the following verses occur:—14. "The Ṛik verses love him who is awake, the Sāman verses proceed to him who is awake. This soma-libation says to him who is awake: 'I am pleased with thy friendship.' 15. Agni is awake; him do the Ṛik verses love: Agni is awake; to him do the Sāman verses proceed. Agni is awake; to him does this Soma say, 'I am pleased with thy friendship.'"

The 151st hymn of the xth book of the R.V. is addressed to Śraddhā, Faith. It is as follows:—1. "Through faith the fire is kindled; through faith the oblation is offered,* with our words we proclaim faith (to be) upon the head of good fortune.† 2. O faith, make this which I utter acceptable to

* That is, according to Yāska, Nirukta ix. 31, "is well kindled," "is well offered."

† *I.e.*, according to the commentary on the Taittirīya Brāhmaṇa, ii. 8, 8, 6 ff., where the hymn is quoted, "Faith is the cause of good fortune to men." "Sāyaṇa in his explanation of this hymn, however, defines *Śraddhā* to be "a particular desire which a man has."

him who gives, and to him who desires to give, and to liberal worshippers. 3. As the gods caused faith in (the minds of) the fierce Asuras, so make what we utter [be an object of faith] to liberal worshippers. 4. The gods sacrificing, protected by Vāyu, reverence faith. A man acquires faith through an impulse of the heart: through faith he gains wealth. 5. We invoke faith in the morning, at noon, and at the setting of the sun: O Faith, inspire us with faith." The Taittirīya Brāhmaṇa ii. 8, 8, 8 adds another verse: "Faith dwells in (or among) the gods; faith is the entire universe; with an oblation we exalt faith, the mother of what we desire." The same Brāhmaṇa has the following verses in ii. 12, 3, 1ff.:—

"Through faith a god attains godhead; faith is divine, the support of the world; favouring us, she has come to our sacrifice, having enjoyment for her offspring, and yielding nectar (or immortality).* Faith, the divine, is the firstborn of the ceremonial, the sustainer of the universe, the supporter of the world. Her we worship with an oblation. May she assign to us an imperishable world, she the ruler, the divine sovereign mistress of all that exists."

In several passages of the Atharva Veda also reference is made to faith. Thus, iv. 35, 7: "I cook this all-conquering Brahmaudana offering; may the gods hear me who have faith." vi. 122, 3 (and xii. 3, 7), "Those who have faith attain to this world." ix. 5, 7, and 11, "The goat drives far away the darkness, being given (offered up) in this world by a man who has faith." xi. 2, 28, "Be merciful, O king Bhava, to the worshipper, for thou art the lord of cattle. Be gracious to the fourfooted and twofooted beings of him who believes that the gods exist." xix. 64, 1, "May he Jātavedas (Agni), give me faith and understanding."

The Vājasaneyi Sanhitā has these verses about faith. xix. 30: "By giving gifts faith is obtained, and by faith is gained truth." xix. 77: "Beholding the forms of truth and falsehood,

---

* The commentator quotes here a Smṛiti verse to this effect: "Sacrifices offered, gifts bestowed, or austerity practised, without faith, are called bad (or null), and have no existence either here or hereafter, O son of Pṛithā."

Prajāpati distinguished them ; to falsehood he attached disbelief, and to truth he attached belief (or faith)."

The following is from the Taittirīya Sanhitā i. 6, 8, 1, "He has no faith in what he offers who sacrifices without the exercise of faith. He brings water. Water is faith. He sacrifices exercising faith ; and both gods and men have faith in his oblation." See also Aitareya Brāhmaṇa v. 2, 7, near the end of the section. The Bṛihad Araṇyaka Upanishad iii. 9, 21 (=Śatapatha Brāhmaṇa xiv. 6, 9, 22) thus refers to faith : "On what is sacrifice based ; on largesses, on what is largess based ? on faith : for when a man has faith, he gives gifts ; so it is on faith that largess is based ; on what is faith based ? on the heart : for it has assurance through the heart : it is on the heart that faith is based."

There are many verses about Śraddhā in M. Bh. xii. 2308, 2320. See also M. Bh. iii. 12,732, and 12,734.

CCXLV. For the sources of this and the following pieces, I refer to my "Original Sanskrit Texts," vol. v. In pp. 140 ff., hymn v. 83 is translated, and other passages relating to Parjanya are referred to.

CCXLVI. See translation of Ṛig Veda, x. 168, in "Original Sanskrit Texts," v. 145 f.

CCXLVII. See "Original Sanskrit Texts," v. 155 ff.

CCXLVIII. See the same volume, pp. 181 ff.

CCXLIX. See the same volume, pp. 199 ff.

CCL. In the hymns contained in the earlier books of the Ṛig Veda occasional references occur to a future life as awaiting the worshippers of the gods.* Allusion is made in various texts to the Ṛibhus, who were mortals, but on account of their artistic skill had attained immortality (i. 110, 2 ff. ; i. 161 f. ; iii. 60,

---

* The subject of the following pages is treated in the fifteenth chapter (headed, "das Leben nach dem Tode") of Dr H. Zimmer's recently published Prize Essay, entitled, "Altindisches Leben, die Cultur der Vedischen Arier nach den Samhitā dargestellt."

3; iv. 33, 4; iv. 35, 3; iv. 36, 4). Prof. Roth, however (see his Lexicon, *s.v. Ṛibhu*), is of opinion that the beings so called cannot have been men, but rather belong to the same class of beings as the dwarfs of Scandinavian mythology, who manufactured wonderful instruments for the gods. Another class of beings, the Angirases are, in like manner said in R.V. x. 62, 1, and Sāma Veda, i. 92, to have obtained immortality; or gone to heaven, but Roth, *s.v.*, thinks that this is an attempt to explain their character, which he regards as superhuman. See also Grassmann's Lexicon, under the words. However this may be, there are other texts which can only be understood as referring to the attainment of immortality by men. In i. 125, 5, it is said: "The liberal man abides placed on the summit of the sky; he goes to the gods. 6. These brilliant things are the portions of those who bestow largesses; there are suns for them in heaven; they enjoy immortality, they prolong their life." i. 154, 5. "May I attain to that beloved abode of his (of Vishṇu), where men devoted to the gods rejoice." In i. 164, 23, it is said that those who have some information about particular metres, have attained immortality. In v. 4, 10, the worshipper prays, "I a mortal, who contemplating thee with a heart which lauds thee, continually invoke thee, who art immortal,—O Jātavedas, confer on us renown—may I with my offspring attain immortality." * In v. 55, 4, the Maruts (storm gods), are besought to place their worshippers in a state of immortality; and in v. 63, 2, Mitra and Varuṇa are prayed to bestow rain, wealth and immortality. In viii. 58, 7, the poet exclaims: "When Indra and I go to the world and house of the sun, then may we, having drunk

---

* This clause may also be explained as the Indian Commentator does: "May I attain immortality (consisting of an unbroken line of descendants), through offspring bestowed by thee." And he quotes a Vedic text to the effect, "A man is born in his offspring; this, O mortal, is thy immortality." But even if such be the true sense of this particular verse, the meaning of the other texts I have cited is not thereby affected. Prof. Ludwig renders "may I attain immortality with children." Prof. Grassmann, "may I become immortal through children."

nectar, abide in the thrice seventh * realm of our friend." In the tenth book of the R.V. we have the following texts:—In x. 73, 7, Indra is said to have made beautiful paths by which man goes straight to the gods. In x. 95, 18, the gods promise to Purūravas that if his offspring would worship them he should obtain happiness in heaven. In x. 107, 2, it is said that those who have given gifts abide high in the sky; the donors of horses abide with the sun; those who bestow gold enjoy immortality; the givers of raiment live long." In the other books of the Ṛ.V. as well as the tenth, the fathers or ancestors of the worshippers, or of the existing generation, are recognised as still existing, and are invoked for succour. Passages to this effect may be found in "Original Sanskrit Texts," vol. v. pp. 28 ff.

In the passages of the Ṛik and Atharva Vedas which follow, the subject of a future life is more fully and distinctly treated.

The following are translations of some verses of Ṛig Veda x. 14, and of other passages. "Worship with an oblation King Yama, son of Vivasvat, the assembler of men, who departed to the great heights, and spied out a path for many." [The same verse is varied in Atharva Veda xviii. 3, 13, as follows: "Reverence with an oblation Yama, son of Vivasvat, the assembler of men, who was the first of men that died, the first that departed to this (celestial) world"]. R.V. x. 14, 2. "Yama was the first that found out for us a way. This home is not to be taken from us;—(the place) whither our ancient fathers have departed along their own paths, knowing (the way) thither." In verses 7 ff. are given the words which are addressed to the departed whose obsequies are being performed: "Depart thou, depart by the ancient paths to the place whither our ancient fathers have departed: (there) shalt thou see the two kings, Yama, and the

* In the original the words are merely "thrice seven." The Commentator explains them of the region of the sun as the highest, according to a Brāhmaṇa, which says: "There are 12 months, 5 seasons, these three worlds and the sun the twenty-first. Prof. Grassmann renders the words by "three weeks," while Prof. Ludwig connects them with *sakhyuh* "friend," which, however, is in the singular.

god Varuṇa, exhilarated by the oblation. 8. Meet in the highest heaven with the fathers, meet with Yama, meet with (the recompense of) thy sacrificial and pious acts. Throwing off all imperfection, again go to thy home. Radiant, become united to a body.* Go ye, depart ye, hasten ye from hence. The fathers have made for him this place. Yama gives him an abode distinguished by days, and waters, and lights."

Atharva Veda xviii. 2, 37. "I give this abode to this man who has come hither, if he is mine. Yama, perceiving, says of him, 'Let him come hither to (be part of) my property.'"

R.V. x. 16, 3. "Let his eye go to the sun, his breath to the wind. Go to the sky and to the earth, according to the nature (of thy several parts); or go to the waters, if that is suitable for thee; enter into the plants with thy members. 4. As for his unborn part, do thou, Agni, kindle it with thy heat; let thy flame and thy lustre kindle it; with those forms of thine which are auspicious, convey it to the world of the righteous." [See note 449 in p. 298 of "Original Sanskrit Texts," where, among other illustrative passages, verses 532 ff., of the Supplices of Euripides are quoted: "Ὅθεν δ' ἕκαστον εἰς τὸ σῶμ' ἀφίκετο, ἐνταῦθ' ἀπῆλθε, πνεῦμα μὲν πρὸς αἰθέρα, τὸ σῶμα δ' εἰς γῆν. "But each (element) has departed to the quarter whence it came to the body, the breath to the aether, the body (itself) to the earth."] Vājasaneyi Sanhitā xviii. 52: "Borne by those thine undecaying, flying pinions, wherewith thou, Agni, slayest the Rakshases, may we soar to the world of the righteous, whither the ancient, earliest-born ṛishis have gone." Atharva Veda xviii. 2, 21: "Meet with the fathers, meet with Yama; may soft, refreshing breezes blow upon thee; may the Maruts, bringing, and swimming in, water, bear thee aloft; causing coolness by their movement, may they wet thee with rain." In Atharva Veda iv. 34, 4, it is said of the man who offers a particular oblation that "borne on a car, or on wings, he passes beyond the sky." Ṛig Veda x. 14, 10: "By an auspicious path hasten past those two four-eyed

* See Prof. Roth's article in the Journal of the American Oriental Society, Vol. iii. pp. 342 ff., and note 468 in "Original Sanskrit Texts," v. 303.

brindled dogs, the offspring of Saramā. 11. Entrust him, O Yama, to thy two four-eyed, road-guarding, man-observing watch dogs, and bestow on him prosperity and health." Atharva Veda xviii. 2, 24: "Let not thy mind, let no portion of thy breath, of thy limbs, of thy sense of taste, of thy body, abandon thee." A.V. vi. 120, 3: "In heaven, where our virtuous friends enjoy blessedness, having left behind them the infirmities of their bodies, free from lameness or distortion of their limbs, may we behold our parents and our children." A.V. ix. 5, 27: "When a woman has had one husband before, and gets another, and they present the *aja panchaudana* offering, they shall not be separated. 28. A second husband dwells in the same world with his re-wedded wife, if he offers the *aja panchaudana*," &c. A.V. xii. 3, 17: "Do thou conduct us to heaven; let us be with our wives and children." Ṛig Veda x. 154, 2: "Depart to those who through tapas (austerities) are invincible, and have gone to heaven, &c. 3. Depart to those who fight in battles, those who have died there, or to those who have bestowed thousands of largesses."

In Ṛig Veda ix. 113, 7 ff., the enjoyments of heaven are said to be conferred by Soma, and are thus described: 7. "Place me, O purified Soma, in that imperishable and undecaying world where perpetual light (exists), and the sun is placed. 8. Make me immortal (in the realm) where King Vaivasvata (Yama) dwells, where is the sanctuary of the sky, and those rushing waters flow. 9. Make me immortal in the third heaven, where action is unrestrained, and the regions are luminous. 10. Make me immortal in the world of the sun, where there are pleasures and enjoyments, where ambrosia and satisfaction are found. 11. Make me immortal (in the world) where there are joys, and delights, and pleasures, and gratifications; where the objects of desire are attained."

In A.V. iv. 34, 2, gratifications of a sensual kind are promised in paradise; and it is declared that those who offer a particular oblation shall be borne on cars, and, becoming winged, shall soar beyond the sky.

The virtues which are rewarded by admission to heaven are described in R.V. x. 154, as austerity or self-restraint, heroism in battle, and liberality.

The following texts seem to allude to a place of future punishment, Ṛig Veda, iv. 5, 5. Like brotherless females, unchaste, like evil women who hate their husbands, wicked, unrighteous, and liars, they are destined for that deep abyss." * ix. 73, 8. " Knowing, he beholds all creatures; he hurls the hated and irreligious into the abyss."

CCLI. See the prose translation of this hymn above, in p. 325.

CCLII. Ṛig Veda x. 146. See prose translation in "Original Sanskrit Texts," v. p. 423.

CCLIII. Ṛig Veda ix. 112. See prose version in " Original Sanskrit Texts," v. 424.

CCLIV. Ṛig Veda x. 34. See "Original Sanskrit Texts," v. 426 f.

CCLV. Ṛig Veda x. 107. See "Original Sanskrit Texts," v. 434.

CCLVI. Ṛig Veda x. 117. See "Original Sanskrit Texts," v. 431 f.

CCLVII. Ṛig Veda vii. 103. See " Original Sanskrit Texts," v. 436.

CCLVIII. See "Original Sanskrit Texts," v. 469 f.

---

* Compare the different translations of Wilson, Ludwig, Grassmann, and Zimmer, Altindisches Leben, p. 331.

SUPPLEMENT TO APPENDIX.

In this Supplement parallel passages additional to those given in the Appendix are adduced.

Page 60, line 12.—"And in the sovereign soul is merged." The expression "merged" does not exactly represent the Vedantic doctrine, which, as may be seen from what precedes, is not that there ever was any individual soul distinct from the Supreme Soul, but that all the conditions which necessitated the seeming individual to remain ignorant of his own identity with the Supreme Self being now removed, he no longer imagines himself to be a distinct and separate personality.

Page 79, note, and p. 270, lines 7 ff.—Possibly this verse, which, I have said, seems very Antinomian in its tendency, may be understood as implying that the sinner who sacrifices to the gods, at the same time enters on a new and righteous course of life. Compare the Bhagavad Gītā, ix. 30 f., where it is said: "Even if a man of very evil life worship me, seeking nothing else (*ananyabhāk* = *bhajanaika-prayojanaḥ* Rāmānuja), he must be regarded as good, for he is thoroughly resolved. He quickly becomes righteous, and obtains perpetual tranquility."

Page 87, No. cxxxvi., for "still men's grief," read "share men's grief."

Page 118, note.—The following lines from the Andromache of Euripides, 943 ff., form a parallel to the closing verses of the quotation from the Troades.

Ἀλλ' οὔποτ', οὔποτ', οὐ γὰρ εἰσάπαξ ἐρῶ,
χρὴ τούς γε νοῦν ἔχοντας, οἷς ἔστιν γυνή,
πρὸς τὴν ἐν οἴκοις ἄλοχον εἰσφοιτᾶν ἐᾶν
γυναῖκας· αὗται γὰρ διδάσκαλοι κακῶν.

"But never, never,—for I shall not say it once only—should wise men, who have a wife, permit (other) women to visit their partner in their houses, for these women are teachers of evil."

In opposition to the idea of shutting up women too much indoors, Menander makes one of his female characters speak thus (Meineke, p. 185) :—

Τὸ μὲν μέγιστον οὔποτ' ἄνδρα χρὴ σοφὸν
λίαν φυλάσσειν ἄλοχον ἐν μυχοῖς δόμων·
ἐρᾷ γὰρ ὄψις τῆς θύραθεν ἡδονῆς,
ἐν δ' ἀφθόνοισι τοῖσδ' ἀναστρωφωμένη,
βλέπουσά τ' εἰς πᾶν, καὶ παροῦσα πανταχοῦ,
τὴν ὄψιν ἐμπλήσασ' ἀπήλλακται κακῶν.

. . . . .

ὅστις δὲ μοχλοῖς καὶ διὰ σφραγισμάτων
σώζει δάμαρτα, δρᾶν τι δὴ δοκῶν σοφόν,
μάταιός ἐστι καὶ φρονῶν οὐδὲν φρονεῖ·
ἥτις γὰρ ἡμῶν καρδίαν θύραζ' ἔχει,
θᾶσσον μὲν οἰστοῦ καὶ πτεροῦ χωρίζεται,
λάθοι δ' ἂν Ἄργου τὰς πυκνοφθάλμους κορας.

"What is most important,—a wise man should never keep his wife guarded within the recesses of his house. For the eye desires out-of-door pleasure; and living in the midst of such enjoyments in abundance, and beholding every thing, and being present everywhere, and satiating her sight, she is preserved from evils. . . . But the man who seeks to preserve his wife by bolts, and confinement, while he seems to be doing something wise, is foolish, and thinking as he does, is the reverse of sensible. For any one of us who has her heart out of doors, flies off quicker than an arrow, or a bird, and would elude the many eyes of Argus."

CXXI., p. 129, note.—Compare also Euripides, Hecuba 282.—

οὐ τὸν κρατοῦντα χρὴ κρατεῖν ἃ μὴ χρεών,
οὐδ' εὐτυχοῦντας εὖ δοκειν πράξειν αεί.

"One in power ought not to exercise that power improperly; nor ought the prosperous to think that they shall always enjoy prosperity."

Euripides, Archelaus (Stobæus iv. 23).—

Πάλαι σκοποῦμαι, τὰς τύχας τῶν βροτῶν
ὡς εὖ μεταλλάσσουσιν. ὃς γὰρ ἂν σφαλῇ
εἰς ὀρθὸν ἵστη, χὠ πρὶν εὐτυχῶν πίτνει.

"Of old, I remark that the fortunes of men change: for he who has fallen rises again, while he who formerly flourished falls."

Euripides, in Stobæus, vol. iv., p. 19.—

Οὐ χρή ποτ' ὀρθαῖς ἐν τύχαις βεβηκότα
ἕξειν τὸν αὐτὸν δαίμον' εἰσαεὶ δοκεῖν.
ὁ γὰρ θεός πως, εἰ θεόν σφε χρὴ καλεῖν,
κάμνει ξυνὼν τὰ πολλὰ τοῖς αὐτοῖς ἀεί.—κ. τ. λ.

"A man who is living in prosperity should not think that he will always have the same good fortune. For the god, if god he should be called, is generally tired of abiding always with the same persons."

Euripides, Antiope, *Ibid.*, p. 20.—

Τοιόσδε θνητῶν τῶν ταλαιπώρων βίος.
οὔτ' εὐτυχεῖ τὸ πάμπαν οὔτε δυστυχεῖ,
εὐδαιμονεῖ δὲ καὖθις οὐκ εὐδαιμονεῖ.

"Such is the life of wretched men: it is neither altogether fortunate nor unfortunate: and it is now prosperous and afterwards unprosperous."

P. 208, No. vii.—Compare Euripides; fragment of Phrixus.

ὅστις δὲ θνητῶν οἴεται τοὐφ' ἡμέραν
κακόν τι πράσσων τοὺς θεοὺς λεληθέναι,
δοκεῖ πονηρὰ, καὶ δοκῶν ἁλίσκεταί.
ὅτ' ἂν σχολὴν ἄγουσα τυγχάνῃ Δίκη,
τιμωρίαν τ' ἔτισεν ὧν ἦρξεν κακῶν.

"But if any mortal thinks that when doing something evil daily, he escapes the notice of the gods, he thinks what is evil, and so thinking, he is caught. Whenever Justice has leisure, he suffers retribution for the evils he has wrought."

Fragment in Stobæus: Nauck, fragments of Euripides, No. 969.

οὔτοι προσελθοῦσ' ἡ Δίκη, μὴ τρέσῃς,
παίσει πρὸς ἧπαρ, οὐδὲ τῶν ἄλλων βροτῶν

τον ἄδικον, ἄλλὰ σῖγα καὶ βραδεῖ ποδὶ
στείχουσα, μάρπτει τοὺς κακοὺς ἀεὶ βροτῶν.

"Do not fear that Justice will ever approach thee and smite thee to the heart, nor will she so visit any other unjust man; but silently and slowly advancing, she always seizes the wicked among mortals."

The following passage is taken from the Florilegium Monacense, containing sentiments from Democritus, Epictetus, and others, printed in Meineke's edition of Stob. Anthol., iv., pp. 267 ff.—

P. 208, No. vii.

Ἐὰν ἀεί μνημονεύσῃς, ὅτι, ᾧ ἐργάζῃ κατὰ ψυχὴν ἢ σῶμα θεὸς παρέστηκεν ἔφορος, ἐν πάσαις πράξεσιν οὐ μὴ ἁμαρτῃς, ἕξεις δὲ τὸν θεὸν σύνοικον.

"If thou always rememberest that God stands by, a beholder of all that thou doest with thy soul or thy body, thou wilt not err in all thy acts, and shalt have God dwelling with thee."

P. 210, No. xii. —Compare Æschylus, fragment 163, Stobæus, i. 62.—

Θεὸς μὲν αἰτίαν φύει βροτοῖς,
ὅταν κακῶσαι δῶμα παμπήδην θέλῃ.

"When God wishes entirely to ruin a house, he creates some ground of complaint against mortals."

P. 210, No. xiii.—Euripides, Antigone (Stobæus, Anthol. iv. 34; also in Dindorf and Nauck), considered by some to be of doubtful authenticity.

Μὴ νυν θέλε λυπεῖν σαυτόν, εἰδὼς ὅτι
πολλάκις τὸ λυποῦν ὕστερον χαρὰν ἄγει,
καὶ τὸ κακὸν ἀγαθοῦ γίγνεται παραίτιον.

"Do not therefore vex thyself, knowing that that which vexes, afterwards often brings joy, and evil becomes the occasion of good."

Philemon, Stobæus, iv. 38.—

πόλλ' ἐστὶν ἐν πολλαῖσιν οἰκίαις κακά,
ἃ καλῶς ὅταν ἐνέγκῃς, ἀγαθὰ γενήσεται.

"In many houses there are many evils, which when well borne, shall become good things."

Menander's Plocium. Meineke, p. 147 :—

Ὦ Παρμένων, οὐκ ἔστιν ἀγαθὸν τῷ βίῳ
φυόμενον ὥσπερ δένδρον ἐκ ῥίζης μιᾶς,
ἀλλ' ἐγγὺς ἀγαθοῦ παραπέφυκε καὶ κακόν,
ἐκ τοῦ κακοῦ τ' ἤνεγκεν ἄγαθον ἡ φύσις.

"In life, O Parmeno, there is no good thing which springs up like a tree from one root; but alongside of the good something evil also grows up; and nature brings good out of the evil."

P. 213, No. xiv.—Plautus, Capt., ii. 2.75.—

Non ego omnino lucrum omne esse utile homini existimo.
Scio ego, multos jam lucrum homines luculentos reddidit.
Est etiam, ubi profecto damnum præstet facere quam lucrum.

"I do not regard every gain as useful to a man. I know that gain has rendered many men brilliant. There are also cases, where in truth, it will be better to incur loss than acquire gain."

P. 212 f., Nos. xiii. and xiv.—Plato, Republic x. 11.—

Τῷ δὲ θεοφιλεῖ οὐχ ὁμολογήσομεν, ὅσα γε ἀπὸ θεῶν γίγνεται, πάντα γίγνεσθαι ὡς οἷόν τε ἄριστα, εἰ μή τι ἀναγκαῖον αὐτῷ κακὸν ἐκ προτέρας ἁμαρτίας ὑπῆρχεν; Πάνυ μὲν οὖν. Οὕτως ἄρα ὑποληπτέον περὶ τοῦ δικαίου ἀνδρος, ἐάν τ' ἐν πενίᾳ γίγνηται ἐάν τε ἐν νόσοις ἤ τινι ἄλλῳ τῶν δοκούντων κακῶν, ὡς τούτῳ ταῦτα εἰς ἀγαθόν τι τελευτήσει ζῶντι ἢ καὶ ἀποθανόντι. οὐ γὰρ δὴ ὑπό γε θεῶν ποτὲ ἀμελεῖται ὅς ἂν προθυμεῖσθαι ἐθέλῃ δίκαιος γίγνεσθαι καὶ ἐπιτηδεύων ἀρετὴν εἰς ὅσον δυνατὸν ἀνθρώπῳ ὁμοιοῦσθαι θεῷ. Εἰκός γ', ἔφη, τὸν τοιοῦτον μὴ ἀμελεῖσθαι ὑπὸ τοῦ ὁμοίου.

"And the friend of the gods may be supposed to receive from them every good, excepting only such evil as is the necessary consequence of former sins? Certainly. Then this must be our notion of the just man, that even when he is in poverty or sickness, or any other seeming misfortune, all things will in the end work together for good to him in life and death: for the gods have a care of any one whose desire is to become just and to be like God, as far as man can attain his likeness, by the pursuit of virtue? Yes, he said, if he is like God, he will surely not be neglected by him." (Dr Jowett's translation of Plato, ii. 455).

P. 213, No. XIV.—I give here, both in a verse and prose translation, the remainder of the Hymn to Zeus, by Kleanthes the Stoic Philosopher, of which a portion has been quoted in p. 213. The original may be found in Stobæus, Ecl. Phys., i., 8 ff.

[Kleanthes is stated in Dr William Smith's "Dictionary of Greek and Roman Biography and Mythology," to have been "born at Assos in Troas about B.C. 300, though the exact date is unknown." The substance of the hymn is given and commented upon in Sir A. Grant's "Aristotle," 3d ed., Vol. i., p. 327 ff.]

Of all immortals grandest, many-named,
Almighty lord of nature, ruling all
By law, great Zeus, all hail! on thee we call:
Thee mortal men may all invoke unblamed.

For from thine own high self we claim to spring;
Of creatures all that people earth or air,
We men alone thy reason's impress bear;
Thy greatness, therefore, will I ever sing.

Revolving round the earth the whole array
Of stars obeys that ever-present force
Whereby across the sky thou lead'st its course,
And willing, bows to thy resistless sway.

For such an instrument to quell revolt
Thou wieldest, lord, in thine unconquered hands
As swift response compels to thy commands,—
The two-edged, fiery, living thunderbolt;

All nature quakes where'er its strokes alight.
So dost thou, Zeus, ordain thy law, which all
The heavenly lights pervades, both great and small:
So great a king art thou, of sovereign might.

Apart from thee no work, great potentate,
Is done on earth, in yonder heavenly sphere,
Or deep in ocean's caverns, far or near,
But what the bad in folly perpetrate.

Thou knowest how to make the crooked straight,
From chaos dire can'st order fair create ;
To thee are dear the things which mortals hate.

For so hast thou things good and ill combined,
That all together one grand system make,
To rule reduced by thy controlling mind :
But evil men this wondrous order break,

And neither see nor hear thy law divine,
Which, well and wisely kept, had made them blest ;
But seeking fancied good, they never rest,

Of envied fame, or sordid gain, in quest ;
Or else to ease and joy their lives resign :
Yet disappointed, all at last obtain
The dark reverse of what they hoped to gain.

But all-bestowing Father, wrapt in clouds
From whose dark depths the dazzling lightnings glance,
Sweep far away that mournful ignorance
Whose gloom the souls of mortals now enshrouds ;

And grant them knowledge, yea, vouchsafe that they
May share that wisdom wherein thou confid'st,
Whilst thou aright the course of nature guid'st ;
That honoured so by thee, we men may pay

Thee back with honour, singing aye with awe
Thy deeds, as men beseems :—from age to age
No nobler task can men or gods engage
Than this, with joy to hymn the universal law.

The following is a prose translation of the preceding hymn:—

"O most glorious of the immortals, many-named, ever almighty, Zeus, author of nature, ruling all things with law,—hail! for it is permitted to all mortal (men) to address thee. For we are a race (springing) from thee, having alone of all mortal things that live and creep on the ground, obtained a resemblance of the sound.* Wherefore I shall hymn thee, and ever celebrate thy might. This entire universe, revolving round the earth, obeys thee wheresoever thou mayest lead, and is willingly governed by thee. Such a minister thou holdest in thine unconquered hands, the two-edged (or forked), fiery, ever-living thunderbolt. For from its blow the whole of nature shudders; whereby thou directest the common order which pervades all things, blending with the greater and the lesser lights . . . thou who art such a supreme king universally. Without thee, O God, no work is done on earth, nor at the divine ethereal pole, or in the sea, save only those things which the wicked perpetrate through their own senselessness. But thou understandest, too, how to make uneven things even, and to order the things that are disordered; and things which are not dear are dear to thee. For so hast thou fitted all good things into one with the bad, that there is but one reason [or account, to be given] of all things ever existing;—which [reason] all wicked mortals shun and neglect; hapless men, who, always longing after the possession of good things, neither see nor hear this universal law of God, by wisely obeying which, they would lead an excellent life. But abandoning what is noble, they rush in pursuit of different objects; some carrying on a bitter struggle for fame, some turning to the unfair pursuit of gain, and others seeking after ease and bodily gratifications, . . . they are carried away in different directions, but prepare for themselves things altogether the opposite of these (for which they are striving). But, O all-bestowing Zeus, wrapped in dark clouds, darter of vivid lightnings, rescue men from mournful ignorance, dispelling it from their souls, O Father; and impart to them wisdom; in which trusting, thou governest all things aright; [do this] that so, being honoured of thee, we may repay thee with honour, celebrating continually thine acts, as befits a mortal; for there is no higher privilege either for men or for gods than ever rightly to sing the universal law."

---

* This is a literal rendering of the corrupt reading in the MSS., which it has been attempted to improve by various conjectures. Meineke has proposed an alteration (ἐκ σοῦ γὰρ γενόμεσθα, λόγου—

No. xxiv. p. 220, line 7 f. from the top. Compare Claudian, Cons. Hon. iv. 296.—

In commune jubes si quid, censesve tenendum,
Primus jussa subi ; tunc observantior æqui
Fit populus, nec ferre negat, cum viderit ipsum
Auctorem parere sibi : componitur orbis
Regis ad exemplum ; nec sic inflectere sensus
Humanos edicta valent, ut vita regentis.
Mobile mutatur semper cum principe vulgus.

"If thou ordainest any thing, or esteemest that it should be observed by the public, be the first thyself to submit to what thou commandest. The people then becomes readier to obey what is right, and cannot refuse to yield when it sees the author of the ordinance obey himself. The world conforms to the example of the king. Nor do edicts avail so much as the life of the ruler, to influence their feelings. The changeable vulgar always changes with the prince."

P. 226, No. xxx.—Compare Menander (Ramage p. 34.)—

ὅταν εἰδέναι θέλῃς σεαυτὸν ὅστις εἶ,
ἔμβλεψον εἰς τὰ μνήμαθ' ὡς ὁδοιπορεῖς·
ἐνταῦθ' ἔνεστιν ὀστέα καὶ κούφη κόνις
ἀνδρῶν βασιλέων καὶ τυράννων καὶ σοφῶν,
καὶ μέγα φρονούντων ἐπὶ γένει καὶ χρήμασιν,
αὐτῶν τε δόξῃ, τῷ τε κάλλει σωμάτων·
καὶ οὐδὲν αὐτῶν τῶνδ' ἐπήρκεσεν χρόνον
κοινὸν τον ᾅδην ἔσχον οἱ πάντες βροτοί.
πρὸς ταῦθ' ὁρῶν γίνωσκε σαυτὸν ὅστις εἶ.

"When thou wishest to know thyself, what thou art, look at the tombs, as thou passest along the road. In them lie the bones, and the light dust, of kings, and despots, and sages, and of men who were proud of their high birth, and their wealth, and their renown, and their bodily beauty. But none of these things could ward off (the influence of) time. All mortals

κ.τ.λ.), which may be thus translated: "For we spring from thee, having alone, &c., . . . obtained the resemblance of (thy) reason." This I have followed in the metrical version.

find a common grave. Regarding these things, know thyself what thou art."

P. 226, No. xxxi.—Propertius iii. 5, 13.—

Haud ullas portabis opes Acherontis ad undas :
Nudus ab inferna, stulte, vehere rate.

"Thou shalt carry none of thy wealth to the waves of Acheron ; O fool, thou shalt be ferried across naked on the infernal boat."

P. 232, No. xxxvii.—Moschus (Ramage, p. 341.)—

Αἰαῖ, ταὶ μαλάχαι μεν ἐπὰν κατὰ κᾶπον ὄλωνται,
ἢ τὰ χλωρὰ σέλινα, τὸ τ' εὐθαλὲς οὖλον ἄνηθον,
ὑστέρον αὖ ζώαντι, καὶ εἰς ἔτος ἄλλο φύοντι·
ἄμμες δ' οἱ μεγάλοι καὶ καρτεροὶ ἢ σοφοὶ ἄνδρες,
ὀππότε πρῶτα θάνωμες, ἀνάκοοι ἐν χθονὶ κοίλᾳ
εὕδομες εὖ μάλα μακρὸν ἀτέρμονα νήγρετον ὕπνον.

"Alas, when the mallows have died in a garden, or the green parsley, or the blooming crisp dill, they live again afterwards, and grow up in another year. But we, the great, the brave, the wise, when once we die, no longer hearing aught, sleep in the hollow earth a very long unending sleep, that knows no waking."

P. 235, No. xlv.—Ovid. Ep. ex Pont. ii. 3, 17.—

Nec facile invenias multis ex millibus unum
Virtutem pretium qui putet esse sui.
Ipse decor, recti facti si prœmia desint,
Non movet, et gratis pœnitet esse probum.

"You will not easily find one out of many thousands who regards virtue as its own reward. Its own lustre, if the prizes of right action are wanting, does not affect any one ; and he repents having been good for nothing."

Claudian, Cons. Mall. Theod. 1.—

Ipsa quidem virtus pretium sibi, solaque late
Fortunæ secura nitet, nec fastibus ullis
Erigitur, plausuve petit clarescere vulgi :
Nil opis externæ cupiens, nil indiga laudis,
Divitiis animosa suis, immotaque cunctis
Casibus, ex alta mortalia despicit arce.

"Virtue is its own reward; it alone shines far and wide, indifferent about fortune, is not elevated by any proud emotions, does not seek to become illustrious by the applause of the vulgar. Desiring no outward wealth, in no need of praise, bold by its own resources, unmoved by all chances, it looks down on the life of mortals from its lofty citadel."

P. 235, No. li.—Compare the following from the so-called golden Pythagorean verses, for a copy of which I am indebted to a friend.—

> Μηδ' ὕπνον μαλακοῖσιν ἐπ' ὄμμασι προσδέξασθαι
> Πρὶν τῶν ἡμερινῶν ἔργων λογίσασθαι ἕκαστον·
> Πῇ παρέβην; τί δ' ἔρεξα; τί μοι δέον οὐκ ἐτελέσθη;
> 'Αρξάμενος δ' ἀπὸ πρώτου ἐπέξιθι, καί μετέπειτα
> Δεινὰ μὲν ἐκπρήξας ἐπιπλήσσεο, χρηστὰ δὲ τέρπευ.

"Nor should one allow sleep to visit his tender eyes before he has examined each of the day's deeds; in what have I transgressed? what have I done? what duty have I failed to fulfil? Beginning at the first, go over all thine acts; and if thou hast done anything dreadful, reproach thyself; if thou hast done well, be glad."

> "Each night, before, in soft repose,
> Thy tired and languid eyelids close,
> Of thine own self the questions ask:
> "Have I fulfilled my daily task?
> What virtuous action have I done?
> Or, ah! have I accomplished none?
> What have I done amiss this day?
> From virtue's path how gone astray?"
> When thou hast thus, from first to last,
> Thine actions all in survey passed,
> If thou hast evil done, be sad;
> If thou hast nobly done, be glad."

Pages 246 ff., Nos. lxxiv. and lxxv.—Although only some of the following Greek passages manifest any resemblance, and that not a very close one, to the pantheism of the Upanishad, I think them worthy of being adduced here:—

Aratus. Stob. Ecl. Phys. i. 7.

'Εκ Διὸς ἀρχώμεσθα, τὸν οὐδέποτ' ἄνδρες ἐῶμεν
ἄρρητον, μεσταὶ δὲ Διὸς πᾶσαι μὲν ἀγυιαί,
πᾶσαι δ' ἀνθρώπων ἀγοραί, μεστὴ δὲ θάλασσα,
καὶ λιμένες, πάντῃ δὲ Διὸς κεχρήμεθα παντες
τοῦ γὰρ καὶ γένος ἐσμεν.

"Let us begin with Zeus; whom we men will never leave unnamed. And all streets are full of Zeus, and all the market-places of men, and the sea too is full, and the ports, and we everywhere stand in need of Zeus. For we are his offspring."

The following lines form the commencement of a long so-called [Orphic] passage in Stobæus, Ecl. Phy. p. 10 :—

Ζεὺς πρῶτος γένετο, Ζεὺς ὕστατος ἀργικέραυνος,
Ζεὺς κεφαλή, Ζεὺς μέσσα, Διὸς δ' ἐκ πάντα τέτυκται.
Ζεὺς ἄρσην γένετο, Ζεὺς ἄμβροτος ἔπλετο νύμφη,
Ζεὺς πυθμὴν γαίης τε καὶ οὐρανοῦ ἀστερόεντος·
[Ζεὺς πνοιὴ πάντων, Ζεὺς ἀκαμάτου πυρὸς ὁρμή·
Ζεὺς πόντου ῥίζα, Ζεὺς ἥλιος ἠδὲ σελήνη·]
Ζεὺς βασιλεύς, Ζεὺς αὐτος ἁπάντων ἀρχιγένεθλος·
ἓν κράτος, εἷς δαίμων γένετο, μέγας ἀρχὸς ἁπάντων·
ἓν δὲ δέμας βασίλειον, ἐν ᾧ τάδε πάντα κυκλεῖται,
πῦρ καὶ ὕδωρ καὶ γαῖα καὶ αἰθὴρ νύξ τε καὶ ἦμαρ,
καὶ μῆτις, πρῶτος γενέτωρ, καὶ ἔρως πολυτερπής.
πάντα γὰρ ἐν Ζηνὸς μεγάλῳ τάδε σώματι κεῖται. κ.τ.λ.

"Zeus, the darter of the flashing lightning, is the first, the last, the head, the centre: all things are formed from (or by) Zeus. Zeus is (or became) a male, the immortal Zeus a maid. Zeus is the foundation of the earth and of the starry heaven. [Zeus is the breath of all, the fury of the ceaseless fire. Zeus is the root of the ocean, Zeus is the sun and the moon]. Zeus is the king, Zeus is himself the progenitor of all things. There is one power, one deity, the great ruler of all things; and one royal body in which all these things are revolved, fire and water and earth, and æther, and night and day, and wisdom, the first generator, and much-delighting love: for all these things lie in the great body of Zeus."

Aristotle de Republicâ vii. 1.—This and the following three passages are quoted, but not all fully, by Ramage, p. 102 f. They are cited, not on account of anything corresponding in the Sanskrit, but for their theistic and elevated sentiments. The treatise from which the last three are taken is not, however, generally regarded as Aristotle's.*

Ditto, de Republicâ vii. 1.—

Ὅς εὐδαίμων μέν ἐστι καὶ μακάριος, δι' οὐδὲν δὲ τῶν ἐξωτερικῶν ἀγαθῶν, ἀλλὰ δι' αὑτὸν αὐτός.

"(God) who is happy and blessed, not through any good external to himself, but himself through himself."

Treatise de Mundo 5.—

Γῆν τε πᾶσαν καὶ θάλασσαν αἰθέρα τε καὶ ἥλιον καὶ σελήνην καὶ τὸν ὅλον οὐρανὸν διεκόσμησε μία ἡ διὰ πάντων διήκουσα δύναμις, . . . τὰς ἐναντιωτάτας ἐν αὐτῷ φύσεις ἀλλήλαις ἀναγκάσασα ὁμολογῆσαι καὶ ἐκ τούτων μηχανησαμένη τῷ παντὶ σωτηρίαν.

"One power, that which reaches through all things, arranged the entire earth, and sea, and æther, and sun and moon, and the whole heaven, . . . compelling the most opposite natures in it to harmonise, and from these things devising safety for the whole."

De Mundo 6.—

Ταῦτα χρὴ καὶ περὶ θεοῦ διανοεῖσθαι, δυνάμει μεν ὄντος ἰσχυροτάτου κάλλει δὲ εὐπρεπεστάτου, ζωῇ δὲ ἀθανάτου, ἀρετῇ δὲ κρατίστου. διότι πάσῃ θνητῇ φύσει γενόμενος ἀθεώρητος ἀπ' αὐτῶν τῶν ἔργων θεωρεῖται.

"These things, too, we ought to think in regard to God, who in might is most strong, in beauty is most fair, in life immortal, in virtue most excellent, because, being unperceivable by mortal natures, he is perceived by his works themselves."

De Mundo 7.—

Κρόνου δὲ παῖς καὶ χρόνου λεγεται, διήκων ἐξ αἰῶνος ἀτέρμονος εἰς ἕτερον αἰῶνα.

"And he is called the son of Kronus and of time, continuing from one age without limit, to another."

* On Aristotle's conception of the Deity, see Sir Alexander Grant's "Aristotle" pp. 175 ff., in Mr Lucas Collins' "Ancient Classics for English Readers."

Flor. Monacense. Stob. iv., p. 267.—

Θεὸς ου ληπτός εἰ δὲ ληπτὸς οὐ θεός.

"God is not comprehensible. If comprehensible, he would not be God."

P. 247, line 2, above the note.—"Without an interior, or an exterior." This cannot be properly said of a lump of salt. It is, however, said of Brahma in ii. 5, 19 of this Upanishad, where the commentator explains *anantara* as "having no succession of births," while he gives *avāhya* as "having no exterior." But it would seem that *anantara*, as the opposite of *avāhya*, is intended to bear the sense of "having no interior."

Page 248, line 27.—Professor Cowell thus expresses himself on the subject:—"It seems to me that the ultimate meaning of *moksha*, as of *Brahma*, (on which it of course depends), is almost beyond our conception. It is the thin ether into which Kant's "dove" hopes to fly up to find perfect freedom of flight. The ordinary ideas of us Europeans do not rise higher than *aham* and *Brahmā*, or Īśwara. But Brahma seems to me utterly impersonal; and therefore Brahmā is as far off from it as we are; and yet our usual idea of God is Īśwara. I cannot help believing that the Vedānta distinction of *pāramārthika* and *vyāvahārika* must extend through all worlds and all eternity; the highest existence, conceivable by us, is infinitely removed from *pāramārthikatva* (reality). God's personality (as conceived in western thought) removes him at once from the *pāramārthika;* for surely all consciousness implies three, the subject, and the object, and the relation; and Brahma is *ekam advitīyam.* His *chaitanya* has no object, it is simple thought." (*Pāramārthika* means *real ; vyāvahārika*, phenomenal or apparent; and *chaitanya*, cognition.)

P. 51, lines 11 ff. from the foot. This view of the commentators, must, however, be regarded as modern. Its falsity as applied to ancient times is shewn by the cases of Maitreyī, Gārgī, and Sulabhā, mentioned in pp. 250 f.

Page 255, Note *. Prof. Cowell draws my attention to the fact that Śankara proposes as an alternative reading instead of *gatiḥ*, viz., *agatiḥ* (= *anavabodho 'parijnānam*) with the sense: "There is not miscomprehension of it, if it is spoken by a non-dualist teacher." This, he observes, is the same meaning as is brought out by my proposed reading, only expressed conversely.

P. 265, No. lxxxii.—Though Indian caste is a different thing from Grecian slavery, the following texts relating to the latter are akin in spirit to the passage from the Mahābhārata:—

Euripides, Ion, 854.—

Ἓν γάρ τι τοῖς δούλοισιν αἰσχύνην φέρει,
τοὔνομα· τὰ δ' ἄλλα πάντα τῶν ἐλευθέρων
οὐδὲν κακίων δοῦλος ὅστις ἐσθλὸς ᾖ.

"For one thing brings shame to slaves,—the name. But in all other respects a slave who is a good man is in nothing worse than those who are free."

Philemon (Stob. Anthol., ii. 365.)

κἂν δοῦλος ᾖ τις, οὐδὲν ἧττον, δέσποτα,
ἄνθρωπος οὗτος ἐστιν, ἂν ἄνθρωπος ᾖ.

"If any one be a slave, my master, he is no less a man, if he be a man."

Euripides, Melanippe (Stob. Anth., ii. 366.)

Δοῦλον γὰρ ἐσθλὸν τοὔνομ' οὐ διαφθερεῖ·
πολλοὶ δ' ἀμείνους εἰσὶ τῶν ἐλευθέρων.

"For the name will not destroy a good slave. For many (slaves) are better than the free."

Ditto, Phrixus.—

Πολλοῖσι δούλοις τοὔνομ' αἰσχρόν, ἡ δὲ φρὴν
τῶν οὐχὶ δούλων ἐστ' ἐλευθερωτέρα.

"To many slaves the name is a disgrace: while their soul is freer than that of others who are not slaves."

Philemon, Meineke, p. 410.—

Κἂν δοῦλός ἐστι, σάρκα τὴν αὐτὴν ἔχει·
φύσει γὰρ οὐδεὶς δοῦλος ἐγενήθη ποτέ·
ἡ δ' αὖ τύχη τὸ σῶμα κατεδουλώσατο.

"Even though he is a slave, he has the same flesh, for no one was ever a slave by nature; but destiny has enslaved his body."

P. 265, No. lxxxiv.—Euripides, Dictys (Stob. Anthol., iii. 153).—

Εἰς δ' εὐγένειαν ὀλίγ' ἔχω φράσαι καλά.
ὁ μὲν γὰρ ἐσθλὸς εὐγενὴς ἔμοιγ' ἀνήρ,
ὁ δ' οὐ δίκαιος, κἂν ἀμείνονος πατρὸς
Ζηνὸς πεφύκῃ, δυσγενὴς εἶναι δοκεῖ.

"I have little good to say of noble birth. For in my estimation, the good is the nobly-born man, while he who is unjust, even if sprung from a father superior to Zeus, is to me ignoble."

Other similar sentiments are cited in the same place by Stobæus.

P. 270, line 15, No. cx.—The translation of the first line of this passage has been omitted here. It runs as follows: "The unlearned man, who has no faith in righteousness, and who constantly sacrifices with means unjustly gained, shall not obtain the rewards of righteousness."

P. 270, No. cxii.—Menander (Ramage, p. 339), but regarded by Meineke, p. 306 f., as spurious.—

Εἴ τις δὲ θυσίαν προσφέρων, ὦ Πάμφιλε,
ταύρων τι πλῆθος ἢ ἐρίφων, ἢ, νὴ Δία,
ἑτέρων τοιούτων, ἢ κατασκευάσματα
χρυσᾶς ποιήσας χλαμύδας ἤτοι πορφυρᾶς,
ἢ δι' ἐλέφαντος ἢ σμαράγδου ζῴδια,
εὔνουν νομίζει τὸν θεὸν καθιστάναι,
πλανᾶτ' ἐκεῖνος καὶ φρένας κούφας ἔχει.
δεῖ γὰρ τὸν ἄνδρα χρήσιμον πεφυκέναι, κ.τ.λ.

. . . . .

ὁ γὰρ θεὸς βλέπει σε πλησίον παρών.

"If any one, O Pamphilus, offering in sacrifice a multitude of bulls or goats or the like, or fashioning gilt or purple mantles, or images of ivory, or emerald, thinks thereby to render the deity propitious to him, he errs, and is foolish. For the man (who hopes for this) must be a good and useful man . . . . for God is near at hand, and beholds thee."

In the Florilegium Monacense printed in Stob. Anthol. iv. 287, the following saying is ascribed to Socrates :—

Ὁ αὐτὸς ἔφη, οἱ τὰ ἀπὸ κακῶν ἔργων εἰς τὰς καλὰς ἀναλίσκοντες λειτουργίας ὅμοιον ποιοῦσι τοῖς ἀπὸ ἱεροσυλίας εὐσεβοῦσι.

"The same person said that those who expended the gains derived from wrongdoing on excellent rites of worship acted similarly to those who performed pious acts with means gained by plundering temples."

P. 271, line 2 ("a gift bestowed with contempt," &c.) and p. 272, No. cxxi.

Philemon, Meineke, 422.—

Ἐὰν ὁρῶν πένητα γυμνὸν ἐνδύσῃς,
μᾶλλον ἀπέδυσας αὐτόν, ἐὰν ὀνειδίσῃς.

"If thou should'st clothe a poor man who is naked, thou hast rather stripped him if thou should'st reproach him."

P. 275, No. cxxxvi.—From the Florilegium Monacense. Stobæus iv. 267 f.

Θεῷ ὅμοιον ἔχει ἄνθρωπος τὸ εὖ ποιεῖν, ὅταν τὸ εὖ ποιεῖν μὴ καπηλεύηται.

"A man is like God when he does good, and does not make a gain of well-doing."

Τιμήσεις τὸν θεὸν ἄριστα, ὅταν τῷ θεῷ τὴν διάνοιαν ὁμοιώσῃς δι' ἀρετῆς. ἡ γὰρ ἀρετὴ τὴν ψυχὴν ἕλκει πρὸς τὸ συγγενές.

"Thou wilt best honour God when thou in mind resemblest him through virtue: for virtue draws the soul to that which has an affinity to it."

Οἱ ἄνθρωποι τότε γίνονται βελτίους, ὅταν τῷ θεῷ προσέρχωνται. ὅμοιον δὲ δείκνυσι τῷ θεῷ τὸ εὐεργετεῖν καὶ ἀληθεύειν.

"Men then become better when they draw near to God, Beneficence and truthfulness evince likeness to God."

Page 275, No. cxxxix.—The following saying of Diogenes is given in the Florilegium Monacense in Meineke's edition of the Anthology of Stobæus, vol. iv., p. 281.—

'Ο αὐτὸς ἐρωτώμενος πῶς ἄν τις ἀμύναιτο τὸν ἐχθρόν, εἶπεν "εἰ σύγε καλὸς καὶ ἀγαθὸς αὐτῳ γένοιο."

"The same sage being asked how a man could defend himself against his enemy, replied, 'If thou shouldst act fairly and kindly towards him.'"

Page 275 f., Nos. cxxxix. and cxl.

Menander in Stobæus, i. 113, and Meineke, 35.

Οὗτος κράτιστος ἐστ' ἀνήρ, ὦ Γοργία,
ὅστις ἀδικεῖσθαι πλεῖστ' ἐπίσταται βροτῶν.

"He is the best man, O Gorgias, who knows how to suffer most injustice."

Philemon in Stobæus, i. 300, Meineke, 364.

Ἥδιον οὐδὲν οὐδὲ μουσικώτερον
ἐστ' ἢ δύνασθαι λοιδορούμενον φέρειν.
ὁ λοιδορῶν γάρ, ἂν ὁ λοιδορούμενος
μὴ προσποιῆται, λοιδορεῖται λοιδορῶν.

"There is nothing pleasanter, or meeter than for one who is reviled, to bear it; for if the reviled does not take it to himself, the reviler is himself reviled."

I give the enclosed from the Floril. Monacense (in Stobæus, iv., 278), though there is nothing corresponding to it in the Sanskrit.

Οἵ τ' αὐτῷ κακὰ τεύχει ἀνὴρ ἄλλῳ κακὰ τεύχων·
ἡ δὲ κακὴ βουλὴ τῷ βουλεύσαντι κακίστη.

"He who devises evil against another devises evil against himself; and the evil design is worst for the designer."

P. 277, No. cxliii. — Although there is nothing quite parallel to this in the Sanskrit, it is worth quoting.

Philemon in Meineke, p. 415.—

Ἐκ τοῦ παθεῖν γίνωσκε καὶ τὸ συμπαθεῖν,
καὶ σοὶ γὰρ ἄλλος συμπαθήσεται παθών.

"From suffering learn sympathy; for so shall another who has suffered sympathize with thee."

P. 277, No. cxlv.—From Menander, cited by John of Damascus in Stob. iv. 167.—

οὐδείς ἐστί μοι
ἀλλότριος ἂν ᾖ χρηστός· ἡ φύσις μία
πάντων, τὸ δ' οἰκεῖον συνίστησιν τρόπος.

"No man is to me an alien, if he be a good man. All men have one nature; but character commends anyone as a kinsman."

Stob. ii. 63, from Plutarch.—

Ἀργεῖος ἢ Θηβαῖος, οὐ γὰρ εὔχομαι
μιᾶς· ἅπας μοι πύργος Ἑλλήνων πατρίς.

"Whence Hercules said well: 'I am an Argive, or a Theban; for I do not profess to be of one country. Any Greek tower is my country.'"

P. 279, No. cliii.—Pythagoras, Stob. Flor. ii. 220.—

Ποίει ἃ κρίνεις εἶναι καλά, κἂν ποιῶν μέλλῃς ἀδοξεῖν· φαῦλος γὰρ κριτὴς παντὸς καλοῦ πράγματος ὄχλος. διόπερ ὧν ἂν τῶν ἐπαίνων καταφρονῇς, καὶ τῶν ψόγων καταφρόνει.

"Do what thou judgest to be right, even though by doing this thou shouldst incur bad repute. For the crowd is a bad judge of all noble acts. Despise therefore the blame of those whose praises thou wouldst contemn."

Page 279, No. cliv.—Sophocles, Aletes.—

Ἀνὴρ γὰρ ὅστις ἥδεται λέγων ἀεί,
λέληθεν αὑτὸν τοῖς ξυνοῦσιν ὢν βαρύς.

"For the man who delights to be constantly speaking, does not observe that he is disagreeable to his associates."

Stobæus, vol. ii., p. 36.—

οὐκ ἄν τις εἴπῃ πολλὰ θαυμασθήσεται,
ὁ μικρὰ δ' εἰπὼν μᾶλλον ἂν ᾖ χρήσιμα.

"A man shall not be admired if he speaks much, but rather if he speaks a little which is profitable."

P. 281, No. clxvii.—Euripides (Stob. Anthol., i. 258).—

Πότερα θέλεις σοι μαλθακὰ ψευδῆ λέγω
ἢ σκλήρ' ἀληθῆ; φράζε, σὴ γὰρ ἡ κρίσις.

"Dost thou desire that I should speak to thee smooth lies, or hard truths? Tell me; for with thee rests the decision."

P. 281, No. clxvii.—Euripides, Ino. Stobæus, i. 259.—

Εμοὶ γένοιτο πτωχός, εἰ δὲ βούλεται,
πτωχοῦ κακίων, ὅστις ὢν εὔνους ἐμοί,
φόβον παρελθὼν τἀπὸ καρδίας ἐρεῖ.

"Let me have a poor man, or if he wishes, worse than a poor man, who, being well disposed to me, will set aside fear, and say what he thinks."

P. 282, No. clxxiii.—Apollodorus in Ramage, "Beautiful Thoughts from Greek Authors," p. 58.—

Οὐδέποτ' ἀθυμεῖν τὸν κακῶς πράττοντα δεῖ,
ἄνδρες, τὰ βελτίω δὲ προσδοκᾶν ἀεί.

"The man who is unfortunate should never despond, but always hope for better things."

P. 286, No. cxciii.—Philemon, Meineke, p. 399, No. xv.—

Πρόσεστι δὲ τῷ πένητι ἀπιστία.
κἂν σοφὸς ὑπάρχῃ, κἂν λέγῃ τι συμφέρον,
δοκεῖ τι φράζειν τοῖς ἀκούουσιν κακῶς·
τῶν γὰρ πενήτων πίστιν οὐκ ἔχει λόγος·
ἀνὴρ δὲ πλουτῶν, κἂν ἄγαν ψευδηγορῇ,
δοκεῖ τι φράζειν τοῖς ἀκούουσιν ἀσφαλές.

"A poor man is not believed. Even if he be wise, even if he say something profitable, he appears to those who hear him, to speak badly: for the word of the poor receives no credence. But a rich man, even if he lie exceedingly, appears to the hearers to say something certain." See also the quotation from the Danae of Euripides, under No. cxcix., at the foot of p. 288.

P. 288, No. cxcix.—Sophocles, Aleadæ.—

Τα χρήματ' ἀνθρώποισιν εὑρίσκει φίλους,
αὖθις δὲ τιμάς. κ. τ. λ.
καὶ γὰρ δυσειδὲς σῶμα καὶ δυσώνυμον
γλώσσῃ σοφὸν τίθησιν εὔμορφον τ' ἰδεῖν.

"Wealth obtains friends for men, and further, honours," &c. . . . "For [wealth] makes even a man with an ugly body and rude in speech, wise and handsome."

Menander (Stob. Anth. i. 234).—

Ἔργον εὑρεῖν συγγενῆ
πένητος ἐστιν. οὐδὲ εἷς γὰρ ὁμολογεῖ
αὑτῷ προσήκειν τὸν βοηθείας τινὸς
δεόμενον· αἰτεῖσθαι γαρ ἅμα τι προσδοκᾷ.

"It is a difficult task to find a kinsman of the poor man, for no one acknowledges that one who needs any help belongs to him; for he at the same time expects to be asked (for some help)."

Floril. Monacense (Stob. iv. 272.)—

Ἐν εὐτυχίᾳ φίλον εὑρεῖν εὐπορώτατον, ἐν δὲ δυστυχίᾳ πάντων ἀπορώτατον.

"In prosperity it is most easy to find a friend, and in adversity the most difficult of all things."

Ibid.

Πολλοὶ τοὺς φίλους ἐκτρέπονται, ὁπόταν ἐξ εὐπορίας εἰς σπάνιν περιπέσωσιν· οἱ γὰρ πλεῖστοι τῶν χρημάτων, οὐ τῶν ἐχόντων εἰσὶ φίλοι.

"Many turn away from their friends when they fall from ease into want. For most men are friends of wealth, not of those who possess it."

Eurip., Hecuba, 1226.—

Ἐν τοῖς κακοῖς γὰρ ἀγαθοὶ σαφέστατοι
φίλοι· τὰ χρηστὰ δ' αὔθ' ἕκαστ' ἔχει φίλους.

"For in adversity friends most distinctly show themselves such. But prosperity in every case is attended by friends."

Eurip., Orestes, 727.—

Πιστὸς ἐν κακοῖς ἀνὴρ
κρείσσων γαλήνης ναυτίλοισιν εἰσορᾶν.

"The man who is faithful in times of calamity, is better to regard than a calm is to mariners."

Eurip., Orestes, 665.—

Τοὺς φίλους
ἐν τοῖς κακοῖς χρὴ τοῖς φίλοισιν ὠφελεῖν·
ὅταν δ' ὁ δαίμων εὖ διδῷ, τί δεῖ φίλων;
ἀρκεῖ γὰρ αὐτὸς ὁ θεὸς ὠφελεῖν θέλων.

"Friends should aid friends in the time of calamity. When Providence gives prosperity, what need have men of friends? for the god, being willing to benefit them, is himself sufficient."

The following is a very noble sentiment:—

Menander (Stob. Anthol., iv. 114; and Meineke's Menander, pp. 176 and 266).—

Τοῦτ' ἐστὶ τὸ ζῆν, οὐχ' ἑαυτῷ ζῆν μόνον.

"This is life, not to live to one's self only."

P. 289, No. cci.—Philemon (in Stob. Anthol. i. 189.)—

Ἀνὴρ δίκαιος ἐστιν οὐχ ὁ μὴ ἀδικῶν,
ἀλλ' ὅστις ἀδικεῖν δυνάμενος μὴ βούλεται,
οὐδ' ὃς τὰ μικρὰ λαμβάνειν ἀπέσχετο,
ἀλλ' ὃς τὰ μεγάλα καρτερεῖ μὴ λαμβάνων,
ἔχειν δυνάμενος καὶ κρατεῖν ἀζημίως.
οὐδ' ὅς γε ταῦτα πάντα διατηρεῖ μόνον,
ἀλλ' ὅστις ἄδολον γνησίαν τ' ἔχων φύσιν,
εἶναι δίκαιος κοὺ δοκεῖν εἶναι θέλει.

"The just man is, not he who does not act unjustly, but who when he is able to do so, does not desire it; nor, again, he who has abstained from taking a little, but he who resists taking great things, when he can have and hold them with impunity; nor, again, is the just man he who only observes all these things, but he who possessing an honest and noble nature, desires to be, and not to seem, just."

P. 289, No. cci.—Plato, Gorgias, 174.—

. . . . *ὡς εὐλαβητέον ἐστὶ τὸ ἀδικεῖν μᾶλλον ἢ τὸ ἀδικεῖσθαι, καὶ παντὸς μᾶλλον ἀνδρὶ μελετητέον οὐ τὸ δοκεῖν εἶναι ἀγαθὸν ἀλλὰ τὸ εἶναι, καὶ ἰδίᾳ καὶ δημοσίᾳ.*

"And of all that has been said, nothing remains unshaken but the saying, that to do injustice is more to be avoided than to suffer injustice, and that the reality and not the appearance of virtue is to be followed above all things, as well in public as in private life." (Dr Jowett's translation, 1st edition).

P. 290, No. ccv.—ccvii., from Florilegium Monacense in Stob. Anthol. iv. 277.—

Αλλων ἰατρὸς αὐτὸς ἕλκεσιν βρύων.

"A healer of others, himself full of sores."

Sosicrates in Stob. i. 342.—

Αγαθοὶ δὲ τὸ κακὸν ἐσμὲν ἐφ' ἑτέρων ἰδεῖν,
αὐτοὶ δ' ὅταν ποιῶμεν, οὐ γινώσκομεν.

"We are all skilled in perceiving evil in the case of others; but we are not aware when we do it ourselves."

Menander, Stob., i. 342.—

Οὐθεὶς ἐφ' αὑτοῦ τὰ κακὰ συνορᾷ, Πάμφιλε,
σαφῶς, ἑτέρου δ' ἀσχημονοῦντος ὄψεται.

"No one clearly perceives his own bad points, Pamphilus, but will observe when another does anything unbecoming."

Menander, Meineke, p. 243.—

ὅταν τι μέλλῃς τὸν πέλας κατηγορεῖν,
αὐτὸς τὰ σαυτοῦ πρῶτον ἐπισκέπτου κακά.

"Whenever thou seekest to blame thy neighbour, first consider thine own faults."

Phædrus, iv. 10.—

Peras imposuit Jupiter nobis duas:
Propriis repletam vitiis post tergum dedit,
Alienis ante pectus suspendit gravem.
Hac re videre nostra mala non possumus;
Alii simul delinquunt, censores sumus.

"Jupiter has placed upon us two wallets; he has put one filled with our own faults behind our backs, and has hung one heavy one filled with the faults of others before our breast. Hence we cannot see our own bad acts, but as soon as others offend, we censure them."

Cicero, Tusc. Quæst., iii. 30.—

Est proprium stultitiæ aliorum vitia cernere, oblivisci suorum.

"It is a part of folly to see the faults of others and forget one's own."

P. 291, No. ccx.—Aeschylus, Prometheus 263.—

Ἐλαφρὸν ὅστις πημάτων ἔξω πόδα
ἔχει παραινεῖν νουθετεῖν τε τὸν κακῶς
πράσσοντ'.

"It is easy for the man who is not involved in calamities to advise and exhort him who is unfortunate."

Philemon, Sicilicus i.—Ramage, "Beautiful Thoughts from Greek Authors," and Meineke, p. 381 f.

Ἄνθρωπον ὄντα ῥᾴδιον παραινέσαι
ἐστίν, ποιῆσαι δ' αὐτὸν οὐχὶ ῥᾴδιον.
τεκμήριον δὲ τοὺς ἰατροὺς οἶδ' ἐγώ,
ὑπὲρ ἐγκρατείας τοῖς νοσοῦσιν εὖ σφόδρα
πάντας λαλοῦντας· εἶτ' ἐὰν πταισωσί τι,
αὐτοὺς ποιοῦντας πάνθ' ὅσ' οὐκ εἴων τότε.
ἕτερον τό τ' ἀλγεῖν καὶ τὸ θεωρεῖν ἔστ' ἴσως.

"It is easy for a man to advise, but not for a man himself to act accordingly. As a proof of this, I know physicians all speaking very wisely to the sick regarding temperance; but when they are themselves suffering, I know them doing the very things which they then would not allow. Perhaps it is one thing to suffer and another thing to speculate."

Euripides, Alcestis, 1078.—

Ῥᾷον παραινεῖν ἢ παθόντα καρτερεῖν.

"It is easier to advise than it is to endure suffering."

Demosthenes, Olynth. iii. p. 33 (Stob. i. 343).—

Διόπερ ῥᾷστόν ἐστιν ἁπάντων ἑαυτὸν ἐξαπατᾶν· ὃ γὰρ βούλεται, τουθ' ἕκαστος καὶ οἴεται. τὰ δὲ πράγματα πολλάκις οὐχ οὕτω πέφυκε.

"Wherefore it is the easiest of all things to deceive one's self: for every one imagines what he desires. But the things are often not so (as we suppose)."

Terence, And. ii. 1, 9 (in Ramage, "Beautiful Thoughts from Latin Authors.)—

Facile omnes quum valemus, recta consilia ægrotis damus.

"We all, when we are well, easily give right advice to the sick."

P. 293, No. ccxvii.—Herodotus, viii. 140.—*καὶ γὰρ δύναμις ὑπὲρ ἄνθρωπον ἡ βασιλέος ἐστὶ καὶ χεὶρ ὑπερμήκης.*

"For the (Persian) king's power is beyond that of men, and his hand is exceedingly long."

Ovid, Heroid, xvii. 71.—

An nescis longas regibus esse manus ?

"Dost thou not know that kings have long hands ?"

To which Dr Ramage adds, "This is the Greek proverb"—

μακραὶ τυράννων χεῖρες.

"The hands of princes [or tyrants] are long."

P. 293, No. ccxix.—A parallel to this insidious maxim may be found in the Florilegium Monacense, in the 4th vol. of Meincke's edition of the Anthology of Stobæus, p. 276. It does not appear who was the author of the saying.—

Τὸν ἐχθρὸν ἀεὶ προσγέλα καὶ προσαγόρευε· δοκῶν γὰρ εἶναι αὐτῷ φίλος ῥᾷον κακόν τι δράσεις.

"Always smile upon, and address, your enemy; for seeming to be friendly to him, thou shalt móre easily injure him."

P. 293, No. ccxix.—I give here some specimens of the artful and immoral counsels alluded to under No. ccxix. in p. 293.

The texts below quoted as parallel differ more or less in diction. M. Bh. i. 5606 (= xii. 5259), "Let a man be very hum ble in speech, but in heart sharp as a razor; let him speak with a smile, when bent on a terrible act." i. 5607 (= xii. 5263), "He who wishes to succeed should join his hands, should swear an oath, should conciliate, should raise hopes," (in the parallel passage—"should wipe away tears"). xii. 5290[b], "Let a man inspire his enemy with confidence for some real reason, and then smite him at the proper time, when his foot has slipped a little." i. 5560, "By kindling fire, by sacrifice" ("by attention, by silence," xii. 5292[b]), "by a beggar's saffron garb, by braided hair, and clothing of skin, let a man fill his enemy with confidence, and then seize him like a wolf." xii. 5293[b] (= i. 5593), "A son, a brother, a father, or a friend, who present any obstacle to one's interests are to be slain:" ("a father or a teacher are to be treated as enemies by him who seeks success," i. 5593). i. 5617 (= xii. 5296[b], "without cutting into his enemy's marrow, without doing something dreadful, without smiting like a killer of fish, a man does not attain great prosperity." Then come in xii. 5299[b], these verses, the first of which seems inconsistent with the context: "Men should always be free from ill-will and strive after kindness and benevolence; and restraint should be practised by one who seeks to prosper." 5300[b], "When about to strike, a man should speak affectionately; and when he has smitten, with more than affection; having cut off his enemy's head with a sword he should grieve and weep."

When thou on hostile acts art bent,
With craft disguise thy fell intent.
Whilst thou 'gainst truth thy breast dost steel,
With humble words thy hate conceal;

Affecting calm, with artful smile
Thine unsuspecting foe beguile:
Then wait thy time, and strike the blow
Which lays thy careless victim low.

With kindly words address thy foe
When thou design'st to lay him low.

When thou hast struck the deadly blow,
Then let thy tears profusely flow.

If sons, or brothers, sires, or friends,
By hostile acts obstruct thine ends,
Thy hand let no weak scruples stay;
Without remorse by kinsmen slay.

These counsels are succeeded by a remark of the speaker to this effect. xii. 5317, "Thus has been declared what is designated as deceitful action; let no one practise this. But that you may know how to act ? (or to perceive it ?) when it is practised by another, I have declared it, wishing your welfare." But this looks very like a subsequent interpolation, made by some one who had scruples as to the doctrines inculcated. For in the next verse it is said that "The king of Surāshṭra" (to whom the advice had been given), "hearing these words of the Brahman" (Bharadvāja), "who was his wellwisher, acted accordingly, with boldness of spirit, and attained brilliant prosperity, along with his kinsmen."

Pp. 295 ff., Nos. ccxxi—ccxxv.—The following passages are found in the Anthology of Stobæus, iii. 2 f.—

Euripides.—

Οἰκοφθόρον γὰρ ἄνδρα κωλύει γυνὴ
ἐσθλὴ παραζευχθεῖσα καὶ σώζει δόμους.

"A good wife, united to a man who is a prodigal, restrains him, and saves the household."

Menander.—

Ἓν ἔστ᾽ ἀληθὲς φίλτρον εὐγνώμων τρόπος.
τούτῳ κατακρατεῖν ἀνδρὸς εἴωθεν γυνή.

"There is one true love-charm (philtre)—a kindly [or considerate] disposition; by this a wife is wont to win her husband."

Hippothoon.—

Ἄριστον ἀνδρὶ κτῆμα συμπαθὴς γυνή.

"A man's best possession is a sympathetic wife."

Euripides, Phrixus.—

Γυνὴ γὰρ ἐν κακοῖσι καὶ νόσοις πόσει
ἥδιστόν ἐστι, δώματ᾽ ἢν οἰκῇ καλῶς,

ὀργήν τε πραΰνουσα καὶ δυσθυμίας
ψυχὴν μεθιστᾶσ'. ἡδὺ κἀπάται φίλων.

"For in calamities and sicknesses a wife is most sweet to her husband, if she manage the family concerns well, softening anger, and diverting the spirit of her husband from dejection; even the wiles of friends are pleasant."

Menander, Meincke, p. 228.—

Οἰκεῖον οὕτως οὐδέν ἐστιν, ὦ Λάχης,
ἐὰν σκοπῇ τις, ὡς ἀνήρ τε καὶ γυνή.

"If thou wilt consider the matter, O Laches, there is nothing more intimately allied than a man and his wife."

Menander, Meineke, p. 269.—

Τὰ δεύτερ' ἀεὶ τὴν γυναῖκα δεῖ λέγειν,
τὴν δ' ἡγεμονίαν τῶν ὅλων τὸν ἄνδρ' ἔχειν.
οἰκία δ' ἐν ᾗ τὰ πάντα πρωτεύει γυνὴ
οὐκ ἔστιν ἥτις πώποτ' οὐκ ἀπώλετο.

"A wife ought always to speak second; and the husband to bear rule in all things. There has never been a house in which a woman stood first in everything which was not ruined."

Philemon, Meineke, p. 413.—

Ἀγαθῆς γυναικός ἐστιν, ὦ Νικοστράτη,
μὴ κρείττον' εἶναι τἀνδρὸς ἀλλ' ὑπήκοον·
γυνὴ δὲ νικῶσ' ἄνδρα κακόν ἐστιν μέγα.

"It is the part of a good wife, O Nicostrate, not to be mistress of her husband, but to be subject to him. But the wife who conquers her husband is a great calamity."

Philemon, Meineke, p. 421.—

Σαπρὰν γυναῖκα δ' ὁ τρόπος εὔμορφον ποιεῖ.
πολύ γε διαφέρει σεμνότης εὐμορφίας.

"Good character makes even a withered woman beautiful: for dignity is far superior to beauty."

P. 303, lines 9 f., No. ccxxxi.—Euripides, Stob. Anthol. i. 2, and Orion printed in ditto, iv. 266.

Ἀρετὴ δ' ὅσῳ περ μᾶλλον ἂν χρῆσθαι θέλῃς,
τοσῷδε μᾶλλον αὔξεται τελουμένη.

"But virtue grows and is perfected, the more it is practised."

Page 303, No. ccxxxiii.—Compare Sophocles, Oedipus Tyrannus, 56.—

ὡς οὐδέν ἐστιν οὔτε πύργος οὔτε ναῦς
ἔρημος ἀνδρῶν μὴ ξυνοικούντων ἔσω.

"For neither a tower nor a ship is of any value if it is devoid of men to occupy it."

Aeschylus, Persæ, 349.—

Ἀνδρῶν γὰρ ὄντων ἕρκος ἐστὶν ἀσφαλές.

"For where there are men, there is a secure bulwark."

Pages 334, at the top, and p. 335, line 12 ff. Antiphanes, Stob. iv. 132.—

Πενθεῖν δὲ μετρίως τοὺς προσήκοντας φίλους,
οὐ γὰρ τεθνᾶσιν, ἀλλὰ τὴν αὐτὴν ὁδόν,
ἣν πᾶσιν ἐλθεῖν ἔστ' ἀναγκαίως ἔχον,
προεληλύθασιν· εἶτα χἡμεῖς ὕστερον
εἰς ταὐτὸ καταγωγεῖον αὐτοῖς ἥξομεν,
κοινῇ τὸν ἄλλον συνδιατρίψοντες χρόνον.

"But men should not greatly lament their dear (deceased) relatives. For they are not dead, but have gone before on the same road which it is necessary for all to travel. Then afterwards we shall arrive at the same resting place with them, to spend along with them the rest of (our) time."

INDEX.

I. SANSKRIT TEXTS.

PAGE

AITAREYA ĀRAṆYAKA.

78 300

ATHARVA VEDA.

iii. 30.1 . . . 139
iv. 16 . . . 163
x. 8.44 . . . 1

See other passages quoted in pp. 334 ff.

BHAGAVAD GÍTA.

ii. 20 . . . 59
iii. 22 . . . 201
ix. 32 . . . 68
xvi. 1 . . . 33

BHĀGAVATA PURĀṆA.

v. 9 and 10 . . 258
vi. 1.52 . . . 225
vii. 5.37 . . . 144
viii. 7.44 . . . 87
ix. 21 . . . 146
x. 22.35 . . . 87

BHĀMINÍ-VILĀSA.

i. 93 . . . 92

BHARTṚIHARI'S ŚĀNTI-ŚATAKA.

35 37

BHARTṚIHARI . 44

iii. 76 . . . 99

BRAHMA DHARMA.

ii. 2.1 . . . 137

BṚIHADĀRAṆYAKA UPANISHAD.

ii. 4.1 } . . . 51
iv. 5.1 } . . . 246

PAGE

CHĀṆAKYA.

5 . . . 140

DAMPATI-SIKSHĀ.

26 . . . 36

DṚISHTĀNTA-ŚATAKA.

76 . . . 144

HITOPADEŚA.

i. 55 (33) . . . 89
98 (107) . . 111
171 (189) . . 10
ii. 44 . . . 40
iv. 10 . . . 92

KAṬHA UPANISHAD 54

KATHĀ SARIT SĀGARA.

iv. 110 . . . 36

LALITA VISTARA.

115 ff. . . . 145

MAHĀBHĀRATA.

i. 3015 . . . 8
3018 . . . 8
3027 . . . 133
3028 . . . 135
3069 . . . 110
3074 . . . 110
3077 . . . 91
3079 . . . 109
3094 . . . 76
3174 . . . 103
3176 . . . 47
3383 . . . 60

MAHĀBHĀRATA—*continued.*	PAGE
3513	103
3559	94
5560	361
5553	112
5563	113
5593	361
5606	361
5607	361
5613	98
5617	361
5627	112
5915	111
6116	85
6254	85
7045	60
8404	97
ii. 164	100
194	140
223	91
251	91
1945	93
2020	142
2136	96
2424	85
2438	85
2485	93
2669	9
iii. 25	91
50	60
62	101
80	103
84	104
87	9
916	7
1055	142
1124	4
1259	98
1333	111
1395	60
2325	137
6715	103
12470	60, 70
12531	69
13252	85
13253	88
13362	60
13427	60
13434	60
13445	75
13448	73

MAHĀBHĀRATA—*continued.*	PAGE
13461	11
13463	11
13475	85
13649	137
13661	133
13676	60
13684	60
13747	78
13751	37
13754	7
13851	44
13982	48
14075	70
14079	101
14085	102
14649 to 14721	113
15382	102
15398	107
16796	84
17041	36
17042	22
17392	70
v. 863	112
916	7
993	101
1007	109
1010	83
1011	83
1028	80
1088	83
1097	96
1112	100
1125	90
1144	45
1150	140
1155	10
1157	140
1162	140
1164	91
1170	92
1172	93
1222	9
1223	77
1242	38
1248	39
1251	8
1252	8
1266	94
1267	94

Mahābhārata—*continued*.	Page
1270	88
1272	90
1289	77
1318 f.	112
1319	112
1321	111
1348	96
1380	109
1381	77
1382	48
1389	113
1405	113
1430	45
1451	9
1474	37
1492	69
1513	99
1517	84
1518	88
1537	40
1623	75
1680	73
3290	93
3313	81
3314	82
3317	95
4143	94
4157	77
4332	140
4348	94
4494-4637	120
4637	120
4567	103
vi. 1403	33
2008	99
vii. 429	10
5960	81
5961	90
viii. 1817	109
2116	109
x. 115	105
178	93
234	95
xi. 36	100
48	41
55	41
67	101
75	102
76	101
88	27

Mahābhārata—*continued*.	Page
91	59
116	27
184	100
xii. 213	105
293	74
343	73
513	103
514	103
529	50
530	51
751	101
781	47
795	81
828	41
831	45
846	42
854	42
1328	80
2320	79
2363	70, 71
2599	140
2791	8
2797	91
2979	73
2980	11, 12
2998	95
3450	139
3501	113
3531	85
3814	100
3855	9
3892	28
4094	75
4148	101
4167	96
4217	92
4221	97
4225	97
4390	112
4889	98
4908	98
4993	86
5259	361
5263	361
5264	113
5265	122
5290	361
5292	361
5293	361
5296	361

Mahābhārata—continued.	Page	Mahābhārata—continued.	Page
5299	361	9917	50
5300	361	9919	50
5317 f.	362	9925	103
5315	311	10517	21
5497	135	10559	37
5528	88	10576	108
5561	133	10931	68
5623	51	11008	88
5683	41	11014	109
5906	81	11017	72
5961	73	11023	90
6002	76	11380	48
6057	60	11692	48
6132	62	11811	65
6284	95	11812	90
6486	45	12050	26
6497	101	12064	49
6508	47	12078	22
6575	106	12121	50
6609	103	12126	73
6641	50	12131	107
6526	28	12447	22
6712	102	12483	101
6713	103	12494	101
6736	11	12501	41
6939	66	12516	41
6951	60	12521	44
7058	7	12381	45
7063	82	xiii. 343	73
7064	82	651	143
7124	21	1542	71
7447	48	1544	76
7981	50	1550	72
8255	41	2084	60
8307	28	2092	64
8311	31	2160	64
8440	72	2194	12
8752	69	2236	138
8801	67	2496	137
8925	69	2610	68
8929	143	2979	73
8959	48	3010	82
9034	21	3082	72
9064	72	3212	89
9248	84	3380	85
9281	84	3650	76
9667	69	4985	93
9810	77	4986	94
9932	28	5534	37
9972	88	5544	79

Mahābhārata—*continued.* Page

	5571	84
	5861	120
	6073	76
	6612	67
	6781	133
	6783	120
	6799	120
	7163	60
	7213	60
	7412	60
	7574	80
	7593	82
	7595	203
	7597	45
	7607	10
xiv.	592	67
	1455	48
	2784	35
	2788	80
	2835	79

Manu.

ii.	162	72
	238	90
iv.	138	96
	161	8
	170	34
	239	26
vi.	45	143
vii.	8	124
	44	140
viii.	17	26
	84	8
	91	8
ix.	49	300
	314	60, 62
	319	61
xi.	9	84
	228	37

Mṛichhakaṭika.

Act iv.		138

Naishadha Charita.

xvii.	45	13,15

Panchatantra.

i.	15	108
	21	143
	277 (247)	87
	314 (357)	110

Panchatantra—*continued.* Page

ii.	127 (117)	39
iii.	92	142
	104 (103)	86
v.	38	89
	49	142

Praśnottaramālā.

	15	36

Raghuvanśa.

x.	15	2

Rāmāyaṇa.*

ii.	18.23	99
	105.16	41
	24.26	137
	108 and 109	14
vi.	67.10 (Gorresio),	111
	83.14 (Bombay Ed.)	21
	115.41	89
vii.	17	154

* *Note.*—The references are mostly to the Bombay Edition; but the parallel passages in Gorresio's Edition are sometimes given.

Ṛigveda.

i.	48	180
	50	179
	92	180
	113	180
v.	83	177
vi.	75	195
vii.	86.3	316
	89.1	317
	103	194
	88.4	317
ix.	112	190
x.	14	186
	15	186
	16	186
	34	190
	90	325
	107.8	192
	117	193
	121	324
	129	188
	146	189
	151	330
	168	178

Besides numerous passages referred to in pp. 311 ff.

Sāhitya-Darpaṇa.

	322	107

PAGE

SĀRṄGADHARA'S PADDHATI.
4 . . . 39

DITTO DHANAPRASANŚĀ.
12 . . . 107

DITTO NĪTI.
2 . . . 39
34 . . . 90

BILHANA IN.
13 . . . 142

SARVADARŚANA-SANGRAHA 17.18

ŚATAPATHA BRĀHMAṆA.
i. 1.1.7 . . . 312
ii. 2.2.19 . . . 76
x. 5.4.16 . . . 50

SUBHĀSHITĀRṆAVA.
43 . . . 38
64 . . . 108
96 . . . 267
110 . . . 102
255 . . . 36
267 . . . 267
274 . . . 88
275 . . . 110
28,313 . . . 44

ŚVETĀŚVATARA UPANISHAD.
iii. 7 . . . 197
19 . . . 1
vi. 1 . . . 198

PAGE

TAITTIRĪYA ĀRAṆYAKA.
x. 9 . . . 76

TAITTIRĪYA BRĀHMAṆA.
iii. 3.3.1 . . . 300
3.10.4 . . . 300
11.8.1 . . . 54
12.4.7 . . . 300

VĀYU PURĀṆA.
viii. 190 . . . 78

VĀJASANEYI BRĀHMAṆA 300

VĀJASANEYI SANHITĀ.
xxxi. 18 . . . 325
xxxii. 2 . . . 235

VIKRAMA CHARITA.
158 . . . 86
232 . . . 2

VISHṆU PURĀṆA.
iii. 18.30 . . . 17
iv. 24.48 . . . 46

VṚIDDHA CHĀṆAKYA.
x. 17 . . . 11
xi. 7 . . . 267
xii. 22 . . . 40
xiv. 6 . . . 38
xv. 1 . . . 37
xv. 10 . . . 41
176 . . . 38
Ms.p. 32 . . . 99

II. CLASSICAL QUOTATIONS.

AESCHYLUS—Fragment, 205
" . . . 214
" . . . 342
Persæ, 349, . . 367
Prometheus, 263, . 362
Sept. ad. Thebas, 591, 290
ANONYMOUS FRAGMENTS, 211, 342, 352, 355, 356, 357, 359, 361, 363
ANTIPHANES—Fragment, 238
" 367
APOLLODORUS—Fragment, 358
ARATUS—Phœn. 1, . 350
ARISTOTLE de Republ. vii. 1, 351
CEBETIS TABULA, 12, . 232
CICERO—Parad. 6, 3, . 245
CICERO—Tusc. Quæst. iii. 30, 362
CLAUDIAN—
Cons. Hon. iv. 296, . . 347
Cons. Mall. Theod. 1, 348
DEMOSTHENES—Olynth, iii., 363
DIODORUS, 296[b], . . 232
DIOGENES—Fragment, 355
EURIPIDES—Alcestis, 1078, 362
Andromache, 943, . 339
Electra, 1131, . . 288
Hecuba, 282, . . 340
" 1226, . . 359
Hercules Furens, 101, 129
" 655 232
Ion, 854, . . . 353
" 1619, . . . 205

EURIPIDES—*continued.* PAGE
Orestes, 665, 727, . 360
Phœnissæ, 503, . . 103
„ 555, . . 213
Supplices, 214, . . 203
„ 532 . . 335
„ 734, . . 203
„ 1000, . . 297
„ 1080, . . 233
Troades, 647, . . 118
„ 649, . . 300
Fragment of Archelaus, 341
„ Antiope, 341
„ Antigone? 342
„ Bressae, 288
„ Danae, 271, 288
„ Dictys, . 354
„ Ino, . 358
„ Melanippe, 353
„ Phrixus, 341, 353, 365
„ Temenidæ, 224
Fragments of works not named, 271, 277, 291, 341, 365, 367
HERODOTUS, i. 32 ; iii. 40 ; vii. 10 and 46, 322
„ viii. 140, . 363
HESIOD, Op. et Dies., . 236
HILLEL in Oorts Apokriefe Boeken, ... 273
HIPPOTHOON—Fragment, 365
HORACE—Odes, iv. 9, 25, 303
„ i. 16, 52, 235
ILIAD, xix. 137, . . 311
JUVENAL, i. 3, 152, . 242
„ x. 140, . . . 235
„ x. 147, 166, . 242
KLEANTHES' (or Cleanthes) Hymn to Zeus, 213, 344
„ Saying of, . 245
LUCRETIUS, ii. 10, . . 51
MENANDER—
Frag. Kouiazomenai, 212
„ Phocium, . 343
Fragments of unknown works, 340, 347, 356, 357, 359, 360, 361, 365, 366

MENANDER—*continued.* PAGE
Fragment of doubtful genuineness, . . 354
MOSCHUS—Fragment, . 348
ODYSSEY, i. 57, . . 304
„ xxii. 10, . . 212
[ORPHEUS], . . . 350
OVID—
Epist. ex Ponto, ii. 3, 17, 348
Heroid, xvii. 71, . 363
Met. ii. 1, . . . 314
PHILEMON—Fragments, 342, 353, 355, 356, 358, 360, 362, 366
Fragment of Sicilicus, 362
PHÆDRUS, iv. 10, . 361
PLATO—
Gorgias, . . . 361
Phædrus, 147, . . 213
Republic, ii. 18, . 206
„ vi. 2, . . 243
„ x. 6, . . 212
„ x., . . . 343
Theætetus, 81, . . 206
PLAUTUS' Trin. 2, 2, 40, 283
„ Capt. ii. 2, 75, 343
PLUTARCH, Verses quoted by, . . . 357
PROPERTIUS, iii. 5, 13, . 348
„ iv. 13, . 299
PYTHAGORAS, . . 357
PYTHAGOREAN Verses, . 349
SALLUST, Cat. 54, . . 290
SENECA DE IRA, 2, 13, 2, 236
SOCRATES, Saying of, . 355
SOPHOCLES' Aleadæ, frag., 359
„ Aletes, „ 357
„ Electra, 916, 129
„ Oed. Tyr. 56, 367
„ Philoctetes, 1443, 224
„ Fragments, 202, 288
SOSICRATES, frag., . 361
TERENCE, And. ii. 1, 9. 363
„ Heaut. 3, 1, 97, 291
TREATISE de Mundo, 5, 6, 7, 351
VALERIUS MAXIMUS, 4, 4, 1, 245
XENOPHON, Memor. i. 7, 1, 289

III. BIBLICAL TEXTS.

PAGE
Corinthians, 1st Ep. to, xiv., 245
„ „ xv. 33, 278
Deuteronomy v. 9, . 162
Ecclesiastes ix. 10 ; xii. 1, 30
„ ix. 11, . 44
Ecclesiasticus xxxiv. 19 and xxxv. 7, . . . 271
Exodus vii. 1 ff., . . 211
„ xv. 1, . . 318
„ xx. 5, . 162, 316
Ezekiel xviii. 1 ff., 162, 316
Genesis ii. 24, . . 300
Habakkuk ii. 20 ; iii. 8, 314
Hosea vi. 6, . . . 267
Isaiah vi. 1, . . 314
„ i. 11, . . . 267
„ lxiii. 16, . . 319
James iv. 14, . . 26
Jeremiah xxix. 26, . 245
„ xiii. 23, . . 279
„ xxxi. 29, . 316
Job xiv. 7 ff., . . 36
John iv. 44, . . . 305
2 Kings ix. 11, . . 245
Luke xii. 33, . . 24
„ vi. 19, . . 24, 80
Mark vi. 4, . . . 305
Matthew v. 46, . . 87
PAGE
Matthew vii. 3 ff, . 110
„ vii. 6, . . 279
„ vii. 12, . . 86
„ x. 42, . . 231
„ xix. 21, . . 80
Peter, 1st Ep. to, ii. 2 f.; iii. 9, 88
„ v. 8, . 26
Proverbs xv. 8, . . 271
„ xxv. 21, . 88
„ xxx. 18, . 160
„ xiv. 20 ; xix. 4, 7, 288
„ ix. 7 ; xiv. 6 ; xv. 12 ; xxvii. 22, 279
Psalms ii. 4 ; xviii. 7, . 314
„ lvii. 4 ; lxiv. 3, 94
„ xxv. 6 ; lxxx. 49 ; lxxxv. 5, . 162
„ lxxxix. 8 ; xcvii. 19, 318
„ lxxiv. 11, . . 321
„ ciii. 13, . . 319
„ civ. 32, . . 319
Romans, Ep. to, xii. 20, 21, 88
Samuel, 1st Book of, ii. 25, 211
„ „ xix. 20, 244
„ 2d Book of, xii. 12, 25
Timothy, 1st Ep. to, v. 8, 84
Titus iii. 10, . . . 279

IV. GENERAL INDEX.

Benfey, Transl. of R. V. i., 92.10, . . . 328
Gough, Articles in Cal. Rev., . . . 255
Haug's Ved. Räths. sprüche, . . . 323
Hildebrandt's Aditi, . 313
„ Varuna and Mitra, . . . 311
Holtzmann's Agni, . 61
„ Arjuna, . xiv.
Ludwig's Rigveda, . 311
Müller's Hibbert Lectures, . 28, 32, 247, 249
„ History of Anc. Sanskt. Lit., . 247, 256
Pascal quoted, . . 223
Regnaud, Matériaux pour servir à l'Histoire de la Philosophie de l'Inde 255
Reuss. Hist. des Israelites, 49
Scott, Sir Walter, quoted, 134
Tod's Annals of Rājasthan, &c., . . . 132 f.
Weber's Ind. Studien, x. 118, ... 250
Wilson, Theatre of the Hindus, . . . 64, 260
Wilson's Vishṇu Pur., . 199
Windischmann's Philosophie, &c., . . 254, 256
Young's Night Thoughts, 36

www.ingramcontent.com/pod-product-compliance
Lightning Source LLC
Chambersburg PA
CBHW022108290426
44112CB00008B/586
* 9 7 8 3 3 3 7 1 7 7 7 7 5 *